D1760385

HEIDEGGER AND FRENCH PHILOSOPHY

How is it that a difficult German philosopher widely known to have been an enthusiastic Nazi became one of the "master thinkers" of postwar French philosophy?

Heidegger and French Philosophy examines the reception of this highly influential and controversial thinker in France. Tom Rockmore traces the way in which Heidegger's theory has redefined and largely determined the nature of philosophical debate in France, and he investigates the background against which "philosophers" from Sartre through Lacan and Foucault to Derrida, Irigaray and Lacoue-Labarthe have adopted Heidegger's thinking. In doing so, Rockmore delineates some of the main aspects of the French philosophical tradition – in particular its deep humanist commitment.

By arguing for a contextual interpretation of Heidegger, the author engages with the controversy over the philosopher's political affiliation with Nazism and the debate on whether or not this commitment can be reconciled with current French philosophy and its use of Heidegger's theory. *Heidegger and French Philosophy* examines the relations between Heidegger's philosophy and his politics, and contends that for the most part the French reception of his theory – first as philosophical anthropology and later on as post-metaphysical humanism – is systematically mistaken.

Tom Rockmore is Professor of Philosophy at Duquesne University, Pittsburgh. His most recent books include *On Heidegger's Nazism and Philosophy* and *Hegel and Contemporary Philosophy*.

HEIDEGGER AND FRENCH PHILOSOPHY

Humanism, antihumanism and being

Tom Rockmore

London and New York

First published 1995
by Routledge
11 New Fetter Lane, London EC4P 4EE

Simultaneously published in the USA and Canada
by Routledge
29 West 35th Street, New York, NY 10001

© 1995 Tom Rockmore

Typeset in Times by
Ponting–Green Publishing Services, Chesham, Bucks
Printed in Great Britain by
TJ Press Ltd, Padstow, Cornwall

Printed on acid free paper

All rights reserved. No part of this book may be
reprinted or reproduced or utilized in any form or by
any electronic, mechanical, or other means, now
known or hereafter invented, including photocopying
and recording, or in any storage or information
retrieval system, without permission in writing
from the publishers.

British Library Cataloguing in Publication Data
A catalogue record for this book is available from
the British Library

Library of Congress Cataloging in Publication Data
Rockmore, Tom, 1942–
Heidegger and French Philosophy: humanism, antihumanism
and being / Tom Rockmore.
p.   cm.
Includes bibliographical references and index.
1. Heidegger, Martin, 1889–1976–Influence.
2. Philosophy, French–20th century.
I. Title.
B3279.H49R618   1994
193–dc20   93–47961
CIP

ISBN 0–415–11180–3 (hbk)
ISBN 0–415–11181–1 (pbk)

CONTENTS

ACKNOWLEDGMENTS

One of the pleasures of publishing a book is that it provides the occasion to express gratitude for help received in carrying out the project. I would like to record my appreciation to the Noble J. Dick Foundation for a grant that allowed me to acquire books and other materials; to Dr. John J. McDonald, Dean, Arts and Sciences, Duquesne University, for kindly funding a short trip to France that allowed me not only to read a paper but above all to do research in the Bibliothèque Nationale in Paris; and to the American Philosophical Society for a fellowship that enabled me to spend a longer period in the same library.

INTRODUCTION

Denken ist die Einschränkung auf einen Gedanken, der einst wie ein Stern am Himmel der Welt stehen bleibt.[1]

More than 200 years ago, astronomers speculated that a star of sufficient size would, owing to its gravitational pull, absorb rather than emit light and would therefore exert an enormous influence while remaining, literally, invisible.[2] Today, such is the role of Heidegger's philosophy in France. Like a massive, yet rarely visible dark star, Heidegger shapes and determines the nature and course of French philosophical debate. As Michael Roth has stated, "Heidegger's influence on French philosophy can scarcely be overestimated."[3]

In an earlier work,[4] I studied the relation between Heidegger's philosophy and his Nazism. This book continues the concern with the relation between Heidegger's theory and his politics through a self-contained, independent inquiry into the French reception of Heidegger's thought. We need to understand, since it is by no means evident, the process leading to the emergence of a philosophical theory linked to Nazism as the dominant view in the basically humanist French philosophical tradition in postwar France. And we need to grasp the background that makes possible the recent, strange claim of Philippe Lacoue-Labarthe, one of the most important French students of Heidegger, that "Nazism is a humanism."[5]

Study of the French reception of Heidegger's theory is interesting for three main reasons. First, it offers an occasion to delineate some main aspects of the French philosophical tradition, in particular its deep humanist commitment, extending over centuries, that is crucial to the reception of Heidegger's theory in France. Second, it represents a special case of the wider, but little understood relation of philosophy to the history of philosophy. We simply do not know how philosophy relates to the philosophical tradition, nor how philosophical theories are taken up in the later discussion. Third, it provides an opportunity to learn something important about Heidegger's theory through study of its French reception. Simply put, this book contends that in the period after the Second World War, Heidegger became the master thinker of French philosophy, the main "French" philosopher; and it further contends that for the most part the French reception of Heidegger's theory, to begin with as philosophical anthropology and later as postmetaphysical humanism, is systematically mistaken.

The impact of Heidegger's theory in France since the end of the Second World War is comparable to Kant's in Germany after the publication of the *Critique of Pure Reason* toward the end of the eighteenth century. Some philosophers were uninterested in Kant's theory and a few opposed it. But for the most part, it dominated the immediate post-Kantian discussion in German philosophy. Some French philosophers are uninterested in Heidegger's theory and others reject it; but for more than half a century it has continued to exert a decisive influence in French philosophy that still gives no clear signs of abating.

The nature of Heidegger's philosophical dominance in France after the Second World War can be suggested through a Kantian concept. In a famous passage, Kant employs the astronomical metaphor of the Copernican Revolution to describe the central organizing function of the subject with respect to the objects of possible experience and knowledge.[6] If to an increasing extent since the end of the war Heidegger has become the master thinker of French philosophy, if Heidegger's theory is central to French philosophy today, if it forms the horizon in which French philosophy formulates its problems and seeks their solutions, then it is literally comparable to the Kantian subject, the transcendental unity of apperception, in transmitting its categories to the debate, in structuring the French philosophical discussion.

Heidegger's philosophical importance is mainly due to his brilliant early work, *Being and Time*. When this book appeared in 1927, its genuine importance was quickly recognized, and its author was propelled to the center of the philosophical stage almost before the ink was dry on its pages. Otto Pöggeler compares the appearance of this treatise to a flash of lightning that illuminated the philosophical landscape in a new way so that things could no longer remain as before.[7] When Alexandre Koyré introduced the first French translation of Heidegger's texts in 1931, he contended that "[Heidegger's] 'philosophy of existence' would not only determine a new stage of the development of Western philosophy but would form the departure point for an entirely new cycle."[8]

Koyré's contention can be read as a prediction that actually came true in France. An even more radical view is passionately embraced by certain of Heidegger's French followers. François Fédier, one of the French philosophers closest to Heidegger's thought and since Jean Beaufret's death one of Heidegger's most tenacious French defenders against the view that his philosophy and his Nazism are directly related,[9] contends that French philosophy is essentially Heideggerian: "It is very simple: the interest for philosophy today is inseparable from the interest for Heidegger. It follows that if there is a survival of philosophy in France, it is in strict relation [étroitement en rapport] to the gigantic work that Heidegger has carried out in this century."[10] It is, then, hardly surprising that so many French philosophers, convinced that Heidegger's theory is central to philosophy, perceived the renewed controversy about his Nazism, following the appearance of Victor Farías's study in 1987,[11] as an attack on French philosophy.

To point out the French interest in Heidegger's theory is not yet to address the problem as to how to proceed. The two main possible approaches are contextualism and anticontextualism. Philosophical anticontextualists take their cue from the traditional philosophical conception of knowledge as absolute. Absolute knowledge is unlimited in any way, for instance with respect to the cognitive capacities of human beings, their relation to a historical or conceptual context, and so on. Such writers as Descartes, Kant and Edmund Husserl argue that knowledge is in time but not of time, not temporally limited. Others, such as Hegel, Karl Marx, and Maurice Merleau-Ponty, insist that claims to know are not only in time but of time, hence temporally limited.

Contextualists insist that we consider the relation of ideas to context in order to understand and evaluate them. Anticontextualists hold that we can do all these things without examining the link of theory to context. Contextualists hold that if we fail to consider context we arrive at a very different and often erroneous understanding of theories, for instance Heidegger's theory, as when we fail to see Heidegger's theory against the background of his enthusiasm for National Socialism in the context of the later Weimar Republic. Anticontextualists tend to eschew the relation of texts to context in order to concentrate on the texts themselves. Contextualists think that such information leads to a very different understanding of the texts. Anticontextualists, such as Jacques Derrida and many French Heideggerians, tend to engage in ever more elaborate scrutiny of the texts while neglecting information that contextualists maintain is essential to their interpretation. Anticontextualists regard contextualists as falling into sociology of knowledge, as devoting insufficient attention to textual study for which they substitute the gathering of textually peripheral information.

Contextualism, the approach of this book, is widely employed. Arthur Lovejoy, for instance, appeals to this doctrine in an essay on William James when he writes that "All philosophies . . . are the result of the interaction of a temperament (itself partly molded by a historical situation) with impersonal logical considerations arising out of the nature of the problem with which man's reason is confronted."[12]

In the Heidegger debate, anticontextualism is widespread on two levels: in the reading of Heidegger's theory as utterly different from, hence incomparable with, the prior philosophical tradition, and with respect to his Nazism. Heidegger's turning to Nazism has been known for more than half a century. Yet efforts are still under way to save if not the Nazi Heidegger at least the philosopher Heidegger, typically by insisting on a strict separation between Heidegger's theory and his Nazism, on a distinction in kind between Heidegger the great philosopher and Heidegger the ordinary Nazi.[13]

Heidegger was, and on some interpretations remained, a Nazi even after he turned away from real National Socialism.[14] With respect to his Nazi turning, the controversy about how to approach Heidegger's theory, more precisely the relation between his life and thought, divides his defenders and critics. His defenders like to argue that his life and thought are separable and separate, and that his thought does not depend in any basic way on his life. They view his thought as untarnished by, even as unrelated to, his life, including his Nazi turning. His critics tend to argue that his life and thought are inseparable, and that his thought cannot be understood without understanding his life, in particular his endorsement of Nazism.

Those who hold that Heidegger's thought is not affected by his politics – in practice many important Heidegger scholars, whose careers not incidentally depend on their grasp of Heidegger's writings, but also others whose relation to Heidegger's thought is more distant – like to diminish or even to disregard his political commitment as a factor in the comprehension of his thought. Richard Rorty, for instance, the self-described liberal ironist concerned to reduce human suffering, surprisingly regards Heidegger's theory, or the theory of someone apparently unconcerned with human suffering, as relevant to this task.[15]

Some observers deny that Heidegger's thought after his turning to Nazism can be understood without reference to the turbulent context in which it arose. Yet others consider his writings without reference to their context. And others, still more extreme, argue that to do otherwise, even to attempt to understand Heidegger's writings in the context of his political commitment, is to make it impossible to understand them at all.[16]

Yet any effort to "save" Heidegger's theory by reading the texts without reference to their context, by turning away from his politics, is doubly problematic: for it "saves" his theory through an anticontextualist maneuver only at the cost of violating his own contextualist commitment; and it provides a properly "sanitized" reading of his theory that conceals more than it reveals, and finally misconstrues the theory it claims to uncover.

The approach of this book will be resolutely contextualist for two reasons. First, contextualism is specifically appropriate in Heidegger's case since, although he does not use the term, Heidegger is himself a contextualist. In *Being and Time*, he proposes a theory of Dasein, understood as existence, in order to study being as time. He thinks understanding through its existential roots in the preconceptual surrounding world. For Heidegger, assertions of all kinds are based in interpretation; and interpretation is grounded in understanding that, with state of mind and discourse, is one of the fundamental ways in which human being is in the world.[17] Human being's grasp of itself and its surroundings in terms of itself, what Heidegger calls its disclosedness (*Erschlossenheit*), literally depends on the fact that it is understanding situated in the world. For Heidegger, understanding is always and necessarily situated, literally inseparable from the context in which it arises. It follows that if Heidegger's political turning is to be defended or even understood, this must be done on contextualist grounds. It further follows that the widespread effort to interpret or to defend Heidegger's theory from an anticontextualist perspective is misguided on strictly Heideggerian grounds.

Second, this book is contextualist since any other approach, in particular an anticontextualist strategy, would be incompatible with its task of understanding the French reception of Heidegger's thought. French philosophers, like others, are attracted to Heidegger's theory because of its philosophical power that no one denies. Yet there are a number of factors intrinsic to the French situation that need to be elucidated in order to understand, not why French philosophers are interested in Heidegger's theory, but rather why they are so interested, arguably more interested than philosophers elsewhere, and why their interest has taken shape in the way that it has. On methodological grounds there seems to be no other way to understand how and why Heidegger's theory was received in France as it was than through a careful account of some main features of French philosophy. Those who desire a detailed discussion of Heidegger's texts, certainly a legitimate concern, will need to look elsewhere since his writings will be discussed only to the extent that they bear on their French reception. It is easy to anticipate that many of those committed to Heidegger's thought will find the critical remarks scattered throughout this essay to be trivial, based on an insufficient grasp of the master's thought. Yet this discussion may satisfy those who are concerned with the troubling question of how an apparent philosophical genius who was drawn to Nazism has continued to attract attention among many philosophers who do not share his political views, above all those working in the humanist tradition of French philosophy.

Heidegger and French philosophy came together through a double movement in which he turned toward French philosophy and the latter turned toward his theory. Both movements require explanation, and neither can be explained without reference to the context that frames the texts. When he wrote *Being and Time* and even afterwards, Heidegger was uninterested in French philosophy and deeply critical of Descartes's position that has long been central in the French debate. His turn toward French philosophy, which cannot be explained through his prior thought, can only be explained through his own difficult existential situation at the end of the Second World War. Similarly, we need to consider the nature of French philosophy in order to understand why, immediately after the Second World War, it turned toward the difficult theory of an obscure German thinker widely known to have been an enthusiastic Nazi.

The Heideggerian turning of French philosophy can be characterized in language now in vogue as "overdetermined." French philosophy has long been unusually receptive to Heidegger's theory for a number of reasons, including its continued strong link to religion, especially to Roman Catholicism, which appeared to find a distant echo in the theory of a former seminarian; its traditional investment in Cartesianism that Heidegger opposed, which in turn made his theory attractive in the French context striving to break its traditional Cartesian bonds; the widespread French philosophical concern with phenomenology, particularly the Hegelian and Husserlian positions, which created interest in Heidegger's fundamental ontology, a form of phenomenology, and so on.

Like the French political structure, French philosophy is highly centralized. French philosophical centralization is manifest in the phenomenon of the master thinker, someone who tends to dominate the debate for a period, in Descartes's case over hundreds of years. Beside Heidegger, there have been a number of other master thinkers in French culture in this century, including Henri Bergson, Hegel, Alexandre Kojève, and Jean-Paul Sartre. And perhaps most extravagantly of all, there is Jacques Lacan, the Freudian psychoanalyst, who has been described in a nearly untranslatable phrase as *le maître absolu*.[18] From this perspective, Heidegger is merely the latest in a line of "French" master thinkers, not all of whom wrote in French, were French in origin or even French at all.

Another factor is the traditional French philosophical concern with subjectivity going back to Descartes or even earlier to Michel de Montaigne. The opposition between those committed to Cartesian and post-Cartesian views of subjectivity is strikingly apparent in a debate between Michel Foucault, who treats the subject as a concept to be discarded,[19] and Jacques Derrida, who affirms that the lesson of Foucault's supposedly superficial reading of Descartes is that one cannot escape from the Cartesian framework.[20] Heidegger's concern with subjectivity is a constant theme in his position: in the approach to being through the analysis of Dasein dominant in his early view, and in the later turn away from subjectivity through an effort to decenter the subject, which was influential in the French structuralist movement.

These and other factors are certainly important. Yet perhaps the single most important factor for understanding Heidegger's extraordinary French reception derives from the persistent French philosophical commitment to humanism broadly conceived. The humanist revival of classical studies (*studia humanitatis*) in Europe in the fifteenth and sixteenth centuries was accompanied by the development of a philosophy of human being that is particularly strong in France. Not only the writings of literary figures like Rabelais, but a long series of French philosophical theories, going back beyond Jean Antoine Condorcet to Descartes and Montaigne, and continuing to the present, turn on the problem of human being. This theme is widely visible in recent French philosophy: in Alexandre Kojève's celebrated interpretation of Hegel's *Phenomenology of Spirit* as philosophical anthropology,[21] in Sartre's famous lecture *Existentialism is a Humanism*,[22] and in various forms of French structuralist antihumanism due to Claude Lévi-Strauss, Michel Foucault, Jean Piaget, Louis Althusser, and others.

The French Heidegger reception, which began in the late 1920s and early 1930s, received a strong impetus in Kojève's famous lectures (1933–1939) on Hegel's *Phenomenology of Spirit*. Others influential in the initial phase of the French Heidegger reception include Koyré, Henry Corbin, Georges Gurvitch, Emmanuel Lévinas, and later Jean Wahl. Kojève, who insisted on close continuity between the views of Hegel and Heidegger, influenced the initial reception of Heidegger's theory as philosophical anthropology that finally peaked in Sartre's famous lecture after the war. Yet this initial way of reading Heidegger's theory was misleading, as Heidegger himself pointed out. For despite contrary indications in *Being and Time*, and following Husserl, he distinguished sharply between his theory and the sciences of human being of whatever kind, including philosophical anthropology.

We can differentiate between the first and second stages of the French Heidegger reception. The second stage was clearly begun through the publication of Heidegger's "Letter on Humanism," appropriately enough a letter to the French on how to read his writings. It was sustained through the determined efforts of Jean Beaufret, its addressee and from the mid-1940s until his death in 1982 Heidegger's most important French student, to transform the view of this text into the French view of Heidegger.

Heidegger's "Letter on Humanism" is indispensable to appreciate the phenomenally rapid rise to prominence of his theory at the end of the Second World War. In this text, Heidegger distances himself from Sartre's uneasy humanist embrace through a description of his own theory as a new, viable, postmetaphysical form of humanism. His rejection of Sartre's and all other traditional views of humanism in favor of a supposedly new humanism attracted considerable attention to his theory in France immediately after the most inhumane of wars, when humanism was a theme on everyone's mind.

Heidegger's "Letter on Humanism" hinges on the underdetermined concept of the turning (Kehre) mentioned in this text. This concept, which has acquired an important role in the interpretation of Heidegger's later thought,[23] can be interpreted from philosophical and political perspectives. Philosophically, the concept refers to the evolution of the original position that takes place in the later writings of all thinkers, including Heidegger, who are not content merely to repeat themselves. Politically, it suggests a turning away, away from all that, away from National Socialism, toward which Heidegger publicly turned and which he served as rector of the University of Freiburg in Hitler's Germany. Yet it is misleading to read the supposed turning in Heidegger's thought as a further turning away from Nazism. If Heidegger turned away from National Socialism as it existed after he resigned his post as rector of the University of Freiburg in 1934, it was only to transfer his allegiance to an ideal form of National Socialism – a concept that, in his view, the German Nazis failed to put into practice – that he never abandoned.[24] Heidegger's apparently constant fidelity to the allegedly misunderstood "inner truth and greatness of this movement",[25] as he put it in 1953, well after the end of the war, must be kept in mind in interpreting his later writings.

Heidegger's rise to prominence in French philosophy after the war was due not only to the impact of his "Letter on Humanism" but also to the tireless efforts of Beaufret on his behalf. Many other thinkers, such as Kant, Hegel, and Marx have had committed disciples. In an extended sense, as Alfred North Whitehead reminds us, the entire Western tradition is the work of those toiling in Plato's shadow.[26] Yet perhaps no thinker – probably not even Heidegger, whose disciples are notoriously ready to excuse any possible defect in his life and thought, even to the point of presenting a consciously engaged Nazi as simply naive – ever had a closer disciple than did Heidegger in Beaufret. Over a period of more than thirty years, Beaufret, who quickly acquired a preeminent position in French Heidegger studies, devoted himself to Heidegger's life and thought in a way that has few if any precedents in the philosophical tradition and that contributed greatly to Heidegger's growing importance in French philosophy.

There is a distinction between a retrospective analysis of factors ingredient in the French philosophical turn toward Heidegger's theory and the influence of that theory within contemporary French thought. The stunning impact of Heidegger's position in the contemporary French philosophical discussion will be documented below in two ways. One way is through attention to some among the many French thinkers concerned with Heidegger's theory. These include those devoted to its exegesis, those dependent on Heideggerian approaches in studies of phenomenology and the history of philosophy, and those whose own views are crucially dependent on Heideggerian insights, most prominently Derrida. The sheer number and quality of those concerned with Heidegger's theory, and the volume of their writings on that theory, is an impressive indication of its influence.

The influence of Heidegger's theory in French philosophy is further apparent in the way it has tended to shape French philosophical consideration of the complex issues arising from the turning of one of the main philosophers in this century to National Socialism. No treatment of the French Heidegger reception is complete that ignores the efforts of French thinkers since the war to come to grips with the link between Heidegger the ordinary Nazi and Heidegger the great philosopher, between the political engagement and the philosophical theory, from a point located within the thoroughly Heideggerian framework of the French discussion. As the following discussion will show, the widespread French philosophical commitment to Heidegger's thought restrains the ability of French thinkers to analyze the link between Heidegger's thought and his political engagement, between his fundamental ontology and his Nazism. And as the discussion will further show, recent efforts by important French Heideggerians such as Derrida and Lacoue-Labarthe in effect to minimize the political damage to Heidegger's thought continue to presuppose a mistaken reading of his early position as humanism.

The French Heidegger reception illustrates the way in which important theories are understood only much later if at all. There is a French reading

xviii

of Heidegger's theory, as of French philosophy itself, as humanist. Heidegger himself contributed to widespread misapprehensions about his theory as humanism in two systematically ambiguous, but crucial texts: in § 10 of *Being and Time*, which indicates that his fundamental ontology both is and cannot be philosophical anthropology; and two decades later in the "Letter on Humanism", which suggests that his position is a postmetaphysical humanism.

The correction to the first reading of his theory, its misreading as anthropological humanism, was provided in its later reading as nonanthropological humanism, which developed after the war under the influence of the "Letter on Humanism." This later reading, intended to correct the initial reading, only does so through yet another misreading of Heidegger's theory. In his "Letter on Humanism" Heidegger condemns humanism while touting his own theory as a new humanism. Yet if humanism is metaphysics, if his own theory is no longer metaphysics, then it cannot be humanism.

It follows that the frequent French reading of Heidegger's theory as humanism, which has been widely influential, particularly in the American Heidegger discussion, is in fact a misreading of his thought. The predominant French reading of Heidegger's theory depicts it early and late, or as he later cast it himself, at least after the so-called turning in his thought, as a new, deeper form of humanism. Yet this is a demonstrable misreading, possible only because his own antihumanism, or more precisely his indifference to human being and humanist concerns, as illustrated in his later commitment to an ideal form of Nazism, has so often been minimized or even gone unnoticed.

We can end with a word about the nature and intended audience for the present study. Heidegger's work has led to a massive literature, often technical, mainly aimed at Heidegger specialists, a literature that is frequently devoid of criticism of any kind. On the contrary, this book will be critical and as nontechnical and accessible as possible. Naturally, Heidegger specialists will be unhappy with and unconvinced by the discussion, which they will find uninformed, superficial, or both. That much can be safely anticipated. Yet it is normal to be critical of another philosopher, to attempt to determine what, to paraphrase Benedetto Croce's famous approach to Hegel, is living and dead in their theories.[27] Indeed, it is especially important to be critical of the link between Heidegger's philosophical theory and his Nazism since so many writers believe that this link is unimportant or even desire to overlook it on the grounds that Heidegger is an important, even a great philosopher. But I am convinced that unless we try to grasp Heidegger's theory in the context of its times, we cannot understand it.

In this sense, the issues that this book raises are not the concerns of a few specialists but an illustration of the much broader problem of how to comprehend and evaluate ideas in the context of their times. Accordingly, the book is not intended for the Heidegger specialist, but for intelligent men and women of good will, philosophers and nonphilosophers, who, toward the end of our troubled century, are legitimately concerned by the link between philosophy, or philosophers, whose craft is allegedly indispensable for the good life, and the outstanding illustration of evil in our time.

1

HEIDEGGER AS A "FRENCH" PHILOSOPHER

This chapter will have a somewhat sociological flavor due to the need to sketch in some of the contextual background of the French reception of Heidegger. This essay contends that since the end of the Second World War Heidegger has assumed a dominant role in French philosophy. If one overlooks Heidegger's impact on the contemporary French philosophical discussion, one cannot hope to understand its main problems and main approaches to them. There is a measure of truth to Heidegger's boast that when the French begin to think, they think in German.[1]

It is difficult to measure something as nebulous as influence. Even the term is difficult to analyze precisely. Yet in an informal, subjective sense, it is clear that as measured by a variety of criteria – including the sheer size of the discussion concerning his thought, the number of philosophers interested in his position, his impact on the subsequent debate – as we approach the end of this century, Heidegger has attained exceptional status as one of the several most influential philosophers of this period. This is nowhere more clearly the case than in France, where over the last half-century his ideas have left their mark on a wide range of leading philosophers (Lévinas, Derrida, Lyotard, Henry), on philosophers specifically committed to detailed historical studies of such figures as Aristotle (Pierre Aubenque, Rémi Brague), Suarez (Jean-François Courtine), Descartes (Jean-Luc Marion), Schelling (Courtine, Miklos Vetö), Hegel (Kojève, Jean Hyppolite, Dominique Janicaud), as well as on social theorists (Foucault), feminists (Luce Irigaray), psychoanalysts (Lacan), and others.

The relation between Heidegger's theory and French philosophy is not bidirectional, or marked by mutual appreciation, but starkly unilateral. Although Heidegger appreciated some French poets, such as René Char, and philosophers devoted to him and to his thought, such as Jean Beaufret, he was unimpressed by, in fact overtly hostile to, French philosophy. With the exception of his severely negative reaction to Descartes's theory, there is no corresponding French philosophical influence in Heidegger's thought. To the best of my knowledge, there is no evidence that Heidegger was ever influenced in his philosophical thinking, other than in a negative sense, in

1

whole or in part, by French philosophy. In at least one text he makes overtures toward France and French thinkers, but in general he takes a consistently negative attitude towards French thought.[2] This negative attitude is illustrated by his consistently critical attitude, early and late, toward Descartes's theory[3] and his later rejection of Sartre's position.[4] Yet, for reasons to be specified below, Heidegger's negative reactions toward the theories of Descartes and above all of Sartre did not hinder but rather helped bring about the French philosophical turn toward Heidegger.

Heidegger's thought, like that of other important thinkers, is susceptible of different interpretations. It is a matter of record that Heidegger's position receives different treatments in different languages and literatures. In practice, the link between Heidegger's and Husserl's theories is more frequently taken into account in Europe than in America, where students of either tend to have a low opinion and even less knowledge of the other philosopher's theory. In Germany, it is standard practice to understand Heidegger's theory through examination of its relation to Husserl's.[5] In France, where the currently influential Derridean approach to Heidegger's theory is only one of the variants, there is a pronounced tendency to approach Heidegger's thought through its relation to Husserlian phenomenology. In the United States, Heidegger is often understood through the eyes of French postmodernism, with particular attention to the views of Derrida and such associates as Philippe Lacoue-Labarthe, Jean-Luc Nancy, and Françoise Dastur as well as through the influence of writers located in America, influenced by the French reception of Heidegger, such as Gayatri Spivak, Jacques Taminiaux, Reiner Schürmann, John Sallis, David Krell, and others.

Heidegger's influence on French thought has become more important over time. Although Kant's position quickly exerted great influence in the German philosophical debate in the wake of the publication of the *Critique of Pure Reason*, some philosophers, such as Johann Georg Hamann, Johann Gottfried von Herder, and Friedrich Heinrich Jacobi were either unconcerned with or even hostile to Kant's critical philosophy. In the contemporary French philosophical debate, there are exceptions, thinkers who display no interest for, and whose own writings are untouched by, Heidegger's thought. Yet it is fair to say that since the end of the Second World War, Heidegger's influence has steadily increased to the point where it can be said to form the horizon of contemporary French philosophy, the perspective within which French philosophers now tend to think and write.

Even if we acknowledge the importance of his theory, Heidegger's enormous influence on the French philosophical discussion is surprising. Certainly, the views of such other German-language philosophers as Gottlob Frege and Ludwig Wittgenstein, which have long been highly influential in English-language philosophy, have so far failed to attract anything like Heidegger's audience in French philosophy.

The impressive impact of Heidegger's theory in France is surprising since there are some fairly obvious factors that in principle ought to count against any large-scale French interest in Heidegger's thought. We have already noted Heidegger's known antipathy toward French philosophy. Then there is a stylistic barrier. In principle French philosophy still respects the well known Cartesian concern with clarity and distinctness. Heidegger is an obscure German philosopher who formulates his ideas in language that at best is not quite standard German and presents formidable difficulties.

Further, even when we take into account the ongoing *rapprochement* within the framework of the Common Market, there are obvious historical grounds for continuing friction, even animosity, between the Germans and the French, whose deep political differences, apparent in two world wars in this century, testify to the uneasy coexistence of these geographical neighbors. In an assessment of the French turning to Heidegger, it should not be overlooked that in the Second World War France was defeated and occupied by the same Nazi Germany with which Heidegger clearly and unambiguously identified.

To understand the French reception of Heidegger's thought requires a characterization of "French" philosophy as well as of its context or background. To avoid misunderstanding, let me clearly state that it is not my intention to provide a description of French philosophy here, even in outline. My characterization of French philosophy will be limited merely to identifying some aspects important for understanding its attraction to Heidegger's theory.

"FRENCH PHILOSOPHY" ?

French philosophy, starting with the understanding of the term "philosophy," is no better or worse than, but certainly different from, philosophy as practiced elsewhere, say in Germany or the United States. The ambiguous term "French philosophy" may be taken to mean "philosophy in France," or "philosophy written in French," or even "philosophy that conveys a specifically French point of view." The French Heidegger discussion includes not only philosophers working in France but others as well who have contributed to the French-language debate. By "French philosophy" I shall mean philosophy published in France by French writers as well as non-French writers writing in French and an occasional contributor to the French discussion of Heidegger from outside France, such as Alphonse De Waelhens, Marc Richir or Jean Grondin. This means that I will have little or nothing to say about French-language philosophy in other countries, including Belgium, Canada, Switzerland, French-speaking parts of Africa, and so on.

The word "philosophy" has different meanings in different philosophical tendencies and national traditions. On seeing the term *philosophie* a French reader is reminded of "philosophy" in the English or German senses of the term. The French reader is reminded as well of the last year in the *lycée* –

3

often referred to as *philosophie* – devoted to acquiring a general grounding in Western philosophy, with particular attention to Descartes and other French thinkers. A further meaning, familiar to any speaker of French, is the frequent injunction to take things philosophically or, more precisely, stoically.

The French term *philosophe* makes no distinction between technical philosophy and the nontechnical musings of the French equivalent of, say, a Francis Bacon. In France, a philosopher is not only someone concerned with ultimate questions like Plato or Aristotle, Kant or Hegel, Descartes and Jean-Jacques Rousseau, but even someone like Victor Riqueti, the Marquis de Mirabeau, or the Baron Paul-Henri d'Holbach, writers who in the French cultural context count as philosophers. As a matter of policy, the set program featured by the *agrégation* – that nationwide competitive examination that still remains the main hurdle to be negotiated to become a college teacher – excludes the writings of all living philosophers. But among nonliving philosophers, the program is quite likely to include texts by François Marie Arouet de Voltaire, Denis Diderot, or even Blaise Pascal, writers who are not philosophers in the English-language sense of the term. It is, then, not surprising that the *Logique de Port Royal* features a strong emphasis on Pascal as a philosopher.[6]

A further point is the intrinsically scientific status accorded to philosophy in France. Philosophy has long been bewitched by the conception of philosophy as the science of sciences, most recently in Husserl's view of philosophy as rigorous science.[7] Since the rise of the new science in the seventeenth century and the separation of philosophy from science, this model has tended to lose its hold in philosophy in general. Yet at least on the linguistic plane, it continues in French philosophy, which is routinely classified with sociology, psychology, and so on as a human science (*science humaine*).[8]

THE FRENCH INTELLECTUAL

It is important but difficult briefly to characterize the peculiarly significant role of the French intellectual, including the French philosopher.[9] In comparison, the French intellectual tends to function more autonomously, to be taken more seriously, and to regard himself as carrying out a more significant task than elsewhere.

The role of the French philosopher is partly due to the task of the French intellectual, not duplicated elsewhere, in cultural transmission. Vincent Descombes points out that at the beginning of the Third Republic, French academic philosophy, which was given the mission of teaching "the legitimacy of the new republican institutions"[10] naturally tended to depict itself as the *terminus ad quem* of social development.

The importance of philosophy is recognized through the place of philo-

4

sophy in the *classes terminales* of the *lycée*, which culminates in the final year, or *classe de philosophie*, the peak of French secondary studies, appropriately devoted to philosophy.[11] Philosophy is also crucial in the exam, known as the *baccalauréat*, which must be passed to gain a *diplôme*, the French secondary school diploma. The importance of philosophy is further acknowledged through the practice, to my knowledge unparalleled elsewhere, of regularly reviewing philosophical books in *Le Monde*, the main French national newspaper.

In France, intellectuals frequently talk and act as if they were the conscience of society.[12] They are comparatively more willing to take a stand on the important issues of the day, to publish petitions, to participate in public meetings centered on important issues, and so on. A conviction of the importance of the intellectual manifests itself in the concern with intellectual responsibility[13] that, depending on one's point of view, reaches an *apogée* or a nadir in Sartre's conception of *engagement*, or deliberate commitment of each person to everyone else.[14]

The importance of French intellectuals, including philosophers, is magnified by features of the French context that allow intellectuals to acquire an autonomous or semiautonomous status outside the usual academic establishment. Elsewhere, academic intellectuals, including philosophers, depend on the acquisition of a university position as the condition of exerting influence in the academic discussion. For an intellectual, it is usually very difficult to influence the academic debate, let alone be noticed by the wider public, if one is not located within the academy in some fairly obvious way.

In Germany, Heidegger continued to influence the philosophical discussion during the period after the Second World War when he was barred from teaching because of his collaboration with the National Socialists. Yet I am aware of no other similar example in German philosophy. In the United States, where intellectuals, with the possible exception of a few natural scientists, have little influence, it is difficult to reach any real public audience outside the university system. Such instances as the later moral influence of Albert Einstein, made possible by his work in physics, are exceedingly rare in the United States. It is further difficult to exert any influence on American academic life from a position outside the university. Rare examples such as the literary critic Edmund Wilson or the philosopher C. S. Peirce, whose influence has continued to increase despite his failure ever to secure a permanent university post, tend to confirm rather than to question this rule.

French intellectuals, including philosophers, often play an influential role from a position outside the university or even outside the academy. In part, this is due to the presence within the French academic system of a number of parallel institutions that function on a university level but are not part of the university in any formal sense. Among these are the so-called *grandes écoles*, to which students are admitted only on competitive examination. They further include the Ecole Pratique des Hautes Etudes, whose doors, like those of the traditional French university, have traditionally been open – although this is now starting to change – to everyone who receives a *baccalauréat*, but which unlike the universities in the French university system chooses its own faculty rather than accepting appointments made from without. And they finally include the even more prestigious Collège de France.

Throughout this century, French intellectuals have exerted considerable influence from positions within these parallel French institutions, that is from outside the formal university system. There are many well known examples: Pierre Bourdieu, the French sociologist, Merleau-Ponty, Vuillemin, Barthes, and Foucault all taught at the Collège de France; Lévi-Strauss lectured at the Collège and at Hautes Etudes, while Althusser and Derrida have been associated with the Ecole Normale Supérieure as well as, in Derrida's case, Hautes Etudes.

In France, some intellectuals attain a position of great influence through work carried out wholly outside the educational establishment. This is often the case for writers both in France, such as André Malraux, and elsewhere but it is rare for philosophers. Two examples of this phenomenon among philosophers are provided by Simone de Beauvoir and Jean-Paul Sartre. Both took degrees in philosophy, both taught at secondary level before resigning to devote themselves to philosophy and literature, and neither returned to the educational system after the hiatus enforced by the Second World War. Both acquired great influence only after they had left the ranks of French education. Unlike Beauvoir, whose influence was mainly literary, Sartre continued to make important literary and philosophical contributions from his position outside the French academy virtually until his death.

CARTESIANISM

Heidegger is on record as opposed to Descartes and to organized religion. Yet paradoxically, French Cartesianism and the close link of French philosophy to religion have contributed strongly to its Heideggerian turning. Descartes has for centuries held a central place within the French discussion that maintains a religious, often strongly religious character. Although it might appear that the Cartesian and religious aspects of French philosophy are in conflict, this is not the case. In France at least, Descartes's theory has often been interpreted in a sense compatible with a claim for the religious foundations of philosophy, for the continuing effort to ground reason in faith.

Outside France, Descartes is usually regarded as an important philosopher whose significance mainly lies in the influence of his theory within the history of philosophy, as the author of a once centrally important theory that is no longer central to the philosophical discussion. Unquestionably, Heidegger contributed to this view of the Cartesian theory through an effort to show that Descartes's impact on later thought, and his theory itself, are at best illustrative of a deep-seated error. A rather different attitude is common in

France and French philosophy where Descartes's thought is perceived in a mainly positive manner, and where, now as before, it continues to remain close to the center of the French philosophical debate.

A striking example is Bergson's declaration: "All modern philosophy derives from Descartes ... All modern idealism comes from there, in particular German idealism ... All the tendencies of modern philosophy coexist in Descartes."[15] A further, equally striking example is Derrida's response to Foucault's famous study *Histoire de la folie*. In an important passage in the first of the *Meditations*, Descartes raises against his theory the possibility that he is quite simply mad.[16] Foucault's comments on this passage[17] led Derrida to remark that not only did Foucault misread the *cogito* in this work but that his misreading proved that the act of philosophy could no longer be anything other than Cartesian.[18]

Since the seventeenth century, Descartes's impact has continued to be felt widely throughout French thought,[19] including the conception of the well written essay. His influence radiates out beyond the limits of philosophy throughout the far reaches of intellectual life. According to Ernst Cassirer, who relies on Gustave Lanson, "After the middle of the seventeenth century the Cartesian spirit permeates all fields of knowledge until it dominates not only philosophy, but also literature, morals, political science, and sociology, asserting itself even in the realm of theology to which it imparted a new form."[20] The frequent assertion that Sartre is the last of the Cartesians and Merleau-Ponty is the first of the post-Cartesians is false since there are still many Cartesians in French philosophy.

There is a corresponding difference in the respect accorded Cartesian scholars. Elsewhere, scholars of Descartes tend to receive serious but limited respect. In France, the Descartes discussion has long formed a minor cottage industry in which whole careers are built on research into his thought.[21] Even taking into account Heidegger's view, Descartes still casts the longest shadow in contemporary French philosophy.

Heidegger's position in French philosophy as a master thinker was certainly aided by his opposition to Descartes. Heidegger is concerned throughout his work with being in general, as distinguished from beings, or entities. For Heidegger, Descartes provides a central illustration of the incorrect view of ontology that has arisen since the early Greeks and that still blocks our access to the problem of being. Heidegger's *Being and Time*, the central treatise of his early period and the most important work of his entire corpus, contains a violent attack on Descartes[22] that is prolonged in later writings, above all in the important essay on "The Age of the World Picture."[23] In these and other texts, Heidegger argues strongly that the Cartesian position epitomizes a fallacious form of metaphysics arising out of a fateful turn away from the original Greek insights concerning being.

Even if the Heideggerian problem of being has never been a traditional interest in French philosophy, the anti-Cartesian thrust of his thought was certainly important in creating interest for his position as a way to move beyond traditional French Cartesianism. Heidegger's well known antipathy to Descartes's position, extending throughout his entire corpus, is unquestionably attractive to French thinkers still struggling, almost three and a half centuries after Descartes's death, to free themselves from his hold on French philosophy.

PHILOSOPHY AND RELIGION

More than either German or English-language philosophy, French philosophy is distinguished by a strong emphasis on the relation between philosophy and religion, reason and faith. Greek philosophy is essentially secular, focused mainly on reason. Scholastic philosophy represents an effort stretching over centuries to reconcile the concepts of reason and faith in various ways. This effort finally came undone when the entire enterprise was rejected in the Enlightenment reassertion of independent reason as the standard of knowledge, presupposing the emancipation of philosophy from religion, for instance through attention to the distinction between reason and faith.[24]

It has been said that modern philosophy records the displacement of theology in an atheistic world.[25] With the important exception of Thomism, philosophy since the Middle Ages has been engaged in a still unconsummated effort to free itself from religion, for instance in the Enlightenment period, which is often understood through its widespread skepticism toward religion.[26] After Descartes and certainly after Kant, claims to knowledge can no longer be based on the claim to theological insight. Yet the theological impulse has by no means disappeared from the philosophical discussion, in which it has tended to take on new forms. The degree of continuity in French philosophy between philosophical and religious themes is one of its most remarkable features.[27]

Hegel's theory is often understood, or more precisely, misunderstood as essentially philosophy of religion, even as a form of ontological proof.[28] Yet its author typically maintained that the philosophical conception of free thought introduced by Descartes at the beginning of modern philosophy was made possible by the Protestant Reformation.[29] For Hegel, the conception of independent thought,[30] presupposing the separation of reason and faith, or again the principle of the world as regulated through reason, what he calls the Protestant principle, is the central insight of modern philosophy.[31]

Yet despite repeated attempts, philosophy has never entirely emancipated itself from religion, since it has never finally severed the cord linking reason and faith. The same Hegel, for instance, who insisted on the importance of the conception of free thought as the hallmark of modern philosophy, recognized religion as an essential component of knowledge in the absolute sense.[32] Although Hegel's theory is often thought to be the culmination of

8

rationalism, it insists on the inseparable link between reason and faith – since reason itself requires faith, that is faith in reason.[33]

For centuries, French culture has been deeply influenced by Roman Catholicism.[34] The religious element remains a persistent, central aspect of French philosophy.[35] The pandemic religious element in French philosophy can be illustrated by the recent claim, advanced in all seriousness by an important French thinker, that Europe has always been, is now, and will in all probability remain basically Christian, even Roman Catholic.[36] The same religious element in French philosophy can be further illustrated by the French reading of Descartes.

Outside France, Descartes's theory is routinely read as a rationalist effort to emancipate reason from faith in order to pursue knowledge by the natural light alone. Read in this way, Descartes bases his position on what is present to mind, to the "I think" or *cogito*, as opposed to mere revelation. He strives to separate reason from faith through a view of evidence based solely on the certainty of the individual conscience as distinguished from assertions based on belief in God.

This way of reading the Cartesian theory suggests a conflict between philosophy and religion, between reason and faith. In France, however, the Cartesian theory is often, perhaps even mainly read as maintaining the inseparability of reason and faith, hence as presupposing the continuity between philosophy and religion, or theology. In France, the unusually religious character of French thought is often taken to be compatible with a religious reading of the Cartesian theory. In French circles, the distinction between reason and faith, in which many claim to see the resolutely modern character of the Cartesian position, is usually understood as an effort to ground reason in faith, as an instance of the permanent link of philosophy to religion.[37]

Descartes is widely supposed to have dispensed with faith to found knowledge in the rational certainty of the *cogito*, in the conscience of the individual subject as distinct from God – more precisely in the first truth, or *je pense*, from which everything else follows – and to provide certain foundations on an extratheological basis. Yet he can also be read as basing the claim to overcome doubt on awareness of God,[38] on the certainty that God is no deceiver.[39] Although Descartes is often understood as a resolutely secular thinker, the insistence that knowledge depends on the certainty of faith is a persistent doctrine running throughout his writings from the beginning to the end.[40]

Historically, Descartes's concern to link his theory of knowledge to faith failed to disarm theological objections that led to his writings being placed on the *Index*. The difficulty posed by a possible conflict between religion and philosophy in the Cartesian theory is evident in the Port Royal *Logic*, a thoroughly Cartesian work. Pierre Nicole and Antoine Arnauld, the authors, both strongly Cartesian thinkers, suggest that reason and faith do not conflict

9

since they arise from the same source. Yet they candidly admit that the fifth edition, published in 1683, was modified in response to theological objections.[41] One can further speculate that the important role accorded in French philosophy to Pascal – who, other than his purely mathematical writings, is best known for his quarrel with Jansenism – is at least partially due to the French emphasis on religion.

The strongly religious character of French philosophy paradoxically predisposes it to Heidegger's antireligious philosophical theory. As we shall see, Kojève's famous reading of Hegel explicitly presupposes a strong continuity between Hegel's and Heidegger's philosophical atheism.[42] Although Heidegger studied theology and even spent time in a Jesuit seminary, his relations to the Church were later strained, even hostile.[43] Yet in the context of the continuing French philosophical commitment to religion – as part of the ongoing debate between thinkers such as Sartre, who claim to liberate themselves from the constraints of faith, those such as Merleau-Ponty, who strive to think within a semblance of the Christian framework even when their faith has diminished, and those who strive to maintain both personal faith and a Christian framework for religion – Heidegger's interest in being is often seen as compatible with a Christian perspective. Thomists have traditionally been hospitable to Heidegger, particularly French Thomists. For instance, Etienne Gilson, while regretting that Heidegger overlooks the Thomist thesis that the being of beings is God, applauds his return to the Platonico-Aristotelian concern with the relation between beings and being.[44]

THE PHILOSOPHICAL TRADITION

The resolutely historical character of the French philosophical discussion is surprising. History of philosophy has gone out of fashion in English-language circles. Hegel is the main influence on British idealism. It is well known that the analytic philosophical tendency grew out of the revolt against British idealism initiated by Bertrand Russell and G. E. Moore. This revolt, which was not initially antihistorical, later became so in the wake of Wittgenstein. Recent analytic philosophy has retained a resolutely ahistorical and even on occasion frankly antihistorical bias. Although some analytic thinkers are interested in the concept of history, they are in general unconcerned with the historical status of the philosophical discipline or even the historical status of knowledge.[45] They tend, on the contrary, to prefer a positivistic view of philosophical discussion restricted to a concern with ahistorical objects and objectivity understood in an ahistorical manner.[46] The positivistic, ahistorical and even antihistorical nature of analytic philosophy is above all evident in contemporary philosophy of science, which for the most part simply ignores historical discussion in favor of the examination of alternative conceptual models of science.

Heidegger's detailed studies in writings after *Being and Time* of a number of figures in the philosophical tradition strikes a sympathetic chord in French philosophy, which is resolutely oriented in a historical direction. In France, unlike America, the majority of philosophical works are historical and not systematic. The English-language discussion is replete with studies of the main Greek thinkers or Kant, but includes comparatively few other figures in the philosophical tradition. German idealism, for instance, which is rarely studied in English-language thought, is a main topic in France at present.[47] Such writers as Hegel or Schelling or even Fichte are rather frequently studied in French philosophy. The vogue for Hegel studies is in part to be explained through Hegel's continuing role as a master thinker in recent French thought.[48] The emphasis on Schelling, who is perhaps as popular as Hegel, is partly due to the religious element in his thought. As measured by the number of works on his thought or translations of his works into French, France (e.g. Xavier Tilliette, Jean-François Marquet, Vetö, Courtine, and others) is at present unquestionably the world's center of Schelling studies.

The continuing French philosophical concern with historical topics is reflected in the comparative prestige accorded to historians of philosophy. In English-language philosophy – with the exception of Greek thought, where historians such as G. E. L. Owen or Gregory Vlastos can shine – there is little attention to historical themes. Apart from writings on a few selected philosophers, say, Kant, and more recently Wittgenstein, Frege, and the Vienna Circle theorists, it is more than suspect to be concerned with establishing and chronicling the main features of a given body of thought. A historian of philosophy is thought of as someone who does not really do philosophy, certainly not in any essential sense. In French thought, the historian of philosophy is regarded as an equal player in the game, whose historical interests do not require excuses. Examples include such earlier figures as Gilson, Jacques Maritain, Ferdinand Alquié, Henri Gouhier, and Xavier Léon, more recently Aubenque, Vuillemin, and Alexis Philonenko, and at present Marion, Courtine, and Brague.

HUSSERL, HEGEL AND FRENCH PHENOMENOLOGY

When the history of French philosophy in this century is written, phenomenology will loom very large. In France, where phenomenology has long been more important than elsewhere, it is sometimes understood as the main philosophical movement of our time,[49] even as the successor to philosophy at the end of metaphysics.[50]

The French philosophical turning towards Heidegger was aided by the traditional French interest in phenomenology.[51] Heidegger began as a phenomenologist. *Being and Time*, the main text of his early period, is strongly influenced by Husserl's transcendental phenomenology. Husserlian phenomenology originated in Germany but seems to have become even more important in France. Even in Germany, except perhaps during Hegel's lifetime, phenomenology was never the dominant tendency. Attention to phenomenology has considerably declined in recent years as the major representatives (Husserl, Heidegger, Merleau-Ponty, Sartre, Gabriel Marcel, Karl Jaspers) left the scene, and new tendencies, such as hermeneutics, most clearly associated with Hans-Georg Gadamer, Heidegger's student, and Paul Ricoeur, have emerged. But phenomenology has continued to attract strong attention in France, in part because of the continued interest in Descartes, whose thought Husserl claims to prolong in his own transcendental phenomenology.[52]

The French appreciation of the views of Husserl and Hegel contributes to the interest in Heidegger's thought.[53] More than elsewhere, French writers tend to turn to Heidegger because of an interest in Husserl or to combine interests in both thinkers. The turn to Heidegger in French phenomenology is helped, not hindered, by the continuing French concern with Husserlian phenomenology. Important French students of Heidegger, including Emmanuel Lévinas and Derrida, have devoted detailed studies to Husserl as well.[54]

Although there are fewer Husserlians than Heideggerians in France, that is not usually regarded as an indication of the relative importance of the two philosophers. In French philosophy, Husserl's theory is still often understood as approximately equal in importance to Heidegger's. Husserl and Heidegger are often considered together, in dialogue, as it were, something that is rare elsewhere.[55]

This tendency is comparatively unusual. Heidegger scholars outside France either tend not to know Husserl's thought well, or when they do, to consider it relatively unimportant for the constitution of Heidegger's theory. Even Heidegger scholars familiar with Husserl's thought, approach Heidegger's thought with little or no recourse to Husserl's position.[56] In a classic presentation of Heidegger's thought prepared under Heidegger's direction, Otto Pöggeler devotes comparatively little attention to Husserl. Pöggeler accepts Husserl's view that Heidegger failed to build upon the Husserlian basis.[57]

Pöggeler's reading of the views of Husserl and Heidegger as discontinuous is implicitly disputed by Merleau-Ponty's stress on their continuity. According to Merleau-Ponty, Heidegger merely prolongs Husserl's thought, from which he does not basically depart. He maintains that Heidegger's own main text can fairly be understood as the "*explicitation*" of Husserl's idea of the life world (*Lebenswelt*).[58] Although few French philosophers go as far as Merleau-Ponty in stressing the continuity between Husserl and Heidegger, his concern to understand Heidegger against the Husserlian background is typical of the French discussion.

The French emphasis on the Husserlian background in Heidegger's theory is consistent with Heidegger's own view of the matter. *Being and Time* is dedicated to Husserl. Heidegger insists that he was captivated by Husserl's

Logical Investigations. He stresses his repeated effort, over a period of years, to come to grips with Husserl's position.[59] Although it is unclear whether his later position can still be properly regarded as phenomenology,[60] his early fundamental ontology, like Husserl's theory beginning in *Ideas, I*, is widely seen as a form of transcendental phenomenology.

Heidegger's appeal to French philosophy was strengthened by the French philosophical concern with Hegel. At least four factors in the French Hegel discussion call attention to Heidegger's theory. First, French Hegel scholars often insist on a link between Hegelian and Husserlian forms of phenomenology. According to Kojève and Hyppolite, for many years the main French Hegel scholars, and to Wahl[61] and Derrida, Hegel's theory overlaps with Husserl's.[62] This suggests a link, through Husserlian phenomenology, to Heidegger's thought.

Second, there is the role of Heidegger's theory for an understanding of Hegel's. In his famous study of Hegel's *Phenomenology of Spirit*, Kojève relies heavily on the views of Marx and Heidegger. Kojève's immensely influential lectures during the 1930s, the basis for his famous book which appeared in the 1940s, focused attention on Heidegger's theory, which, in his reading of Hegel, in part represented a more recent version of Hegel's own theory. Kojève was one of the first participants in the French philosophical debate to be aware of Heidegger's position. His early interest in Heidegger's theory preceded and partially determined his study of Hegel. He regards Heidegger as presenting the most significant atheistic philosophy since Hegel.

Third, and more remotely, there is the way that Heidegger calls attention to Hegel, something which, in the French context, suggests the need to bring Hegel's and Heidegger's theories together.[63] Heidegger made repeated efforts, in his language, to dialogue with important thinkers on their own level.[64] Beginning with *Being and Time*, Heidegger's writings contain a number of attempts to enter into dialogue with Hegel's thought.[65]

Fourth, there is the enormous influence of Hegel in French thought. In France, from Kojève in the early 1930s until the decline of Marxism at the end of the 1960s, a long string of Hegel commentators, often associated with the French Communist Party, either developed a peculiarly leftwing form of Hegelianism or a Hegelian form of Marxism. Increasingly, Heidegger's theory was seen as representing a viable alternative to this tendency. For the desire to escape from the pervasive influence of what many saw as a disturbing form of leftwing Hegelianism led for many in the direction of Heidegger.

"FRENCH" PHILOSOPHERS AND FOREIGN CONCEPTUAL MODELS

Further aspects of French philosophy relevant to the reception of Heidegger's theory include the fact that so many "French" thinkers are of foreign origin, and the French willingness to assimilate foreign conceptual models. The important role of foreign-born thinkers in French intellectual life is surprising since France has long been a country turned inward on itself. The French Revolution confidently announced the universal ideals of liberty, equality and fraternity and promptly violated them in the great terror to which it gave rise. The ultimately Christian ideal of fraternity, rarely translated anywhere into practice, is even less frequently realized in this largely Roman Catholic, basically xenophobic country. According to Foucault, the institution of the psychiatric hospital has long been used to exclude those who were held to be insane.[66] In the postwar environment, Charles de Gaulle's powerful vision of a France united in defense of itself has been regularly distorted by his supporters and others in the political debate to exclude resident aliens. The same land that brought us the famous egalitarian ideals of the French Revolution, which continue to ring throughout subsequent history, also spawned the authoritarian vision of a Joseph de Maistre[67] and Joseph-Arthur Gobineau's view of history as an Aryan conspiracy.[68]

French intellectual life, like France itself, may initially appear mainly, even wholly, to revolve on its own axis. Its apparent indifference, even hostility, to other views is, however, misleading since it is in fact extremely sensitive to foreign philosophical models and foreign intellectuals. French philosophy is unusually open to foreign, particularly German philosophical models.[69]

The interest in views imported from abroad is not a recent phenomenon, as witness Voltaire's well known efforts over many years to bring the insights of John Locke's *Essay Concerning Human Understanding* and above all Isaac Newton's *Principia Mathematica* to the attention of his French colleagues.[70] What is recent is the tendency to concentrate on Germany as the main such source. As early as the beginning of the second decade of this century, well before the rise in French interest in Hegel or the concern with Heidegger, the great French critic Hippolyte Taine observed that "From 1780 to 1830, Germany produced all the ideas of our historical period, and, during still half a century, perhaps during a century, our great task will be to rethink them."[71]

Obviously Heidegger would not have achieved preeminence in French philosophy if it had not been open to the influence of a foreign intellectual. It has been said that there are four German models of French philosophy: Nietzsche, Heidegger, Marx, and Freud.[72] In fact, we have already noted the presence of others, including Husserl and Hegel, whose thought has exercised a strong influence on French philosophy at least since the end of the 1920s.

The French intellectual context has been exceedingly hospitable to foreign-born philosophers. Recent examples include such well known "French" philosophers as Emmanuel Lévinas, the phenomenologist born in Lithuania; Eric Weil, a German-born thinker who did work on Kant and Hegel, and put forward his own systematic position;[73] Alexandre Koyré, a Russian emigrant who made significant contributions to the history of philosophy and science before emigrating to the United States; Alexandre Kojève, who was also

Russian by birth; Jacques Derrida, who was born in Algeria, at the time a French possession, and many others.

FRENCH ACADEMIC CONSERVATISM

In the United States, college faculty tend to be liberals, whereas in France and Germany they tend to be conservatives. French academic conservatism, partly due to the strong Roman Catholic influence present everywhere in French philosophy and society, is further fostered by the structure of the French academy. It has been said that the entire French system of secondary education is organized around the reproduction of the French educational system.[74] For this reason, leftwing French philosophers have periodically denounced the role of French philosophy in preserving the status quo.[75]

In the present context, it will be sufficient to identify four ways in which the French educational system tends to co-opt future academics, including philosophers, by subjecting them to a series of pressures to ensure that they conform to, rather than deviate from, accepted academic norms as the price of success. College teachers, who generally tend toward conformism, are perhaps even less adventurous and more conformist in France than elsewhere.

One factor is the time, often many years, that many French academics spend in the *lycée* before beginning to teach at university level. In practice, this means that one must often watch one's academic step over a long period of time in order to have any hope of a university career.

A second factor is the structure of the *agrégation*, a nationwide competitive examination based on a different set program in each of the different academic disciplines. The examination consists of two parts, a written exam followed by an oral. In order to pass the exam, it is better to distinguish oneself within the usual academic guidelines than outside them. A famous example is Sartre's effort at brilliance when he first took the exam: he was failed, and passed it on his second attempt.

A third factor was, until recently, the requirement of a second dissertation, or *thèse d'état*, which was normally undertaken only after the young professor, having proven his or her mettle in a series of competitive exams, had passed the *agrégation* in order to become *agrégé*, had acquired a doctorate, most often a *doctorat du troisième cycle*, and had begun to teach. In practice, this meant that at a point in his or her career when a young professor in the United States university system, who has finished the requirements for the degree, need only acquire tenure, the average French professor, who instantly receives tenure on being appointed to a position, nonetheless otherwise remained a student, often for a lengthy period of time, during which the second dissertation was being written. The result was an unusually lengthy period in which the young professor remained subject to external direction, hence to influences tending to bind his or her allegiance to the French educational establishment. Although the second dissertation has recently been abolished, other obstacles have been introduced in its place. Hence, it seems unlikely that the result will weaken the various structures tending to link the average French professor to the corporate structure of French education.

A fourth factor concerns the particular way that French academic talent is identified and nurtured through a system of elite secondary schools. The notion of an elite school system is fairly common in Western countries, which have long maintained elite secondary schools and universities. An obvious example is the English public school system, in reality a number of private schools for students from a frequently wealthy or at least well-to-do background, the best of whom are expected to matriculate at Oxford or Cambridge.

The French system is different, but the results are similar. Even if students in the French elite school system often come from a well-to-do family, emphasis is placed less on the financial background than on the identification and eventual co-optation of the most intelligent students through a system of national examinations. The system,[76] which goes back to Napoleon, includes a number of so-called "grandes écoles" of which the most prominent are the Ecole Polytechnique for future engineers as well as for those interested in mathematics and the physical sciences, the Ecole Normale Supérieure[77] mainly for humanists, and the Ecole Normale d'Administration for future technocrats. These schools take the place of, and are commonly – and correctly – regarded as superior to, an ordinary university education. Those who study in these schools have traditionally enjoyed an enormous comparative advantage in the series of competitive examinations taken by future French teachers at university level.[78] It has been suggested that one does not become but is rather born a *normalien*, or student of the Ecole Normale.[79] Acceptance as a *normalien*, Bourdieu has argued, is a consecration.[80]

One enters this and other elite schools after a period of intense preparation followed by rigorous examinations including both a written, and, for those successful in the first stage, oral portion. Those admitted to the schools take no further examinations while they are there. But on graduation they are expected to play a leading role in France as heads of major companies and, in the case of the *normaliens*, within the university system as teachers of humanities. Instances of such students who go on to play a major role in French society are frequent and frequently well known. Recent examples among French politicians include Georges Pompidou, a former president, who was admitted as first on the list (*cacique*) to the Ecole Normale Supérieure and taught before turning to politics, and Valéry Giscard d'Estaing, Pompidou's successor, who is a graduate of both the Ecole Polytechnique and the Ecole Nationale d'Administration.

The peculiarly rigorous selection process and the subsequent nurturing to which these students are exposed is designed to produce, and in fact produces, an unusually tightly knit group, loyal both to their institution and to the system of which they are arguably the finest flower. The system leads to a clear co-optation of its most important members who, having been identified and fostered through it, naturally tend to defend and to propagate it. The result is a strong, sometimes unconditional loyalty to the very restrictive, rigid academic system, heavily tilted towards a numerical few, the academic elite, in which they themselves have succeeded.[81]

The importance of this background continues to manifest itself throughout the academic career. In France, it is normal for future students to indicate that they are graduates of the Ecole Normale after their names when publishing a book. This background is also a factor in attracting students since, within the French academic establishment, those professors who are well connected, those who are *normaliens*, are more attractive to work with for those students whose goal is to enter into and become a part of the system.[82]

The same system that ensures the co-optation of elite French academics, including philosophers, tends to maintain traditions of all kinds, leading to a resistance to change and a consistent political conservatism. Like others, philosophers live in, and are subject to the pressures of, the prevailing social context. It is well known that Kant deferred the publication of his writings in order not to incur public censure. For decades Hegel has been accused, most frequently by Marxists, of seeking a political accommodation with the political establishment of his day.[83]

This same political conservatism is reflected in Heidegger's own deeply conservative thought. His intrinsic conservatism is evident in his turning to National Socialism, a conservative revolutionary movement, which in the waning days of the Weimar Republic was acknowledged by many intellectuals as a putative third way between liberalism and communism. Heidegger's conservatism is further evident in his insistence on the importance of tradition. In *Being and Time*, he argues for the need for authenticity, understood as an authentic choice of oneself, or "ownmost" possibilities of being. An authentic choice is a choice of what has already been authentically, of one's destiny, in other words a choice of a future that lies in the authentic reenactment of one's past.[84] Hence, yet another reason why French philosophy turned so strongly to Heidegger lies in perceived conservative qualities of his thought, regarded, for that reason, as useful to counter other, more liberal views.

2

HEIDEGGER
AND THE MASTER THINKER
IN FRENCH PHILOSOPHY

The previous chapter identified features of French philosophy tending to turn it toward, or at least to create an atmosphere receptive to, Heidegger's thought. The present chapter will analyze the concept of the master thinker with special reference to French philosophy.

A MASTER THINKER?

The phenomenon of the master thinker is not confined to France. It can be found in other countries, too, and is a common feature in academic and nonacademic disciplines, including philosophy, where the ideas of a few thinkers tend to dominate the ongoing discussion to a disproportionate degree, generating the very framework in which other contributions are received and evaluated. This dominance is apparent in what is often an almost reverential attitude of Marxists toward Marx, of Freudians toward Freud, for instance, and of followers in general toward significant intellectual figures.

In philosophy, too, the phenomenon of the master thinker is widespread, for instance in Anglo-American analytic philosophy. At the beginning of the twentieth century, a small coterie of thinkers at Cambridge University including Russell and Moore, and later Wittgenstein, formulated views that have dominated the discussion ever since. This pattern has endured in more recent analytic thought even as the dominant figures have changed. The ideas of Wilfrid Sellars and W. V. O. Quine, more recently those of Donald Davidson, Michael Dummett,[1] and now Rorty, and perhaps to a lesser extent Hilary Putnam, literally form the horizon of the discussion. Anyone who writes in the analytic vein but fails to take their ideas seriously risks being excluded from serious consideration.

A similar phenomenon is even more widespread in France, particularly in French philosophy, where Descartes has been the master thinker over centuries and others have enjoyed a similar status for briefer periods. The predisposition for the philosophical debate in France – to this day a strongly centralized country in many senses of the term, politically as well as intellectually – to center around the theory of a master thinker was undoubtedly a factor in enabling Heidegger to become the master thinker of French philosophy.

THE MASTER THINKER AND PHILOSOPHY AS DIALOGUE

To comprehend the master thinker phenomenon in philosophy, it will be useful to consider the dialogic structure of the philosophical tradition. Virtually since its origins in ancient Greece, philosophy has been understood, by analogy with the Platonic dialogues, as spoken or written dialogue. The two forms of dialogue can be roughly described as oral, and antitraditional on the one hand, written and based on tradition on the other hand.

The former, or Socratic model, follows the example of the Platonic dialogues, where philosophy is presented as a direct discussion, or conversation.[2] This Platonic notion of philosophy as an oral dialogue is still influential. It underlies so-called Oxford common room approach, still widespread in analytic philosophy, famously illustrated by J. L. Austin. Philosophy, in this model, takes place as a rapid-fire exchange in a direct, face-to-face encounter. A similar idea lurks in the background in infrequent philosophical works presented as largely or even wholly oral in character, as in Saul Kripke's *Naming and Necessity*.[3]

The oral, Socratic model of philosophy as dialogue is characterized by a resolutely antitraditional stance. This antitraditionalism is exemplified, even in views that do not insist on oral dialogue, in the familiar idea that we need to begin again – to begin in awareness of the failure of previous thought (Kant), to make a new beginning (Husserl), to recover the beginning (Heidegger), to ignore the history of philosophy in a resolutely systematic approach (Quine). Such variations on the theme of a new beginning for philosophy assume that the philosophical discussion is discontinous and can start anew, so to speak. Philosophy, on this model, is not understood as a tradition, or a continuous dialogue taking place over time, but rather as a series of discrete, independent discussions.

The rival Hegelian model, though also influenced by the Platonic example, extends the dialogue over time. Philosophy is now viewed as an indirect, ongoing dialogue, a tradition, not as a direct encounter, and, for that reason, not as oral, but essentially as written. In this model, the conversation of philosophy occurs as later thinkers react to and build upon the written views of their predecessors; and the philosophical tradition is a continual, written dialogue in which competing ideas are advanced and rejected in an effort to construct a satisfactory theory. This view is most clearly exemplified by Hegel, according to Heidegger the inventor of the history of philosophy in a philosophical sense,[4] who privileges the written over the spoken,[5] and who consistently strives to take into account and to build upon preceding theories.

The common element in both models is the assumption that philosophy follows some version of the Platonic dialogue. The dispute between them concerns the proper way to model the dialogical form of philosophy, not whether it is dialogical. This problem can be put more provocatively as follows: if we admit that the philosophical discussion assumes the form of a dialogue, are there any further constraints? Does philosophy have any further structure other than the oral or written dialogue between individuals?

We can begin to respond by noting the restrictions upon participants in philosophical dialogue. It may seem as if philosophical dialogue were open on an equal basis to anyone who cared to participate. Yet most of those who take part in the debate do so on a rather unequal footing. For the views of only a relatively small number of thinkers effectively shape the philosophical discussion which they often influence decisively as master thinkers (*maîtres à penser*),[6] masters of the philosophical game.[7]

Histories of philosophy tacitly concede that only a relatively small number of thinkers really influence the philosophical debate. No historian of philosophy attempts to mention all the participants. For the same reason, philosophical movements are usually described through the views of a few central thinkers. Examples include the dominance of Descartes, then Leibniz and Spinoza in continental rationalism, of Locke, Berkeley and Hume in British empiricism, and of Fichte, Schelling and Hegel in German idealism.

Each of these philosophers is important within an important philosophical movement. Each of them can fairly be regarded as contributing to the development of a particular approach, to the formulation of a tendency, to the elaboration of a movement. The philosophical tradition as a whole can be understood as an ongoing struggle among competing approaches tending to exclude each other as the single true or correct theory of knowledge and truth.[8]

WHITEHEAD, KANT AND SARTRE ON THE MASTER THINKER

Under different names, the conception of the master thinker has been discussed from various perspectives. According to Whitehead, on the assumption that "Philosophy never reverts to its old position after the shock of a great philosopher,"[9] an outstanding thinker can be identified through the introduction of a new alternative that permanently displaces the discussion. Yet it is rarely the case that different views coalesce around a single, identifiable position.

To take an extreme example, the phenomenological movement issuing from Husserl's thought is widely regarded as a search for essences. But some of its main proponents (e.g. Heidegger, Merleau-Ponty, Sartre, and others) are not concerned with essences, and it is unclear whether the movement itself has a single essence. Moreover, alternatives to established positions are often recognized through their influence. But there are doubtless many important ideas, alternatives in Whitehead's sense, that fail to attract attention and hence do not displace the succeeding discussion.

Whitehead's conception of the phenomenon of the master thinker remains embryonic. A more developed approach is suggested by Kant's concept of philosophy as a systematic science. According to Kant, a system requires the unity of the various parts of a theory with respect to a single idea.[10] Like Hume, who famously argues that a missing shade of blue can be inferred as absent,[11] Kant assumes that the parts of the theory are interrelated in a natural unity, so that the absence of even one of them can be noticed. A new science is based on a new hypothesis whose elements follow an intrinsic order of which its founder (*Urheber*) is often unaware. He advances and applies a view that is often unclear both to him and his followers but that is to be understood in terms of its rational unity:

> For we shall then find that its founder, and often even his latest successors, are groping for an idea which they have never succeeded in making clear to themselves, and that consequently they have not been in a position to determine the proper content, the articulation (systematic unity), and limits of the science.[12]

Kant expands his argument that a new science is based on a new insight in his revival of the distinction between the spirit and the letter which St. Paul proposed as the basis for interpretation grounded in the Christian faith. Kant reinterprets this distinction to emphasize the contrast between a conception of the whole and the interpretation of passages taken out of context. With this in mind, and in order to protect his own position against misinterpretation, Kant recommends the interpretation of a theory in terms, not of its letter, but of its intrinsic spirit.[13]

The idea of textual interpretation in terms of the spirit and the letter was popular in the German idealist tradition.[14] It is presupposed in efforts by Fichte, Schelling and Hegel to complete the theoretical revolution initiated by Kant,[15] and is related to a conception of orthodoxy influential in the reception of Kant's position. Beginning with Reinhold, a series of writers separately claimed that they were the only one fully to understand the critical philosophy. Kant's frequent indications to thinkers as disparate as Reinhold and Maimon that he alone understood the critical philosophy only encouraged this tendency.

It is virtually a truism – Hegel and Cassirer are important exceptions – that historians of philosophy rarely do original work of their own; their energies are mainly taken up in the arduous, unending task of reading others' views. Yet original thinkers frequently make claims for unusual understanding of prior thought, as in Heidegger's tacit and not so tacit assertions that only his own readings, for instance his own readings of the critical philosophy, are authentic. Heidegger is typically uninterested in Kant's theory for its own sake. He admits that his attempt to dialogue with Kant is violent, but asserts that the violence is justified since it is subject to other criteria.[16] It is fair to say that Heidegger's interest is not simply or even mainly to provide a correct reading of Kant's philosophy but to reread him as a precursor of his own view.[17]

The assertion, frequent in the discussion concerning the *Critique of Pure Reason*, that a particular writer possesses unusual insight into the critical philosophy, is consistent with Kant's own understanding of the relation between an important thinker and his disciples. For Kant, the former utilizes an idea he cannot formulate, and the latter formulate an idea that they cannot utilize. For instance, in a famous passage Kant claims to understand Plato better than he, Plato, understands himself.[18]

Through his modest suggestion that an original thinker often makes use of an insight that he cannot clearly formulate, Kant encouraged his students to suggest exclusive possession of the correct reading of his thought. As concerns the critical philosophy, this claim has been raised on purely philosophical grounds not only by writers who were relatively modest (K. L. Reinhold) but also on occasion by major thinkers (Fichte). Similar claims with clearly political ramifications have been made throughout the Marxist movement with respect to Marx's thought.

Kant agrees closely with Whitehead's conception of the master thinker as someone who launches an idea taken up by the later discussion that turns on grasping and further developing its spirit. A master thinker is someone who dominates the later discussion, which is largely, mainly, on rare occasions nearly exclusively, concerned to work out the implications of his thought. Unlike Whitehead, who ignores the relation of the master thinker to subsequent debate, Kant stresses that the master thinker dominates the later discussion whose task is to come to grips with his thought.

Kant's concept of the master thinker finds a distant echo in Sartre's effort to link the thought of the master thinker to society. Kant's analysis is intentionally abstract since he is concerned throughout with the conditions of the possibility of knowledge in the most general possible sense. For Kant, the master thinker is characterized by an original idea that dominates the later discussion. Sartre's innovation lies in the suggestion that the ability to dominate the later discussion is due to an original idea as well as its relation to contemporary society. For Sartre, a master thinker is someone whose thought captures the nature of society at a given moment.

This concept of what we have called a master thinker arises in embryonic, undeveloped form in Sartre's later, Marxist phase, in his assertion that philosophy is sustained by the practice (praxis) from which it emerges and which it explains. Sartre makes three assumptions in this regard. First, he assumes that there is a single form of social practice that characterizes society at a given moment. According to Sartre, the present period is the epoch of capitalism, which arose in the wake of the Industrial Revolution. For explanatory purposes, other forms of social practice are not significant.

Second, he assumes that at most a single theory can grasp the dominant contemporary form of social practice. He fails to entertain the possibility that more than one theory might be able to explain contemporary social practice or that the understanding of contemporary society might be a question of degree only. Third, he assumes that philosophy is solely concerned to understand social practice. In this way, he silently excludes from consideration all philosophical theories – in practice, the majority of them, including the initial version of his own position – that are not centered on the comprehension of social practice in particular or society in general.

According to Sartre, a theory that understands the society in which it emerges must remain the philosophy of its time for as long as it continues to grasp contemporary social practice. "Thus a philosophy remains efficacious so long as the *praxis* which has engendered it, which supports it, and which is clarified by it is still alive."[19] It follows that there can be only one philosophy of our time, one theory that is both supported by and succeeds in comprehending contemporary social practice. It further follows that, when social practice changes, when society enters another period, what has been the philosophy of the time, the master idea of the contemporary epoch, loses its vitality. The result is a theoretical vacuum created by social change that invites the contribution of a new master thinker.

Sartre's assumption that a master thinker captures the nature of the social context in an unusually penetrating manner can obviously be realized only rarely. He identifies three such occasions in modern philosophy, which he associates with the names of Descartes and Locke, Kant and Hegel, and finally Marx. These three philosophies define the modern philosophical discussion:

> There is the "moment" of Descartes and Locke, that of Kant and Hegel, finally that of Marx. These three philosophies become, each in its turn, the humus of every particular thought and the horizon of all culture; there is no going beyond them so long as man has not gone beyond the historical moment which they express.[20]

The assertion that there are only three important philosophies in the modern philosophical tradition is obviously questionable. So is the claim that either of the odd couples, Descartes and Locke, or Kant and Hegel, represent a single philosophy. Descartes is a rationalist whereas Locke is an empiricist. Hegel intended to bring to a close the movement in thought initiated by Kant. The Young Hegelians and later the Marxists routinely contend that Hegel was successful in that task.[21] In his first philosophical text, the so-called *Differenzschrift*, Hegel argued that there can never be more than one true philosophical system; one can point to basic dissimilarities between the Kantian and the Hegelian positions to deny that there is any single position that Kant and Hegel share. It is even more difficult to identify a single position shared by Descartes and Locke since the former's rationalism and the latter's empiricism seem basically incompatible.

It is clearly controversial to identify Marxism without qualification as the philosophy of our time, as a theory that cannot accept revisionism of any kind.[22] When Sartre offered this claim in 1957, in the wake of the Hungarian Revolution, it represented an acknowledgment of his residual Marxist faith, despite the terrible events in Hungary, in effect the suppression of freedom in the name of freedom. Today, after the tumultuous changes in Eastern Europe, it is considerably more difficult to defend this claim. Either, as Sartre foresaw, as times change a new philosophy must come to the fore; or Marxism in fact never grasped the warp and woof of modern society, never clarified the practice that engendered it.

There is obviously no neutral, universally, or even widely acceptable way of identifying the master thinkers of the philosophical tradition. Unquestionably, Sartre is correct that some thinkers succeed in capturing in thought the social practice of the time in a way that propels them to the center of the discussion. Yet if thought does not have to be socially oriented to be important, this is not a reason to identify master thinkers in this way only. Other thinkers capture only the *Zeitgeist*, the ideas that are in the air, as Heidegger can be said to capture the spirit present at the decline of the Weimar Republic and as Sartre clearly captured the concern with freedom in occupied France.

Since the philosophical tradition can be understood in different ways, it is simply impossible to agree on a short list of the few genuinely great philosophers. Such a list would have to be very short indeed since there are only a few thinkers who are universally or even widely regarded as great philosophers from any perspective. On one reading of the philosophical tradition, it includes no more than four names: Plato and Aristotle, Kant and Hegel.[23] These four thinkers arguably comprise the tiny handful of genuinely great philosophers whose influence extends throughout the subsequent philosophical discussion that takes shape as a series of reactions to their thought. They also exemplify those rare thinkers whose influence extends beyond philosophy to other domains, such as social science, the arts, literature, in short virtually throughout Western culture. Yet from different perspectives, one might want to include Descartes or Hume, Bergson,[24] Wittgenstein[25] or Frege, or St. Thomas, St. Augustine, and others.

Whitehead, Kant, and Sartre agree at least that what I have been calling the master thinker decisively affects the philosophical discussion. After the impact of a major thinker, there is a tendency for later philosophical positions to take shape within his sphere of influence and to revolve around his theory as moons and asteroids move in orbit around a planet, and as planets circle around the sun. The theory of the master thinker exerts a quasi-gravitational influence on the views of others who take up his problems, debate his solutions, and generally continue to think within the gravitational field or conceptual horizon established by his thought. In unusual cases, the conceptual field of the master thinker is so strong that it literally cannot be "seen," as if it were invisible, by virtue of its location at the center of the discussion where, like a giant star it exerts its influence but absorbs all light.[26]

THE MASTER THINKER IN FRENCH PHILOSOPHY: DESCARTES, LACAN, SARTRE

There have always been master thinkers in the philosophical tradition, those whose thought dominated the later debate. Whitehead's famous description of the "European philosophical tradition" as "a series of footnotes to Plato" indicates the impact of Plato's thought in what is routinely known as the Platonic tradition.[27] In modern philosophy, Descartes has been peculiarly influential in two ways: in his discovery of the idea of independent thought as distinguished from faith, which Hegel called the Protestant principle; and in his discovery of the foundationalist strategy for knowledge that has since dominated epistemology.[28] Hegel's influence has been acknowledged by many writers, as in the frequent assertion that later philosophy is largely composed of a series of reactions to his thought.[29]

The fact that a theory attracts attention does not necessarily mean that it was developed by a master thinker. Reinhold, for instance, was widely popular in the discussion of Kant's critical philosophy, but his theory was intrinsically unimportant and has since by and large been forgotten. A master thinker has an organizing or centralizing effect on the later discussion: his views not only influence the debate, they define the boundaries within which it takes place, provide it with a focal point and stake out the positions that may be taken up by the contenders. This crucial organizing function of the master thinker, evident throughout the philosophical tradition, is particularly strong in French thought.

French philosophy has long had a succession of master thinkers (*maîtres à penser*) and seeming master thinkers. Since the 1930s, Hegel, Kojève, Sartre, Lacan, Marx and Heidegger have all at least briefly enjoyed the special status of the master thinker. Merleau-Ponty, Lévi-Strauss, Foucault,[30] and Derrida are writers with important international reputations who never gained the kind of ascendancy in the philosophical discussion long held by Descartes, and for much shorter periods by Hegel, Kojève, and Sartre.

In France, Marx's theory is a special case. For many years his influence was sustained through two different sources: philosophically, through the leftwing Hegelianism popularized first by Kojève and then by Sartre; and politically, through the French Communist Party. The latter was a major force until it was effectively silenced by the election in 1981 of François Mitterand, a socialist, as president and its subsequent political maneuvering. Marx's influence was exceedingly strong until the late 1960s, but after the student rebellion of 1967–1968 it began to recede rapidly. It has all but disappeared at present as the result of the recent political changes in Eastern Europe. But at its peak, French Marxism was an important intellectual movement, particularly in the writings of Louis Althusser, the orthodox Marxist, even Stalinist philosopher.[31]

In its heyday, Marxism, though always dependent on Hegel's thought, nearly equalled it in importance. It was certainly more influential philosophically than the views of Merleau-Ponty, Lévi-Strauss, Foucault, or Derrida. Merleau-Ponty is an extremely solid if unspectacular thinker. Despite his position of influence as professor at the prestigious Collège de France, his main audience has been abroad, particularly in the United States, where his thought has been extensively discussed. Lévi-Strauss is a philosophically trained anthropologist whose thought is one of the main sources of French structuralism. Yet he played only a relatively minor role in the strictly philosophical debate, and then mainly through his controversy with Sartre about the latter's Marxism.[32] Foucault, another highly regarded professor[33] at the Collège de France, has arguably been more influential in the period since his death than he was in his lifetime.[34] Derrida is a deliberately eccentric writer who has long had a much greater audience abroad, occasionally approaching a cult following in Anglo-Saxon lands, and there mainly in literature departments. In France, his thought has not so far elicited the interest of more than a small coterie of close associates who tend to publish with Editions Galilée and/or to be associated with the Collège International de Philosophie in Paris.

In most cases, the career of a master thinker is like a flower that buds, suddenly bursts into full bloom, and withers after a while. Thus, around the turn of the nineteenth century, in the post-Kantian period, Fichte was for a brief moment the brightest star in the philosophical firmament, prior to his decisive eclipse by Hegel. All the master thinkers of French philosophy have enjoyed a similarly transient status – except for Descartes. His influence, which spans several centuries of French thought, apparently remains undiminished.

In the hothouse environment of French culture, the writers identified here as master thinkers in the French philosophical context have distinct, even intimate links with each other. With the exception of Descartes, each of these thinkers has, for a variable time, exercised a strong, decisive, even overwhelming influence on contemporary French philosophy; each of them was influenced by Heidegger; each further propagated Heidegger's influence in the French discussion. And, in comparison to Heidegger's commanding presence as the most important master thinker in French philosophy since Hegel, each was finally only a minor satellite, an asteroid, a lesser body in orbit around an enormously larger gravitational mass.

Lacan is a Freudian psychoanalyst with a worldwide reputation as well as the uncontested doctrinal master of French psychoanalysis.[35] In the inbred world of French culture, he maintained a complex link to philosophy, particularly to Heidegger, Hegel, and Kojève,[36] as well as through the structuralist discussion and his brief psychoanalytic treatment of Beaufret.[37] As will become clear below, the latter more than anyone else created the ongoing French fascination with Heidegger's theory. Lacan's transient contact with Beaufret led to his own direct acquaintance with Heidegger.[38] Although an important intellectual who virtually ruled over Freudian psychoanalysis in France, Lacan willingly deferred to Kojève,[39] whom he acknowledged as his master.[40] Kojève's characteristic concepts, centered around Lacan's own interpretation of the famous master–slave analysis in Hegel's *Phenomenology*, appear throughout Lacan's writings.[41] In point of fact, many of Lacan's fundamental ideas are decisively influenced by Kojève's reading of Hegel.[42]

Sartre's dominant role in French philosophy after the end of the Second World War – *Being and Nothingness* appeared in 1943 – and during the emergence of French structuralism in the early 1960s is well known and has often been described.[43] Like Lacan's, Sartre's theory reflects the influence of the views of Heidegger, Hegel, and Kojève, as well as others, above all Husserl.[44] Husserl was undoubtedly Sartre's first major philosophical master. It was to pursue his studies on Husserl that he spent the academic year 1933–1934 in Berlin. His first major academic publication, the "Essai sur la transcendance de l'Ego," written in 1934, offers a realistic rereading of Husserl's idealist conception of the ego.[45] Like so many French intellectuals, Sartre only came to Heidegger through Husserl's writings. He reports that his initial enthusiasm for Husserl's theory led to an intensive preoccupation with it over a period of four years. He only turned to Heidegger's theory when he was saturated with Husserl's, in order to resolve problems that still remained, in particular solipsism and the elaboration of a realistic perspective.[46] The influence of Hegel's position on his thought, particularly in *Being and Nothingness*, has often been studied.[47] Unlike so many other French thinkers of his generation, Sartre was not introduced to Hegel through Kojève's famous lectures on the *Phenomenology*, although he was certainly aware of Kojève's views through his friends and, apparently, through an article written by Kojève.[48]

HEGEL AS A "FRENCH" MASTER THINKER

Assessments of the importance of Hegel's thought are extremely disparate. While some writers regard his theory as uninteresting, even unimportant, others argue that it is one of the few genuinely important philosophies in the entire philosophical tradition. Lévinas, for instance, a thinker deeply influenced by Husserl and Heidegger, once claimed that "For a philosopher, to locate his thought with respect to Hegel's is as for the weaver to install his loom prior to attaching or removing the cloth that will be woven and rewoven."[49]

Among the long succession of master thinkers in French philosophy, those most important for an understanding of Heidegger's emergence as the leading French philosopher in the postwar period are Descartes, Hegel, and Kojève. Besides Marx, who weighed heavily in the turn to Heidegger and has influenced the French debate via Hegel, Kojève, and the French Communist Party, Hegel and Kojève were the most influential thinkers in French philosophy from the 1930s until the rise of Heidegger at the end of the Second World War.

Hegel's position, like that of other major philosophers, has been interpreted from different, often incompatible points of view. The main approaches to Hegel are already apparent in the dissolution of the Hegelian School after his death in 1831. On the one hand, there were the Young Hegelians, including Marx, who tended to reduce or even to eliminate the religious element in Hegel's thought; the Right Hegelians, on the other hand, stressed its religious aspects; and in between, the Old Hegelians were fighting a losing battle to maintain the middle ground.[50]

French interest in Hegel began in his lifetime in Victor Cousin's discussion of the *Phenomenology of Spirit* in his courses at the Collège de France in 1828.[51] Cousin met Hegel in Heidelberg in 1817 and 1818, became interested in his work, and remained in correspondence with him.[52] In Cousin's wake, French Hegel studies continued in a desultory manner, although until relatively recently the influence of his thought in French circles was never more than minor.

In the last decade of the nineteenth century, Lucien Herr contributed a short, neutral presentation of Hegel's life and thought.[53] At the beginning of this century, Hegel's thought was discussed by a number of French writers. Such discussions include several chapters in a work by Victor Basch on classical German views of political philosophy[54] and a monograph by Paul Roques, the first such work in French devoted to Hegel.[55] Slightly later, in a series of lectures at the Sorbonne, which were eventually published in book form, the Kant scholar Victor Delbos mentioned Hegel in the context of a discussion of "Kantian factors in German philosophy from the end of the eighteenth to the beginning of the nineteenth centuries."[56] In a comprehensive work on scientific explanation, Emile Meyerson wrote at length on Hegel's philosophy of nature (*Naturphilosophie*).[57] The neo-Kantian Léon Brunschvicg contributed a violently critical chapter on Hegel in his account of consciousness in Western philosophy.[58]

Owing to his influence, Brunschvicg's attack on Hegel was important in establishing an unsympathetic climate toward his thought. Brunschvicg, like Husserl, regarded Hegel as part of the romantic reaction to Kant. He described Hegel as "the master of contemporary scholasticism."[59] For Brunschvicg, Hegel suffered the worst fate that could befall a thinker: he proposed a metaphysics of nature that was an anachronism even prior to its formulation.[60] Brunschvicg further maintained, from a clearly Cartesian perspective, that the absence of an appropriate method in Hegel's theory "renders his philosophy of history as inconsistent and feeble as his philosophy of nature."[61]

French interest in Hegel received a decisive new impetus through Wahl at the end of the 1920s[62] – it has been said that Wahl's important study of Hegel and Kierkegaard began the Hegel renaissance in France[63] – through Kojève in the 1930s, and through Hyppolite and Kojève in the 1940s. Since then it has continued strongly, so that at present France is one of the main centers of Hegel research. Hegel has remained so influential that even non-Hegelians give careful attention to his thought.[64]

Elsewhere, particularly in English-speaking countries, it has been relatively easy to ignore Hegel.[65] In a much-quoted passage, which perhaps exaggerates Hegel's influence – as it is unclear how Hegel relates to the discovery of psychoanalysis although his presence in French psychoanalysis is very real – Merleau-Ponty provides an antidote to this neglect, while at the same time warning specifically and very aptly against confusing Hegel's thought with the uses to which it has been put:

> All the great philosophical ideas of the past century – the philosophies of Marx and Nietzsche, phenomenology, German existentialism, and psychoanalysis – had their beginnings in Hegel; it was he who started the attempt to explore the irrational and integrate it into an expanded reason which remains the task of our century. He is the inventor of that Reason, broader than the understanding, which can respect the variety and singularity of individual consciousnesses, civilizations, ways of thinking, and historical contingency but which nevertheless does not give up the attempt to master them in order to guide them to their own truth. But, as it turns out, Hegel's successors have placed more emphasis on what they reject of his heritage than on what they owe to him.[66]

The importance of Hegel's thought in the French discussion, as perhaps elsewhere, cannot be measured by the number of his students. The number of people directly concerned with Hegel's thought in France or elsewhere has never been large. Yet, because of the forceful, insightful way in which his writings, particularly the *Phenomenology*, have been read by his most important French students, Kojève and Hyppolite, it has been exceedingly influential virtually throughout French culture. Those influenced by Hegel's theory include poets like Stéphane Mallarmé or Raymond Queneau, psychoanalysts like Lacan,[67] and philosophers whose main preoccupations lie elsewhere, such as Foucault and Althusser – they both wrote on Hegel for their *DES*, nowadays known as a *Maîtrise de philosophie*, or master of philosophy – as well as Derrida, who has written extensively on Hegel.[68]

Since the 1930s,[69] a small but lively tradition of Hegel studies has developed in France. Its main characteristics, besides the continuing interest in the *Phenomenology*, are a related concern with rationalism, theology, philosophical anthropology, phenomenology, existentialism and Marxism, all features that accord well with the traditional French emphasis on Descartes. Through Descartes, the inventor of so-called Cartesian or continental rationalism, French philosophy acquired a permanently rationalist thrust. This rationalist tendency continues to express itself in the ongoing struggle in French thought between rationalism and irrationalism, in which the latter is linked to a strong interest in such writers as Freud, Nietzsche and Heidegger, all of whom are read as challenging reason. The French discussion of Hegel's thought is largely rationalist, and mainly concerned to emphasize the historical character of reason as it unfolds in social, political, and cultural contexts. This adds a historical dimension to the ahistorical, even antihistorical Cartesian concern with reason, for which history was only a *fabula mundi*, a mere story.

French Hegel interpretation is dominated by a religious, or rightwing reading that corresponds to the strongly Christian impulse in French philosophy. The Christian inspiration behind Hegel's thought is unmistakable, and this in part explains the large number – larger perhaps than in other national traditions – of Roman Catholic thinkers in particular among Hegel scholars in France.[70] The interest in philosophical anthropology is a further development of the conception of subjectivity launched by the Cartesian cogito that according to Heidegger transformed all of philosophy into anthropology.[71] There is a subtle or not so subtle critique of theology implicit in the French concern with philosophical anthropology in general, and in particular in the master–slave discussion central to Kojève's interpretation.[72]

French Hegel interpretation stresses the relation of Hegel's theory to phenomenology and to its stepchild existentialism. The typical emphasis on the continuity between the Cartesian impulse and the phenomenological approach to Hegel is supported by two factors. First, there is the obvious continuity between the theories of Descartes and Husserl manifest in the latter's effort to depict his own theory as a continuation of the Cartesian position.[73] Second, Hegel too calls attention to the link between his theory and the Cartesian view. In suggesting that, had Kant been successful, he would have resolved Descartes's problem, and in further indicating his own concern to complete the Kantian philosophical revolution, Hegel implies that his position prolongs the Cartesian impulse.

The phenomenological reading of Hegel's theory common in French philosophy has at least four levels. One level emphasizes, as noted, Hegel's *Phenomenology*. A second level insists on the phenomenological aspect of Hegel's thought.[74] Third, there is the relation between Hegel's thought and other, more recent forms of phenomenology, particularly Husserlian phenomenology.[75] Kojève, for example, makes use of insights borrowed from Husserl[76] and Heidegger[77] as well as from Marx to interpret Hegel, while Hyppolite reads Hegel in part through Husserl's thought.[78] If existentialism is understood as an offshoot of phenomenology, then the fourth level is the related existentialist reading of Hegel. This reading is mainly due to two disparate sources: Heidegger's impact on Kojève's interpretation[79] and Sartre's impact on Hyppolite's interpretation.[80] If the existentialist readings of Hegel are diverse, it is because the very term "existentialism" is understood in obviously diverse ways and applied to quite disparate authors from Dostoyevsky to Sartre, including writers such as Rilke, Kafka, and Camus, and philosophers such as Kierkegaard, Nietzsche, Jaspers, Heidegger, and Sartre.[81] Since Wahl's study of the relation of Kierkegaard to Hegel, French Hegelians have routinely stressed the existential aspect of Hegelian phenomenology.

Hegel's thought has provoked political controversy since the dissolution of the Hegelian School at his death. Marx was a Young Hegelian or member of the Hegelian left wing, and Marxism has always had a close if uneasy relation to Hegel. The Marxist approach to Hegel's thought is especially appealing in France where until recently the Communist Party played an important political role. From the end of the Second World War to the French student revolution in the late 1960s, nearly every French intellectual of any significance had at one time been a member of the French Communist Party, interested in Marxism, or at least knowledgeable about it.

Until recently, the Marxist approach was a main component of the French Hegel discussion. His advocates included Marxists and non-Marxists alike, ranging from Kojève, the committed Marxist, over Roger Garaudy,[82] a member of the French Communist Party, and Jacques D'Hondt, an eminent French Hegel scholar with a similar political commitment,[83] to more neutral observers such as Hyppolite, who played an important role in the typically French effort to understand Marx through Hegel and Hegel through Marx.[84] Lukács develops a Marxist reading of Hegel throughout his Marxist writings.[85] In his important study of *The Young Hegel*, Lukács interprets Hegel as a reader of Adam Smith who in a sense anticipates Marx's own theory. Examples include Hegel's statement of the tendency of wages to diminish, his view that capitalism turns on the constant tendency of value to expand, his attention to the rise of poverty, and so on. Hyppolite, though not himself a Marxist, follows Lukács in his discussion of Lukács's reading of Hegel.[86]

KOJEVE AS A "FRENCH" MASTER THINKER

Like other major philosophers, Hegel is studied differently in different national traditions. Put simply, if somewhat misleadingly, the English-language discussion has long been concerned with the *Phenomenology*, whereas the German-language discussion tends to focus on the *Science of Logic*, and more recently on the early writings, unpublished during Hegel's lifetime, and on the *Philosophy of Right*. The French discussion of Hegel now centres on his early writings and his *Logic*, but until relatively recently, with some exceptions,[87] its main emphasis and contribution concerned the *Phenomenology*.[88]

In the context of the French discussion, the views of Hegel and Kojève are inextricably intertwined. Although Kojève did not inaugurate French interest in Hegel's work – the credit for that must go to Charles Andler[89] – his seminal reading of the *Phenomenology* lent immense momentum to the Hegel renaissance and has continued to influence not only French Hegel studies, but the French philosophical debate as a whole for several decades; it also helped shape the initial reception of Heidegger's thought.[90]

Thanks to Kojève's famous reading of the *Phenomenology*, Hegel became a central figure in French philosophy,[91] and Kojève himself became a force in French philosophy. Kojève's lecture series transformed a slow but steady interest in Hegel's thought[92] to the point where Hegel quite literally emerged as a master thinker in the French discussion, in which he continues to occupy a distinct philosophical niche.

Ironically, Kojève's lectures on Hegel led to a reversal similar to the one Hegel describes in his brilliant analysis of the master–slave relation in the *Phenomenology*, the very relation strongly emphasized in Kojève's reading of this work. In his analysis, Hegel famously contends that the truth of the relationship is that the slave is the master of the master and the master is the slave of the slave.[93] This same dialectical logic seems to be at work in Kojève's own relation to Hegel. For through a strange quirk indicating the curious status of the master thinker, Kojève, the interpreter, became for a while even more important in French philosophy than the author whose text he construed. Kojève, who presented himself as a mere reader of the thought of one of the most powerful of all philosophical minds, while simultaneously presenting his own views as those of the master, for a short time achieved a prominence within French philosophy greater than Hegel's, as perhaps its greatest master thinker in this period. When the definitive history of French thought in this century is written, it will not be surprising if the most influential "French" thinker of the period between the two World Wars turns out to be Alexandre Kojève who, as Alexandre Kojevnikov, even before he was naturalized, captivated a generation of future leaders of the French intellectual world in his famous lectures on Hegel.

To appreciate Kojève's impact in the French discussion, we need to consider both his charismatic personality and his work. Kojève was a complex, mysterious man of unusual intellectual gifts, with deep interests in oriental thought – he studied Chinese, Tibetan, and Sanskrit – and physics as well as philosophy. After fleeing his native Russia in the wake of the Russian Revolution, apparently in order to continue his education, he retained a lifelong sympathy for Marxism. He studied in Germany for years, earning a doctorate in philosophy under Karl Jaspers in Heidelberg with a dissertation on the thought of Vladimir Soloviev, the Russian religious thinker, before emigrating to France. Obliged finally, after dissipating his fortune, to earn a living, through the intervention of Alexandre Koyré,[94] his friend and fellow Russian emigrant, he began to give courses on Russian philosophy at the Ecole pratique des Hautes Etudes. He also wrote paid reviews of books covering a bewildering variety of topics for *Recherches philosophiques*, a journal that Koyré had a hand in founding.

When Koyré has to interrupt his courses on Hegel's philosophy of religion (*la philosophie religieuse de Hegel*), Kojève stepped into the breach with his own lectures on Hegel's *Phenomenology* from 1933 to 1939. He seems to have had a mesmerizing effect on his students.[95] The extraordinary list of regular auditors at his courses included such future leaders of French intellectual life as Raymond Queneau, Jacques Lacan, Georges Bataille,[96] Pierre Klossowski, Alexandre Koyré, Eric Weil, Maurice Merleau-Ponty, Raymond Aron, Gaston Fessard, Aron Gurwitsch, Henry Corbin, Jean Desanti, and André Breton.[97]

At the end of his lectures, in which he proclaimed the end of history,[98] lectures which paradoxically ended even as the Second World War erupted to show that history had not ended, Kojève was mobilized into the French army. Without academic ambition – his famous book on the *Phenomenology* is no more than the transcript of his lectures edited by Raymond Queneau, the French poet[99] – he later became an important French civil servant, negotiating on behalf of his adopted land, confining his work in philosophy to his leisure time. In a final irony, he died in 1968 during a meeting of the Common Market in Brussels, at a moment when France was caught up in the student revolution that nearly toppled the Gaullist government to which Kojève, justly regarded as a revolutionary intellectual and perhaps even as an intellectual revolutionary, had devoted his working life.

There is a close, still not fully clarified relation between the Hegel interpretations of the two Russian immigrants to France, Koyré and Kojève.[100] Koyré was a member of Husserl's Göttingen circle in 1910.[101] He later regarded Husserl, who knew little about the philosophical tradition, as a decisive influence on his own approach to the history of philosophy.[102] But in Göttingen his main teacher was Adolf Reinach.[103] When he emigrated to France, Koyré brought with him an unorthodox form of Husserlian phenomenology.[104] His unorthodoxy manifested itself in various ways, for example in his course on Hegel's philosophy of religion at the Ecole Pratique des Hautes Etudes from 1931–1932, in which he concentrated mainly on Hegel's Jena writings at a time when they were still relatively unknown.

Kojève's lectures were intended to continue the main themes of Koyré's course through a study of Hegel's *Phenomenology of Spirit*. He read the *Phenomenology* as a description of human existence[105] from an antireligious, atheistic perspective[106] including a critique of the extension of dialectic to nature[107] and an antidialectical view of method as basically the same in Husserl and Hegel.[108]

Kojève believed that the religious themes could not be isolated from the philosophical anthropology that, in his interpretation, characterizes the work as a whole.[109] This has been taken as suggesting that his views of Hegel were mainly, perhaps overwhelmingly, derived from Koyré.[110] Yet although Kojève took over Koyré's course on Hegel and his problems, it is not possible to deduce or otherwise to anticipate his own reading of Hegel from Koyré's.[111] Koyré may have held similar views of Hegel; but it is Kojève's statement of these views, not Koyré's, that influenced subsequent generations of French philosophy.

It is admittedly difficult to evaluate Kojève's reading of Hegel's theory. All observers agree on the importance of Kojève's Hegel interpretation, but opinions about what it represents vary widely. At the heart of the controversy is the question of whether Kojève offers insight into Hegel's thought, in perhaps the most important book ever written on Hegel,[112] or whether he silently substitutes his own view for Hegel's.[113]

Since Kojève himself was a controversial figure, it will come as no surprise that in the French discussion, too, opinions are sharply divided. Vuillemin, who sees Kojève as an atheistic existentialist, claims that one cannot exaggerate the importance of Kojève's study, which shows that Marx's *Capital* is the real commentary to Hegel's *Phenomenology*.[114] According to Bataille, Kojève understood that Hegel had already reached the outer limits of thought, which led him to renounce the idea of an original theory in favor of the explanation of Hegel's.[115] For Jean Lacroix, Kojève was simply the only real Hegelian of his time.[116] Henry sees Kojève's denial that dialectic applies to nature – also urged by Hyppolite – as unfaithful to Hegel's position.[117] According to Elizabeth Roudinesco, the French historian of psychoanalysis, Kojève's reading lies somewhere between history and fiction.[118] Aron – who remarks that one can admire various insights in Kojève's interpretation that, regarded as a whole, cannot be defended – holds that Kojève presents his own theory under the cover of a reading of Hegel's.[119] According to Patrick Riley, Kojève simply had no intention of presenting an accurate reading of Hegel.[120] Descombes, who studies Kojève in more detail, to the point where Kojève and Hegel seem to merge in one giant intellectual figure, simply refuses to address the question of the link between Kojève's account of the *Phenomenology* and Hegel's original work.[121] Others, more critical, distinguish between Kojève's commentary on, and his interpretation of, Hegel's *Phenomenology*.[122] For Pierre Macherey, Kojève was in effect a conceptual terrorist.[123] He maintains that Kojève abused the right of the commentator in presenting his own theory under the guise of an interpretation of Hegel's text.[124]

There is an evident disparity between the views of Kojève and Hegel, between Hegel's text and Kojève's reading of that text. For a time, this disparity was effectively covered up within the French philosophical debate, and the Marxist Kojève – who, like Lukács,[125] has been described as trying to be more Hegelian than Hegel[126] – briefly seemed to loom larger than Hegel.

It was possible to study the complex nature of the philosophical debate in the middle of this century as if it were determined mainly by Kojève in isolation from Hegel, who existed only, or mainly, as seen through Kojève's eyes.[127] Yet French Hegel scholarship, which Kojève helped to foster, was later to free itself largely or even wholly from Kojève's reading through a more standard interpretation introduced by Hyppolite.[128] The latter attended Kojève's lectures before going on to develop his own reputation as a major Hegelian scholar. It is fair to say that contemporary French Hegel scholarship is largely shaped by the views of Hyppolite, not those of Kojève. The paradoxical result is that, although Kojève provided a decisive influence for the French Hegelian tradition, his influence fostered an indigenous tradition of French Hegel scholarship that no longer or at most only rarely makes reference to him and that mainly functions as if he had never written.[129]

We need to distinguish between Hegel's theory, which Kojève regarded as the final possible position, and Kojève's own position. Although the two are obviously linked, they are different and should not be conflated. Hegel is a great philosopher, one of the great thinkers of the Western philosophical tradition, a master thinker both in the French discussion and throughout philosophy since the beginning of the nineteenth century. Kojève is at most an important Hegel interpreter, one of the most authoritative readers of Hegel's thought in a long line of important Hegel interpreters, with Lukács one of the two main Marxist readers of Hegel, one of the best known and certainly most influential French Hegel students.

In a letter, Kojève himself stresses his silent revision of essential Hegelian doctrines in his reading of the *Phenomenology*.[130] His interpretation stresses a number of ideas, some of which have been very influential, but not all of which can simply be ascribed to Hegel. Claiming to derive his position from Hegel, Kojève proclaims the end of history.[131] According to Kojève,

> Hegel was able to bring the history of philosophy (and, hence, history in general) to an end and to initiate the era of wisdom (whose light already shines on us, but also burns us, more than it warms us, which sometimes seems to us to be revolting) in identifying the Concept and Time.[132]

This idea has been widely echoed, for instance in Derrida's view of "absolute knowledge as closure or as the end of history."[133] Yet Hegel never claims to bring philosophy to an end in his system; in fact, he explicitly disclaims this possibility in his insistence that philosophy, which comes after the fact, is condemned to meditate on previous forms of thought.[134] If textual interpretation is still relevant, then it is worth while pointing out that nowhere in Hegel's texts is there any evidence for Kojève's famous claim that Hegel saw the end of history[135] in the figure of Napoleon at the battle of Jena – actually, Hegel only wrote in a letter that he had seen the world-soul on horseback.[136] And there is absolutely nothing in Hegel to support Kojève's enigmatic revision of that claim – an instance of his Stalinism that so irritated

Aron[137] – to the effect that the end of history arrived not in Napoleon but in Stalin. The closest Hegel ever comes to this sort of assertion is in his comment in the *Phenomenology* that we are now assisting at the birth of a new period.[138] Indeed, he seems to take back even that claim later on, in the *Philosophy of Right*, when he insists that the owl of Minerva, or philosophy, flies only at dusk.[139]

We can usefully compare Kojève's Hegel interpretation to that of his onetime student Hyppolite.[140] Kojève, and Hyppolite are well known for their important, but strikingly dissimilar studies of Hegel's *Phenomenology*.[141] Hyppolite's study of Hegel is widely regarded, even by those not sympathetic to it, as a model of objectivity and detachment in which there is considerably more Hegel than Hyppolite.[142] Hyppolite was a major, but considerably more orthodox Hegel scholar. He taught Hegel's theory to students who later became important in French philosophy such as Michel Foucault, Gilles Deleuze, Louis Althusser, Jacques Derrida[143] and Michel Henry. Kojève was even more important for an earlier generation of French intellectuals who became distinguished in an enormous range of cultural fields stretching from philosophy over political science, sociology and literature to Islam.

Kojève's famous interpretation of Hegel's theory is further comparable to Lukács's slightly less famous, equally insightful, and equally arbitrary Marxist reading of Hegel's *Phenomenology*. Working within the general framework of leftwing Hegelianism, both offer readings downplaying the religious side of Hegel's thought and stressing its anthropological aspect.[144] Unlike Lukács, who, after he became a Marxist, prided himself on his fidelity to Marxism, Kojève's Marxism was never orthodox. In his lectures, Kojève, despite his Marxist leanings, denied the Marxist application of dialectic to nature as well as its Hegelian origin.[145]

It has been said that Kojève's influence came into being when his study of Hegel appeared in 1947 with its strange mixture of Hegel, Heidegger and Marx.[146] But his impact on the wider public, though certainly facilitated by the publication of his course notes in the form of a book, had already been set in motion by his influential Hegel lectures. His rise to prominence was at least partly due to his unusual intellectual gifts, including his philosophical brilliance. For Aron, Kojève was more impressive than Koyré and Weil, more intelligent than Sartre,[147] someone who either had already thought or was capable of thinking any idea of his own.[148] Gadamer considered Heidegger to be only slightly less important than Kant and Hegel; Aron is reported to have had a similar opinion of Kojève.[149] Yet Kojève's personal brilliance is not sufficient to explain his rise not only to prominence but even dominance in the often dazzling intellectual atmosphere of the French philosophical discussion. His rapid ascendance depends as much on his foreign origin, his mesmerizing style, the work he made central to his own thought, Hegel's *Phenomenology*, on his view, which met a sympathetic reception in France, that history had come to an end with Napoleon, and the particular historical moment.

They say that *le style, c'est l'homme*. Even if this is not always the case, it clearly helped Kojève in the struggle for influence in the French philosophical discussion. Others, particularly Weil, who knew Hegel's text in similar detail, never attracted as much attention.[150] Hegel himself was apparently a poor lecturer, whose dry delivery was enlivened only by the power of his thought. Kojève's reading of Hegel, by contrast, was carried out in a virtuoso manner that fascinated his audience. Here is Aron's description:

> Kojève translated, to begin with, several lines of the *Phenomenology*, stressing certain words. Then he spoke, without notes, without ever tripping over a word, in impeccable French to which a Slavic accent added an originality and charm. He fascinated an auditorium of superintellectuals inclined to doubt or to criticize. Why? The talent, the dialectical virtuosity were part of it. I do not know if his oratorical capacity remains intact in the book that depicts the last year of the course; but this capacity that had nothing to do with eloquence, was due to the topic and to his person. The subject was both universal history and the *Phenomenology*. Through the latter, the former was explained. Everything acquired a meaning. Even those who were skeptical about historical providence, who suspected artifice behind art, did not resist the magician; at the moment, the intelligibility that he accorded to time and to the events functioned itself as a proof.[151]

Beyond his foreign origins and his mesmerizing style, the single most important philosophical factor in Kojève's emergence as a French master thinker was undoubtedly his choice of topic. The *Phenomenology*, a philosophical masterpiece, is Hegel's first major work. It is unusual in that Hegel, who conscientiously revised everything, did not see fit to revise it, and on some accounts it is Hegel's most significant study. Yet for a variety of reasons, including the rapidity with which it was composed, it is a very dark work that requires detailed commentary. In the French intellectual context, Kojève's lectures had the result of making available the main work of a major philosopher that was still unavailable in translation.

In virtue of its acknowledged importance, the *Phenomenology* has long attracted commentators but repulsed translators. Hegel is exceedingly difficult to translate. Obscure even in German, his discussion is even more difficult to follow in another language. The book was first translated into English in 1910,[152] but unavailable in French before Hyppolite's translation, which only appeared well after Kojève had finished his lectures. The mastery of foreign languages, which all French students are required to study in secondary school, has traditionally been rare. Kojève, who left the Soviet Union in 1919, spent years studying philosophy in Heidelberg. When he arrived in France in 1928, he was equipped with a thorough grounding in

Hegel and in the German language.[153] This and his mastery of French made him uniquely suited to provide an intelligent discussion of a fundamental, untranslated philosophical work, a work, moreover, that introduced reason to history at a time of historical ferment as France and all of Europe were moving uneasily towards the Second World War.

As we have already noted, Kojève's Hegel interpretation also appealed to the French because of his extraordinary claim, somewhat at odds with his emphasis on the historical component in Hegel's thought, to perceive through it the end of history. The related claim that philosophy has come to an end in Hegel's thought has long been popular with leftwing Hegelians, and particularly with Marxists ever since it was made by that first Marxist, Engels.[154] Kojève widens this claim to encompass the end of human being as well, a notion that runs through recent French philosophy, notably the views of Foucault and Derrida.[155] According to Kojève, here influenced by Marx, the end of history[156] is also the end of human being, the end of the free, historical human individual, following from the end of wars, revolutions and philosophy.[157]

The resolutely leftwing character of Kojève's reading of Hegel also attracted attention in the politically polarized French intellectual context. Leftwing Hegelians, who uniformly devalue the religious element in Hegel's thought, privilege finite over infinite views of subjectivity as well as the anthropological concept of human being over ideas of God. The key to all so-called leftwing readings of Hegel's thought, including Kojève's discussion of the *Phenomenology*, is the stress on the anthropological approach. Kojève maintains this approach, if necessary even against Hegel, when he insists that the *Phenomenology* is philosophical anthropology whatever Hegel may have thought.[158] From his anthropological angle of vision, Kojève emphasizes the priority of the interaction between subject and object,[159] in particular the complex relation between master and slave whose natural resolution lies in their reconciliation[160] at the end of history when all oppositions will have been overcome.[161] Hegel, argues Kojève, is not the first philosophical anthropologist: he is preceded on that path by such Christian thinkers as Descartes, Kant, and Fichte from whom he differs in his essentially pre-Christian, pagan conception of human being.[162]

Kojève's impact on the French discussion was further heightened by the particular historical moment that turned attention toward history and, by extension, toward historical rationality. His lectures coincided with the period of tremendous social instability from the moment that Hitler took power until the outbreak of the Second World War. The decline of the Weimar Republic, the rise of National Socialism in Germany, and the unstable political and economic situation in France – shortly to culminate in the *front populaire* (1936) – each called attention to a philosophical work intended to comprehend historical rationality, the historical character of reason and the rational character of history, the same theme that animated Marxism.

And lastly, there is a wonderfully dramatic, even fateful aspect to Kojève's reading of Hegel. Philosophers have long stressed the indispensable character of their stock in trade. At the dawn of the Western tradition, Plato maintained that philosophy was the minimal condition of the good life. In a famous passage in the *Phenomenology* Hegel suggested that history was at a turning point.[163] In his discussion of being, Heidegger grew more and more confident that this was the central problem of human history. And he maintained that through his account of metaphysics he was able to interpret the present and even the future.[164] An assiduous reader of both Hegel and Heidegger, Kojève, in a time of historical crisis and in terms recalling Heidegger's view of being, melodramatically draws attention to the link between the historical moment and Hegel's texts: "In the final analysis, perhaps the future of the world, and, hence, the meaning of the present and the comprehension of the past depend on the way in which we today interpret Hegel's writings."[165]

3

GERMAN PHENOMENOLOGY, FRENCH PHILOSOPHY, AND SUBJECTIVITY

As part of the effort to understand Heidegger's emergence as the master thinker of recent French philosophy, preceding chapters have studied the anatomy of French philosophy in general with an eye toward those features predisposing it toward a favorable reception of Heidegger's thought. Particular attention has been given to the important phenomenon of the master thinker in the French philosophical debate. This chapter will extend the effort to grasp Heidegger's appeal to French philosophy through remarks on the theme of the subject, or subjectivity.

A common interest in subjectivity is an important factor in the *rapprochement* between French philosophy and Heidegger. Subjectivity has been an important theme throughout much of the history of philosophy. It already looms large in the thought of such premodern writers as Augustine and Pico della Mirandola, and with the writings of French thinkers such as Montaigne and Descartes it becomes one of *the* problems of philosophy. Modern philosophy has made the question of subjectivity one of its main concerns.

Modern French philosophy has often been understood, for instance by Heidegger, as deriving from the Cartesian concept of subjectivity, the conception of the *cogito* that is basis of Descartes's theory. Subjectivity is further a main component of Heidegger's position, whose initial formulation depends on a highly original analysis of Dasein, or human being concerned with being, as the clue to being. Heidegger's rejection of the Cartesian position and, in his later thought, of metaphysics and philosophy in favor of so-called thinking can be understood through his rejection of the Cartesian view of the subject.[1]

This chapter will discuss some main modern approaches to the vast area of subjectivity. To avoid misunderstanding, let me clearly state that it is not my intention to provide a general history, or even an outline, of the conception of subjectivity in modern philosophy, or even recent French philosophy. The purpose of this chapter is merely to point to the importance of this theme for an understanding of Heidegger's role in recent French philosophy.

CARTESIAN SUBJECTIVITY AND KNOWLEDGE

Although the concern with subjectivity is much older, it emerges as an explicit theme only in modern philosophy. It arises in the context of, and is determined by, an interest in the problem of knowledge as early as Parmenides. In modern philosophy, as part of the continued focus on knowledge, there is a shift in emphasis from the object to the subject of knowledge. Any claim to know obviously requires a conception of the knower, the subject that knows, and of the object that is known, or subjectivity and objectivity.[2] Philosophers concerned with the theory of knowledge tend to comprehend subjectivity and objectivity as functions of the requirements imposed by their respective, normative conceptions of knowledge.

In terms of the subject–object distinction, it is fair to say that ancient philosophers mainly stress the object pole. Plato and Aristotle share a similar commitment to a conception of knowledge as objective. Plato's conception of ideas and Aristotle's conception of *ousia* satisfy a normative requirement for an invariant object understood as a necessary condition of knowledge.

In ancient thought, issues surrounding the nature and possibility of objective knowledge are mainly discussed without explicit reflection on the problem of the subject to whom knowledge is communicated, or through whom knowledge comes to be. Yet a concept of the subject is silently presupposed in ancient theories of knowledge as well as throughout Greek culture: in artistic depictions of the ideal human form and in Greek literature, where the relation of human beings to the gods is a frequent topic, as in the Homeric poems or the *Oresteia*. An idea of the subject looms large in Greek philosophy, for instance in the *Republic*, in Plato's discussion of the ideal state modeled on the structure of the mind, and in Aristotle's view of ethics that explicitly invokes a philosophical anthropology.

The rise of the modern view of the subject is dependent on the concept of the individual, which is still lacking in Greek thought.[3] This concept only enters the philosophical tradition in later Christian thought, for instance in the attribution of individual human responsibility for the fall from divine grace. This conception of individual responsibility presupposing the notion of individuality is already present in the writings of Augustine.[4]

Numerous writers have stressed the continuity between the Augustinian and Cartesian views of the subject.[5] Post-Cartesian epistomology emphasizes knowledge-claims which are resistant to sceptical objections of any kind. The modern concern with epistemological objectivity is not diminished but strengthened through a shift to a concept of the subject as the condition of objective knowledge. This shift is equally apparent in the Cartesian cogito and the Kantian transcendental unity of apperception, in the Hegelian substance becoming subject, in Husserl's transcendental ego, and in Heidegger's Dasein. Each of these concepts is introduced to support a claim to know not in a subjective but in an objective sense, a claim raised and sustained through an idea of subjectivity as the key to objectivity.

There is a reciprocal relation between scepticism, which is younger than the concern with knowledge to which it responds, and the proposed solutions that scepticism attempts to defeat. Descartes's theory has routinely been understood against the background of the Pyrrhonian scepticism reintroduced into the modern philosophical discussion by Montaigne. Descartes can be regarded as succeeding, or from another perspective, as failing in the effort to defeat the new Pyrrhonism, as gloriously rescuing or as heroically failing to save knowledge from scepticism.[6]

The Cartesian theory of knowledge turns on a conception of the cogito as an indubitable ground with clearly Augustinian roots. Augustine is neither a philosopher nor concerned with epistemology in the modern sense. But his work offers important philosophical insights for the theory of knowledge. In discussing freedom of the will, he aims to resolve the problem of evil encountered in his own progression from Manichaeism to Roman Catholicism. In his decision to go back into himself to find objective truth instead of going forth into the world, in his development of the idea of inner sense, he gives new meaning to the Delphic motto, "Know thyself."[7] He further adumbrates, although not under that name, the Cartesian idea of the cogito. As Descartes will later do, Augustine argues for the existence of God from his own existence, presented as indubitable. An anticipation of what will later become the Cartesian cogito is manifest in at least two passages in his analysis of freedom of the will. He writes: "Since it is clear that you exist, and since this would not be clear to you unless you lived, it is also clear that you are alive. So you understand that these two points are absolutely true."[8] And he adds: "Furthermore, it is very certain that he who understands both *is* and *lives*."[9]

Descartes did not initially possess a conception of the cogito. In the "Rules for the Direction of the Mind" (1628), his earliest philosophical work, he insists on "sound and correct judgments," "sure and indubitable knowledge," not on conjecture but on "what we can clearly and perspicuously behold and with certainty deduce," and on "the need of a method for finding out the truth."[10] In the "Rules," he elaborates his conception of method through the proper ordering of the objects of knowledge, beginning from the simple and rising to the complex, constantly relying on intuition, being careful to omit nothing, and so on.[11]

The introduction of the cogito in the "Discourse on Method" is a decisive new step in the formulation of the Cartesian view on method. The method secures a privileged source of certain knowledge through a strategy that has come to be known as foundationalism, or epistemological foundationalism. The foundationalist view of knowledge dominates the philosophical discussion in the modern period.

There are different ways to understand "foundationalism" and its denial, or "antifoundationalism."[12] In his influential, original formulation of his strategy for knowledge, Descartes recognizes only mental intuition and deduction.[13] He insists that knowledge is possible only through self-evident intuition and necessary deduction.[14] From this perspective, "Cartesian foundationalism" can be understood as the assertion that "indubitable knowledge is possible if and only if there is an epistemological ground or foundation that can be known with certainty and from which true statements encompassing the entire domain of what is to be known can be rigorously derived."

In his idea of the cogito, Descartes transforms the Augustinian return into the self into the path to universal knowledge. In the fourth part of the "Discourse," appealing to a normative conception of knowledge as that which is beyond any reasonable doubt, he introduces the cogito as a concept of the subject that can be thought of as entirely certain, or indubitable. According to Descartes, since the claim to think cannot be denied, it can serve as the basis of his philosophy. In an important passage, he states that

> whilst I thus wished to think all things false, it was absolutely essential that the "I" who thought this should be somewhat, and remarking that this truth "*I think, therefore I am*" was so certain and so assured that all the most extravagant suppositions brought forward by the sceptics were incapable of shaking it, I came to the conclusion that I could receive it without scruple as the first principle of the Philosophy for which I was seeking.[15]

Descartes's approach combines an antitraditional attitude with the effort to establish certain, or indubitable, foundations for knowledge. The cogito, or claim that when I think that I am I cannot deceive myself or be deceived, is, and is explicitly recognized as such by Descartes, here and elsewhere, the answer to his concern to elicit the foundation of all of his positive claims to know.

In the first of the *Meditations* he voices his conviction "that I must once for all seriously undertake to rid myself of all the opinions which I had formerly accepted, and commence to build anew from the foundation, if I wanted to establish any firm and permanent structure in the sciences."[16] This same antitraditional attitude is still present in his last work on "The Passions of the Soul," where he feels "obliged to write just as though I were treating of a matter which no one had ever touched on before me."[17] Through his conception of the cogito as an Archimedean point, he validates the appeal to clear and distinct ideas as necessarily true. Further following Augustine, he also turns to the proof of the existence of a greater perfection, or higher being.[18] Here and in his later writings, the capacity to prove the existence of God is acknowledged as the key to acquiring other, further knowledge.[19]

CARTESIAN AND KANTIAN VIEWS OF SUBJECTIVITY

There is a crucial difference between a theory of knowledge and an account of the nature of human being. A concept of subjectivity that follows from a normative conception of knowledge obviously cannot be employed without qualification to describe a human subject. Descartes fails to clarify, in fact tends to confuse, the issue in his description of the cogito as in effect an epistemological placeholder postulated in order to satisfy an epistemological condition of knowledge.

From an idea of subjectivity invoked to sustain a normative view of objective knowledge, no inferences follow with respect to the nature of human being. On the basis of the Cartesian cogito, it is not possible to describe or otherwise characterize human subjects any more than it is possible to characterize human individuals on the basis of the Kantian view of subjectivity as the transcendental unity of apperception. Descartes's description of himself as a thing which thinks, or thinking being, must not be misunderstood as a description of people who obviously both think and have bodies.[20] The perspective of epistemological theory, in which we wonder with Descartes whether men passing in the street are robots, is not that of ordinary life.[21] Human beings are both active and passive, joyous and sad, hungry and sated. In the "Discourse," the Cartesian allusion to man as "the spectator of all,"[22] the basis of his famous spectator theory of knowledge, does not refer to human being but rather to a view of the problem of knowledge, more precisely the claim to know an independent, already constituted object in terms of clear and distinct, or self-validating perceptions.

The Cartesian view of the subject as an abstract epistemological posit, and as a passive spectator rather than as active, follows directly from his normative view of knowledge. Building on others' views, Descartes insists on subjectvity as a requirement for objective knowledge. Kant follows Descartes's idea that objectivity, or objective knowledge, depends on subjectivity.

The Kantian conception of subjectivity differs in two main ways from the Cartesian view. First, Kant, unlike Descartes, carefully distinguishes between subjectivity and the human subject, between the requirements of a rigorous theory of knowledge and the very different task of arriving at a viable comprehension of human being. Second, Kant transforms what in Descartes's view is a mere passive spectator into an actor as the condition of knowledge. This Kantian move, which in the critical theory is known as the Copernican Revolution, is basic to any form of modern idealism. It is still not widely known that the move itself did not originate with Kant, but had been widely anticipated elsewhere, for instance in Vico's early form of anti-Cartesianism that depends on the idea that *verum et factum convertuntur.*[23]

Kant's interest in the problem of human being is linked to his well known interest in Rousseau. In an early work, Rousseau differentiates the problem of enabling man to realize himself through his own efforts from the more important but also more difficult problem of the nature of man.[24] Kant's interest in comprehending human being is evident in his corpus on many different levels. In a letter, he remarks that nothing is more useful than consideration of the problem of man if there is to be the least possibility of making progress in this direction.[25] He further taught a course in anthropology that resulted in a book, *Anthropologie in pragmatischer Hinsicht* (1798). In this work, Kant contends that man can only be studied from two perspectives: from the physiological point of view – what would now be called the biological perspective – to see what nature has made of man; or from the pragmatic vantage point, under the presupposition that man is a freely acting being (frei handelndes Wesen), to see what man can, ought, or in fact does make of himself.

Kant distinguishes sharply between his anthropological and his epistemological concerns. In his epistemological writings, he typically expresses interest in, but warns against, the attempt to respond to questions about the nature of human being understood as a subject. In a well known passage in the *Critique of Pure Reason*, he famously refers to three questions as combining the interests of reason.[26] In his *Introduction to Logic*, he reproduces and supplements this passage through the addition of a fourth question, "What is Man?," which he describes as the most useful but also the most difficult one.[27] In his work on logic, he insists that metaphysics, the topic of the *Critique of Pure Reason* as well as of the *Prolegomena*, is confined only to the problem of what we can know. And in the same text he analyzes the limits of our knowledge of human subjectivity in his discussion of the paralogisms. In his distinction between logic and psychology, he specifically warns against what Husserl would later call psychologism, roughly a confusion between the conditions of the possibility of knowledge and what we in fact do.[28] Logic, including transcendental logic, which is central to the critical philosophy, abstracts from all content and is a priori; psychology is a posteriori, or experiential.[29]

Kant understands metaphysics as epistemology, not as a claim about ontology. For Kant, metaphysics is solely concerned with answering the question of what we can know.[30] Following Descartes's view that knowledge requires a subject, Kant sketches his view of the abstract subject of knowledge, or "I think," that must be able to accompany all representations, in his concept of the original synthetic unity of apperception.[31] The continuity between the Cartesian and Kantian conceptions of subjectivity is as obvious as it is instructive for an understanding of the critical philosophy. It is, then, surely no accident that Kant's "I think" (*ich denke* [denken = to think]) is an exact translation of Descartes's (*cogito* [cogito, cogitare = to think]).

Kant follows Descartes in understanding the epistemological subject, not as a human being, but through the requirements of a normative conception of knowledge. His break with the Cartesian conception of the subject as passive is determined by the Copernican Revolution, the basic epistemo- logical insight in the critical philosophy. In claiming that knowledge is impossible if intuition must conform to the constitution of objects, Kant rejects in principle the effort, common to rationalism and empiricism, to know an independent object.[32] According to Kant, knowledge is possible only on the supposition that objects conform to our knowledge,[33] since, as he also says, reason can know only what it produces.[34] Yet if the epistemological subject can know only what it produces, then it is not passive but necessarily active as a condition of the possibility of knowledge.

With respect to Descartes, Kant's epistemogical innovation results in a dissimilar view of the subject of knowledge. Two main differences concern revisions in the nature of the subject and of its relation to the object. Kant's understanding of the subject as active is a basic theme not only in the *Critique of Pure Reason* but throughout the critical philosophy. His three *Critiques* can be regarded as analyses of the possibility of theoretical, practical, and aesthetic knowledge, whose possibility depends on three types of reason, or rational activity, attributed to the knowing subject. Descartes's insistence on the subject as the key to knowledge is accompanied by a view of the object as already constituted and, hence, as independent of the subject. Kant's idea that we know only what we produce reaffirms the importance of subjectivity for objectivity while forging epistemological and ontological links between them. To assert that we know what we produce is to say that epistemology is grounded in ontology. We can know what we produce since we are its producers, and what we produce is transparent to the structure of the mind.

SUBJECTIVITY AFTER KANT

We have so far identified three distinct views of the subject of knowledge: a Greek approach de-emphasizing, or at least not stressing, the subject in order to concentrate on objectivity, in one reading the self-manifestation of objectivity that Heidegger much later makes central to his disclosure theory of truth; and the modern, Cartesian and Kantian approaches to objective knowledge that respectively stress concepts of subjectivity as passive and as active.

Each of these approaches to the subject of knowledge has been influential in the later philosophical debate. Thinkers in the German idealist tradition mainly tend to follow Kant's view of subjectivity as active in whole or in part, whereas more recent German thinkers tend to return either to Descartes's view of passive subjectivity or to what I have called the Greek view. Husserl's theory is influenced by Kant's, but his conception of the subject of knowledge is closer to Descartes's. Heidegger's understanding of the subject reflects a variety of influences. Simplifying somewhat, one can say that Heidegger follows both the Cartesian and the Greek conceptions of subjectivity in different periods of his thought; and that under Heidegger's influence, recent French philosophy has tended to follow a modified Greek view of subjectivity.

The famous Kantian Copernican Revolution leads to an anti-Cartesian conception of the subject widely influential in later German idealism. If knowledge is possible if and only if the subject produces what it knows, then the Copernican Revolution commits Kant to an active view of subjectivity as well as to a relation of identity between subject and object. If the subject produces what it knows, then in knowing the subject obviously knows what it has produced. In other words, objectivity is cognizable by, or transparent to, the subject, hence knowable, since objectivity depends on, and is identical with, subjectivity. The identity between the knower and the known, subject and object, subjectivity and objectivity, which Hegel called "the principle of speculation,"[35] runs like a red thread from the critical philosophy through later German idealism, the so-called philosophy of identity (*Identitäts-philosophie*), including Marx's theory.

As Hegel acknowledged, the principle of speculation is present in Fichte's theory, which Hegel regards as capturing the spirit of Kant's critical philosophy,[36] specifically in Fichte's identification of subjectivity and objectivity.[37] It is also present in Hegel's famous description of substance becoming subject in the *Phenomenology*. And it is present in Marx's theory. Marx's concepts of alienation and of value, two fundamental themes in his position, presuppose a relation of identity between the worker who produces a commodity, or product destined for sale, and the product thus produced. According to Marx, value is generated in the process of production when the worker concretizes his work in the form of the product. But the worker can only be alienated in virtue of the fact that he can be separated from his product, that is, since the product can be regarded as himself in the form of externality, as separated from himself.

Although all the later German idealists, including Marx, are influenced by Kant's theory, none follows the Kantian conception of active subjectivity in more than a loose fashion. Later ideas of subjectivity in German idealism and in much of later philosophy choose one of two alternatives: either they respond to and elaborate further alternative approaches present in a state of uneasy coexistence within Kant's critical philosophy, or they attempt a qualified return to alternatives rejected by the critical philosophy.

The various views of the subject in later German idealism are influenced by tensions in the Kantian view of subjectivity. Kant inconsistently combines his interest in a transcendental analysis of knowledge through an abstract view of the subject with an interest in real human being. In the critical philosophy, the idea that the subject produces what it knows as a necessary condition of knowledge clearly has, but is just as clearly not meant to have, an anthropological ring. Kant rigorously isolates epistemological and anthropological elements within his position. Although his theory of pure reason is intended to identify the conditions of knowledge whatsoever without regard to the nature or limits of human being, it inevitably has an anthropological aura that is finally destructive to the view he defends. It is unsatisfactory to claim that the subject is necessarily active unless one also elucidates the nature of this activity. Kant's failure to do so, for instance in his notoriously obscure allusion to an unknown capacity hidden within the human soul,[38] suggests the need to reconceptualize the subject in other, more human terms as a human being.

The post-Kantian evolution of the idea of the subject can be understood as a series of reactions to the Kantian view. Since Kant's rejection of the Cartesian spectator theory in favor of the subject as an actor remains within the framework of the Cartesian alternatives, the latter, including the re-interpretation of activity in anthropological terms, provides the boundaries of the ensuing debate. In the simplest terms, in German idealism after Kant, there is a gradual move away from the idea of the subject as an abstract epistemological placeholder, a mere principle assumed for purposes of knowledge, toward a rival view of the subject as a human being rooted in the social, political and historical world. Typically this move is not completed within the German idealist tradition since none of the main theories, including Marx's, which is most clearly committed to an anthropological perspective, is based solely on a conception of the subject as a human being. In post-Kantian German idealism, the main views of subjectivity all exhibit a tension between the abstract view of the subject as active that Kant proposes and the concrete view of the human being as the real subject toward which his theory implicitly refers. These aspects, in principle separable, are in practice intertwined within all later German idealist positions. Later forms of German idealism invariably emphasize either one or another of these aspects of his view (Fichte, Marx), or both at once (Hegel).

The post-Kantian moment in German idealism offers a complex discussion turning on the relation of the finite and the infinite, or absolute views of knowledge and subjectivity. Schelling, who understood the finite subject through the infinite, or absolute, differs as a special case from other major German idealists in that regard. If, for present purposes we ignore the distinction between Marx's supposed materialism[39] and German idealism in order to understand his theory within the German idealist movement, it is tempting to see a progression from abstract (Fichte), through abstract and concrete (Hegel), to exclusively concrete (Marx) views of the subject. Yet such a classification would finally be inaccurate since each of the views combines finite and infinite dimensions, or an understanding of the subject as both a real human being rooted in the real world and an abstract epistemological principle. The difference between them, then, is a matter of degree, or emphasis. For in each case, the German idealists, including Marx, offer dualistic appreciations of human being as a finite, concrete, human subject as well as an infinite, abstract view of subjectivity.

Marx's supposed materialism has mainly been understood, above all in the Marxist tradition, as the antithesis of idealism, above all as the antithesis of its Fichtean variety. Yet Fichte's abstract conception of subjectivity has clear parallels with Marx's own view. Through his critique of Hegel's view of the subject, Marx clearly moves in Fichte's direction.[40] Both Fichte and Marx initially base their theories on a view of the subject as active; both identify subjectivity and human being; and both are later driven through the logic of their respective theories beyond the initial view of the finite subject to a transfinite or absolute subject.

Most important philosophers are misunderstood, but Fichte more than most. A grasp of his theory is not helped by his hermetic style or his exaggerated claims, rebuffed by Kant, to be the only correct interpreter of the critical philosophy. Fichte's view of the subject is closely Kantian in two main ways. First, he insists on a conception of the subject, in his language the self (*das Ich*), as active.[41] In this way, he inverts Kant's argument. Kant analyzes types of knowledge and experience through types of activity, but he is unable to think the conception of a unified subject other than in the abstract sense of a transcendental unity of apperception. Fichte begins, then, with the result toward which Kant points in the critical philosophy but cannot attain. Second, in his theory of the self he develops the consequence of Kant's insistence on the original synthetic unity of apperception. The three fundamental principles of the *Science of Knowledge* (*Grundlage der gesamten Wissenschaftslehre*, 1794) Fichte's first and most influential statement of his position, develop the consequences of Kant's view of apperception through a conception of the subject, or self, the object, or not-self, and their interrelation.[42]

Hegel's view of subjectivity features a revised view of the absolute and a surprisingly fragmented analysis. The term "absolute," which Kant regarded as one of the few words that we cannot do without,[43] reappears in Fichte's absolute self, or self understood in hypothetical isolation from all context, and in Schelling's indifference point (*Indifferenzpunkt*). Hegel, who criticizes Schelling's featureless view of the absolute,[44] is often read as following Schelling's ontological reinterpretation of it. For Hegel, the absolute is a result that only fully is in the end.[45] The *Phenomenology* famously provides a three-fold analysis of the subject of experience as the immediate subject, then as all humanity rising to consciousness through the spiritual odyssey that Hegel describes, and finally as substance becoming subject, or the absolute.

Despite the strongly synthetic thrust to Hegel's thought, he ultimately fails to bring together the three different aspects of his conception of subjectivity, unable, just like Kant, to think the unitary subject of experience. Marx's critique of Hegelian idealism from the angle of so-called real human being is afflicted by a similar difficulty. Marx studies subjectivity on three interrelated, but different levels: in early writings, such as the *Economic and Philosophical Manuscripts*, through a concept of human being; in the

German Ideology and elsewhere through the idea of class, a concept that he never really defines; and in later, more economic writings, including *Capital*, through a theory of capital as the "real" subject of capitalism. The Marxist assertion that Marx advances beyond Hegel and philosophy in general to discover the real subject of human history in the concept of the proletariat[46] presupposes a unified Marxian view of subjectivity that Marx in fact never formulates.

EXCURSUS ON HUSSERL

What I am calling the pre-Kantian conception of subjectivity represents a qualified return either to the "Cartesian" view as in the theories of Husserl and the early Heidegger, or to a "Greek" view as in the later Heidegger. With the important exception of Husserl, later German idealism has continued the Kantian stress on the subject as active while making a slow transition away from the epistemological placeholder version of subjectivity advanced by Descartes and restated by Kant. Some writers stress Husserl's relation to Kant.[47] Not surprisingly, in virtue of his insistence on the continuity between his own position and Descartes's, Husserl retreats from various Kantian and post-Kantian changes in the conception of the subject to a pre-Kantian, more closely "Cartesian" view.

Husserl's never sharply delineated view of subjectivity combines Kantian and Cartesian elements. Like Kant and Descartes, he sharply distinguishes the subject of knowledge from human being. In the second edition of *Ideas* in 1913, he introduces the phenomenological reduction that he continues to regard, in all his later writings, as the cornerstone of phenomenology.[48] Owing to his commitment to transcendental phenomenology, Husserl insists on the difference between the empirical and the transcendental ego. It is from the perspective of the latter that eidetic phenomenology is possible.[49]

Husserl's retreat from the Kantian view of the subject to a more Cartesian, even Augustinan view leads to an ultimately ambiguous understanding of the relation between the subject and object of knowledge. Husserl wavers on the Kantian claim that knowledge is possible if and only if the subject produces its object. He employs the term "constitution" to refer to the relation between subjectivity and objectivity. Yet this neutral word, which is apparently never clearly defined, reflects his own inability to clarify this key aspect of his theory.[50]

There is no point in attempting here to settle a dispute between Husserl scholars about the proper interpretation of his theory. Yet as late as *Cartesian Meditations*, where he stresses the many connections between his own view and the Cartesian position, Husserl's conception of phenomenological constitution was either systematically ambiguous or at least undefined. For he held that transcendental phenomenology is the systematic analysis of the contents that constitute themselves in consciousness, of what is constituted in us; and he also held that the subject constitutes itself and its objects.[51] At the very least, Husserl appears to retreat in a Cartesian direction from Kant's view that we know only what we produce.

HEIDEGGERIAN SUBJECTIVITY

The frequent, but mistaken claim that Heidegger has destroyed the modern theory of subjectivity[52] misreads the genuine continuity between his own view and the preceding philosophical tradition. To comprehend his view of subjectivity, it is helpful to consider the relation of Heidegger's theory to Husserl's. In *Being and Time*, Husserl's influence is apparent in specific commitments to phenomenological truth as transcendent truth (*veritas transcendentalis*)[53] and to a form of a priorism as the genuine meaning of philosophical empiricism.[54] The Husserlian retreat from the Kantian view of active subjectivity is accelerated in Heidegger's thought: initially through a qualified return to the Cartesian spectator view, and later through a so-called decentering of the subject. Despite Heidegger's publicly anti-Cartesian stance, his initial view of the subject as Dasein is both Cartesian and anti-Cartesian. By contrast, Heidegger's later effort to decenter the subject, so influential in recent French thought, is resolutely pre-Cartesian, closer to the Greek concern with knowledge in the absence of any explicit reflection on the subject.

Heidegger's suggestion that the only positive influences on his thought lie in the ancient Greek tradition tends to cover up its many links to modern philosophy. The two main periods in the evolution of Heidegger's position are separated by what he later called a turning (*Kehre*) in his thought, a topic to which I will return below. What I am calling Heidegger's "Cartesian" view of subjectivity is central to his earlier, better known view of phenomenological ontology formulated in *Being and Time* (1927), his first and most influential philosophical work. The evolution of Heidegger's view of subjectivity is explicable through his lifelong fascination with being. As his view of being changed, it required a change in the view of the subject through which the concern with being is raised.

In *Being and Time*, Heidegger recasts Husserlian phenomenology, as he understands it, for his own ontological purposes. Heidegger's main theme – for Heidegger, an important thinker has only a single concern[55] – is the problem of being running through his entire corpus. In *Being and Time*, he poses the question of the meaning of being,[56] where being, or being in general, is distinguished from beings, or entities. Heidegger identifies phenomenology with ontology. He writes: "Philosophy is universal phenomenological ontology, and takes its departure from the hermeneutic of Dasein, which, as an analytic of *existence*, has made fast the guiding-line for all philosophical inquiry at the point where it *arises* and to which it *returns*."[57]

The term "Dasein" is an ordinary German word that is routinely used by philosophers within the German tradition to mean "existence," as in Kant's discussion of the existence (Dasein) of God.[58] "Dasein" is Heidegger's term for human being as well as for man's being. "As ways in which man behaves, sciences have the manner of Being which this entity – man himself – possesses. This entity we denote by the term *Dasein*.[59] The result is a three-valued ontology including entities, or things, being in general, or the being of beings, and Dasein, or human being that mediates between beings and being.

In *Being and Time*, Heidegger stresses the connection of Dasein with existence and being. According to Heidegger, Dasein is concerned with and understands being, at least in a preliminary way.[60] It understands itself in terms of its own existence.[61] And its various ways of being exhibit a concern with its being.[62] The main claim that Heidegger advances in this work is that being is time. But the entire treatise is devoted to an analysis of Dasein in two parts: the preparatory fundamental analysis of Dasein, and the later analysis of Dasein and temporality. Just as for Plato human being is the middle term between appearance and reality, so for Heidegger human being or Dasein is the link between beings and the comprehension of their being.

Being and Time strongly criticizes Cartesian ontology, including Descartes's failure to investigate the being of the cogito.[63] Heidegger's view of Dasein as existence follows from an anti-Cartesian, anti-anthropological view of subjectivity. On the basis of his own anti-anthropologism,[64] Husserl mistakenly thought that Heidegger had relapsed into basing a philosophy on anthropology.[65] Heidegger's agreement with Husserl's basic anti-anthropologism is clear in his effort to distinguish his own analysis of Dasein, or subjectivity, from anthropology as well as psychology and biology, the three sciences of human being.[66] His continued opposition to philosophical anthropology of any kind is frequently reiterated throughout his later writings.[67] The point of calling Heidegger's early view of Dasein "Cartesian" is to indicate that, despite his anti-Cartesianism, he continues the Husserlian retreat toward a modified Cartesian spectator view of the subject.

The "Cartesian" dimension in Heidegger's view of Dasein is particularly noticeable in his idea of truth as disclosure.[68] According to Heidegger, the disclosure view of truth is doubly rooted in Dasein: in Dasein's disclosedness, and in Dasein as both in truth and untruth.[69] Disclosure to the subject of knowledge consists in bringing to light what is hidden since "the entities *of which* one is talking must be taken out of their hiddenness; one must let them be seen as something unhidden (alethes); that is, they must be *discovered*."[70]

In saying that the early Heideggerian conception of the subject is "Cartesian," I am not saying that one view can be reduced to the other. Heidegger differs from Descartes and Husserl in his insistence on the way that Dasein, whose name literally means "existence," is rooted in the world.[71] Heidegger stresses the opposition between the Husserlian and Cartesian views of the subject as conscious and of Dasein as existence.[72] This opposition is, and is meant to be, fundamental. In thinking the subject through its existence, Heidegger intends to break with the modern philosophical tradition that he regards as beginning in Descartes, as continuing in Kant, and as reaching a new peak in Husserl. Yet Heidegger's view of subjectivity as the source of ontological truth remains strongly "Cartesian" since for Heidegger, as for Descartes but unlike either Husserl or Kant, the object of knowledge is already constituted independent of the subject. Just as the Cartesian cogito scrutinizes the contents of consciousness in order to determine which ideas are clear and distinct, so Dasein discloses truth by wresting uncoveredness from entities.

After the turning (*Kehre*) in his thought, at some point after the appearance of *Being and Time* in 1927, perhaps as early as that year but in all probability after 1930, Heidegger abandons his earlier effort to know being through Dasein in favor of a view of being as self-disclosing. This change is linked to a deepening of Heidegger's anti-Cartesianism, manifest in a gradual turn against metaphysics and philosophy. Kant had rejected bad metaphysics in order to ascertain the conditions of metaphysics as a science.[73] In *Being and Time*, Heidegger tries to recover a supposedly authentic, ancient Greek form of metaphysics that was covered up in the later philosophical tradition. Heidegger later came to believe that the effort to revive a genuine form of metaphysics was misguided. In his later thought, he equates Descartes's theory with Western metaphysics, or philosophy. For Heidegger, the introduction of the cogito inevitably transforms philosophy into philosophical anthropology that can only be overcome by overcoming Western metaphysics.[74] In a famous passage, meant to offer an alternative to the subject of the *Meditations*, Heidegger writes:

> Being subject as humanity has not always been the sole possibility belonging to the essence of historical man, which is always beginning in a primal way, nor will always be. A fleeting cloud shadow over a concealed land, such is the darkening which that truth as the certainty of subjectivity – once prepared by Christendom's certainty of salvation – lays over a disclosing event [Ereignis] that it remains denied to subjectivity itself to experience.[75]

This passage signals a fundamental change in Heidegger's view of subjectivity from a "Cartesian" to a qualified Greek conception, from a view that we can only comprehend being by analyzing Dasein to a view that being simply discloses itself to us. If being discloses itself, it is no longer necessary for human beings to disclose it. In this way, Heidegger retains his view of truth as disclosure – now modified only in the change from truth as disclosed through Dasein in favor of the view that truth is disclosed to Dasein – while avoiding the "Cartesian" error of an anthropological conception of the subject.

SOME RECENT FRENCH VIEWS OF SUBJECTIVITY

Heidegger's view of subjectivity has influenced French Hegel scholarship, French existentialism, and French structuralism. Heidegger's theory began to affect French views of subjectivity as part of the Hegel revival in the 1930s. Although Wahl[76] and Koyré[77] each wrote articles on Heidegger's position, it did not significantly influence their readings of Hegel's thought. Yet in his collection of essays on James, Whitehead, and Marcel, Wahl's reading of Heidegger's thought served as a philosophical benchmark against which to consider rather different views.[78] Heidegger's influence is stronger in the views of Hyppolite and above all Kojève. Hyppolite developed a momentary interest in Heidegger after his views on Hegel had taken shape. Kojève's reading of Hegel, by contrast, and in particular his conception of subjectivity, was from the outset strongly influenced by Heidegger's thought.

Hyppolite's most important work on Hegel, including his translation and study of the *Phenomenology*, was in print before the end of the 1940s. His early work on Hegel is entirely exempt from any Heideggerian influence. He later wrote at least three articles on Heidegger.[79] The detection of a slight Heideggerian influence in a later study of Hegel's logic[80] has been used to argue that Hyppolite later shifted his attention from Hegel's theory to Heidegger's, or from humanism to being.[81] There are indeed a couple of passages where Hyppolite employs Heideggerian terms.[82] Yet his influence on Hyppolite's work is obviously transient, hardly even worthy of the name. For in Hyppolite's very next study of Hegel's view, Heidegger's name and terminology are wholly absent.[83]

We have already noted that Kojève's Hegel interpretation is influenced by both Heidegger and Marx. Heidegger's influence on Kojève's interpretation of Hegel's thought is often underestimated. Kojève understands Heidegger's theory in an anthropological way widely present in the initial French reception of his thought but later explicitly rejected by Heidegger in his "Letter on Humanism." Heidegger influences Kojève's Hegel interpretation in two specific ways: in his anthropological reading of the *Phenomenology*, and in his concentration on the theme of death.

Kojève particularly stresses the significance of the concept of death for Hegel's position. Hegel has little directly to say about death either in the *Phenomenology* or in other writings. Yet death is a major theme in Heidegger's early work.[84] Following Heidegger, Kojève emphasizes this theme in his reading of the *Phenomenology*.[85] Since to understand man as free is to understand him as finite, Hegel's anthropological theory is essentially a philosophy of death.[86] The difference between Christian anthropology and Hegel's view lies in Hegel's introduction of the idea of death.[87] According to Kojève, Heidegger returns to Hegel's ideas about death although he neglects the related themes of struggle and work; Marx insists on struggle and work while neglecting the problem of death; and both

Heidegger and Marx fail to perceive the importance of the Hegelian theme of revolutionary terror.[88]

Existentialism is a diverse movement grouping together a wide variety of writers, including, depending on the interpretation of "existentialism," Søren Kierkegaard, Nietzsche, Miguel de Unamuno, Heidegger, Jaspers, Rudolf Bultmann, Paul Tillich, Sartre, Albert Camus, Beauvoir, Merleau-Ponty, and others.[89] Heidegger's impact on existentialism, particularly French existentialism, is important, in part because of the widespread, persistent, but mistaken French view of Heidegger as an existentialist putting forward a philosophical anthropology. It is always arbitrary to assign fixed temporal limits to a conceptual movement, but clearly French existentialism predates Sartre's main work, *Being and Nothingness*, which only appeared in 1943. If, as has been suggested, French existentialism came into its own as early as 1938,[90] then it clearly overlapped with Kojève's lectures on Hegel.

There is a link on several levels between French existentialism and Heidegger's thought. Vuillemin follows the interpretation of Heidegger as an existentialist in his argument that the transition from phenomenology to existentialism is parallel to, in fact coincident with, the reinterpretation of Kant's critical philosophy.[91] Lévinas points to the anthropological interpretation of Heidegger. He remarks that, with the possible exception of Marcel, French existentialism largely derives from phenomenology. And he further points out that existentialism is not only due to the anthropological side of his position that Heidegger himself rejected.[92]

Heidegger's impact is visible throughout French existentialist writings. One obvious link is the persistent insistence on existence, for instance, in Sartre's phenomenological ontology, and later in Merleau-Ponty's critique of Sartre's still Cartesian view of subjectivity as inadequate for a concrete view of existence.[93] Merleau-Ponty is aware of Heidegger, but his strongest phenomenological influence lies in Husserl's thought. Among French existentialist writers, it is Sartre, prior to his Marxist turn, whose view of subjectivity is most clearly influenced by Heidegger's theory. Sartre's main philosophical influences include the theories of Hegel, Heidegger and Husserl.[94] Sartre claims that Heidegger taught him the meaning of authenticity and historicity just when these concepts were rendered necessary by the outbreak of the Second World War.[95] He appeals to what he curiously calls Heidegger's "free assumption of his historical moment"[96] for help in assuming the burden of a French soldier in 1940.[97]

Heidegger influenced Sartre directly through the latter's reading of Heideggerian texts and indirectly through the views of others, particularly Kojève. The numerous Heideggerian influences in *Being and Nothingness* include the ideas of *engagement* and responsibility, both of which are modeled on the Heideggerian view of resoluteness (*Entschlossenheit*), which Sartre interprets in a concrete sense; Sartre's analysis of temporality as three ecstases recalls Heidegger's similar analysis; his conception of nothingness also derives from Heidegger via Kojève's reinterpretation;[98] Sartre's idea of the phenomenon is reminiscent of Heidegger's own analysis, and so on.

Heidegger's effort to comprehend being through Dasein leads naturally to an anthropological misreading of his fundamental ontology. *Being and Time* culminates in §74 in a "Cartesian" conception of the subject obliged to choose to be authentic, to choose itself. In Sartre's *Being and Nothingness*, everything happens as if the subject were understood on a "Cartesian" model. There is a clear parallel between an anthropological reading of Heideggerian Dasein as existence – in Sartrean language in situation, or according to Heidegger confronted with the resolute choice of itself – and Sartre's view of human being condemned to choose to be authentic. The prominence of "Cartesian" subjectivity, what Sartre later called its humanism,[99] is a major factor in existentialism of all kinds, for instance in Merleau-Ponty's view of the subject as the lived body that is the basis of perception[100] and in his critique of Sartre's perceived antihumanism.[101] Yet it is conspicuous by its absence in structuralism.

Conceptual movements are rarely uniform, or homogeneous, but structuralism is even more heterogeneous than most.[102] The very span of structuralism is indicated by the way that it ranges from mathematics, over natural and social sciences, including psychology and linguistics, to philosophy.[103] Structuralism is obviously concerned with "structures"; but what this means has been understood in different ways: as a relational rather than substantial approach to the objects of the human sciences;[104] or as the view that structures can be grasped in terms of concepts of totality, transformation, and auto-regulation;[105] or again as the relation of meaning to truth and being.[106] Sartre increasingly dominated the French cultural context from the early 1940s, when *Being and Nothingness* appeared, until the rise of what came to be known as structuralism in the 1960s. The French structuralist movement has been understood as a widespread revolt against Sartre's influence leading to a broadly antiphenomenological stance.[107]

The main source of structuralism was Saussure's linguistics, but Heidegger's theory also played an important role. Structuralism arose at a time when Heidegger was central to French philosophy. Heidegger's position directly influenced some of the French structuralist thinkers and indirectly influenced others. Recalling the later Heidegger's concern with being as self-manifesting, various structuralists aim to elucidate structures by minimizing or even wholly avoiding recourse to a conception of the subject. Although some structuralists, such as Lévi-Strauss, owe nothing discernable to Heidegger's thought, others, such as Lacan, or, depending on one's view of structuralism, Derrida, are deeply influenced by it. With the exception of Derrida, whose view of deconstruction, which has been seen as a form of structuralism, originates in phenomenology[108] – structuralism in general gives the impression that, following the break with first Sartre and then phenomenology there has been a turn from a "Cartesian" view of the subject to a disembodied, epistemological placeholder view of subjectivity,[109] similar to the decentered conception of subjectivity featured in the later Heidegger.

Although any number of French structuralist figures, including Barthes, Derrida, Deleuze, Piaget, Goldmann,[110] and others could be mentioned, this point can easily be illustrated through the theories of Lévi-Strauss, Althusser and Foucault. Piaget, who is typical of structuralists in that regard, is concerned to avoid a conception of the subject that has anything to do with lived experience.[111] Barthes substitutes a concept of the author writing for the concept of the person.[112]

The structural anthropologist Lévi-Strauss advances a conception of history independent of human being, in which history is the starting point but not the end point of a quest for intelligibility.[113] In the *Critique of Pure Reason*, Kant makes the possibility of knowledge dependent on an unconscious and unknowable activity through which a conceptual subject produces the knowable object of experience.[114] Lévi-Strauss takes a similar line in maintaining that all culture can be understood as a result of the unconscious imposition of form by the human mind that is basically the same in all times and places.[115] This view has been taken to imply the claim, for instance, that although there are myths there are no authors.[116]

Althusser's so-called theoretical antihumanism is on display in his structuralist Marxism[117] that refuses any form of anthropology. His antihumanism is intelligible against the background of the Marxist debate roughly since Lukács's brilliant *History and Class Consciousness*. The emphasis on alienation in Lukács's book, which was later confirmed by the publication of several unknown, early Marxian texts, led to the idea of a Marxist humanism.[118] The formulation of a humanist, anthropological, resolutely philosophical reading of Marx's position threatened the Marxist view of Marx, current since Engels, as transcending philosophy in a science of history and society.[119] Althusser's intervention in the debate was meant to defend the Marxist view of Marxism as a science by admitting the existence of Marx's early philosophical writings – once they were published it was hard to deny this fact – while denying their importance.[120] His antihumanist reading of Marx, more precisely his claim that Marx breaks with the very idea of a universal essence of man in favor of a specific analysis of levels of human practice,[121] is intended to show that in his mature work Marx moves beyond anything resembling a conception of the subject in order to carry out a scientific study of practice. His intent, which cannot be understood apart from the political struggle to maintain Marxist orthodoxy, is to abolish the subject as Marx understood it in order to "save" the Marxist view of Marx.

Foucault's relation to Heidegger's thought is important for an understanding of his own theory. Although he indicates that Nietzsche is more important to him than is Heidegger – a Nietzsche read through Heideggerian lenses – he sees the latter as the essential philosopher.[122] Foucault's attack on a certain conception of human being is exceedingly radical. Yet it is misconceived as an attack on human being as such, or as antihumanism, since it is limited to an analysis of the concept or the representation of human being.[123] Foucault's aim in his early works is in part to show how human being became an object of science in the seventeenth and eighteenth centuries.[124] And his later work centers precisely on tracing various forms of human practice.[125]

Among the structuralists, Lévi-Strauss and Althusser put subjectivity into parentheses in order to constitute structuralist anthropology and Marxism as social sciences. If, as has been claimed, "structuralism" is nothing but a superficial effort to formulate a general methodology for the human sciences,[126] then Foucault is not a structuralist. He objects to the very idea of social science as in principle mistaken. Social sciences are not only false sciences; they are not even sciences at all since they rely on a conception of human being that cannot be known, that cannot be the object of a science.[127] Influenced by both Kojève[128] and Heidegger, Foucault maintains that the conception of human being is "finished" (*fini*).[129] It came into being in the eighteenth century between two types of language, when human being gave itself a representation in the interstices of language temporarily in fragments.[130] Our task today is to think the disappearance of human being since it is now in the process of disappearing. As Foucault later put it, the result is an anonymous system without a subject that marks a return to the seventeenth century; but man has not been put in the place of God since there is only "an anonymous thought, knowledge without a subject, theory without identity ... ''[131] Like the later Heidegger, in a famous passage Foucault emphasizes the impermanence of the conception of human being. Just as the conception of human being arose in a change in the situation of knowledge, so a further change may see human being "erased, like a face drawn in the sand at the edge of the sea."[132]

4

HEIDEGGER, SARTRE, AND FRENCH HUMANISM

Having identified a number of factors likely to have facilitated Heidegger's rise to importance within the French philosophical discussion, we now need to consider how Heidegger's rise to prominence in fact occurred.

This will be the first of three chapters dealing with the role of humanism in Heidegger's emergence as the master thinker of recent French philosophy. In examining aspects of the humanist misreading of Heidegger's thought, as well as the broader theme of humanism in French philosophy and Heidegger's theory, the intention is to identify a link between the traditional French concern with humanism and the French Heidegger reception. This chapter will show how the revival of the French interest in humanism naturally led toward Heidegger. The next chapter will consider the effect of Heidegger's "Letter on Humanism" on the French reception of his thought. Finally, a third chapter will examine the relation between Heidegger's political involvement and humanism. We shall see that many French philosophers turned to Heidegger in the mistaken belief that he shared their humanist concern.

There is a difference between the specifically philosophical concerns that dominate a given philosophical position, those that lead to its initial formulation and later reformulation, and those often quite different concerns, which may or may not be philosophical in nature, that lead to its rise to prominence in the discussion. Attention to Heidegger's theory in Germany after the publication of *Being and Time* (1927) was independent of any capacity to awaken a widespread interest in his claim, underlying his initial position, that the problem of being had been forgotten. With the possible exception of a few philosophical colleagues, almost no one in the immediate discussion was clearly aware of, or even prepared to deal with, this assertion. On the contrary, Heidegger's theory become prominent in contemporary German cultural life because of his remarkable ability to capture widespread contemporary concerns in philosophical language that appealed widely to his philosophical colleagues.[1]

In the particular historical situation, dominated by the decline of the Weimar Republic, the deepening of a worldwide economic depression, the search for a third way between a liberalism commonly thought to have failed and a Bolshevism so widely feared, and the rise of National Socialism, Heidegger was able to translate his technical ideas into language that expressed the contemporary *Zeitgeist*. Examples include themes of authenticity, resoluteness, being with others, anxiety, and so on, all existential themes in a Germany struggling to preserve self-respect and to assert individuality in a difficult period between two world wars. Heidegger's enormous rhetorical capacity to capture in philosophical language the spirit of the times is above all on display in the famous rectorial address delivered in May 1933 when Heidegger, who had just publically joined the Nazi party, solemnly assumed office as the rector of the University of Freiburg.[2]

Heidegger's thought attracted attention in France as early as the late 1920s and early 1930s, but it was only later that it suddenly became central to the French discussion. This did not happen when Hegel became an important factor in French philosophy, in large part through Heidegger's influence on the French appropriation of Hegel's thought. Nor did it happen as soon as Heidegger's writings began to be available in French translation in the early 1930s. Nor again did it happen when writers such as Sartre made use of Heidegger's fundamental ontology in the formulation of their own positions. It only finally happened when, in the aftermath of the Second World War, the problem of humanism was raised again in the French philosophical context. The ensuing debate led to a turn toward Heidegger's theory that has since become one of the few relatively stable points in the volatile French cultural context.[3]

HUMANISM

Humanism is an unclear concept, used in many, often incompatible ways.[4] It apparently has no natural or non-normative meaning. Philosophers have often rejected the association between philosophy and humanism on the grounds that humanism is incompatible with rigorous philosophical thought.[5] But it is compatible with philosophy, or at least some forms of philosophy. In the "Letter on Humanism," the same text in which he attempts to drive a wedge between philosophy and humanism, Heidegger insists on the humanist character of his own theory.[6]

There is a long, but still not clarified link between philosophy and humanism. European humanism did not spring into being in a particular theory or in a particular text, but has emerged only gradually over a long period. A concern with humanism is already present in the Roman tradition. Cicero and Varro distinguish between humanitarianism, or the love of humanity in general, and humanism (*humanitas*), understood in the sense of the Greek *paideia*, meaning education. Following Cicero and Varro, Benda distinguishes two senses of "humanism": the desire to know human being animating Kant, Goethe and other Enlightenment figures; and the more general concern with knowledge.[7] In the latter sense, humanism is associated with the discovery of the idea of human being in the Renaissance,[8] and the emergence of various kinds of individuality[9] in the second part of the fourteenth century. The idea of human being is an idea that later spread throughout Europe, and that is often taken to mark the end of the Middle Ages. Yet as the older view of classical studies did not disappear when the conception of human being emerged, this whole period is marked by a continual oscillation between the revival of the humanist tradition and the emergence of a philosophy of human being.[10]

"Humanism" is notoriously difficult to define since it means different things to different observers. For example, Höffding writes: "Humanism denotes, then, not only a literary tendency, a school of philologists, but also a tendency of life, characterized by interest for the human, both as a subject of observation and as the foundation of action."[11] Höffding's definition usefully evokes the return to classical studies as well as the novel Christian conception of human being that emerges in the wake of Augustine's attention to the notion of personal responsibility. Yet it omits a central philosophical element of humanism: the self-congratulatory, broadly humanist understanding of philosophy as indispensable for the good life.

Discussion of humanism often tends to equate the genus with one of its species.[12] For present purposes, three forms of "humanism" can be distinguished: the revival of classical letters; the stress on human being; and a claim for the social relevance of philosophy.

Understood as the revival of classical letters, humanism is the effort to develop the rational faculties without regard to discipline. This conception is manifest in the educational reform undertaken in Bavaria by Friedrich Immanuel Niethammer, Hegel's friend and sometime patron, who was appointed as Central School Counselor in 1808. Niethammer represented a so-called new humanism (*Neuhumanismus*) that aimed to provide a general development of human faculties through the study of the ancient world, in particular through the revival of classical letters.[13] When Hegel became rector of the Egidium Gymnasium in Nuremberg, no less than 13 of the 27 weekly class hours were devoted to Greek and Latin materials.[14]

Understood as the concern with human being, humanism is specifically influential in a long line of philosophical positions. This view of humanism, which can be illustrated in the writings of Pico della Mirandola and Ludovicus Vives, naturally ranges widely over such themes as freedom, naturalism, historical perspective, religion, and science. In a famous passage, Pico della Mirandola stresses the idea of human freedom:

> I have given you, Adam, neither a predetermined place nor a particular aspect nor any special prerogatives in order that you may take and possess these through your own decision and choice. The limitations on the nature of other creatures are contained within my prescribed laws. You shall determine your own nature without constraint from any

barrier, by means of the freedom to whose power I have entrusted you. I have placed you at the center of the world so that from that point you might see better what is in the world. I have made you neither heavenly nor earthly, neither mortal nor immortal so that, like a free and sovereign artificer, you might mold and fashion yourself into that form you yourself shall have chosen.[15]

Humanism is often regarded as central to the Enlightenment. Pope's famous couplet is frequently taken as a motto of Enlightenment interest in the study of man: "Presume not then the ways of God to scan / The proper study of mankind is man." Yet treatment of the Enlightenment in terms of humanism is by no means a universal tendency. Foucault, for instance, usefully distinguishes between the Enlightenment as an event and humanism as the decision to focus on a theme or given set of themes.[16] Observers differ widely in the importance they attach to humanism as a theme in the Enlightenment period. As knowledgeable a writer as Ernst Cassirer managed to compose a detailed discussion of the period in which he scarcely even mentions humanism other than to refer to Pope;[17] on the contrary, in Peter Gay's books on this topic, humanism figures prominently.[18]

Philosophy, which is only one of the many strands in the growth of culture during the Enlightenment period, tends to stress an anthropological approach. This tendency is particularly evident in Hume's writings. In *A Treatise of Human Nature*, David Hume writes: "Human Nature is the only science of man; and has been hitherto the most neglected."[19] Clearly anticipating Marx's famous claim that all the sciences are sciences of man, Hume asserts: "'Tis evident, that all the sciences have a relation, greater or less, to human nature."[20] He further writes:

He straightforwardly holds that all scientific questions are finally questions about man: There is no question of importance, whose decision is not compriz'd in the science of man; and there is none, which can be decided with any certainty, before we become acquainted with that science. In pretending therefore to explain the principles of human nature, we in effect propose a compleat system of the sciences, built on a foundation almost entirely new, and the only one upon which they stand with any certainty.[21]

It is precisely this science of man that Hume intends to construct through empirical observation: "As the science of man is the only solid foundation for the other sciences, so the only foundation we can give to this science itself must be laid on experience and observation."[22]

Hume's anthropological approach to philosophy is further strengthened in modern German philosophy. Here the Enlightenment stress on reason is accompanied by an increasingly secular, even Promethean view of human being as central to the world and as the master of human fate. Thinkers like the Danish writer Kierkegaard, who understand human being as authentic only through a particular relation to God, are an exception to this tendency. Although Kant famously seeks to limit knowledge to make room for faith,[23] his position throughout is rigorously secular. He continually stresses reason as the main, in fact the only admissible, component in his analyses of various types of experience. Even his discussion of reason is conducted within the bounds set by reason that, from his very rationalist viewpoint, cannot be rationally transgressed.

The anthropological element in Kant's critical philosophy is partly traceable to Hume's well known influence in awakening him from his self-described dogmatic slumber.[24] In his theory of ethics, Kant insists on freedom as the necessary but indemonstrable presupposition for ethics through a conception of human being as wholly free from external influences, hence able to determine the principles of action in an entirely rational fashion. He stresses a similar concept in his famous definition of the Enlightenment as "man's emergence from his self-imposed immaturity."[25] In his writings on history, Kant emphasizes that human being matures through history in the progressive internalization of the moral law.

A closely Kantian insistence on human being as rational and free is a main theme in later German idealism. Although Kant develops a theory of history in his minor writings, he is never able to integrate it into his view of reason, which remains resolutely ahistorical.[26] With respect to the critical philosophy, post-Kantian German idealism differs mainly in an ever increasing awareness of the historical character of reason. Here Kant's Copernican turn, invoked for strictly epistemological reasons in order to account for the possibility of knowledge in general, is given a historical, even a historicized reading. Fichte's view of striving (*Streben*), Hegel's idea of freedom as the goal of history, and Marx's conception of the emergence of genuine individuality at the beginning of human history are different versions of the way in which human being expands the range of human activity in social, cultural, political, and historical surroundings.

After Gottfried Wilhelm Leibniz and Christian Wolff, modern German philosophy grows increasingly secular, as reflected in the importance of secular humanism. Fichte, Schelling, and Hegel were all deeply influenced by Protestantism; there is a strongly religious element in each of their positions, especially in Fichte's after the celebrated controversy on atheism (*Atheismusstreit*) that cost him his teaching position. Unlike Schelling's thought, which cannot be understood from a secular perspective, the views of Fichte and Hegel can be read in an entirely secular manner.[27] This is further the case for Marx's theory where a disinterest in religion – which in Marxism has often taken the rather different form of a frank attack on religion – is combined with a secular stress on human action as the mode of human development through a secular idea of salvation.

Philosophy itself can be regarded as broadly humanist in inspiration due to its claims for intrinsic social relevance. Socrates' idea that the unexamined life is not worth living is transformed by Plato into the double claim that only philosophy yields knowledge and that philosophical knowledge is socially indispensable. The latter idea has often met with resistance. Aristotle's view that philosophy satisfies wonder only, Hegel's insistence that philosophy always comes too late, the Marxist contention that philosophy is ideology, or false consciousness, inadequate to resolve the problems that are solved by Marxist science, and Wittgenstein's effort to show that philosophical problems arise from the misuse of language are only some of the manifestations of a widespread philosophical uneasiness about this claim. Nonetheless, many philosophers support the broadly humanist view of the philosophical discipline as not only useful but essential for the good life initially formulated by Plato.

A broadly Platonic conception of the social utility of philosophy echoes through the modern philosophical tradition. Kant, the apostle of pure reason, comprehends philosophy, or reason's highest form, not only as the condition of ethics understood as a pure science[28] but as a conception of the world intrinsically concerned with the ends of human being. Kant's disarmingly simple but also simplistic depiction of philosophy as "the science of the relation of all knowledge to the essential ends of human reason (*teleologia rationis humanae*)"[29] and of the philosopher as "the lawgiver of human reason"[30] is widely followed. Any short list of variations on the Kantian conviction of the intrinsic social utility of philosophy would include Husserl's notion of transcendental phenomenology as the concealed secret of all modern times[31] as well as Heidegger's conviction that human being depends on the problem of being.

FRENCH HUMANISM

With important exceptions, French philosophy is basically humanist. The most varied aspects of French thought routinely lay claim to the humanist label. Recent examples include Hyppolite's study of Hegel's view of human being,[32] Mikel Dufrenne's defense of the concept of human being[33] and Roger Garaudy's humanist dialogue with such distinct tendencies as existentialism, Catholic thought, structuralism, and Marxism.[34]

The emergence of a secular philosophical approach in German philosophy is often seen as the result of Luther's influence.[35] In France, where there has been no Lutheran Reformation, where the natural tie between theology and philosophy remains strong, the situation regarding humanism is more complex. In other countries and literatures, the dissociation of the temporal and the eternal, the rational and the religious, is often incomplete. Perhaps this separation has never been fully carried out. Philosophy and religion are strongly interrelated in the positions of later German idealists. In our own time, no one has gone further toward the elaboration of an atheistic philosophy than Sartre, although even he understands human being through a conception of an absent God.[36]

In the United States, which broke away from Great Britain in part to secure religious freedom, reason has never been strongly associated with religious faith. In France, where the tendency to dissociate reason and faith has been relatively weak, certainly weaker than in Germany, there is a permanent tension stretching over centuries between competing secular and religious conceptions of humanism. This tension can be regarded as an opposition on many levels between an understanding of the world centered on a view of human being, and a view of the world and of human being centered on a religious commitment, hence as a difference between essentially irreligious, or pagan,[37] and religious, or antipagan conceptions of man. In the French discussion, the antireligious thrust of secular humanism is often rejected from the point of view of religious humanism as a negation of human being and as anti-Christian. In a typical passage, Henri de Lubac writes:

> Positivistic humanism, Marxist humanism, Nietzschean humanism: much more than atheism in the strict sense, the negation of what is at the base of each of them is an antitheism, and more precisely an anti-Christianism. As opposed as they are to each other, their implications, hidden or manifest, are numerous, and although they share a foundation in their rejection of God, they also have the same consequences, above all the crushing of the human person.[38]

In French thought, the well known opposition between competing forms of humanism is sometimes regarded as a struggle pitting the views of the Encyclopedists, as well as all free thinkers of the rights of man, and the enthusiasts of universal reason against those of the spiritualists, often of Christian inspiration.[39] The competition between incompatible humanist conceptions results in a struggle between secular humanists, who regard Christianity, particularly the Roman Catholic Church, as a major obstacle to the new doctrine and as a source of obscurantism,[40] and the Church, which has always sought to combat secular humanism as representing a fall away from true Christian doctrine.

It has been claimed that the Enlightenment was only possible because at the time Christianity was moribund.[41] In reality the situation has always been more complex, since even those strongly committed to organized religion are often equally committed to the Enlightenment view of human being. For instance, Pierre Gassendi, who today is chiefly known as the author of the fifth set of objections to Descartes's *Meditations*, a Catholic priest whose orthodoxy is not suspect, shared a commitment to humanism, as indicated in Diderot's remark: "Never was a philosopher a better humanist, nor humanist such a good philosopher."[42]

The French humanist tradition follows rather than precedes the Italian Renaissance.[43] The revival of classical letters is emphasized by Rabelais in

1532 in *Pantagruel*. Gargantua's famous letter to his son Pantagruel mentions the restoration of humanistic studies, the importance of learning the ancient languages, especially Greek, the role of the art of printing, and so on.[44] At least as much as in Italy, humanism in France was associated with the philosophy of human being.

Philosophical humanism begins in France as early as Montaigne who, rather than Descartes, is sometimes regarded as the founder of modern philosophy.[45] Montaigne is renowned as a sceptic, above all for the ideas expressed in his famous "Apologie de Raymond Sebonde." Yet he is centrally concerned with human being. His work can be read from different perspectives: as a theory of knowledge, suggested by his concern with scepticism, or as a philosophy of life.[46] The main theme of his celebrated *Essays* is himself, a theme that has evoked widely different attitudes from his readers.[47] He says in the preface: "Thus, reader, I am myself the content of my book [Ainsi, lecteur, je suis moy mesme la matière de mon livre]".[48] The third book of his essays is concerned with his ego, his thoughts, his moods, and so on. It has been suggested that in his writings, "humanism" takes on a new meaning concerning what is fully human.[49] Even his scepticism has been read as leading to the view that truth must be founded on the subject, on himself.[50]

In the same way, Descartes's theory can also be read from epistemological or humanistic angles of vision. In the Anglo-Saxon discussion, Descartes is mainly studied as the prototype of the modern epistemologist, as the founder of foundationalism,[51] as the discoverer of a method to secure knowledge against scepticism. Yet the French tradition, while preserving an epistemological emphasis, links it to a reading of the Cartesian theory as the basis of modern philosophical humanism, even as anticipating later existentialism.[52] In France, emphasis is often placed on the link in the Cartesian theory between science and human being, between knowledge and the human mastery over the world, on the thinker who substitutes reason for prejudice. French discussions emphasize a humanist view of Descartes as the thinker who answered Montaigne's question of "what can I know? [que sais-je?]" by demonstrating the limitless possibilities for progress of the human spirit.[53] In French circles, Descartes is understood less as an epistemologist than as a humanist whose idea of reason dominates the later Enlightenment debate culminating in Kant's critical philosophy and continuing to our own time.

If we acknowledge the humanist aspects of Montaigne's and Descartes's theories, we must also acknowledge the continuity between them. Montaigne's scepticism requires a turn to the self in order to found knowledge. His Pyrrhonian scepticism profoundly influences Descartes's later effort to overcome scepticism of all kinds through the cogito. There are echoes of Montaigne's thought throughout the Cartesian corpus, especially in the "Discourse on Method." His celebrated conception of human being as the spectator of all[54] and his resolve to make himself the subject of study[55] both continue Montaigne's similar concerns.

Descartes's interest in humanism is clear in the title of his first text, "The Treatise on Man", which was completed in 1633 and immediately suppressed. His more famous "Discourse on Method" from 1637 depends on a turn to the subject that is only reinforced in his refusal of the analogy between human beings and machines,[56] an analogy later exploited by the philosophical materialist Julien Offray de La Mettrie. The "Meditations on First Philosophy" were originally meant to be called "Project of a Universal Science Able to Bring Our Mind to Its Highest Point of Development [Projet d'une science universelle qui puisse éléver notre esprit à son plus haut degré de perfection]." Descartes's humanist impulse is still present in his last work, the "Passions of the Soul [Les passions de l'âme]" written in 1645–1646, where he stresses that, with respect to the free will, a person is similar to God.[57]

Descartes's influence was immediate and profound on both the secular and the religious strands of French humanism. The secular strand of French humanism is already present in the Cartesian emphasis on the idea of progress that follows his stress on the supremacy of reason and the invariability of the laws of nature.[58] His emphasis on reason as distinguished from faith set the tone for the later discussion. The Enlightenment grouped together such widely disparate thinkers as the mechanist Bernard Fontenelle, the theist Voltaire, the materialist Claude Adrien Helvétius, and others, all thinkers who, within the climate of Cartesian reason, shared the Cartesian commitment to reason, to the scientific method, and to evidence.[59] It was further developed in the *Encyclopedia*, whose tone was set by Diderot's statement in the article "Encyclopedia" that everything begins and ends with man. Confident of reason as the only guide, Diderot writes:

> For this reason we have decided to seek in man's principal faculties the main divisions within which our work will fall. Another method might be equally satisfactory, provided it did not put a cold, insensitive, silent being in the place of man. For man is the unique starting point, and the end to which everything must finally be related if one wishes to please, to instruct, to move to sympathy, even in the most arid matters and in the driest details. Take away my own existence and that of my fellow men and what does the rest of nature signify.[60]

The idea of limitless human progress, of the perfectability of human being initially mentioned by Rousseau,[61] inspired Kant. It was given a gigantic helping hand in the practical sphere by the French Revolution which sought to realize the famous ideals of liberty, equality and fraternity, as well as democracy and progress. It was worked out in much greater detail in Condorcet's writings, in his related ideas of human being as indefinitely perfectible and of human perfection as basically limitless. Taking a stance against Rousseau, in his famous study of human progress Condorcet emphasizes "destruction of the inequality between nations, the progress towards equality in a single people, finally the real perfection of man."[62]

The secular humanism represented by Condorcet and others is in permanent tension with religious humanism. This tension is certainly not confined to the French context. It can be illustrated by two philosophers writing in reaction to Hegel: Ludwig Feuerbach and Kierkegaard. Feuerbach, a leftwing Hegelian, privileges the anthropological over the religious aspect in Hegel's thought. Kierkegaard, who insists on existence against Hegelian idealism, can be located, through his insistence on the religious dimension, within rightwing Hegelianism. Secular humanism tends to deny God in order to make room for human being, for instance in Feuerbach's inversion of the usual conception of the dependence of human being on God in favor of a dependence of God on human being.[63] Human being seeks its salvation through its own works. Religious humanism takes the contrary view, expressed by Kierkegaard, that human salvation must be sought in the return to God.[64]

The tension between starkly opposed, mutually exclusive forms of humanism runs through French thought and society on many different levels. It is present, for instance, in the struggle between innovation and tradition, between those who favor the maintenance of a strong centralized state closely tied to the Roman Catholic Church and those who oppose it. The same French Revolution that attempted to realize the social contract theory by proclaiming the rights of man before violating them in the terror that followed, abolished the privileges of the nobility and restricted the Church. The effort to found government on the will of the governed aimed at equality before the law against hierarchy and liberty against the traditionally divine right of kings. The predictable result was a tension that has lasted over more than two hundred years. It features irreconcilable views, opposing those who regard the French Revolution as a permanent contribution to the development of human freedom, bought at the price of loosening the ties between Church and state; and those who regard it as a betrayal of the human rights it invoked,[65] a view represented ouside the French discussion by Edmund Burke.[66]

The desire for autonomy that fueled the French Revolution was only partially realized in an event that eventually substituted one form of autocratic centralism for another through Napoleon's rise to power. Since that time, the problem has remained unresolved as France has continued to maintain a strong central state with centralized institutions. In practice, French political centralization has given rise to a resistance to central direction that occasionally verges on anarchism. Not surprisingly, anarchism is a political doctrine that has long been popular in France.[67] Like so many other institutions, French education is highly centralized, rigid, and autocratic. It is, then, not surprising that the 1968 French student revolution has been regarded as merely a further attempt to gain autonomy, as symbolized by a systematic questioning of traditional educational methods, of the relations between students and teachers, and so on.[68]

Both sides in the tense struggle between proponents of secular and religious humanism rely on the same Cartesian theory that can be read either as supporting or as challenging the link between religion and philosophy.[69] It is not by chance that Descartes's writings were quickly placed on the Index. For as he was aware, notwithstanding his efforts to disarm possible religious opposition, the very attempt "to build anew from the foundation"[70] in order to secure scientific knowledge presupposes a radical break with authority and tradition in the name of self-subsistent reason. Despite his explicit disclaimer, his very concern to study questions about God and the Soul – as he puts it in an inopportune statement from the dedication preceding the *Meditations* intended to still possible disquiet – "by philosophical rather than theological argument"[71] does not comfort, but rather threatens revealed theology.

The dispute between secular and religious humanists frequently concerns the proper attitude toward tradition. Traditionalists like Heidegger or, following him, Gadamer frequently resist the effort to separate tradition from reason, bending their efforts to preserve tradition. On the contrary, Descartes and others like him regard the break with tradition as a necessary condition for the beginning of science, as a necessary prerequisite to the liberation of human being through reason and the domination of nature.[72]

The tension between the modern commitment to reason that mandates a break with tradition and the traditional commitment to authority, often to religious authority, separates thinkers into different, incompatible camps. This complex tension is present on occasion in the thought of an individual writer, such as Pascal,[73] a writer who, in that respect, is divided against himself. Pons has perceptively noted an unresolved conflict between Pascal the man of science and Pascal the believer. This is a tension between Pascal who accepts the Enlightenment idea of infinite progress, including the Baconian idea of the perfection of human being over time, and the same Pascal who deplores the illusion of human progress since, despite the apparent changes, human being remains inalterably the same.[74] This is the Pascal whose commitment to reason leads to his acceptance of Pyrrhonian scepticism that in turn leads him back to his religious faith.[75] And this is the same Pascal, who, despite his important contributions to mathematics, insists, following Augustine and Aquinas, on the separation between the objects of sense, or reason, and of faith, the three principles of our knowledge.[76]

HEIDEGGER'S "HUMANISM" AND FRENCH PHILOSOPHY

If Heidegger is a humanist at all, he is not a humanist in any ordinary sense of the term. For he rejects many usual humanist ideas, such as the ideas of progress and human perfectibility as well as the so-called metaphysical conception of humanism. Yet Heidegger does not break, but rather reforges, the philosophical link to humanism from the perspective of his concern with being.[77]

Both the initial interest in Heidegger's position at the beginning of the 1930s and the broad turn to his theory immediately after the war were fueled by its perceived relevance to humanist themes. Beyond the traditional French interest in humanism, broadly conceived, at least five further factors called attention to Heidegger's thought from a humanist perspective at this time. First, there was the worldwide economic collapse that affected the social and political structure throughout Europe, including France. This difficult economic situation drew attention to existential factors of all kinds in a way that some saw as corresponding to Heidegger's "existentialism."

Second, there was traditional French Roman Catholicism, including philosophical interests in Thomism and spiritualism of various kinds, as well as an incipient personalism associated with Emmanuel Mounier. Heidegger's political conservatism attracted support to his position by those concerned to refute other, more liberal views of a philosophical or political nature.

Third, there was a lengthy French socialist tradition. Thinkers in this tradition have long been interested in the full development of the human individual. French socialism has long taken a variety of forms, including, after the Russian Revolution, the emergence of a powerful French Communist Party. In France as in Germany and elsewhere, the concern to resist Bolshevism was a strong motivating factor in the turn toward rightwing theories, including conservative philosophical views.

Fourth, there was the renewed attention to Hegel, including the emergence of a leftwing form of Hegelianism.[78] Although all these factors played a role in the French appropriation of Heidegger's thought under the sign of humanism, the precipitating factor was undoubtedly the leftwing form of Hegelian interpretation elaborated by Kojève.

Fifth, there was the ambiguity in Heidegger's own texts that permitted, in fact even suggested, an anthropological misreading of his theory. In §10 of *Being and Time*, he explicitly distinguishes his analysis of Dasein from any form of human science. Yet as will emerge in the discussion below, this same paragraph inconsistently leaves open the possibility of an anthropological misreading of his thought.

Being and Time, Heidegger's first major publication brought him to the attention of German philosophers in 1927. Until around 1930, Heidegger's theory was known at most to only a few French scholars. It started to become better known in France in the early 1930s in various ways, directly through articles on Heidegger's thought and through translation of some of his writings, indirectly through the influence of his theory on the renewed French interest in Hegel's thought.

Translations have always been particularly important for French philosophers. Unlike Germans, who are often fluent in English, although less often in French, French philosophers share the Anglo-Saxon lack of language background. Except for the views of Wittgenstein and Frege, Anglo-American analytic thinkers are by and large uninterested in other cultures and tradition.

French philosophy, as already noted, developed a deep interest in German thought early in the nineteenth century. At the present time, the French discussion of German thought has a strongly philological perspective. Yet until relatively recently, since the French philosophical command of German tended to lag well behind the interest in German philosophy, French philosophers were highly dependent on translations into French.

Heidegger's thought first appeared in French translation in a rendering of his celebrated lecture, "What Is Metaphysics?," delivered on assuming Husserl's chair in Freiburg in 1929. As early as the same year, Henry Corbin, who later attended Kojève's famous Hegel seminar and made a name for himself as a leading French Islamist, offered a translation to the NRF.[79] Corbin's translation, which was initially rejected, finally appeared in the journal *Bifur* with a short preface by Alexandre Koyré. This was quickly followed by a rendering of *"Vom Wesen des Grundes"* under the title *"De la nature de la cause"* in April 1931 in the first issue of a new journal, cofounded by Alexandre Koyré, *Recherches philosophiques.*[80]

Koyré's preface set the tone for the initial Heidegger reception in France. Koyré begins by describing Heidegger as "one of the great metaphysical geniuses whose thought determines that of an entire period."[81] For Koyré "the philosophy of existence" will not only determine a new philosophical stage but constitute the beginning of an entirely new part of the discussion.[82] Heidegger's theory, which is important as the first one after the war to have spoken to us of ourselves, is concerned with a double theme: consciousness of oneself, and the revelation of one's own being to oneself.[83] Heidegger's most important contribution is to insist, against those who are religiously or mystically inclined, that nothing comes from nothing. In this way, he acknowledges "the solitary grandeur of human finitude thrown and plunged into nothingness."[84]

Although Heidegger consistently maintains that his thought is solely concerned with the problem of being, Koyré neglects this problem in order to concentrate on Heidegger's conception of human being understood solely through itself. Koyré thus anticipates the view of Heidegger's theory as philosophical anthropology that dominates the early French Heidegger reception. Koyré's identification of Heidegger's thought as a philosophy of existence further anticipates Sartre's effort immediately after the war to identify his own brand of existentialism and Heidegger's fundamental ontology as both humanist.

Koyré only returned to Heidegger in an article that appeared some fifteen years later.[85] Yet his brief introduction to Corbin's translation was immediately influential. Jean Wahl followed Koyré's claim for the importance of Heidegger's thought in *Vers le concret* (1932) that provided a detailed discussion of Heidegger's relation to Kierkegaard's position.[86] Meanwhile, in 1938 Corbin offered a volume of Heidegger translations, including a preface by Heidegger.[87] Hence, as early as the late 1930s, there was a growing literature on Heidegger in French and his thought was beginning to be made available to the French public.

Many of the earliest publications in French concerning Heidegger were due to *émigrés* to France with access to the German texts. Koyré, a Russian emigrant, studied in Germany before emigrating to France. Other publications on Heidegger by foreign-born scholars include a book by Georges Gurvitch who also spent time in Germany before emigrating to France;[88] a detailed article by Emmanuel Lévinas[89] who, after his emigration to France, studied with both Husserl and Heidegger in 1928–1929, and finished his dissertation on Husserl's thought;[90] and a number of reviews by Kojève of books directly or indirectly about Heidegger.[91]

Kojève's often caustic reviews invariably give the impression that he knows the material better than the author. An example is his remark that Alois Fischer's study of Heidegger's conception of being neglects the concept of time, basic for fundamental ontology, resulting in a critique of a position that has no common link with Heidegger's.[92]

To rely on the publication of translations of Heidegger's texts and articles on his thought would produce an inaccurate reading of Heidegger's initial French reception; for it would fail to reveal the widespread tendency to approach Heidegger's thought as a form of anthropological humanism. For instance, in a survey of recent German philosophy, Georges Gurvitch typifies the emerging anthropological reading of fundamental ontology, as well as later tendencies to seek an ethics in this view or to conflate it with existentialism: "Heidegger's moralism offers itself in precisely this manner, leading to a cult of humanity as the basis of the being of existence."[93]

This anthropological approach is already present in Lévinas's study of Heidegger's ontology, one of the first to appear in French.[94] Lévinas provides an excellent discussion of Heidegger's ontology keyed to his conception of human being as Dasein. He maintains that the modern analysis of the subject–object relation resulting in the idealist destruction of time for a subject is not surpassed in Heidegger's posing of the question of being in relation to time. Heidegger inverts the familiar starting point in consciousness since human being is essentially its existence; and for Dasein to be is to understand being. Instead of the usual intellectual effort to achieve the unity of the subject, Heidegger describes the unity of human being within existence.

In a later article on Heidegger's temporal ontology, Lévinas correctly notes that Heidegger's understanding of human being through being yields a tragic vision of finite human being devoid of support in the eternal.[95] His focus on the Heideggerian conception of human being is typical in the early French debate, unusual only in the depth and precision of his discussion. Although Lévinas avoids a conflation between Heidegger's conception of Dasein as existence and an anthropological form of philosophy, he focuses attention on the conception of human being following from Heidegger's concern with being.

The anthropological reading of Heidegger is further underscored in the French revival of Hegel studies. Now this is clearly ironic since, despite repeated efforts, Heidegger never comes to grips with Hegel's dialectical position, basically different from his own nondialectical theory.[96] In § 82, the penultimate section of *Being and Time*, Heidegger compares Hegel's supposedly radical version of the ordinary conception of time with his own view.[97] Heidegger's discussion of the Hegelian concept of time reads like an invitation to dialogue between two major thinkers that never took place, in fact could not occur since Heidegger was neither well versed in nor sympathetic to Hegel's position.[98] Although never uninteresting, Heidegger's later texts on Hegel's thought reflect an embarrassing inability to comment on more than isolated aspects of the Hegelian system.

In the French context, the anthropological approach to Heidegger was greatly reinforced through Kojève's famous lectures on Hegel's *Phenomenology of Spirit*. Except for the reference to Hegel, Kojève agrees with Lévinas in understanding Heideggerian Dasein as a conception of man without God, finally as an atheistic conception of human being. Like other leftwing interpreters of Hegel's theory, Kojève emphasizes human being at the expense of the Absolute. We have already noted Kojève's claim that Heidegger's "remarkable authentically philosophical" philosophical anthropology "finally adds nothing new to the anthropology of the *Phenomenology of Spirit*."[99] Through Kojève's influential Hegel seminar, his anthropological reading of Heidegger's thought was indirectly transmitted to numerous students who later figured prominently in French culture.

Kojève's anthropological reading further directly affected the translation of Heidegger's thought. Heidegger contends that through translation, through the transposition of thought from one language to another, it is inevitably transformed.[100] This view can be illustrated by the French translation of the term "Dasein," a key concept in Heidegger's early thought. The word "Dasein," based on the adverb "da", meaning "there," and the verb "Sein", meaning "to be," occurs often in German philosophy, for instance in Kant's discussion of God's existence (*Dasein Gottes*), where it means "existence."[101] But this word is difficult to translate into other languages, including French.[102]

In his initial Heidegger translation, Corbin, following precedent, translates "Dasein" as "existence." In his volume of Heidegger translations that appeared in 1938 and that served as the fundamental source of Heidegger's writings in French translation for the first phase of the French Heidegger discussion,[103] he replaces the earlier rendering of "Dasein" as "existence" by the neologism "réalité - humaine." The result was to deepen the typically French, anthropological misreading of Heidegger's thought.

Corbin was a student in Kojève's seminar. His revised translation of "Dasein" as "réalité-humaine" can be traced to the influence of Kojève's view of Heidegger. On the first page and thereafter throughout his book,

Kojève writes of "human reality", for instance in the second paragraph when he remarks, in support of Hegel and in criticism of alternative theories, that an analysis of thought, of reason, and so on, "never discovers the why or the how of the origin of the word "me" and, following it, self-consciousness, that is to say human reality [la réalité humaine]."[104]

Corbin, who added a hyphen but otherwise followed Kojève on this point, justifies this particular rendering in some detail in the preface to his volume of translations. In *Being and Time*, Heidegger distinguishes between the fundamental, or existential, structures of human existence that concern its existentiality, and the particular, or existentiell, ways in which human being exists.[105] In a remark presumably directed against his own earlier translation practice, Corbin contends that the result of translating "Dasein" as "existence" is to conflate Heidegger's distinction between the existential and the existentiell although Heidegger's *Existenzphilosophie* (philosophy of existence) does not intend to return to the old debate between essence and existence. In substituting "réalité-humaine" for "existence" as the proper translation of "Dasein," Corbin intends to provide the basic technical vocabulary needed to translate Heidegger's texts into French.[106] He further reinforces the anthropological reading of Heidegger's theory when, at the close of his preface, he speaks of the "hommage" to an author arising from a genuine "understanding that grounds human reality, which makes human coexistence possible."[107]

Corbin's influential translation of this key Heideggerian term and his classification of Heidegger's thought were singularly important in the context of a French discussion largely dependent on translations for access to Heidegger's thought. His classification of Heidegger's view as a philosophy of existence was later influential in French existentialism. It pointed toward the conflation between the views of Heidegger and Sartre that the latter exploited immediately after the Second World War in his depiction of existentialism, in response to his critics, as a humanism.[108]

Sartre's reading of Heidegger was always overly generous. He consistently attributes to Heidegger's theory doctrines that were his own, on occasion doctrines even incompatible with Heidegger's. An example among many is his classification of Heidegger's position as existentialist, a description which Heidegger later pointedly rejected in his "Letter on Humanism" in a determined effort to distance himself from Sartre's thought.

The tendency to classify Heidegger as an existentialist affected other, more critical writers, including Jean Beaufret, who was to become Heidegger's main spokesman in the second phase of the French Heidegger debate. Following Heidegger's lead, Beaufret later rejected any perception of a positive link between Heidegger's philosophical thought and a modern philosophical theory. Yet in an early article he had no hesitation in analyzing Heidegger's theory as one of the forms of existentialism.[109]

Corbin's rendering of "Dasein" as "human reality," his claim that "the being of man" is precisely "the human reality in man,"[110] reinforced the emerging anthropological reading of Heidegger's thought that dominates the first phase of the French Heidegger discussion. This led to the evident conflation that Heidegger had been at pains to anticipate in *Being and Time* between the subject of phenomenological ontology and the very different subject of the human sciences.

In principle, Heidegger's insistence on a radical distinction between phenomenological ontology and the sciences of human being – be they anthropology, psychology, or biology – excluded this identification. Yet the introduction of the French term "réalité-humaine" for "Dasein" was regarded as authorizing an anthropological conception of subjectivity within philosophy and science. In his *Esquisse d'une théorie des émotions* (1939), Sartre follows Corbin's suggestion when he writes:

> Now *man* is a being of the same type as the *world*. It is even possible that, as Heidegger, thinks, the concepts of world and of "human-reality" ["réalité-humaine"] (Dasein) are inseparable. Precisely for this reason psychology must resign itself to missing human-reality, if at least this human-reality exists.[111]

This same tendency also infected French sociology. In his summary of a paper by Michel Leiris, Jean Wahl evokes the future constitution of "a science of human realities".[112] The use of the term was still current as late as 1960, when Beauvoir employed it.[113]

SARTRE, FRENCH PHENOMENOLOGY, AND HEIDEGGER

In the French humanist misreading of Heidegger, Jean Wahl played an important role. An early, enthusiastic, but critical student of Heidegger's thought, Wahl taught and wrote on Heidegger over many years. In a paper delivered in 1937 before the French Philosophical Society, he suggested that the relation of Heidegger's and Jaspers's views to Kierkegaard's is similar.[114] At the time, he saw important parallels between the views of Heidegger and Jaspers.[115] Later he became more critical of Heidegger's thought. In a book from the early 1950s, he suggested that it is incorrect to regard Heidegger as a philosopher of existence.[116] Still later, he came to the conclusion that Heidegger's meditation on being is fundamentally sterile.[117]

Wahl's role as one of the best French Heidegger scholars is recognized, for instance, by Pöggeler, one of the best German Heidegger specialists. According to Pöggeler, although Wahl makes a real effort to understand Heidegger, he finally fails to grasp how Heidegger interprets the problem of being.[118] This view was further shared by Heidegger himself. In a letter to the French Philosophical Society (Société française de philosophie) in 1937, following Wahl's paper, Heidegger protests against the existentialist reading of his thought.[119]

Sartre did not invent the familiar existentialist misreading of Heidegger's thought. Yet he played a decisive role in helping to propagate it. Sartre, who followed Kant in stressing absolute freedom as absolute responsibility, acquired great intellectual fame, exceedingly rare for a philosopher, after the publication of *Being and Nothingness* in 1943, in then occupied France, through his insistence that we are always utterly and irrevocably free to choose. He maintains this view not only on the theoretical but also on the practical level. In a typical passage about the lot of the French during the German occupation, Sartre writes:

> Never have we been as free as during the German occupation. We had lost all our rights, beginning with the one of speaking; we were insulted everyday and we had to shut up; we were deported en masse, as workers, Jews, political prisoners; everywhere on walls, in newspapers, on the screen we found that bland and repulsive face which our oppressors wanted us to have of ourselves: because of all that we were free. Since the Nazi venom snuck even into our thoughts, every correct thought was a conquest; since an all-powerful police tried to keep us silent, every word become precious like the weight of commitment. . . .
> The choice that each one of us made was authentic since it was made in the presence of death, since it could always be expressed in the form of 'Rather death than . . . .[120]

Had Sartre been unknown, had he remained simply an obscure writer fascinated with words, someone whose verbal virtuosity was equally manifest in his philosophical fiction and his philosophy, his influence would have been minimal. In virtue of his enormous prestige, the captivating effect his writings had on so many readers, his dependence on Heidegger's theory, and his misreading of it, Sartre played a decisive role in the initial phase of the French Heidegger reception. This connection was only magnified in Sartre's famous lecture, *Existentialism is a Humanism* when, immediately after the War, he again drew attention to Heidegger's conception of human reality in a discussion of atheistic existentialism, freedom, commitment, and responsibility.

Sartre's influence, his status as a master thinker, even as a kind of intellectual guru, weighs heavily in the French interest in three major philosophers that continues to this day: Husserl, Heidegger, and Hegel. In the French context, it is fair to say that Sartre reinforced the rising interest in Hegel, that he provided an important impetus to the concern with Husserl,[121] and that – in virtue of the overwhelming importance of Heidegger's theory for *Being and Nothingness* – he offered an even more influential, basically incorrect reading of Heidegger.

From this angle of vision, Sartre's influence in French philosophy has proved surprisingly durable. French philosophy has long since turned away from Sartre's thought. With the exception of Merleau-Ponty, who was extremely critical of his existentialist colleague, Sartre has no major follower in later French philosophy. But French philosophy has yet to escape from Sartre's influence in its continued fascination with the "three Hs" that remain dominant, above all as concerns Heidegger.[122]

Although an original thinker, often unjustly demeaned in the swing away from his thought beginning with the rise of French structuralism, Sartre was also heavily dependent on others. His early position is heavily indebted to the views of Husserl, Heidegger and Hegel, and his later thought is equally beholden to the theories of Marx and Marxism. After the appearance of *Being and Nothingness*, his first major work, Sartre's prestige was a factor in calling attention to Husserl, Hegel, and above all Heidegger as thinkers in the background of his position. Beaufret, the French Heideggerian most responsible for the shape of the second phase of the French Heidegger discussion, is typical of many others in having initially been drawn to Heidegger through Sartre: "[F]or a long period I thought of Heidegger only as the background of what seemed to me to be of major importance: Sartre. And when I made the trip to Freiburg, I was still motivated by my curiosity about what could have made *Being and Nothingness* possible."[123]

Sartre's intellectual dependence on prior thinkers is paradoxical since he rarely read anyone else with care, rarely studied the texts, preferring either to assimilate ideas that were in the air or through haphazard readings. Even if we acknowledge that Sartre is an original thinker without scholarly pretensions, we must concede that his careless use of others' ideas inevitably results in distortion, even radical distortion. His relation to Hegel's thought is a case in point.[124] For Juliette Simont, Sartre had not read Hegel when he wrote *Being and Nothingness*, although he later studied the *Phenomenology of Spirit* with care.[125] Christopher Fry, who has provided a detailed examination of Sartre's relation to Hegel, contends that the former never read the latter in a more than desultory manner. He says that Sartre's view is an "alchemical *caput mortuum*" of Hegel's and that there is no name for Sartre's use of Hegel.[126]

Sartre devoted considerable study to the works of Husserl and Heidegger. Yet he persistently misunderstood Heidegger's thought, or rather always grasped it through the lens of his own preoccupations. Heidegger stresses the links between his position and the pre-Socratics, whereas Heidegger scholars point to the influences deriving from his reading of texts by Aristotle, the neo-Kantians, and so on. Sartre viewed things rather differently. According to Beauvoir, he drew a connection between Heidegger and the French author Antoine de Saint-Exupéry.[127]

Like French philosophy since Descartes, Sartre's thought is dominated by the problem of humanism. His main concern from beginning to end, including both his earlier existentialism and his later Marxist period, is the concept of the human subject, including human freedom. His early study of the Husserlian idea of the subject in the *Transcendence of the Ego*, his analysis of the For-itself (*Pour-soi*) in *Being and Nothingness*, his offer of the existential concept of human being to prevent the collapse of Marxism in *Search for a Method*, the popularized version of his view he presented in *Existentialism is a Humanism*, his study of human praxis in the *Critique of Dialectical Reason*, and his enormous study of Flaubert in *The Family Idiot* are all aspects of Sartre's continuing interest in human being as his central philosophical theme.

Sartre was not only interested in human being; he further desired to ground his philosophical theory in philosophical anthropology. An indication among many of Sartre's concern to base his philosophy on a conception of human being is provided by a passage from his Marxist period. In a discussion of the Marxist concept of praxis, after a remark on Heidegger, he states that "any philosophy that subordinates the human to the other than human, be it an idealist existentialism or Marxist, is based on and leads to the hatred of human being."[128]

Sartre's position, certainly in its earlier existentialist period, presupposes a fundamental conflation, even an amalgamation, between two philosophers of freedom at the antipodes of the intellectual universe: Descartes and Heidegger. We can illustrate this point through the ruminations of Sartre, the intellectual soldier in search of himself. While others were engaged in fighting a war to the death with fascism, he was busy keeping a diary,[129] writing plays, and preparing his philosophical *magnum opus*. Raising the problem of humanism in November 1939, Sartre rejects the idea of human being as a species as no more than an abasement of human nature. Since Heidegger's position offers a unitary conception of the subject that is not essentialist, it can be said to surpass the Cartesian theory to reach a common goal. In a passage that refers backward to his realist criticism of Husserl's transcendental ego and forward to his own conception of human being as free, Sartre writes:

> Nothing shows better the urgency of an effort like Heidegger's and its *political* importance: determine human nature as a synthetic structure, as a totality devoid of essence. Certainly, it was urgent at the time of Descartes to define spirit through methods inherent to spirit itself. In that way it was isolated. And all the later efforts to constitute the whole man by adding something to spirit were destined to fail because they were only additions. Heidegger's method and those [of the thinkers] that can come after him are at the bottom the same as Descartes': study human nature with the methods inherent to human nature itself; know that human nature is already defined by the way in which it questions itself.[130]

Sartre consistently sought to comprehend human being through the theme of freedom that Kant regarded as the indemonstrable presupposition of morality.[131] Sartre's famous account of freedom in *Being and Nothingness*, the longest single section in the book, develops a view of human conscious-ness as independent of its surroundings,[132] and of human being as possessing a freedom that forces the individual to choose.[133] According to Sartre, one can only be wholly determined or wholly free, and human being is wholly free.[134] As in his account of human being, so in his view of human freedom Sartre brings together Descartes and the anti-Cartesian Heidegger. In a letter to Simone de Beauvoir, written during his captivity, he typically writes that he has "read Heidegger and never felt so free."[135]

Sartre's feeling of freedom derived from Heidegger had little to do with Heidegger's own view. For Heidegger, freedom is essentially a conservative notion whose authentic expression requires the repetition of the past in the future in order to conserve rather than to depart from tradition.[136] Here and later, Sartre regards freedom, not from a traditional angle of vision, but rather as the entirely unencumbered choice of oneself and others. For Sartre, freedom entails a responsibility to choose and authentic choice accepts this responsibility.

The idea that one can assume responsibility for oneself and everyone has always attracted two groups of equally unrealistic supporters: young people who are not yet enmeshed in such social relationships as commitments to spouses and children, and philosophers who typically consider philosophical thought as wholly independent. Arthur Danto, who in this regard is typical, was sufficiently charmed by Sartre's idea to suggest that Sartre led an exemplary life and perhaps achieved authenticity.[137] Although Sartre later modified his understanding of freedom to take account of circumstances,[138] he regarded his view of total human freedom as the recuperation of Des-cartes's view and as the essential basis of humanism. In an important essay on "Cartesian Freedom" he writes: "Two centuries of crisis will be necessary – spiritual crises, scientific crises – for human being to recuperate the creative freedom that Descartes gave to God and to suspect this truth, the essential basis of humanism, human being and being whose appearance causes a world to exist."[139]

HEIDEGGER, SARTRE, AND HUMANISM

Important theories can never be reduced to those of their predecessors. Since Sartre is an important thinker, it is a mistake to overestimate the dependence of his own theory on Heidegger's. Early on, Sartre was aware of and annoyed by this dependence.[140] Yet Sartre's position cannot simply be understood as a variant of Heidegger's, or indeed of any other predecessor's, but needs to stand on its own. Yet the perception of that dependence popularized a misapprehension of Heidegger's thought dominant in the first phase of the French Heidegger reception.

Even in France, the wider public does not read philosophy, certainly not such technical philosophical treatises as *Being and Nothingness*. Sartre had an enormous capacity to attract attention to his writings and, through them, to himself. The link between Heidegger's and Sartre's thought present in that work was considerably strengthened in the latter's famous public lecture, *Existentialism is a Humanism*, where he publicly enlisted Heidegger in the cause of his own existentialism, now characterized as humanism.[141]

Although Sartre follows the early Heidegger in his focus on human being, they comprehend it in basically different ways. Heidegger focuses on human being in terms of the problem of being that was never a Sartrian concern. Heidegger's interest in being is certainly one of the reasons behind his turn to Nazism, for instance, in the "Rectorial address" where he straight-forwardly insists on the need to found National Socialism in fundamental ontology, not only for its own sake, but ultimately for the sake of being.[142] He understands responsibility in the first instance as leading to an authentic repetition of the past and then as the realization of the German people as the heirs to authentic metaphysics in order to know being. On the contrary, Sartre insists on political commitment conjoined to the choice, not only of oneself, but, distantly following Kant, of all human beings, for each of us is responsible for the whole world, so to speak. Heidegger is an anti-Cartesian whose rejection of Cartesianism deepens in his later thought, above all in his effort to decenter the subject. Sartre begins as and finally remains a Cartesian[143] whose effort to understand human being in situation, even in his Marxist phase, never abandons its Cartesian roots.[144]

There is, then, a deep and finally unbridgeable chasm between Heidegger's and Sartre's conceptions of human being. Unquestionably Sartre's thought was influenced by Heidegger's, and for a time Sartre seems genuinely to have thought that Heidegger had anticipated some aspects of his own humanism. Yet if Heidegger is a humanist, his humanism is very different from Sartre's. And although Sartre discerned a close relation between his conception of the human individual and Heidegger's, he in fact offers a different, or at least basically revised notion of subjectivity.

5

JEAN BEAUFRET AND THE "LETTER ON HUMANISM"

French philosophy since the sixteenth century has been concerned with humanism understood as a philosophy of human being in a broad sense. The preceding chapter showed that and how the initial phase of the French Heidegger reception stressed an interpretation of Heidegger as a humanist thinker.

Heidegger's thought is not humanism in any obvious, ordinary sense, although he suggests – and his suggestion is widely followed – that his theory is a new form of humanism. The term "humanism" (*Humanismus*) does not occur in *Being and Time*. From Heidegger's angle of vision, the French humanist reading of his thought relies on an uncritical assumption of the traditional understanding of humanism.

This assumption, suggested by Kojève, reaches a peak in Sartre's enthusiastic, erroneous, but highly influential conflation between his own existentialism and Heidegger's thought.[1] Kojève was never popular with more than a small intellectual circle, but Sartre was popular with the general public. His enthusiastic embrace of Heidegger's thought on the basis of his own humanism helped to popularize Heidegger's theory through a false interpretation that quickly spread throughout the French discussion. Yet around the same time that Sartre's humanist misreading of Heidegger emerged into public view in Sartre's public lecture, a reaction against any anthropological reading of Heidegger's theory was also beginning to emerge.

The first and second phases of the French reading of Heidegger's theory agree in their insistence on its basic humanism. The difference between them does not concern the approach to Heidegger's theory as humanism that remains constant throughout the French reading of Heidegger's theory but rather the association of humanism with philosophical anthropology. In general terms, the first reading ignores the transcendental side of Heideggerian phenomenology in favor of philosophical anthropology in the interpretations of Kojève, Wahl, Sartre, and others. On the contrary, the second reading, intended as a revision, or course correction, restores its transcendental side at the price of a calculated retreat from philosophical anthropology while still maintaining the view of Heidegger's theory as humanism, albeit in a novel sense. This chapter will study the second phase of the French Heidegger reception as a reaction against the initial humanist reading of Heidegger's thought.

SARTRE, HEIDEGGER, AND HUMANISM

For more than fifteen years dating from the appearance of *Being and Nothingness* until the emergence of structuralism, Sartre increasingly dominated French philosophy and the intellectual context in general.[2] Dominant thinkers attract detractors, those who rebel against their thought, and Sartre attracted more than his share. During his life, Sartre's person attracted not only attention but strong emotions.

According to John Gerassi, a recent biographer, who devotes a whole chapter to the topic, no one was more hated than Sartre.[3] Those who hated Sartre ranged from those who denounced him, say, for collaboration with the enemy (André Malraux) or being a foreign agent (François Mauriac), to Pope Pius XII who placed Sartre's writings on the Index in 1948, extending even to two abortive efforts to assassinate him in 1962.[4] Others, aware of Sartre's repeated pleas for intellectual engagement,[5] were annoyed by his decision to continue to publish in occupied France,[6] or believed that his celebrated commitment was mainly a commitment to himself.[7]

In this respect, Foucault's reaction is instructive. Foucault, who was earlier a member of the French Communist Party, later turned against communism and Marxism as Sartre moved in that direction, eventually writing his *Critique of Dialectical Reason*. Foucault spoke for others when in an interview he satirized Sartre as a man whose thought belonged to an earlier period: "The *Critique of Dialectical Reason* is the magnificent and pathetic effort of a man of the nineteenth century to think the twentieth century. In this sense, Sartre is the last Hegelian and, I would even say, the last Marxist."[8]

Yet Sartre's thought was highly influential. If the two main movements of French postwar thought are existentialism and structuralism, then it is a measure of the importance of the man and his continued influence on French philosophy that French existentialism is largely identified with his theory and that French structuralism can be understood as a concerted effort to throw off its shackles.[9] The desire to break free of Sartre's claustrophobic influence as a *monstre sacré* was a strong motivating factor in French intellectual life immediately after the war. For the young Foucault, Sartre's journal, *Les Temps Modernes*, represented a form of intellectual terrorism.[10] According to Didier Eribon, the end of Sartre's intellectual hegemony on French intellectual life was only signaled by Lévi-Strauss's direct attack on his thought in *La Pensée sauvage*.[11] Significantly, Pierre Bourdieau understood this work as indicating a new, different route to follow.[12]

Humanism was not originally a central theme in Sartre's philosophical thought. In his first novel, *Nausea*, where he emphasizes the absurdity of life, he satirizes the humanist as the gay narrator who blindly loves man but hates individuals.[13] In *Being and Nothingness*, where he stresses personal commitment, humanism is still not an explicit theme. He only turned explicitly to humanism in the aftermath of the war when a similar concern swept through France.

Although different observers understood this word in different senses,[14] humanism became a central theme at this point in time virtually throughout French life: in Sartre's existentialism, in Marxism as well as in religion.[15] In politics, this theme figures in the exchange in 1945 between French socialist leaders. Léon Blum appealed to the transformation of the human condition through a humane socialism, and Guy Mollet objected to an erroneous humanism.[16] It is exemplified in literature in André Malraux's famous novel about *La Condition humaine*.

From the humanist perspective, Sartre's growing inclination to Marxism at the end of the war was problematic. Marxism, especially as linked to the French Communist Party, was dominant in France over about a dozen years from 1944 until the the short-lived Hungarian Revolution and subsequent Soviet invasion in 1956.[17] Although some Catholics, such as Emmanuel Mounier and his colleagues at *Esprit* maintained close ties to Marxism and the French Communist Party,[18] Marxism long attracted two kinds of opposition: from those concerned with or members of organized religion, particularly Roman Catholics, who were troubled by the official Marxist commitment to atheism; from some intellectuals, such as Raymond Aron, Albert Camus, or Maurice Merleau-Ponty. These were some of the many writers and intellectuals who either initially or later feared the link between Marxism and Bolshevism or Leninism. Merleau-Ponty, for instance, Sartre's former colleague on *Les Temps Modernes*, turned from an initial enthusiasm about political Marxism[19] to a sober concern to distance himself from it.[20] In France as in Germany, although there were many intellectuals who were genuinely enthusiastic about fascism, others turned to fascism on the grounds that it was a lesser evil than international communism.[21]

In the aftermath of the war, questions were also raised about the quality of Sartre's humanism, say, the extent of his commitment to the French resistance movement.[22] It seems clear that Sartre's political engagement was mainly theoretical until rather late in his career. This point has a clear existential significance. During the war, while Sartre was busy furthering his intellectual career, other French intellectuals, such as Paul Nizan,[23] his former room mate at the Ecole normale superieure, Georges Politzer, the communist sociologist,[24] Marc Bloch, an important historian and co-founder of the *Annales*, the famous historical journal, and Jean Cavaillès,[25] a brilliant young philosopher of science, were paying for their commitment to freedom with their lives.

Sartre's ambiguous position did not go unnoticed. Representing the French communist party, Roger Garaudy denounced existentialism, with a violence inhabitual even in the French context, as exemplary of "the sickness when thought is separated from action" and in the claim that "the rich and well born [la grande bourgeoisie] are titillated by the intellectual fornications of Jean-Paul Sartre."[26] Slightly later, Jean Wahl, who was philosophically more sophisticated, wrote that "existentialism has become not only a European problem but a worldwide problem."[27]

Sartre, who was aware of these criticisms, chose to answer them on the philosophical plane through an identification of his own theory with Heidegger's. This was the kind of anthropological misreading of the master's position that Heidegger rejects in *Being and Time* and later explicitly proscribes in a letter to Jean Wahl in 1937.[28] Sartre's famous lecture, *Existentialism is a Humanism*, was initially delivered to the Club Maintenant on Monday, October 28, 1945, and published, in slightly modified form, in March 1946.[29] This lecture immediately attracted the widespread attention that *Being and Nothingness*, published during the War, failed to attract. As a short, accessible version of Sartre's more technical thought,[30] indeed a travesty of it, it was widely and easily accessible in a way that his main philosophical contribution was not.

Sartre begins his lecture on existentialism by reviewing some of the more salient objections to his philosophical theory. Medieval thinkers, such as Thomas Aquinas, traditionally make existence dependent on essence.[31] According to Sartre, who inverts the relation of these categories, all existentialists agree that existence precedes essence.[32] He classifies existentialists in terms of Catholicism, such as Jaspers and Marcel, or atheism for Heidegger and himself. Sartre identifies his own atheistic existentialism with Heidegger's view of human reality, or the idea that fundamentally human being exists.[33] This leads to a theory of total commitment (*engagement*)[34] that alone accords dignity to human being.[35] He rejects the traditional form of humanism centered on human being as an end in itself,[36] for instance in Kant's theory, in favor of a view of human being as a constant project outside itself that causes its own existence.[37] Against criticisms that he professes a quietism allied to a contemplative view of philosophy, such as the Cartesian "I think,"[38] he stresses action beginning with Cartesian certainty.[39]

Sartre's view attracted many objections, for instance from Gabriel Marcel, the proponent of Christian existentialism, made uneasy by Sartre's emphasis on absolute freedom and the inherent meaninglessness of human existence. In his lectures, Sartre responds by emphasizing the importance of a coherent atheism,[40] since God's possible existence is irrelevant[41] to human being. Yet his lecture did not allay but only increased doubts about his theory. His silence with respect to the limitations to human freedom imposed by the social and political context was attacked as antihumanism by Jean Kanapa, his former student turned communist, and Henri Lefebvre, another communist who was later expelled from the French Communist Party.

Kanapa, who criticizes Sartre, not wholly unfairly, as an intellectual opportunist, regards existentialism as a covert form of anti-Marxism. He opposes any form of Christian humanism in which human being is made to capitulate before God[42] and argues that humanism is meaningful only as Marxism.[43] For Kanapa, humanism entails the struggle for human being. Although the existentialists present themselves as revolutionaries, they are finally only an ineffectual bunch of bourgeois intellectuals.[44] He further stigmatizes the existentialist claim that human being is free as a return to Bergsonism and as a modern form of sophistry.[45]

Kanapa, the editor of *La Nouvelle critique*, was a staunch Stalinist. His inflammatory pamphlet, mainly directed against Sartre, is less impressive than Lefebvre's philosophically more mature study of existentialism. Lefebvre correctly regards Sartre as self-inflated. He begins his book with an interesting autobiographical account that usefully mentions many of the future intellectuals of his generation, in the process of explaining how he, who earlier adhered to existentialism, became a Marxist and a communist.[46]

According to Lefebvre, in 1946 existentialism is less a movement than a new form of academic thought[47] that has the advantage of attracting a few cultural stars and assorted snobs.[48] Following orthodox Marxism, he depicts existentialism as the concentration on the individual following the breakup of Hegelian idealism.[49] Husserl preaches a form of abstract rationalism, in which the phenomenological reduction corresponds to the isolation of the individual.[50] Heidegger transforms Husserlian rationalism into an irrationalism in his metaphysics of the *Grand Guignol*. Heidegger is a profascist philosopher, whose exaltation of destiny and death provide a Hitlerian "affective tonality."[51]

Sartre, who does not rate a chapter of his own in Lefebvre's study, is discussed within the chapter on Heidegger. Here his theory is simplistically depicted, much as he himself depicts it in his lecture, as the continuation of Heidegger's. The latter's existentialism is a form of adventurism, and in Sartre's theory being and nothingness are separated by Heideggerian existentialism.[52] Sartre, who closely follows Heidegger, mixes together literature and philosophy. His theory is continuous with Heidegger's philosophy in the style of Hitler's SS. Sartre's initial thought adds nothing either to Husserl's or to Heidegger's.[53] His inconsistent view is located somewhere between a philosophy of inhumanism and a concern for the human.[54]

HEIDEGGERIAN CRITICISM OF EXISTENTIALISM

Heidegger and Karl Jaspers both became well known in France after the war, although Heidegger more so than Jaspers.[55] Heidegger was not yet the main "French" philosopher, although he quickly achieved this status when the war came to a close. At the end of the war, there was a very broad range of attitudes toward Heidegger. These included those indifferent to his thought, those concerned to study it from a careful, increasingly critical perspective, such as Wahl, those whose own positions were influenced by Heidegger's, such as Lévinas and Merleau-Ponty, those who appropriated it, often on the basis of a superficial reading, such as Sartre, or Gilson, and those, the Heideggerians, such as Henri Birault and Beaufret, who identified with Heidegger's thought, even, in extreme cases, with Heidegger himself.

After the war, French Heideggerians were under pressure from several sides, including the anthropological misunderstanding of the master's thought that reached its height in Sartre's conflation of his own existentialism with fundamental ontology and humanism, and the effort by French communists, who consistently opposed Sartre, to focus attention on Heidegger's allegiance to National Socialism. Sartre's facile lecture exhibited his verbal capacity more than his ability for strict philosophical reasoning on display in *Being and Nothingness* and in other technical philosophical writings. His lecture failed to placate but only annoyed his philosophical critics.

Responses followed from the right and the left, from Christians and communists, from other existentialists and from their opponents. Etienne Gilson, the noted French Thomist, attempted to divide and conquer in claiming that Thomism is only existentialism properly understood.[56] This suggests that existentialism is finally an imperfect form of Thomism. Gilson held that the initial premise of Sartrean existentialism, in his view the premise that human being is only what it does, is a purely gratuitous affirmation.[57]

Sartre's equally facile philosophical embrace of Heidegger's doctrine only enraged the growing ranks of Heidegger's French adherents. Among French Heideggerians, the annoyance generated by Sartre's identification with Heidegger continued to rankle over time. The writings of Beaufret and Derrida illustrate the reaction to Sartre's uncritical embrace of Heidegger by French Heideggerians.

In a sense, relative rank is not a concern among French Heideggerians who, like the philosophically orthodox in all times and places, subordinate themselves to the "orthodox" reading of the master thinker's thought. Yet just as Althusser became centrally important in French Marxist circles for his identification of the "correct" form of Marxism, so in the legions of French Heideggerians, several figures stand out for their service to the Heideggerian "cause." More than anyone else, Jean Beaufret worked successfully to correct the anthropological reading of Heidegger dominant in the first phase of the French Heidegger discussion. After Beaufret's death in 1982, Jacques Derrida, his onetime student, became the central French Heideggerian. In the highly charged political atmosphere of the French Heidegger discussion, roughly since the middle 1960s François Fédier has for many years been Heidegger's most important defender against any attempt to link his philosophical thought to his politics.

Right after the war, Beaufret, Lévinas, and Birault were among the most important figures to speak up for Heidegger's theory. Beaufret was not the only orthodox French Heideggerian in this period, but he was certainly the most visible and most orthodox of them all. Lévinas, although never an orthodox Heideggerian, perhaps never even a Heideggerian at all, was distinctly favorable to Heidegger's thought at this time. In an article in the *Revue de métaphysique et de morale* from 1951, he went so far as to claim that in Heidegger's position the problems of the present and the abstract question of being come together.[58] Birault, in an article in the same issue, presented a detailed, uncritical reading of Heidegger's thought that served as the model for many young students in the 1950s unable to read Heidegger's as yet untranslated writings.[59] He maintained this orthodox perspective many years later in his book, *Heidegger et l'expérience de la pensée*, intended to show how to think with Heidegger.[60]

In his early, influential article, Birault affirms without qualification the status of Beaufret as the most authorized interpreter of Heidegger's thought in France.[61] Beaufret closely follows the model of Heidegger, who typically declines to "criticize" others. Unlike many French writers, Beaufret is not polemical, preferring to "correct" expressed views rather than to confront his opponents.

Beaufret's analysis of the views of Sartre and Heidegger changed radically over time. In a long article from 1945,[62] he gives credit to Sartre for leading him to Heidegger's theory that Sartre understands better than anyone even if he expresses his understanding of it inadequately.[63] The translation of "Dasein" as "human reality" (*réalité humaine*) adopted by Sartre fails to grasp the eruption of presence.[64] Existentialism pushes phenomenology to existence, the human condition, whose analysis depends on Heidegger's conception of Being-in-the-world.[65]

At this point, immediately after the war, when Sartre's star was at its zenith, before the reaction had reached its peak, Beaufret's attitude towards Sartre was respectful but increasingly critical. Only two years later in another article,[66] he distanced himself from Sartre on behalf of Heidegger. Sartre's analyses have a merely psychological validity that lacks Heideggerian radicality.[67] Heidegger's view of Dasein is not, as Heidegger says, a means to avoid the cogito whose presupposition it reveals.[68] Heidegger's notion of existence as the essence of human being is unlike Sartre's conviction that subjectivity inexhaustibly reinvents itself.[69]

In his later writings, Beaufret further increases his view of the distance between Sartre and Heidegger. Heidegger's return to the Greeks is "a little too rustic" for the contemporary sages headed by Sartre.[70] The latter's conviction that Husserl has freed us from interior life (*la vie intérieure*) is only half true, since this requires a return with Heidegger behind the cogito to Dasein.[71] In accepting Marxism as the source of contemporary knowledge (*savoir*), Sartre uncritically accepts the traditional view of philosophy.[72] Sartre's existentialism is no more adequate than Husserlian phenomenology to dialogue with Marxism.[73] For Sartre fails to see the point of considering

87

Nietzsche as a philosopher.[74] Sartre resembles Karl Löwith, Heidegger's first graduate student, in his failure to understand the master thinker's thought.[75]

HEIDEGGER'S FRENCH OFFENSIVE

Heidegger's "Letter on Humanism" forms the second phase in an offensive undertaken by Heidegger to attract attention in the French discussion and, I believe, to distract attention from his commitment to National Socialism.

The full dimensions of Heidegger's allegiance to real National Socialism as it in fact existed are still unknown since relevant portions of his *Nachlass* have still not appeared and the Heidegger Archives in Marbach are not open to the public. It is also significant that the ongoing edition of his *Collected Works* will not include his letters, since the letters from his period as rector of the University of Freiburg could reasonably be expected to shed light on his precise relation to the NSDAP and his view of real Nazism.

In the immediate postwar atmosphere, information about Heidegger's precise link to Nazism was even scarcer than at present. Later, after the war, when Heidegger began to devote extensive attention to creating his own legend, he sought above all to disguise the nature and extent of his commitment to real and then to an ideal form of National Socialism, a commitment that began prior to Hitler's rise to power and continued, even after the war, until the end of his life.

Writing in 1947, Wahl, who was sympathetic to Heidegger, notes that when Hitler came to power Heidegger "made a resolute decision to join the Nazi leaders."[76] Wahl, who attributes Heidegger's adherence to Nazism to the merely formal character of fundamental ontology, is willing to face the problem posed by Heidegger's turning to National Socialism on the basis of Heidegger's philosophical thought. Others in the French discussion take a much harder line. In the discussion following Wahl's talk, Georges Gurvitch describes Heidegger as a basically dishonest thinker who employs a form of existentialism to effect a transition from his original scholastic philosophy to the Nazi philosophy.[77]

Our immediate concern is less with Heidegger's Nazism than with its influence on his turn towards toward France and French philosophy. Elsewhere I have argued in detail that Heidegger's philosophical and political views are inextricably intertwined.[78] After the war, the dimensions of Heidegger's commitment to Nazism were only partly known, although enough was known to raise serious questions for some observers. Yet it is only possible to understand Heidegger's appeal to French philosophers if we note that in France his thought was accepted in isolation from his political commitment. Paradoxically, although a long line of French intellectuals, including French philosophers, have been directly engaged on the political level, Heidegger's theory achieved a preeminent status in part through abstraction from its political dimension.

In the present context, there is no need to rehearse the details of Heidegger's commitment to National Socialism. Suffice it to say that in 1933, almost immediately after Hitler came to power Heidegger was elected rector of the University of Freiburg i. B. by his academic colleagues. In May of that year, he delivered the notorious "Rectorial Address" in which he publicly placed his philosophical resources in the service of National Socialism.[79] At that time, Ernst Röhm was head of the SA (*Sturmabteilung*) opposed to the SS (*Schutzstaffel*) led by Hermann Göring. After the assassination of Röhm on June 30, 1934, with whom he may have been allied,[80] Heidegger resigned from his post as rector and returned to teaching. At the end of the war, like other Nazi collaborators in the German academy Heidegger was called to account for his actions. He immediately took steps directed at self-exculpation, or at least at damage control, that he and his some of his closest followers continued until the end of his life, and that his followers have still not abandoned.

Despite his antipathy to Descartes, Heidegger twice turned toward France, in "Ways to Discussion [Wege zur Aussprache]," a short text written in 1937, that is in the period between Heidegger's resignation from the rectorship and the beginning of the war, and later in the "Letter on Humanism." The former is a little known text,[81] written after the end of the Weimar Republic, when Hitler had come to power, as Germany was slowly proceeding down the path toward what was to become the Second World War.

At present, when France and Germany are together striving to live together in the framework of the Common Market, relations between the two continental neighbors are exceedingly good. In retrospect, Heidegger's little text is surprising in the context of then politically difficult relations between France and Germany that have often been only slightly better on the philosophical plane. Since Heidegger's antipathy to Descartes runs throughout his thought from beginning to end, it is surprising from a philosophical point of view that in "Ways to Discussion" he turns toward France and French philosophy. Heidegger's appeal to a neighboring country is more comprehensible from the political perspective. It was something that was in the air at the time, for instance in the art historian A. E. Brinkmann's appeal for cultural collaboration between European peoples.[82]

In his text, Heidegger ostensibly reexamines the Hegelian theme of the conditions of agreement between the French and the Germans. He maintains that any agreement must be based on mutual respect whose conditions are listening to each other and the courage for "proper self-limitation [eigenen Bestimmung]."[83] In the second paragraph of this essay, he states his view of understanding among peoples in a description of the authenticity of a people, in a startling passage that requires full quotation:

Authentic [Echtes] understanding among peoples [Völker] begins and fulfills itself on one condition: this is in a creative reciprocal discussion leading to awareness concerning the historically shared past and present

89

conditions. Through such awareness each of the peoples is brought back to what is ownmost to it [je Eigene] and grasps it with increased clarity and resoluteness [Entschiedenheit]. The ownmost in a people is its creativity [Schaffen], through which it grows into its historical mission [in seine geschichtliche Sendung hineinwächst] and so first comes to itself. The main feature [Grundzug] of its mission has been indicated for the historically cultured peoples in the present world situation [Weltstunde] as the rescue of the West [Rettung des Abendlandes]. Rescue here does not mean the simple maintenance of what is already present to hand [Vorhandenen], but rather signifies the originary, newly creating justification [Rechtfertigung] of its past and future history. Reciprocal understanding of neighbor peoples in their most ownmost means rather: for each the ownmost task [je eigene Aufgabe] is to know how to give oneself the necessity of this rescue. The knowledge concerning this necessity springs all the more from the experience of need, which arises with the innermost menace of the West, and from the power of the plan concealing [Kraft zum verklärenden Entwurf] the highest possibilities of Western man [abendländischen Daseins]. Just as the menace of the West drives toward a full uprooting and general disorder [Wirrnis], so, on the contrary, the will to the renewal from the ground up must be led through the final resolutions [Entscheidungen].[84]

This passage, composed after the rectorate, when Heidegger has returned to teaching, contradicts his description of the implicitly apolitical character of "a conversation of essential thinking with itself [Selbstgespräch des wesentlichen Denkens mit sich selbst]."[85] Although Heidegger gave up his rectorate in 1934, here and in later writings he continues to insist on an aim common to Nazism and his own thought – expressed here in Spenglerian terms, on the basis of his own view of authenticity – for the German people to realize itself in the future historical context. The mere fact that he here calls upon the French to do likewise in no sense alters the fact that he continues to mobilize the resources of his philosophy for an end in view which has not changed.

Heidegger clearly describes his view of the practical, hence political, role of so-called authentic philosophy. Unlike Hegel, who held a retrospective view of philosophy which looked back on what had already taken place, for Heidegger authentic philosophical knowledge is prospective, a form of anticipation for which the problem of theory and practice does not arise.

By itself authentic philosophical knowledge [Wissen] is never the backward-looking addition to the most general representations on already known things, but rather the anticipatory opening through knowledge of the consistently hidden essence of things. And precisely in this way it is never necessary to make this knowledge immediately useful. It is effective only mediately in that philosophical awareness prepares new points of view and standards for all attitudes and resolutions [Entscheiden].[86]

Heidegger leaves no doubt here of the intrinsic purpose of authentic philosophy. In the midst of the social, political, and historical circumstances that were shortly to lead to the Second World War, he takes an aggressive view of the philosophical task, reminiscent of the early Marx's insistence on philosophy as tranforming the masses, as transforming the consciousness of the people.[87]

> If an authentic self-understanding is achieved in the basic philosophical position [in der philosophischen Grundstellung], if the power and the will for it can be correspondingly awakened, then the dominant knowledge [das herrschaftliche Wissen] rises to a new height and clarity. It prepares the way for the first time for a transformation of the peoples which is often invisible.[88]

This passage provides an important insight into Heidegger's adherence to Nazism as an ideal even after his resignation from the rectorate. Heidegger here relies on his conception of authenticity, which he applies to philosophy and to the German *Volk*. He clearly insists on the revolutionary role of authentic philosophy in bringing about the realization of the true destiny of the German people.[89] Like Brinkmann, who insists on German spirituality as a higher synthesis that justifies and saves the lesser tendencies of so-called French rationalism and Italian sensualism, so the aim of Heidegger's proposed dialogue with French thinkers is to present German philosophy as the conceptual solution to the existential problems of both the French and Germans.

HEIDEGGER'S LETTER TO BEAUFRET

"Ways to Discussion" is important as the initial phase in Heidegger's turning toward France and French philosophy, a turning that he pursued with renewed vigor, in a second phase, at the end of the war. At about the same time that Sartre was publicly embracing Heidegger's theory to justify his claim that existentialism is humanism, Heidegger was seeking to free his view from this embrace, to distance it through a clarification of the meaning of the term "humanism" in his own theory. Heidegger's "Letter on Humanism" is useful to understand the later evolution of his thought, but crucial for an understanding of the emergence in the second phase of the French Heidegger reception of a nonanthropological, postmetaphysical but humanist reading of his position.

The "Letter on Humanism" is the response to a letter from Beaufret carried to Heidegger by Jean-Michel Palmier, a young German-speaking Alsatian, in the fall of 1945, immediately after the end of the Second World

War. Heidegger's initial response to Beaufret, in a letter dated 23 November 1945,[90] contains a number of flattering comments about Beaufret's remarks on the translation of "Dasein" in the latter's article, "A propos de l'existentialisme." He sent Beaufret a longer text in December 1946 in the form of a letter that he then revised and published in 1947 under the title "Über den 'Humanismus'. Brief an Jean Beaufret, Paris."

Heidegger's "Letter on Humanism" responds to specific theoretical, or philosophical and practical, or political imperatives. This text is an important document in the slow elaboration of Heidegger's later thought. It is located approximately halfway between the first phase that reaches an early high point in *Being and Time* (1927) and, depending on one's reading, comes to an end in "What Is Metaphysics?" (1929) and the later thought leading up to "The End of Philosophy and the Task of Thinking" (1964).

Heidegger's "Letter on Humanism" cannot be understood merely as a reaction to Beaufret's letter by which it was elicited. When Beaufret wrote to Heidegger immediately after the war, he was still an unknown philosopher, certainly not known for his developing interest in existentialism, known, if known at all, for his interest in Marxism. It is fair to say that he was not then, nor did he later become, despite his indefectible allegiance to Heidegger, someone whose thought was ever important in itself, ever worthy of the attention of an important thinker for other than strategic reasons.

If it is a mistake to consider the "Letter on Humanism" solely as an occasional document written with no further intentions, or solely for the specific occasion of Beaufret's letter to Heidegger, it is a further mistake to neglect the political aspects of Heidegger's text that connect it to the historical context. One factor is the political maneuvering for advantage that affects philosophers with about the same frequency and to the same degree as others. Philosophers are rarely equal to their public pronouncements. Sartre's fabled notion of selfless commitment is mainly a personal commitment, an interest in himself that is fully duplicated by Heidegger's constant effort to maneuver in the German academy, in a difficult period leading up to and later away from the Second World War, for personal advantage.

Even Heidegger's most occasional texts have a clearly philosophical side. Yet texts such as the "Rectorial address" cannot be fully grasped without considering both the strictly philosophical and the political imperatives that they express. The same imperatives describe the "Letter on Humanism" as well. This document elicited by Beaufret's inquiry, upon which Heidegger fastened for his own purposes, clearly responds to a number of specific factors which concerned Heidegger at the end of the war. These include Heidegger's desire to correct a misinterpretation of his thought, his effort to seek help in a personally difficult situation, and his concern to forestall the incipient French debate on his Nazism.

In his initial letter to Beaufret, after his earlier letter to Wahl, Heidegger insists on the importance of Beaufret's refutation of the mistranslation of

"Dasein" as "human reality." As Borch-Jacobsen points out, in this respect Heidegger's text is as much a response to Sartre as it is to Kojève, who first proposed this rendering,[91] and perhaps even to Corbin, whose pioneering translations of Heideggerian texts initially propagated it.

All thinkers desire to be understood, or at least not too severely misunderstood. It is, then, not difficult to understand Heidegger's concern to correct the prevalent French anthropological misunderstanding of his thought. Yet there is an obvious disparity between a mere misunderstanding of his philosophical position that, disagreeable as it was, could not reasonably be construed as a direct or even a major threat to his life and thought, and other, more immediate threats in the postwar environment to his life in philosophy and his philosophical lifework. The mere interpretation of his philosophical thought pales as a factor when viewed against the background of his "existential" situation in the aftermath of the Second World War, in which other, more immediate threats to his person and thought almost certainly took precedence in his mind.

Obviously, Heidegger was concerned about his difficult personal situation immediately after the war, when, as Germany's greatest living philosopher, he was, like others, as part of the denazification process called to account for his identification with National Socialism. As a result of this process, Heidegger – the German philosopher who initially thought of himself as the authentic heir to the mantle of Plato and Aristotle, and later with Parmenides, Heraclitus and Anaximander as one of only four real thinkers of being – was excluded from the university and forbidden to teach. In his time of need, Heidegger appealed unavailingly to his closest philosophical ally, Karl Jaspers.[92] Heidegger's difficulties in the aftermath of the war, including his "rustification" in disgrace, the loss of his pension rights, the threatened confiscation of his house and personal library, as well as his failure to find support among other German academics, naturally led him to seek support elsewhere.

His turning toward France may have been influenced by three specific factors: his exclusion from the German delegation to the Descartes conference in Paris in 1937 that rankled sufficiently for him to complain about it as late as the *Spiegel* interview in 1966, his apparent inability to accept an invitation to address the French Philosophical Society at their meeting of December 4, 1937, and the fact that since Freiburg was in the French occupation zone in the denazification process he had to deal with the French military authorities.

Certainly the latter factor makes it reasonable for Heidegger to have thought that he had to cultivate, correctly as it turned out, a potentially fruitful relation to French philosophy. For in appealing to French philosophers for philosophical dialogue, Heidegger, the anti-Cartesian philosopher, was appealing to his French philosophical colleagues on the level of his own *discipline* and, through French colleagues, to the French nation, including the French occupying forces.

It is possible that in difficult personal straights, even more than his person or his family Heidegger was concerned to protect his philosophical thought whose integrity was clearly threatened, in fact is still threatened by his Nazi turning. If this is the case, then a further factor in the composition of his "Letter on Humanism" lies in the emergence of the controversy about Heidegger's Nazism that, since it began, has gone through various phases but has never ended. This controversy has long persisted as a threat not only to his person during the remainder of his life – during his "rustification" it cost him his livelihood – and after his death as a menace to his thought.

The controversy about Heidegger's Nazism began immediately in the wake of his "Rectorial Address," at the zenith of his ascendancy in Nazi Germany. From the first, it opposed important thinkers like Jaspers who congratulated Heidegger for his willingness to act on his convictions[93] and Benedetto Croce who claimed that he dishonored philosophy.[94] The disagreement between those who condemned and those who praised Heidegger's Nazism, those concerned to probe the link between his political thought and his political turning and those more inclined to absolve his thought of any political blemish by impeding any such interrogation, did not, in fact, could not occur in Germany where almost every philosopher who remained in the German University during the war had inevitably been politically compromised.

The first, incomplete phase of the debate on Heidegger's Nazism took place in France after the end of the war, when attention was focused on Heidegger through Sartre's existentialism, in the pages of Sartre's journal, *Les Temps Modernes*. Hence, another reason for Heidegger to address himself to French philosophers on the subject of humanism was to practice damage control in the growing French discussion of his Nazism, to protect the integrity of his thought against probing intended to reveal its political consequences not only in the French philosophical debate but, as an easily anticipated consequence of any extended French debate of this theme, in Germany as well.

HEIDEGGER'S "LETTER ON HUMANISM"

If Heidegger's intent in writing his "Letter on Humanism" was not only further to develop his thought but also to influence the French philosophical discussion – through correcting the anthropological misinterpretation of his thought, then through securing allies abroad for his person and thought when few were available in his own country, and finally through limiting the threat to his own person and thought represented by the incipient debate on his Nazism – then he succeeded brilliantly.

His success in this regard surpassed any reasonable or even unreasonable expectation. He was not only able to correct the misreading of his position and to secure allies in a neighboring country, and, at least for a time to keep the lid on the debate concerning his Nazism. His success went still further since he was even able to displace Sartre who, prior to Beaufret, was his main

French disciple, in order to become the master thinker of French philosophy, the main "French" philosopher in the postwar discussion. And he was able to influence the French philosophical debate in a durable fashion, in the most diverse ways, including even Althusser's Marxist antihumanism.[95]

Heidegger's "Letter on Humanism" is a complex document, difficult to interpret.[96] This text has attracted attention in the Heidegger literature,[97] particularly in France, where its importance in the French discussion was heightened by the relatively tardy appearance of *Being and Time*. The French, who are traditionally less able to read texts in foreign languages than the Germans, also translate relatively little and then usually after a lengthy period. The complex process of rendering Heidegger into French, arguably more difficult than into English, was rendered even more difficult by such other factors as the dispute about the correct translation of "Dasein." Beaufret's remark in his initial article that "if German has its resources, French has its limits"[98] was significantly praised by Heidegger in his initial response.[99] Despite intense French interest, the first half of *Being and Time* was only rendered into French in 1964[100] and 21 years elapsed before further progress was made. *Being and Time* was finally only made available for the first time in a full, but pirated translation in 1985[101] and in an "authorized" translation in 1986.[102]

In the absence of a complete translation of Heidegger's main treatise, his "Letter on Humanism," which was quickly available in translation some 32 years before *Being and Time*, assumed a crucial role.[103] In this text, Heidegger publicly responds to a series of queries posed by Beaufret: How can one give a new meaning to "humanism?" What is the relation of ontology to a possible ethics? How can one save the element of adventure in philosophy? These questions are significant in themselves. They were particularly significant in the immediate postwar French context, concerned practically with the restoration of a humane society in the wake of the Nazi occupation and theoretically with Sartre's suggestion that existentialism offers the required conceptual aid. From that angle of vision, Beaufret's questions should be read less as a hostile reaction to Sartre than as an effort to go beyond Sartrean existentialism to the philosophical background on which it claimed to rely. His questions provide a useful occasion for Heidegger further to elaborate a position that had already shifted and to respond through his own position to pressing French concerns.

Three themes dominate the "Letter on Humanism." First, there is Heidegger's public effort to distance his theory from that of Sartre, the reigning French philosophical guru. More than anything else, his success in vanquishing Sartre led to Heidegger's emergence as the master thinker in French postwar thought. Second, there is Heidegger's opportunistic concern at a time when this problem had been raised in France to clarify the notion of humanism in his own thought. This text contains the first and last discussion of this problem in his writings. Heidegger's treatment of humanism in this text is even more important since the debate on his Nazism had raised significant questions about his own humanism on political grounds. Third, Heidegger indicates a fundamental evolution, or turning, in his thought. In the highly charged political atmosphere prevalent in the aftermath of the war, the result was to invest a philosophical claim, an observation about the development of his philosophical thought, with political meaning, in effect – the word is not too strong – to "sanitize" German phenomenology for French philosophical consumption.

Heidegger is unusually aware of other philosophies, indeed of the entire history of philosophy. He magisterially suggests the uselessness of criticism. Yet his writings are replete with critical remarks on other views, as in his comment, in his initial letter to Beaufret, that the supposedly canonical reference to "Jaspers and Heidegger" is *the* misunderstanding par excellence."[104] In the "Letter on Humanism," Heidegger's criticism of Sartre, whose effort to compare or even to ally himself to the master thinker is rejected as entirely misbegotten, is sharp, direct, and devastating. Heidegger's discussion reaffirms his conviction, on display in *Being and Time* and all later writings, of the primacy of the concern with being. It purports to show that his theory of being is not only different from but prior to Sartrean existentialism and all other philosophical theories.

In his response to Beaufret, Heidegger employs Sartre's own strategy against Sartre. Both Sartre and Heidegger reject traditional humanism, supposedly unsatisfactory to respond to social concerns, in favor of a new, socially useful kind of humanism. In "Existentialism Is A Humanism" – the only work by Sartre to which Heidegger clearly refers – there is no evidence that he has read *Being and Nothingness* – Sartre responds to criticism by affirming that existentialism, properly understood, offers a new type of humanism that requires each of us to be responsible for everyone, for the whole world. Heidegger similarly argues that thinking, the name that has replaced fundamental ontology as the designation for his theory, is a new form of humanism; but Sartre's view is merely another type of the traditional, unsatisfactory humanist genus. It follows that Sartrean existentialism merely pretends unsuccessfully to be the new, socially useful form of humanism that is realized in Heidegger's view.

Heidegger develops his claim in a discussion clearly based on *Being and Time* and later texts. His repeated references to Hölderlin and to Nietzschean nihilism allude respectively to his intervening lecture series on the poet[105] and the philosopher.[106] In *Being and Time*, Heidegger approaches being through human being. Conversely, his view of humanism represents an approach to human being through being.

This strategy quickly emerges in writings later than *Being and Time*. For instance in a lecture series from 1929/30, during the worldwide economic depression, he contends that various social problems are symptomatic of the turn away from being.[107] He elaborates this idea here in his notion of thinking, or the authentic thought of being, intended as the alternative to traditional metaphysics that turns away from being. For Heidegger, the alienation of human being[108] has its roots in the "homelessness of modern man,"[109] supposedly symptomatic of the forgetfulness of being. Marx's theory is important in addressing history, although neither he, nor Husserl, nor even Sartre sees the link to being.

Heidegger reserves special treatment for Sartre's theory that, since it merely reverses traditional metaphysical categories, remains metaphysical.[110] The priority of existence over essence justifying the appellation "existentialism" has nothing in common with *Being and Time* whose discussion moves on a deeper plane. Authenticity does not refer to action as opposed to thought but rather to thought in the light of being that is already action. Human being cannot be understood in itself but only comprehended through being, in a word as existence. A metaphysical theory such as humanist existentialism cannot resolve human problems that require an understanding of human being beyond metaphysics.

Heidegger's analysis of humanism presupposes the prior acceptance of his view of ontology. His binary form of argument resembles the Christian view of human history as the story of the fall away from and return to God. Ordinary humanism is metaphysics, and metaphysics turns away from being, resulting in homelessness and alienation. Conversely, a new humanism reverses this turn away by turning back, by returning to being, in order to find one's home and to overcome alienation. In an important passage, he writes: "To think the truth of Being at the same time means to think the humanity of *homo humanus*. What counts is *humanitas* in the service of the truth of Being, but without humanism in the metaphysical sense."[111]

Heidegger's new, postmetaphysical humanism based on the return to being is meant to take the place of the old anthropological, metaphysical humanism. This new humanism, or thinking beyond philosophy, is in many ways reassuring: it eschews the materialism associated with Marx and Marxism[112] and even nationalism;[113] it is not inhumane but precisely humane in thinking man, as Heidegger says, through the nearness to being;[114] nor is it nihilism;[115] it holds no opinion at all about God; it further discards views of subjectivity leading to "biologism" and even "pragmatism."[116] This new thinking is no longer philosophy that is concerned with theory and practice but deeper than philosophy,[117] which, as metaphysics, fails to resolve, in fact contributes to, human problems following from the turn away from being. "Communism" and even "Americanism" are related to the forgetfulness of being.[118] Indeed, Heidegger goes so far as to claim that human destiny is revealed through the history of being.[119]

Heidegger's new humanism was specifically reassuring in the French context and may even have been formulated with that end in mind. His text can be read as representing another phase in the slow evolution of his philosophical thought, or as combining his philosophical concerns with a skillful bid for influence in the French debate, or as both. Heidegger's new form of humanism constitutes an attractive alternative to a series of positions jockeying for influence in the difficult postwar period. These include Sartre's atheistic existentialism, leftwing, Marxist Hegelianism with which Sartre was closely allied, and the French Communist Party that emerged greatly strengthened from the war, all of which were fundamentally unacceptable to the overwhelmingly conservative French intellectual community.

Heidegger's text contains a subtext that spoke directly to conservative French intellectuals worried by forms of secular humanism influential in the postwar debate. Although he praises Marx's attention to history, Heidegger stigmatizes materialism as another form of metaphysics.[120] He distances himself from the political activism represented by Sartre and Marxism by praising thought as action.[121] He further reassures readers concerned by his relation to National Socialism through the rejection of "biologism," a danger that he now, in a wave of the conceptual wand, attributes to Sartre's attachment to subject philosophy. Any residual doubt is dissipated through Heidegger's allusion to a turning (Kehre)[122] in his thought, a suggestion that he has turned over a new leaf so to speak, and in this way broken with any objectionable part of his past. Yet Heidegger also undercuts this suggestion by emphasizing the continuity between the original position and its later version.

Heidegger's references to religion in this text are particularly important. Although he was earlier attracted to Catholicism and at one time desired to become a Jesuit, he later left the Church when he married a Protestant. Heidegger is throughout a philosophical atheist. He clearly insists that philosophy must in principle be atheistic whatever one's personal religious beliefs.[123] As Beaufret points out, Heidegger's philosophical atheism is founded on a nonidentity of God and being,[124] in essence an anti-Thomistic attitude. Yet in this text, he is especially careful to distance himself from philosophical or other forms of atheism – he mentions God no less than twenty-nine times in this essay[125] – by taking a reassuring, neutral stance toward religion, clearly at odds with his own deeply held conviction.[126]

Perceptive readers of Heidegger were clear that his own theory rested on a separation between philosophy and theology, which it strove to surpass.[127] Yet Heidegger's apparently friendly attitude to religious belief in this text could hardly fail to please in largely Roman Catholic France. Henri Birault, one of the most orthodox French Heidegger commentators, went so far as to claim that Heidegger, who claimed that atheism is the condition of philosophy, offered a position that allows us to avoid despair through returning to God.[128]

HEIDEGGER'S "LETTER ON HUMANISM" AND THE TURNING IN HIS THOUGHT

The central idea of the "Letter on Humanism" is the concept of the turning. This difficult, controversial concept requires further discussion. It might be thought that the contextualist reading provided here misses or otherwise distorts a philosophical idea that needs to be understood, as it has mainly been understood, within the context of Heidegger's thought, hence without reference to the wider context. To the best of my knowledge, Heidegger only addresses his view of the turning in his thought in two passages that are found respectively in the "Letter on Humanism" and in his letter to William Richardson, an American Heidegger scholar.

In the "Letter on Humanism," after distinguishing his new, or other thinking from that in *Being and Time*, he writes:

> The adequate execution and completion of this other thinking that abandons subjectivity is surely made more difficult by the fact that in the publication of *Being and Time* the third division of the first part, "Time and Being," was held back . . . . Here everything is reversed. The section in question was held back because thinking failed in the adequate saying of this turning [Kehre] and did not succeed with the help of the language of metaphysics. The lecture "On the Essence of Truth," thought out and delivered in 1930 but not printed until 1943, provides a certain insight into the thinking of the turning from "Being and Time" to "Time and Being." This turning is not a change of standpoint from *Being and Time*, but in it the thinking that was sought first arrives at the location of that dimension out of which *Being and Time* is experienced, that is to say, experienced from the fundamental experience of the oblivion of Being."[129]

In comparison to his other writings, this passage is extremely clear, as if Heidegger were going to unusual lengths to get across his view of the turning. Heidegger maintains a similar view of the turning in his letter to William Richardson, the American Heidegger scholar. This letter, written in April 1962, was initially published in a Festschrift for Jean Beaufret.[130] Here he insists that the turning only mentioned in 1947 was part of his work ten years earlier. He maintains that being as such can only be thought out of the reversal. He insists that the reversal leading to the study of what was designated in *Being and Time* as "Time and Being" was already contained in that work. And he asserts his earlier view is not left behind but rather contained within his later position.[131]

Heidegger's twin accounts of the turning in his thought are straight-forward, but unsatisfactory. To begin with, there is the discrepancy between statements that the thinking of the turning was already apparent in 1930, and that the matter of the turning already moved his thought a decade before 1947,[132] hence in 1937. A second series of problems concerns the nature of this event. Heidegger's description of his original project in *Being and Time* foresaw a turning from being and time to time and being. This suggests a distinction between the turning foreseen in the original project and another turning resulting from the difficulty of carrying out that project. What if there were more than two turnings, even turnings not constrained by the failure of thinking within the original project?

Heidegger's description of the turning in his thought has been often been uncritically taken as the main clue in its interpretation.[133] Following Heidegger, Alberto Rosales argues that a contradiction between the basic presuppositions of Heidegger's original theory as he worked it out led to the turning.[134] He maintains that his interpretation is supported by a review of Heidegger's relevant writings.[135] For Jean-François Mattéi, the references to the turning in the "Letter on Humanism" and the letter to Richardson are insufficient to understand it.[136] He sees the idea of the turning as already present in Plato's premetaphysical thought.[137] Jean Grondin distinguishes between the radicalization of human finitude, the problem of *Being and Time*, concerned with the destruction of traditional ontology, and the other turning that in fact took place in the 1930s. For Grondin, following Rosales, there is, then, a turning in the turning due to the difficulty in carrying out the turning that was foreseen in *Being and Time*.[138]

Rosales, Mattéi and Grondin independently support Heidegger's claim for a turning following from the weakness of thought in carrying out the original project in *Being and Time*. We can test this Heideggerian view by consulting the texts. Before we do so, two remarks are in order. First, the German language is extremely rich in words etymologically or conceptually linked to "Kehre," literally "turn or bend," such as "Umkehrung," or "overturning, conversion, reversal, or inversion," "Umkehr," or "return, change, conversion, reversal," "Bekehrung," or "conversion," and so on, as well as "Drehung," or "turn, or rotation," "Umdrehung," or "turning, or revolution," "Eindrehung," or "turning inward," and so on. We will need to be alert to these and other related terms as ways in which Heidegger refers to the idea of a turning in his thought, in Western philosophy, in being, and so on. Second, the idea of a turning is frequent in modern philosophy, beginning with Kant's famous Copernican Revolution, essentially a turning away from theory of knowledge as it had so far existed, Feuerbach's turning of religion into philosophical anthropology, Marx's inversion (*Umstülpung*) of idealism as materialism, and so on.

Even a rapid survey of Heidegger's writings will detect a multitude of turnings in his thought, in and with respect to his original project, other thinkers, the philosophical tradition, metaphysics, poetry, politics, as well as a turning by other thinkers, and so on. Attention to these multiple turnings suggests that the turning is more complex than it initially seems and that to understand it we must refer both to Heidegger's writings as well as to his historical situation.

Although the concept of the turning only becomes prominent in Heidegger's thought after the war, it occurs prior to the war and even the appearance of his main treatise. He refers to this concept in a remark on the transformation of ontology into ontical metaphysics in a lecture course given during the period when he was writing the book.[139] In § 8 of *Being and Time*, he provides the design of the treatise within the framework of a larger project in three parts. The published portion of *Being and Time* includes the first and second parts of the first of two parts. Part two and the third division of the first part have never appeared. The third division of part one, time and being, was intended to contain a reversal of the analysis of being and time in the published treatise.

In § 44, *Being and Time* offers an important analysis of the concept of truth as disclosure. In the lecture "On the Essence of Truth," Heidegger reverses his earlier view of the question of truth that is now held to arise out of the prior question of the truth of the essence.

> The present undertaking takes the question of the essence of truth beyond the confines of the ordinary definition provided in the usual concept of essence and helps us to consider whether the question of the essence of truth must not be, at the same time and even first of all, the question concerning the essence of truth. But in the concept of "essence" philosophy thinks Being.[140]

In writings after this point, Heidegger often employs the idea of a turning. So in his 1936 lecture course on Schelling, he mentions a "turning [Wandel] of European existence out of a ground that to this day remains dark to us."[141] Later in the same text, he writes that "the question concerning the truth of being . . . turns [kehrt sich um] into the question concerning the being of truth and of the ground . . . . "[142]

The idea of a turning is an important theme in Heidegger's Nietzsche lectures and in the study that emerged from them. In his study, he mentions the idea of a turning (*Umkehrung*) several times in the early chapter on *The Will to Power* and in a later chapter concerning truth in Platonism and positivism.[143] In the former, Heidegger describes Nietzsche's nihilism as a countermovement to nihilism within nihilism. Nietzsche's procedure, he maintains, is a constant reversal (*ständiges Umkehren*).[144] In the discussion of Nietzsche's philosophy as an *Umkehrung* of Platonism, he remarks on the need to change the order so that the *Umdrehung*, or turning around, will become a *Herausdrehung*, or twisting free, from Platonism.[145] Yet a turning (*Drehung*) is not necessarily a reversal (*Umkehrung*), since, as he later reminds us, it can rather be a kind of penetration (*Eindrehen*).[146]

In his Nietzsche lectures, Heidegger not only considers Nietzsche's theory as a failed turning against the Platonic philosophical tradition. He further suggests that in these lectures he himself came to grips with, hence turned against, Nazism. In the famous *Spiegel* interview, he maintains that "Anyone with ears to hear heard in these lectures a confrontation with National Socialism."[147]

Following Heidegger, Hannah Arendt maintains that Heidegger's turning against Nazism occurred in the transition from the first to the second volume of the Nietzsche lectures, in which Heidegger comes to grips with "his brief past in the Nazi movement."[148] Pierre Aubenque affirms that in 1935 Heidegger tried to save an internal truth of National Socialism but that beginning in 1936 in the Nietzsche lectures he rejected Nazism as a possibility.[149] For Silvio Vietta, Heidegger's analysis of Nietzsche's view of nihilism constitutes a recognition of the intrinsic nihilism of Nazism.[150] Others dispute the very idea that in his study of Nietzsche Heidegger turned away from National Socialism. Otto Pöggeler, for instance, maintains that Heidegger's study of Nietzsche and the pre-Socratics led him to National Socialism.[151]

We find another turning in the recently published *Beiträge zur Philosophie*, a controversial study composed during the period 1936–1938, while Heidegger was giving his Nietzsche lectures. "Ereignis," the master word of this difficult book, is roughly synonymous with "Geschehnis," "Erlebnis," and other terms connoting "an event or an occurrence." In a section devoted to the "Turning in the Event [Die Kehre im Ereignis]," Heidegger writes: "The event [Ereignis] has its innermost occurrence and its widest result [Ausgriff] in the turning [Kehre]."[152] He further states with evident hyperbole that the problem of whether "the turning will still become history is decisive for man's future."[153]

The idea of the turning also occurs in Heidegger's later discussion of technology. Under the heading "Insight Into What Is," Heidegger held four lectures on December 1, 1949 in Bremen. In the fourth and last lecture, "The Turning [Die Kehre]," he insists on the danger resulting from a turning away from being, a main theme in his later writings. In a typical passage in this difficult, poetical text, he writes: "In the essence of the danger essences [west] and dwells a favor [Gunst], namely the favor of the turning of the forgetfulness of being in the truth of being."[154]

If this is a representative sample of the concept of the turning in Heidegger's thought, we can distinguish at least the following kinds of turning in Heidegger's theory:

1 The turn in *Being and Time* against the history of ontology and toward Dasein in order to grasp being as time.
2 The turn in Heidegger's thought from being and time to time and being that failed due to Heidegger's inability to think through the project as originally conceived.
3 The turn from the essence of truth to the question of the truth of the essence in the lecture "On the Essence of Truth."
4 The turn from philosophy to poetry in the first series of Hölderlin lectures as part of the turn beyond philosophy to thought.[155]
5 The turn to Nietzsche in the Nietzsche lectures since he alone has recognized the primordial event that since the beginning determines Western history and Western metaphysics.

102

6 The analysis of Nietzsche's failed effort to turn against the Platonic tradition of which, for Heidegger, he is its final member.

7 In the *Beiträge zur Philosophie* the triple turn from Dasein to being as self-manifesting, the turn from the first beginning to the other beginning in the same text, and finally the turn to *Ereignis* as the master word of the later writings. In fact, since this term is already prominent in Heidegger's first series of lectures in 1919, the turn to *Ereignis* marks a return to an earlier concept.[156]

7 The political turn to and later turn away from real National Socialism, as well as the turn toward the supposedly misunderstood truth and greatness of the movement, a philosophical, or ideal form of Nazism.

8 The effort in the "Letter on Humanism" to portray himself as having turned over a new page, of having turned away from politics while he nonetheless held fast to what he continued later to describe as the misunderstood truth and greatness of the movement.

9 The turn to technology as a fall or turn away from being.

It follows that the turning is not the univocal event determined solely by the working out of the original position that Heidegger depicts. In fact, that turning may never have occurred since it is at least arguable that, although the original view evolved, the basic concern with being remains constant throughout. Clearly, there is more than one turning in his thought, including a turning toward Nazism. And although in the "Letter on Humanism" Heidegger implies that he has turned against National Socialism, this claim is contradicted by other, later texts in his corpus.[157]

6

HEIDEGGER'S "LETTER ON HUMANISM" AND FRENCH HEIDEGGERIANISM

The preceding chapter drew attention to the link between French humanism and Heidegger's "Letter on Humanism." Then as now, Heidegger's "Letter on Humanism" is important for philosophical and extraphilosophical reasons. Philosophically, it offers a way into Heidegger's later philosophical position; and extraphilosophically, it represents a way to counter the growing, but for some unacceptable, influence of secular humanism.

The preceding chapter analyzed factors in the French debate leading to a strongly positive reception for Heidegger's "Letter on Humanism." The present chapter will consider aspects of the French Heidegger debate under the influence of this text. In reaction to the anthropological misreading of Heidegger's thought dominant in the first phase of the discussion, in its second phase, influenced by the "Letter on Humanism," a series of writers, including Beaufret and Derrida, presented a nonanthropological, postmetaphysical but still resolutely humanist reading of Heidegger's theory. The result was to create a Heideggerian orthodoxy that, in the aftermath of the renewed, often bitter debate on Heidegger's Nazism, endures to this day.

FRENCH HEIDEGGERIAN ORTHODOXY AND THE "LETTER ON HUMANISM"

The French Heidegger debate is part of the complex process, still under way, of the assimilation of Heidegger's theory. Heidegger's theory is obviously, by any standard, an unusually important philosophical theory. Now any such philosophical theory, any philosophical position that breaks with received wisdom, that departs from previous views in significant ways, that opens a new chapter in the debate, requires a complex, often lengthy process of reception, sometimes extending over centuries, in which its insights are made available and eventually assimilated as part of the philosophical debate.

There is no single way in which important philosophical theories are received. Philosophy supposes the capacity for disagreement founded in reasoned discussion. Yet certain philosophical theories create a form of conceptual orthodoxy that precludes disagreement about anything other than the "correct" interpretation of the position in question. The significance of Kant's Copernican revolution in philosophy was widely acknowledged. On the basis of a shared assumption that there is no more than a single correct way to read the critical philosophy, a number of writers, including Reinhold and Fichte, sought to provide the only "correct" interpretation of Kant's theory.[1] In similar ways, ever since Friedrich Engels, the first Marxist, a series of Marxists, most prominently Lukács, most recently Althusser, have sought to determine the "correct" interpretation of Marx's thought.

The Heidegger debate, particularly in France, has long turned on a total or nearly total identification with the master thinker. Its uncritical, even unphilosophical character is at least partially due to the essential Platonism of Heidegger's theory reputed for its anti-Platonism. Plato advanced a conception of truth disclosed only to a few gifted individuals, and then only after appropriate preparation, a conception astonishingly similar to certain mystical religious doctrines.[2] A link between the Heideggerian and the Platonic models of truth is even more apparent in Heidegger's later writings, where he increasingly stresses reverence toward being, for instance in the idea of letting be (*Gelassenheit*)[3] as the prerequisite enabling being to show itself. If Heidegger, the master thinker, is the most pious of the pious towards being, and if being can only be known through intuition, then the master's disciples must not question but receive and propagate his privileged insights about being.

To the uninitiated, the Heidegger discussion frequently sounds like a debate among true believers. The master's best students implicitly dispute the mantle of orthodoxy in a vain effort to furnish an absolutely seamless reading of the master's doctrine. Heidegger's students are devoted to the exposition and the elucidation, but rarely to the critical appraisal of the master's thought. In the Heidegger discussion criticism is often timid, even more often nonexistent. Like members of an organized religious faith, followers of the master are expected to, and often do, renounce criticism of any kind. For the role of the true disciple is to follow unquestioningly while restricting criticism to criticism of others, non-Heideggerians.

The highly orthodox, uncritical nature of the Heidegger literature is not threatened by the influence of the "Letter on Humanism." *Being and Time*, the central text of Heidegger's early period, is still the center of Heidegger's focus in his later thought. This type of relation between earlier and later aspects of an important position is fairly standard. Fichte's later evolution is largely centered on the restatement of his initial position in new ways through constant revision of the *Foundations of the Science of Knowledge [Grundlage der gesamten Wissenschaftslehre]*, his early, major text; similarly Heidegger's later evolution is largely composed of a series of rereadings and interpretations, from an evolving angle of vision, of *Being and Time*.

Heidegger consistently emphasizes that his thought was in motion, not arrested, as in the choice of the slogan "*Wege, nicht Werke*" for his collected works. Since many of his later texts are either based on or presented as interpretations of *Being and Time*, his later thought can be regarded as a series of revisions of that work. The "Letter on Humanism" is one of a number of such rereadings at a period when Heidegger's initial view was still under way, so to speak, as Heidegger continued to rethink his original position.

Yet this text is more than Heidegger's latest rereading of his initial position. In the context of his elaborate written response to Beaufret's questions, it is a letter from Heidegger to the French philosophical community. Unlike any other text in Heidegger's enormous corpus, it is filled with specific indications as to how to interpret or, as the case may be, to reinterpret particular passages in *Being and Time* from his later angle of vision. Examples include the concept of the "they" in §§ 27 and 35,[4] the view of language in § 34,[5] the word "essence" from p. 42 of the German edition,[6] a reference to time and being on p. 88 of this edition,[7] a series of repeated references to the phrase "The 'substance' of man is existence" on pages 117, 212, 314 of the German text,[8] an allusion to the concept of care on pp. 226ff. in § 44 of the German original,[9] and so on. These and other unusually specific references to Heidegger's main philosophical treatise suggest that everything happens in this text as if Heidegger were trying to instruct the French on how to read *Being and Time*.

Heidegger wrote the "Letter on Humanism," according to some observers the best introduction to *Being and Time*,[10] after the so-called turning in his thought, after significant changes in the original position. These changes occur gradually in a series of writings composed after Heidegger's central text. In the same passage in which he introduces the conception of the turning, Heidegger also introduces notions of the forgetfulness of being and thought beyond metaphysics. If, as Heidegger increasingly came to believe, metaphysics is philosophy,[11] or at least Western philosophy, then what he calls thinking in this text is no longer philosophy. If that is the case, then the line of thought originally presented under the heading of fundamental ontology, as an effort to recover a question supposedly ignored since the Greeks, is no longer valid, at least not valid as originally formulated.

If the original formulation of the question of the meaning of Being is no longer valid, then both the question and the response require revision. Other changes are demanded by the turbulent times in which Heidegger lived and wrote as Germany, continuing to suffer from the loss of the First World War, moved steadily towards the Second World War. Changes in his theory after *Being and Time* have become even clearer with the recent publication of the *Beiträge zur Philosophie*. Whatever the verdict on this controversial treatise – alternatively praised as the single most important work in Heidegger's entire corpus[12] and dismissed as characteristic of his dogmatic, prophetic way of conducting a seminar without argument of any kind[13] by equally knowledgeable observers – it is at least clear that this book sounds all the themes of his later thought.[14]

Discussion of the "Letter on Humanism," has already mentioned such changes in the original position as the concept of the forgetfulness of Being (*Seinsvergessenheit*) that is first mentioned under that name in this text,[15] the conception of the turning in Heidegger's thought whose initial public reference also occurs in this text, and the idea of thinking as beyond metaphysics and philosophy in general.

In a work solely on Heidegger, the modifications of his later thought would require detailed discussion. In the present context, it is sufficient to note a difference in perspective arising in the difference between direct study of his original position and indirect access to it through the lens of his "Letter on Humanism." *Being and Time* belongs to his early period. The "Letter on Humanism" belongs to the later evolution of his thought, when his original philosophical theory had changed to the point where, as he clearly said, it was no longer philosophy: "The thinking that is to come" he writes, "is no longer philosophy, because it thinks more originally than metaphysics – a name identical to philosophy."[16] The degree of continuity in the evolution of Heidegger's position, which should not be minimized, ought not to obscure the genuine differences between his later and his earlier thought, hence the different understanding of the position that results when it is viewed immediately or, on the contrary, mediately through one of its later phases.

There is a French Heidegger, a particular view of Heidegger's thought specific to the French philosophical debate that has recently been appearing with some regularity in English. In France as elsewhere, *Being and Time* is and will in all probability remain the central text in Heidegger's corpus. That is not in dispute; but since texts do not read themselves but must be read, there is room for dispute about how this is to be done, how to appropriate this text. It is one thing to read *Being and Time* directly on its own terms and something entirely different to read the same text through the focus provided by his later thought. If the French Heidegger were mainly attached to *Being and Time* understood only in terms of itself, then it would mainly be concerned with the early Heidegger, Heidegger's theory before it evolved in a long series of later writings that eventually took him, at least in his own mind, beyond philosophy. Since in France Heidegger is mainly read through the lens of his "Letter on Humanism" and other later writings, it is hardly surprising that the French reading of *Being and Time*, hence of Heidegger's overall position, occurs mainly from the perspective of the later Heidegger.

BEAUFRET AND THE COUNTEROFFENSIVE

In France, Heidegger's stunningly influential "Letter on Humanism" affected no one more than Jean Beaufret, to whom it was sent. Before he wrote to Heidegger, there is apparently little in Beaufret's biography to explain the extraordinary devotion – the word is not too strong – that he later manifested for Heidegger's thought and even his person. In the inbred French intellectual world, where all the main players in the game have ties, even close links, to one another, Beaufret did not initially belong to any particular intellectual circle. When he began his dialogue with Heidegger that was to last to the end of their lives – Heidegger died in 1976, Beaufret in 1982 – he was a young French philosopher, who had been active in the Popular Front, and was attracted to socialist ideas, especially Marxism. During the war, after being captured and escaping, he became interested in phenomenology, eventually in Heidegger. He turned to Heidegger very early, during the German occupation, on his own account in 1942 before the end of the war, like Sartre, after studying Husserl.[17] Perhaps one can say that Beaufret was destined – one is tempted to say destined by being, since for the later Heidegger thought is destined by being – to become Heidegger's main representative in France.

In comparison with *Being and Time*, Heidegger's "Letter on Humanism" was rapidly translated into French. Yet the dozen years between its original appearance in German and its translation into French sufficed for Beaufret, whose inquiry provided the official excuse for Heidegger to compose this text, to acquire a commanding position in the French Heidegger debate. In retrospect, beyond his growing attachment to Heidegger's thought, several factors enabled Beaufret to acquire ascendancy in this debate. One factor was the politically impeccable past of a soldier captured in the war that helped to calm a certain political uneasiness about Heidegger's less than politically impeccable past, which in turn affected the reception of his theory. Another factor was Beaufret's undoubted linguistic ability, including his sensitive command of German.

Although he did not have the necessary spoken command of the language to begin with, as indicated by his need to be represented by Jean-Michel Palmier, he soon acquired it. In France, Beaufret's ability to read Heidegger in the original German, combined with the traditional French insistence on textual analysis (*explication de texte*), quickly secured for his Heidegger interpretations a status analogous to Kojève's Hegel studies. Unlike Kojève, who later lost his preeminent role in the French Hegel discussion, Beaufret has maintained his dominant position in the French Heidegger discussion even after his death. Pierre Bourdieu, who insists on the importance of Beaufret's role in initiating his students into the the arcane mysteries of Heidegger's obscure texts, describes the general situation of colleagues and students dependent on the Kojèves and the Beaufrets for access to their authors of predilection. After noting that there were few translations of the thinkers in vogue, Beaufret writes:

> The most zealous admirers could only receive an often approximative and deformed understanding *ex auditu*, through eclectic retranslations in magisterial-style courses [du cours magistral]. Everything happened as if the cult fastened by preference on texts and authors who were

esoteric, obscure, even, as in the cases of Husserl and Heidegger, practically inaccessible because of the lack of translations . . . .[18]

Heidegger's initially lavish praise of Beaufret that was clearly disproportionate to the importance of the occasion – a simple inquiry from an unknown French student of phenomenology, unless, as seems likely, Beaufret's letter was merely a pretext – only increased in later communication between them.[19] Beaufret, who was clearly flattered by Heidegger's attention, became Heidegger's disciple to an almost unimaginable degree. He reports that he went to see Heidegger for the first time in September 1946 and made the decision to study Heidegger's writings seriously. This was only the first of many trips during a "dialogue" between two thinkers on very unequal levels that was to last some thirty years.

During this period, Beaufret let pass no occasion to demonstrate his loyalty to Heidegger through what was never less than a relation of utter orthodoxy. Philosophy differs from religion in its intrinsic unorthodoxy, in its need to declare its independence, to refuse to submit either to tradition or to dogmatic assertion, to demand proof instead of assurance, argument instead of reassurance. In modern philosophy since Kant the idea of orthodoxy has taken on new proportions.

With the possible exception of Marxists and Freudians, Heideggerians have no rival for their concern with orthodoxy. Heidegger talked of Dasein as the shepherd of being; Beaufret was the shepherd of Heidegger's being, the most orthodox among the orthodox, a representative whose loyalty was literally boundless, in some ways even the court fool of Heideggerianism.

Beaufret's boundless acceptance of, and identification with, the master's thought is strikingly illustrated in his four volumes of dialogues with Heidegger, his interviews with Towarnicki, and his discussion of Parmenides from a Heideggerian perspective without so much as a single critical remark. Another illustration is Beaufret's resistance to the very idea that there could be any, even the slightest impairment in Heidegger's thought. If the philosophical debate does not come to an end in a given theory, then the reception of any theory that is not wholly rejected can only aim toward a partial appropriation through the determination of what is living and dead in a given thinker's thought. Yet Beaufret, who desires his Heidegger whole, as it were, resists the distinction, in his words, between "an acceptable Heidegger and an inadmissible Heidegger" through his rejection of the very idea of a merely partial recuperation of his thought.[20] Still a further illustration is a seminar in 1948, during the period when Heidegger was banned from teaching in the University, at which, according to Beaufret, he was the only participant.[21]

Beaufret's personal relation to Heidegger was an important factor in his own rise to prominence in the French Heidegger debate. Heidegger scholarship is marked, some might say marred, by unequal access to the primary texts. It is difficult to argue with someone who bases an argument on privileged access to the texts, or who possesses a text that is not in the public domain. Beaufret illustrates this phenomenon in his reference at crucial points to information available only to him. If, as seems likely, Heidegger utilized his ongoing dialogue with Beaufret as a means to influence the French discussion of his thought, then it is plausible to think that Heidegger further provided privileged information to his French acolyte with the same end in view.

Beaufret began this practice early on, soon after entering into dialogue with Heidegger. In an article from 1947, the year that the "Letter on Humanism" appeared, he employs an unpublished letter from Heidegger on Heraclitus's fragment 119 to refute Sartre's reading of Dasein.[22] In an article from 1958, he writes: "Heidegger once told me, concerning the *metaphysics* of Aristotle: "This *metaphysics* is not at all a "metaphysics," but a phenomenology of what is *presence*."[23] He continues this practice throughout his later writing on Heidegger. A particularly flagrant example occurs in a passage on the quadripartite, where Beaufret enlists Heidegger's oral comment to him in 1950 concerning the manner in which "ent-schwindet" disappears from Heidegger's later texts without "verschwinden." Beaufret buttresses this point through citing a passage seven lines long that, he says, Heidegger dictated to him in 1952.[24] Slightly later, he avoids even the appearance that Heidegger's position is anything other than a seamless web in stating that a passage omitted from the transcript of Heidegger's Thor lecture series showed that Heidegger meant "Ereignis" beginning in the "Letter on Humanism" although he continued to write the term "Sein."[25]

The uncritical way in which Beaufret cleaved to Heidegger's thought was matched only by Beaufret's weight in the ensuing French Heidegger debate. We have already noted that in France the brightest students are identified by competitive examinations and educated in a parallel system of elite schools. A teacher in these schools, many of which are in Paris, has an opportunity to influence unusually capable French students who frequently go on to become the leaders of French society. After the war, after he turned to Heidegger, Beaufret taught for 27 years in such Parisian schools. During this period, he was able, by his own account, to awaken a real interest for Heidegger among a number of students who later became prominent in the French Heidegger debate, including François Fédier, François Vézin, Jean-Luc Marion, Jean-François Courtine, Emmanuel Martineau, Alain Renaut, Dominique Janicaud, and so on.[26] According to Beaufret, who exaggerates the point, among all these students there was only one who later "appeared to prefer the legend to history,"[27] in short, on his account, only one who rejected Beaufret's orthodox view of Heidegger's theory.

Beaufret indicates the significance of this remark in a short description of his teaching methods. He notes that he frequently visited Heidegger and so remained up to date on the latter's thought. In his teaching, the accent was not on "criticizing" Heidegger but on "studying the philosophy by not stopping at the study of Kant, Nietzsche or Husserl but in going on to a more important point [un point plus brûlant] that my students and I held for *fragwürdig* – let us say: problematic [problématique]."[28] For Beaufret, then, unquestionably Heidegger could not be compared with the greats of the prior philosophical tradition, whom he surpassed, with whom he finally had nothing in common. If one had to stop to question, the questioning could and should be directed only to the elucidation of Heidegger's thought. Beaufret transmitted this idea of Heidegger through his uniquely faithful teaching of the master's thought that, he himself insists, was unparalleled in the Parisian postwar environment.

Beaufret, who is aware of the degree of attachment to Heidegger's thought that he describes, simply concedes that it was easy to look on the whole as being "an exercise in teleguided persuasion,"[29] Yet at the very least, it is clear that he contributed strongly, often decisively, as he clearly desired to do, to the formation of a generation of Heidegger students, some of whom, like Beaufret, are no more critical with respect to the master thinker than their mentor.

BEAUFRET AND THE RISE OF FRENCH HEIDEGGERIAN ORTHODOXY

Beaufret, the main figure in the second phase of the French Heidegger debate, is also the main architect of French Heideggerian orthodoxy. Pierre Aubenque, who correctly notes that Beaufret was not the only one to introduce Heidegger into France, nor the sole guardian of Heideggerian influence,[30] regards the French Heidegger reception as normal.[31] Yet it is normal only if it is normal for the disciple to regard the master's thought as entirely flawless, as if it were the revealed truth. If man is the shepherd of being, then it is not too much to consider Beaufret, as he apparently considered himself, as the shepherd of Heidegger's being.

Beaufret's allegiance to Heidegger's person and thought is unusual, even extraordinary. It is questionable whether Heidegger, or indeed any other thinker, ever had a more loyal disciple than Beaufret, someone who cheerfully subordinated his entire identity to Heidegger's needs at a time when this was not yet popular.[32] In Germany, Heidegger's leading disciple has long been Friedrich-Wilhelm von Hermann, the editor of the ongoing edition of his collected works. If, as has been said, von Hermann's entire bibliography consists in a series of variations of Heidegger's texts, then Beaufret's writings after his Heideggerian turn, beginning at least as early as 1947, consist increasingly in a restatement of the master's thought in the form of an authentic repetition, in an echo of revealed truth.

Heidegger took pains to create his own legend in a series of texts. These include the 1945 article where he depicts his rectorship at the University of

Freiburg as a meaningless episode,[33] the *Spiegel* interview withheld until his death which can be regarded as a kind of intellectual testament, the "Letter on Humanism" instructing French philosophers in the interpretation of *Being and Time*, the "Letter to Richardson" providing an authorized interpretation of the notion of the turning,[34] and above all the wholly uncritical edition of his collected works, following his explicit instructions, now in progress. Heidegger's own view of his theory is further available in a series of texts prepared with his cooperation, often under his explicit direction, in the main contemporary philosophical languages: in German in von Hermann's work on Heidegger's own self-interpretation[35] and in the initial but *not* the later editions of Pöggeler's early study,[36] in Richardson's book in English,[37] and in all of Beaufret's many writings on Heidegger.

Beaufret's writings on Heidegger present an accurate, insightful, but wholly uncritical statement of Heidegger's own self-interpretation. Although Heidegger desires to dialogue with great philosophers on their own level, Beaufret is not a great or even an important thinker. His entire legacy is bound up with his effort over many years to transmit a particular image of Heidegger in the French discussion. It is fair to regard Heidegger's lengthy dialogue with Beaufret as an effort to provide an authoritative interpretation of his view that will stand the test of time.

Disciples often devote a number of articles or a volume, sometimes two, rarely more, to the master's thought. In this as in other respects, Beaufret is an exception. His Heidegger interpretation is expounded in numerous places, including an early introduction to philosophies of existence,[38] four volumes of dialogue with Heidegger patched together out of many articles and lectures on various aspects of his thought,[39] a study of Parmenides based on Heidegger's interpretation of this thinker,[40] a couple of volumes of interviews concerning Heidegger,[41] ten radio talks on Heidegger's thought, and so on.[42]

Heidegger's grasp of the history of philosophy is unusual. In comparison, Beaufret's command of the philosophical tradition is shallower, but still impressive. His writings reflect a thorough knowledge of French and German thought, as well as scholasticism, with a deep grounding in Greek philosophy. Beaufret's writing on Heidegger is consistently characterized by his own wide philosophical culture. In his early texts on Heidegger, he uses that culture to understand Heidegger as one among the other important philosophers. At this point, Beaufret accepts Sartre's later view that the only two contemporary philosophies worth taking seriously are existentialism and Marxism. Beaufret inclined to Marxism prior to his turn to Heidegger, and there are many knowledgeable, sympathetic remarks on Marx and Marxism in his works. Perhaps the most unfavorable reference to Marx in Beaufret's writings is a remark in passing that Nietzsche understands Greek thought better than Marx.[43]

Yet when Beaufret enters into dialogue with Heidegger, his attitude towards Heidegger's theory changes. After the "Letter on Humanism," he accepts without reservations of any kind Heidegger's claim that he is not a philosopher since philosophy is concerned only with false ideas of being.[44] This idea consistently forms the cornerstone of Beaufret's later writing on Heidegger, where he uses the same wide philosophical culture to argue for the radical discontinuity between Heidegger's and other views, for the radical discontinuity between Heidegger's theory and philosophy.

There is a conceptual break in Beaufret's reading of Heidegger's relation to other philosophers and to philosophy itself. Like Hegelians and Marxists, who regard Hegel and Marx respectively as bringing the philosophical tradition to an end, Heideggerians tend to see Heidegger's theory as sui generis, as without significant relation to prior thought.[45] Whereas Beaufret initially detects continuity with differences in the relation of Heidegger's theory to those of earlier thinkers, he later detects only differences. In an early article, in line with the French tendency to approach Heidegger's theory through its link to Husserl's, he sees Heidegger as building upon Husserl's view. In his conception of being in the world (l'être-au-monde), Heidegger follows Husserl who followed Brentano. Heidegger builds on the Husserlian notion of intentionality that he transforms through the discovery of our "irremediable *facticity*."[46]

Yet later, after the appearance of the "Letter on Humanism," Beaufret regards the effort, parenthetically characteristic of the French Heidegger discussion, to understand Heidegger's theory through a purported link to Husserl's as mere eclecticism. The change in Beaufret's perspective reflects two points that Heidegger raises in his text: his claim to go beyond philosophy; and his objection to a comparison between his position and Jaspers's and, by implication, his position and any other. Following Heidegger's self-interpretation, Beaufret rethinks the relation between the views of Husserl and Heidegger not as a development through continuity but as a discontinuity, as a conceptual break. Despite the essential relation of the theories of Heidegger and Husserl, he now holds that to counterpose them, to consider them on the same level, as in the phrase "Husserl and Heidegger," leads to a deep misunderstanding. Husserl's analysis of the prehistory of the conception of science is strictly incomparable with Heidegger's meditation on the Greek origins of *logos*. Their views are radically unlike and, hence, discontinuous since Heidegger subjects to radical scrutiny what Husserl merely assumes.[47]

Beaufret steadily refined his reading of Heidegger's position over more than thirty years. The final, richest version of his Heidegger interpretation is presented in two places: in a lecture given in 1977,[48] and in another lecture given in 1981 at the first French Heidegger conference.[49] His final view of Heidegger's theory is later repeated in simplified form, often in the same words, in a volume of interviews with Beaufret on Heidegger's thought arguably intended, like the latter's *Spiegel* interview, to present that thought to the widest possible public.[50] Here Beaufret offers a coherent, interesting reading of Heidegger's later position as a lengthy meditation on Greek philosophy, in particular on the Aristotelian idea that it is difficult to grasp the *topos*. For Beaufret, then, the central thread running throughout all Heidegger's later writings is the nonmetaphysical or postmetaphysical concern to work out the topology of being that, on his interpretation, was only beginning in 1927.[51]

Beaufret partly bases his interpretation of Heidegger's theory on a reading of the celebrated turning in the latter's thought. Apparently unaware of Heidegger's letter to Richardson, he situates the turning in 1927, in a transition from the "first beginning" to "another beginning" in "a still *unknown* book."[52] This transition turns on the forgetfulness of being that is no longer, as in *Being and Time*, due to a simple human oversight, but is now attributed to being:

> The forgetfulness of Being is no longer a simple inadvertency as the reader of *Being and Time* might still believe. It is the concern of Being, not ours. In other words, the locution: forgetfulness of Being, an objective genitive, is turned into a subjective genitive. The forgetfulness comes from Being.[53]

This transformation is communicated initially in public fashion in the lecture "On the Essence of Truth" in 1930. According to Beaufret, here we find the theme of all of Heidegger's later thought.

This simple linguistic observation refers to the change in Heidegger's theory according to which being is no longer known through, but rather makes itself known to, human being. Beaufret interprets the transformation of an objective genitive into a subjective genitive as a withdrawal of being. And he further interprets the so-called withdrawal of being as fundamental to history viewed as an event, or *Ereignis*.[54] Relying once more on his uniquely close relation to the master thinker, Beaufret remarks, now citing the master, that in 1949 Heidegger once told him that "man is penetrated [transi] by Being to the point of becoming *Dasein* and this event *Ereignis* is the truth of Being to which Dasein essentially belongs."[55]

Beaufret usefully distinguishes a number of meanings of the term "Ereignis" that Heidegger regarded as untranslatable.[56] These include meanings associated with Greek poetry, the birth of Greek philosophy as a separate entity, and the history of philosophy since this moment until the point at which it was surpassed through modern technology.[57] The last, decisive meaning emerges from a long meditation on modern technology as *Ereignis* – as the successor of a theme that could always have been studied but that is only initially studied in *Being and Time* – with respect to "the *other beginning*, the initiating of the step which disengages itself from metaphysics through moving back . . . ."[58]

There is a difference between the formulation and the dissemination of an authoritative interpretation of a master theory, and its defense against nonorthodox, or even dissident readings that disagree with the attempt to establish an orthodox reading. A disciple whose entire career is devoted to a master thinker, who relies at crucial points in the debate on privileged information to provide what can only be regarded as the "authorized" interpretation, is unlikely to welcome interpretations conflicting with his own. Although Beaufret's refutations of other Heidegger interpretations can be regarded as instances of his concern to correct misinterpretations, they are not only that. Quietly but firmly, Beaufret goes to considerable lengths to discredit other readings of Heidegger's thought in the process of asserting his own preeminence in this domain.

Examples include his refutation of rival interpretations of Heidegger's thought due to Renaut, Vuillemin, Merleau-Ponty, Ricoeur, Löwith, and Pöggeler. Alain Renaut is a former Beaufret student and a Heidegger apostate, according to Beaufret – who did not live to appreciate the more recent evolution of the French Heidegger reception in which many of his former students have now either begun to or already distanced themselves from his own overly clement interpretation of the master's thought[59] – the only one of his students to reject his authorized reading of Heidegger's thought.[60]

In an article, Renaut raises questions concerning the French translations of Heidegger's seminars at Thor (1966, 1968, 1969) and Zähringen (1973).[61] As for the "Letter on Humanism," the latter seminar was provoked by a letter from Beaufret. The manuscripts of both seminars were reconstructed from notes by Beaufret and translated by Claude Roëls, a collaborator, and himself. In questioning the relation of these texts to Heidegger's corpus, the accuracy of their reconstruction, and the rendering of particular terms, Renaut implicitly threatens Beaufret's privileged role in the French Heidegger establishment and his authorized reading of Heidegger's thought.

The vigor of Beaufret's response,[62] nearly twice as long as Renaut's paper, indicates how seriously he takes this challenge to his authority. In response, Beaufret makes four points: He describes Renaut as a disgruntled former student, by implication not someone whose word about Heidegger should be given undue weight, certainly not against the view of a ranking French Heidegger scholar; he provides a brief restatement of the entire development of Heidegger's later position in order to demonstrate his own mastery of the topic; he indicates in detail reasons governing his translations of particular terms and his translation practice in general while deprecating Renaut's competence to object to specific renderings;[63] and he provides a detailed account of his intimate personal links to Heidegger over many years.

Renaut's article challenges the latter's preeminence in the French Heidegger debate but does not challenge Heidegger's theory. On the contrary, Merleau-Ponty, Vuillemin and Ricoeur elicit responses from Beaufret not because they threaten his preeminence in the French Heidegger debate but because they challenge Heidegger's theory. In a well known book, Jules

Vuillemin, for many years professor at the Collège de France, studies the positions of Fichte, Hermann Cohen, the great neo-Kantian, and Heidegger as three responses to Kant's Copernican Revolution in philosophy.[64]

For a determined Heideggerian, a study of this kind obviously undermines the extraordinary importance of the master thinker whose thought, which by his own claim surpasses philosophy, is literally incomparable, and hence not comparable with that of even the most important philosophers. Beaufret's unusually sharp response can be regarded as an effort to discredit Vuillemin's book that he characterizes as "apparently documented," as "a novel in which Heidegger is one of the protagonists," and as belonging to "the fantasies of erudition" whose faults are easily overcome through "simple textual study."[65]

In Beaufret's eyes, Maurice Merleau-Ponty, the important French phenomenologist, commits a similar mistake. His suggestion that *Being and Time* can be seen as no more than an effort to work out the later Husserlian idea of the life world[66] implies a relation of continuity between the two positions. Following Heidegger's rejection of the locution "Jaspers *and* Heidegger," Beaufret resists the "eclecticism" apparent, despite the "essential connection" of Heidegger to Husserl, in the similar locution "Husserl *and* Heidegger."[67] Once again, Beaufret's strategy is to insist on the discontinuity between Heidegger and any other thinker, in this case Husserl. In a manner recalling Heidegger's rejection of Cartesian subjectivity in the1938 lecture,[68] Beaufret maintains that in *Being and Time* Heidegger abandoned "all subjectivity in favor of an earlier question, namely, ek-sistence [ek-sistence] as the fundamental dimension of the Greek experience."[69]

Paul Ricoeur, the important French phenomenologist, an honored colleague, is another significant foe whose objections cannot be answered merely through insisting on one's own importance or by simple ridicule. In his response, we begin to see the rather modest limits of Beaufret's own philosophical capacities that are inversely proportional to his attachment to Heidegger's theory. In an article on the relation between Heidegger and theology,[70] Beaufret refers to objections brought by Ricoeur against Heidegger's later effort simply to equate metaphysics and philosophy,[71] and Heidegger's supposed "*prétention*" to bring the history of being to an end through the notion of *Ereignis*.[72]

Ricoeur's criticisms touch on the core of Heidegger's later position, that is his intention indicated in various ways – through the turning in his thought, what in the *Beiträge zur Philosophie* he called the transition from the first beginning to the other beginning, in short by means of a substitution of a subjective genitive for an objective genitive and other devices – to bring philosophy to an end, in short to escape from the philosophical tradition to something beyond it called thinking.

In response to the first point, Beaufret insists that Heidegger's crucial contribution, like Hegel's, is to restrict the term "philosophy" to thought in the deepest sense arising out of the Greek tradition.[73] Yet his flattering comparison between Heidegger and Hegel fails to respond to the objection that, if allowed, simply destroys Heidegger's effort to transcend metaphysics and philosophy in general.

Beaufret's response to the other point raised by Ricoeur is even weaker. In effect, he changes the subject and introduces a weak *ad hominem*. In declaring that Heidegger is not a pretentious person although it is "affected" to accuse him of affectation and "fatuous" to accuse him of fatuity,[74] Beaufret implies that Ricoeur is pretentious. This strategy consists in a double transformation of a philosophical question into a personal one, and a personal question into a question concerning the questioner. Yet it fails to respond either to the letter or even to the spirit of Ricoeur's objection that questions Heidegger's success in bringing metaphysics to an end and even the general possibility of reaching this end.

Beaufret's attitude towards his French colleagues is influenced by his concern to protect a favored interpretation of the master's writings and his personal struggle for influence in the French Heidegger debate. On the contrary, his attitude towards his German colleagues, as illustrated through his remarks on Löwith and Pöggeler, is presumably influenced only by his concern to maintain Heideggerian orthodoxy.

Karl Löwith, Heidegger's first graduate student and later colleague, is an important philosopher. In the French Heidegger discussion, he is further important as one of Heidegger's severest German critics as well as the author of the article that began the French debate on Heidegger's Nazism in the pages of Sartre's journal, *Les Temps Modernes*.[75]

Beaufret's attack on Löwith, which is unmotivated by any specific criticism, is intended to show Löwith's ignorance of even the most elementary aspects of Heidegger's thought, in effect to disqualify him as a critic without, however, responding to specific objections. In a comparison of Löwith's and Sartre's views of Dasein with Heidegger's self-interpretation, the same Sartre whom Beaufret initially regarded as a keen student of Heidegger, Beaufret writes: "To think otherwise is to miss the departure point, namely, to miss everything from the beginning, as Sartre does simplistically when, in *Being and Nothingness*, he criticizes Heidegger for 'refusing' as he says or at least 'avoiding' through Dasein the cogito."[76]

Otto Pöggeler, one of the important German scholars of both Heidegger's and Hegel's theories, is the author of a well known study of Heidegger's thought, prepared under the close supervision of the master. It would be implausible to suggest that Pöggeler is less than deeply familiar with Heidegger's thought. It is not implausible to suggest that certain nuances escape him that are, however, by implication known to Heidegger's chief disciple. Beaufret makes this point with respect to Pöggeler's observation, which he accepts, that Hölderlin's poetry led Heidegger to introduce the notion of the fourfold. For Beaufret, Pöggeler fails to elucidate the choice of

Hölderlin. Relying once more on an oral comment by Heidegger, Beaufret remarks that it is because alone among the poets Hölderlin raises "the problem of the singular relation of our world to its Greek origins."[77]

It is obvious that Beaufret will tolerate no criticism of Heidegger in any form, no deviation from the "authorized" reading of his thought. Someone concerned to protect Heidegger's theory is aware that it requires protection not only against unauthorized, even deviant interpretations but also, especially in the postwar French environment, against politically motivated criticism deriving from his turning to National Socialism. Beaufret's handling of the political dimension of Heidegger's thought is a model for later French discussion. Like those who deny the problem of evil, Beaufret in effect denies that there is any political problem to be addressed as concerns Heidegger's relation to National Socialism.[78]

Beaufret's infrequent remarks on Heidegger's political turning are invariably exculpatory. In an early response to Sartre's remark that Heidegger rallied to National Socialism through lack of character, Beaufret demurs, insisting that it was surely a consciously premeditated act. He wonders if Heidegger turned to Nazism through the naive view that it was an authentic form of resoluteness in the face of death, before suggesting that such naïveté is due to a bourgeois lack of attention to social infrastructure.[79] At this stage, the most that Beaufret is willing to countenance is a certain naïveté on the part of the philosopher of being, presumably unaware of, or at least unschooled in, political realities.

In later writings, Beaufret portrays the same Heidegger who perhaps naively, but honorably rallied to National Socialism as a staunch opponent of Nazism. According to Beaufret, Heidegger's lecture on the "Origin of the Work of Art" delivered several times in 1935 and 1936 was a clear act of defiance of Goebbels's Nazi view of culture. Heidegger's only mistake is "to have believed that Hitlerism could be overcome through the force of thought."[80] Once more Heidegger is guilty of nothing more than being a little naive, presumably like all philosophers.

Yet even the minimal admission in texts addressed to philosophical colleagues that Heidegger is possibly politically naive is taken back in the harder line formulated in interviews intended for public consumption. Here Beaufret weaves an absolutely seamless web devoid of flaws of any kind. He maintains that Heidegger did nothing that could possibly justify the allegations raised against him and that the political interrogation of his thought reflects only the philosophical mediocrity of his detractors.[81] Further adopting an Olympian attitude, he maintains that it is demeaning for a thinker like Heidegger to respond to criticism and that, following Heidegger's explicit wish, he will not do so.[82] Presumably criticism concerning Heidegger's position and his politics are on the same plane. Going further, Beaufret suggests, in a transparent allusion to Marxism, that to accuse an important body of thought is equivalent to interpreting philosophy as ideology.[83]

Yet as the facts have continued to emerge, it has become ever clearer that, in Beaufret's language, Heidegger did a number of things that might justify the allegations raised against him, such as denouncing his colleagues to the National Socialists.[84] While most of Heidegger's critics are philosophically less significant figures, it does not follow that their criticisms are either incorrect or politically motivated. Yet if political questions cannot be asked then intellectual responsibility, on which Heidegger insists in his conception of resoluteness, disappears. And if important theories are not subject to criticism, then they are literally incomparable, *sui generis*, beyond evaluation of any kind, merely an object of admiration. This is perhaps the deeper message of Beaufret's determined defense of Heidegger against all criticism of any kind.

FRENCH HEIDEGGERIAN ORTHODOXY

Beaufret's influential reading of Heidegger's theory offers a selective affirmation of the main themes of the "Letter on Humanism" that became the basis for French Heideggerian orthodoxy. The official pretext of this text is Sartre's overly enthusiastic claim to base his own existentialism in Heidegger's fundamental ontology. Yet Heidegger, who seems initially to have believed in his hour of need that his salvation would come from Sartre,[85] was certainly aware that the stakes were considerably higher.

In Beaufret's influential reading of Heidegger, three themes predominate: the approach to Heidegger's earlier thought through its later evolution; the idea that Heidegger's theory is beyond philosophy; and the effort to defend Heidegger's position against criticism motivated by his political involvement. These themes further predominate in the orthodox French Heidegger discussion that concentrates on a strictly philosophical, anticontextualist reading of the master's thought. Following Beaufret's lead, there is a tendency to isolate Heidegger's thought from his political commitment or, if that is not possible, to present the most favorable view of Heidegger's politics.

The authoritative *Cahier de l'Herne* devoted to Heidegger illustrates the latter strategy.[86] In a presentation of his thought as a whole, it is obviously not possible to avoid mention of his commitment to National Socialism. Yet this obvious danger is defused in two ways: through a selective reproduction of Heidegger's writings that presents only his side of the issue; and through the publication of articles in the section on politics that either do not address his turn to National Socialism[87] or tend to excuse it.

Following Heidegger's own *Spiegel* interview, Jean-Marie Veysse discusses the famous "Rectorial address" as a meditation on the essence of the German university without consideration of its link to Heidegger's Nazism.[88] A more accurate picture of this speech would have been presented by reproducing the talk. Jean-Michel Palmier, author of a work on Heidegger and politics,[89] contributes a discussion of Heidegger and National Socialism that refutes any claim for a connection between Heidegger's thought and his political turn by the simple device of restricting the discussion narrowly to a very short chronological period.[90]

The widespread tendency in orthodox French Heideggerianism to interpret Heidegger's early writings through his later thought and his thought through itself produces a strongly conservative approach to Heideggerian texts. In the analysis of Heideggerian writings, French textual interpretation sometimes takes on a nearly hierophantic quality in which questions of truth are bracketed in favor of elaborate, extended, ever more ingenious textual readings. Everything happens as if for certain views of the sacred writings Heidegger's ideas are known to be true and the only relevant question is how to depict them.

After Beaufret's death, his mantle as the most important French reader of Heidegger's thought was gradually assumed by Jacques Derrida. Unlike Beaufret, Derrida is an original thinker but he is also distinguished by a deep devotion to Heidegger's thought, which he interprets in an almost Talmudic fashion, often paragraph by paragraph or even line by line.[91] Although he is deeply influenced by Heidegger, it is a mistake to conflate Derrida's own thought with Heidegger's. Yet as we shall see below, when he has finished with his intricate reading of Heidegger's writings, considered as an interpretation, the result is often indistinguishably similar to the orthodox form of Heideggerianism established by Beaufret.[92]

HEIDEGGERIAN HUMANISM: AN ORTHODOX READING?

We have discussed aspects of French Heideggerian orthodoxy created by Beaufret. The image of French Heideggerian orthodoxy presented here is necessarily stereotypical, an ideal type, exhibiting general characteristics exhibited in different ways by recent French students of Heidegger. It is not necessary for any single French student of Heidegger's thought to exhibit all the features of the later Heideggerian reading of his theory through the lens of the "Letter on Humanism" to maintain that this cluster of features is widely exemplified in the French Heidegger discussion.

We can illustrate contemporary French Heideggerian orthodoxy through the work of Michel Haar, a young French Heideggerian, with solid ties to orthodox Heideggerian circles in France and abroad. Haar's work, which is representative of the best contemporary French Heidegger scholarship, is distinguished through his grasp of the entire Heideggerian corpus, a solid knowledge of German, a relatively spare, neutral writing style, unusual in the Heidegger discussion, a useful capacity, infrequently in evidence in the Heidegger debate, to contrast Heidegger's ideas with those of other writers, and a growing willingness to criticize. Yet in other respects Haar is typical of the orthodox tendency to approach Heidegger's initial theory through his later writings, to view that theory as beyond philosophy, and to minimize or eliminate Heidegger's political involvement as a factor in judging his theory.

Haar is one of the few French Heideggerians to concentrate on the Heideggerian concept of human being. He raises this theme in two recent books, indirectly and less critically in a study of the idea of the earth, that place where human beings live, from a late Heideggerian perspective,[93] and more directly and more critically in a study of Heidegger's concept of human being[94] that is, as Haar points out, so strangely silent on the place of the individual in history.[95]

The first book is a study of what the Greeks called *physis* from the perspective of the later Heidegger. According to Haar, this concept is absent in *Being and Time*. It is initially elucidated in Heidegger's study, "The Origin of the Work of Art." For Haar, following Heidegger, the Greek temple refers not only to the cultural world but to all of nature. He presents Heidegger's theory as a non-Hegelian approach to the history of being from Greek *logos* to modern technology that implies something that is not exhibited, that is held back, in terms of which history is destiny. In this theory, each epoch forms a unity, but each is also held back with respect to being.

Ereignis is the discovery of this limit of history. Through this idea we can go out of the history of being in order to grasp it as a finished whole and to "remember" it without arriving at a Hegelian totalization. *Ereignis* is, hence, the condition of acceding to a nonmetaphysical experience of the world that Heidegger describes as letting be:

> *Ereignis* hence causes to appear the limits and the disposition of the wordly disposition, thought through its historical provenance, as the purely *metaphysical* basis. Is this scientific and technological basis, derived in a distant and complex manner from the "first principles" of philosophy, the *soil* [*sol*] on which man walks or stands? Certainly not. Even if man begins to distance himself from the planet towards cosmic space, he still inhabits this earth that in no sense signifies for him a "planet" among others ("planet" means etymologically "wandering star"). Although in the last phase of the History of Being the earth has already become "planetary," it however gives to man the originary experience of place.[96]

The book is divided into three parts, concerning being and the earth, the limits of history, and art and the earth. In the first part, after some remarks on animality, Haar takes up the question of human being through the idea of mood (*Stimmung*). The third section discusses the primacy of mood over the corporeal character of Dasein. Haar concedes that *Being and Time* has no analysis of what Husserl's *Ideas, II* or the early Merleau-Ponty describe as the original site of truth under the names of *Leib, Leiblichkeit, corps propre, chair, corporéité*, and so on.[97] Yet this is not a defect, since mood and

121

thrownness (*Geworfenheit*), themes that Heidegger analyses in detail, are prior to the body.[98] In fact, mood reveals thrownness. It is also the basis of all emotions. He follows Heidegger in differentiating mood and basic mood (*Grundstimmung*). "The *Grundstimmung* not only reveals the situation in the world, but the situation *of the world* concerning the earth, the divine and history."[99]

In this book, written prior to the raging discussion on Heidegger's politics that took place in France in 1987–1988, Haar is respectful of Heidegger, including Heidegger's view of human being, concerned to expound and defend rather than to criticize, as close as possible to Heidegger's own view as he reads it. His approach evolves in his more recent study, written after the discussion of Heidegger's politics, which is squarely centered on Heidegger's theory of human being.

In the later book, Haar rapidly dismisses Heidegger's political turning as due merely to a moment of "voluntarism"[100] without inquiring into its effect on the later theory. This aspect of the discussion is uncritical. Haar simply claims that Heidegger declined both racism in virtue of its biologism and the *Führerprinzip* because of its elitism. Yet there is now reason to believe that, if anti-Semitism is racism, Heidegger may have been a racist after all,[101] and his public support of the *Führerprinzip* is a matter of record.[102]

Haar's treatment of Heidegger's political turning is excentric, not central to his book. It is only significant in virtue of his unwillingness to be more than faintly critical of Heidegger, critical in a way that basically challenges the theory on any single point. He is slightly more critical of Heidegger's conception of man. Yet the criticism is muted by the fact that it presupposes rather than intends to question the bases of the Heideggerian edifice. Whereas some writers exaggerate the importance of their criticism, Haar minimizes his. He seems to want to question, but not to place in question Heidegger's conception of the essence of man.

According to Haar, Heidegger's analysis of Dasein innovates through a concept of man's unitary essence that is independent of the prior discussion.[103] Echoing Sartre's view that Marxism requires the existentialist concept of man, Haar contends that the traditional metaphysical view of being as presence requires Heidegger's concept of Dasein as a finite being.[104] Haar identifies three Heideggerian motives: to refuse the traditional philosophical idea of man as a rational animal, including the identification of a metaphysical essence with an animal grasped as a thing, the idea that reason (logos, ratio) understood as a simple faculty loses its link to being, and the idea that human being is only a special case of the metaphysics of subjectivity.

Haar's critique of Heidegger's essentialist conception of human being is developed punctually in the discussion, notably with respect to the idea of being-toward-death. He defends Heidegger against the charge of antihumanism due, he contends, to a misreading of Heidegger's antianthropologism.

What is sometimes unreflectively [étourdiment] called "antihumanism" is principally a radical rupture with the anthropocentrism that dominates since the dawn of Modern Times. Man does not produce himself. He does not create being. He does not possess the final possibility of his own capacities. He does not master the provenance or the secret necessity of the structures of the world. He can only administer them. He only perceives rarely and dimly the possibility of the Earth that is received through art."[105]

This passage toward the end of the book confirms that Haar basically accepts Heidegger's conception of man as Dasein, man as defined through his relation to being, man as a dependent being. This is a view of human being that has lost the modern humanist insistence on such characteristics as freedom or naturalism, as in the idea that man is part of nature, characteristics that have been replaced by the idea that man depends on and can point to being.

The book ends with two critical remarks concerning Heidegger's "excesses." First, Heidegger suppresses not only the metaphysical subject but its individuality.[106] Through his concern with being, Heidegger fails to preserve what is particular about different human beings, what makes them artists, or poets, and so on. Second, Heidegger pretends that "being would have the *force* to manifest itself spontaneously, by and through itself."[107] For Haar, Heidegger's later effort, after decentering the subject, to approach being directly, is unintelligible without the subject to which being manifests itself. In reference to Heidegger's late essay, "The End of Philosophy and the Task of Being," where he discusses the idea of the clearing (*Lichtung*), Haar writes: "If one follows *Being and Time*, it is Dasein itself that is the *Lichtung*!"[108]

Haar, who addresses the limits of Heidegger's conception of human being from an angle of vision located within Heidegger's thought, does not draw the conclusion of his remark that is simply devastating for the later evolution of Heidegger's theory and for the theory itself. If we follow Haar, the later development of Heidegger's thought, including the decentering of the subject, the emphasis on being as self-manifesting, in short the content of the celebrated turning, is in fact a turning away from the valid kernel of his theory. If it is excessive to regard being as self-manifesting, and if being can only manifest itself to human being, then Heidegger should not later have turned away, but rather held fast to the analysis of Dasein, the central insight of his fundamental ontology.

Haar could accept this point, since his purpose seems to be to call attention to what he regards as valid in Heidegger's early thought. What he could not accept is the further implication of his remark. For if the earth precedes the world, if human beings raise the problem of being, then it is mistaken to understand human being through being. Hence, the wider implication of Haar's analysis is simply to question the foundations of Heidegger's original analysis of human being as the clue to being. Although this is not his intention, his discussion of Heidegger's view of the essence of human being threatens that view as well as the deeper concern, animating his entire theory, with being.

FRENCH HEIDEGGERIAN ORTHODOXY FOR EXPORT

French Heideggerianism is a form of philosophical orthodoxy that, like orthodoxy in general, turns on uncritical fidelity. This orthodoxy stands in for the critical examination of truth claims that are presupposed but rarely if ever tested. In the orthodox French reading of Heidegger, orthodoxy is assured by the reading of Heideggerian texts anticontextually, that is without regard to time and place, in abstraction from their genesis, merely in terms of themselves. When stress is placed on the interpretation of an author, any author, merely through that author's texts, then the resultant reading lacks ordinary standards of comparison required to evaluate theories of any kind. An approach to Heidegger's early writings through the focus of their later development, useful in revealing reasons for the transformation of the initial position, is also philosophically conservative in precluding any assessment of the theory. The resultant reading of Heidegger's theory through the focus of his own "Letter on Humanism" tends to apply his own reverential attitude towards the authentic repetition of tradition to the reverential repetition of his view of his own thought.

The orthodox character of the French Heidegger discussion, as illustrated by Beaufret, serves to render a master thinker immune to criticism. Heideggerians everywhere employ techniques designed to sacralize the master thinker while impeding evaluative discussion. Yet it would be illusory to regard philosophical orthodoxy as confined to Heidegger's students or to French thought. This practice is unfortunately widespread in the philosophical discussion in France and elsewhere that continually evades even the most determined effort to measure its claims, especially its persistent claims for social utility, against the reality of the situation.

It will be useful to end this chapter with a brief note about the influence of French Heideggerianism in American circles. French Heideggerianism, including its orthodox variant, like French wine, is a product that travels well, that can be exported to other countries, particularly to North America. It was introduced, popularized and disseminated by important scholars active in America interested in Heidegger, such as Reiner Schürmann,[109] but above all through the growing American reputation of Derrida. The latter acquired an American audience for his thought, including his particular brand of French Heideggerianism through his association with a group of Yale literary critics with philosophical inclinations, including J. Hillis Miller, Geoffrey Sammons, Harold Bloom, and especially Paul de Man. Although with the exception of de Man none of these writers is particularly Heideggerian, there was at least a receptivity, and in the case of de Man, an active concern with certain Heideggerian themes[110] that helped create an interest in Derrida. This interest was quickly increased through translation of his writings as well as through his frequent teaching forays to the United States.

There is an increasing penetration of French Heideggerian orthodoxy in American cultural circles, including departments of literature, French, comparative literature, and philosophy. This tendency is stronger in France, where its influence is felt in the Collège international de philosophie and in the publications of Editions Galilée. Those in France under Derrida's influence, that is paradoxically weaker than in America, include Jean-Luc Nancy, Philippe Lacoue-Labarthe, Françoise Dastur, Sarah Kofman, and others. In America, those who take an orthodox French Heideggerian line mediated through the influence of Derrida, that is mediated through John Sallis's journal *Research in Phenomenology* and his book series at University of Indiana Press, Studies in Continental Philosophy, include Sallis, David Krell, and Charles Scott. As in French Heideggerian orthodoxy, the common thread linking together all these writers is the triple concern to turn away from or at least severely to minimize Heidegger's political commitment, to read the earlier Heidegger through the later writings, and to consider Heidegger's writings either without reference to the philosophical tradition or mainly, even solely, through his own reading of it.

At present, when the rise of French Heideggerian orthodoxy is still under way, it is difficult to predict the outcome. It is too early to say whether like wine it will continue to improve with age over a fairly long period or whether like cheese it will ripen and then quickly spoil. Yet it is likely that the emergence of detailed discussion of Heidegger's political misdeeds will eventually lead to a revision of the rather too charitable, uncritically orthodox French reading of his thought in French and American philosophical circles. In fact, this may already be happening. As the recent publication of Krell's critical study of Heidegger makes clear, even his staunchest supporters are now revising their view of Heidegger and Heidegger's theory.[111]

7

ON HEIDEGGER AND CONTEMPORARY FRENCH PHILOSOPHY

A master thinker is influential with respect to the ensuing discussion that, on one interpretation, takes form in the horizon formed by the master's thought. Precisely this status was claimed for Heidegger in Koyré's introduction to the initial translation of Heidegger's writings into French. This claim is meaningful only if it can be shown that Heidegger's theory exerts a dominant influence in the contemporary French philosophical debate. This is the first of two chapters that will demonstrate the dominant influence of Heidegger's theory within contemporary French philosophy.

Suggestions of influence are easy to grasp but difficult to evaluate. "Influence" is intrinsically vague. Virtually any relation between two thinkers might be construed as indicating the influence of one on the other. Yet many forms of influence are unimportant, certainly philosophically unimportant. Although Hegel saw Napoleon on horseback at the Battle of Jena, it is philosophically unimportant to know the color of the horse. Yet it is philosophically important to understand how Hegel's observation of Napoleon relates to the Hegelian concept of the role of the great man in history.

To illustrate Heidegger's influence in contemporary French philosophy, it is useful to distinguish between three types of philosophical discussion: that devoted mainly or even solely to Heidegger's theory; that which makes use of Heideggerian insights as an aid in studying the philosophical tradition; and that so-called creative philosophical work that draws on Heideggerian insights to develop a position that may or may not remain within the Heideggerian orbit.

HEIDEGGERIAN EXEGESIS

Heidegger specialists, whose work is devoted to preparing editions of his writings, to their translation, and to interpretation of his ideas, obviously tend to be influenced by his theory. Here the relevant factor is the very size of the French Heidegger debate in which in recent years as many as fifteen or more books on the master's thought have been published each fall. It is easy to pick out a Heidegger scholar, or at least no more difficult than it is to pick out, say, a Plato scholar. Frequently those whose work consists in scrutinizing texts in the closest possible way are reluctant to do more than that, particularly reluctant to criticize. There seems to be an inverse relation between detailed, expert knowledge of any philosopher's thought, especially Heidegger's, and the desire or willingness to raise, or even to entertain, objections to the position.

It must be highly unusual for someone to devote himself to detailed exegesis of the thought of a writer held to be less than first rank. Those whose theories receive and merit such scholarly devotion are usually the very few thinkers of the highest philosophical importance. One way to measure Heidegger's influence in contemporary philosophy is through the sheer number of philosophers engaged mainly or wholly in some form of Heideggerian exegesis in the wider sense of the term, those who regard their primary or perhaps sole philosophical task as preparing the texts or as getting out the Heideggerian message.

In French philosophical circles, those committed to Heideggerian exegesis seem more numerous than elsewhere. In part, we have already considered Heideggerian exegesis through the instructive example of Jean Beaufret who, in many writings devoted to Heidegger's theory, presents an insurpassably orthodox view of the master's own theory, including his reading of selected figures in the philosophical tradition. But there are many others who, while they may not adopt the seamlessly orthodox interpretation that Beaufret favors, are close, often very close to it. They include, in no particular order, such writers as François Fédier, Emmanuel Martineau, Henri Birault, Jean Greisch, Alain Boutot, François Vézin, in certain of his moods Jacques Derrida, and others.

Heidegger's theory is at best difficult to understand. There is certainly room for a faithful effort to explain the main lines of a difficult theory without criticism. Such careful explanation is different from a further, more orthodox effort at what can fairly be called philosophical hagiography. An admittedly extreme, recent example is provided by the short presentation of Heidegger's thought due to Boutot,[1] who earlier published a study of Heidegger and Plato.[2] Even when we take into account the fact that this little study is written mainly for the wider public, it exhibits an extreme type of orthodoxy simply antithetical to philosophy that has here been replaced by a kind of philosophical cult of personality.

In his book, Boutot simply reproduces the usual clichés of orthodox Heideggerianism without criticism of any kind. Examples include the idea that Heidegger is incontestably one of the major thinkers, even the major thinker of this century, that his thought moves through all the controversies it has engendered without any damage whatsoever, that the history of philosophy since the early Greeks is the history of the forgetfulness of being, that we still have not begun to think, and that Heidegger's thought is one of those rare views that end up by transforming all of human existence.

HEIDEGGER AND FRENCH INTERPRETATION OF PHENOMENOLOGY

It is not difficult to pick out those who specialize in Heideggerian exegesis. It is more difficult to distinguish between those employing Heideggerian insights to read other views and those employing such insights to so-called original philosophy. In practice this distinction is mainly honored in the breach, for instance in Heidegger's theory which, like Hegel's and many others, combines insights borrowed from the philosophical tradition with systematic discussion. It is likely, then, that no firm distinction between the history of philosophy and systematic philosophy can be drawn since this distinction is at best relative and never absolute.[3] In fact, many French philosophers present interesting, original theories in part through the guise of a novel reading of prior philosophy, most recently in Dominique Janicaud's discussion of the theological transformation of French phenomenology.[4]

Heidegger's influence in French cultural life is wider than the philosophical discussion. It includes, for instance, the views of the psychoanalysts Julia Kristeva and Jacques Lacan. The latter's peculiar form of Freudianism is influenced directly by his reading of Heidegger and indirectly through Heidegger's influence on Kojève's Hegel interpretation. Lacan's well known thesis that "the unconscious is structured like a language,"[5] deriving from the later Heidegger's turn to language,[6] is understood by him as a form of anti-Hegelianism.[7]

Heidegger's impact on contemporary French studies of the history of philosophy is difficult to overestimate. An example is the interpretation of Kierkegaard, whom some writers regard as the first important existentialist thinker. For Lévinas, who acknowledges that Henri Delacroix and Victor Basch already studied Kierkegaard at the beginning of the century, we owe to Heidegger the philosophical reading of Kierkegaard.[8]

In France, Heidegger is still commonly regarded as a phenomenologist. Heidegger profoundly influences French interpretation of phenomenology, as well as the development of the French phenomenological tradition. French studies of Husserl may overlook Heidegger,[9] but even in the most orthodox treatment Husserl's theory invariably or nearly invariably figures in the works on Heidegger's.[10] In part through Lévinas's continuing influence, French Husserl studies have never been free from a certain Heideggerianism.

According to Paul Ricoeur, a major contributor to French phenomenology as well as a scholar and translator of Husserl's thought, French Husserlian studies were literally founded by the appearance of Lévinas's first book, *Théorie de l'intuition dans la phénoménologie de Husserl* in 1930.[11] This

128

work, which was Lévinas's dissertation, is ostensibly devoted to Husserl. Yet Lévinas, who studied with both Husserl and Heidegger, was never only a Husserlian. In fact, he has always provided a somewhat violent reading of Husserl's thought,[12] with important Heideggerian components.

The Heideggerian element in French Husserl studies is stronger in the writings of those closer to Heidegger, including former Beaufret students Jean-François Courtine, Jean-Luc Marion,[13] and above all in the works of Jacques Derrida.[14] Courtine and Marion are both exceptions to the frequent French philosophical tendency, encouraged by Heidegger and practiced by Beaufret, to consider Heidegger's thought as beyond comparison with philosophical theories. With others, such as Jacques Taminiaux[15] and Marion, Courtine has for years been concerned with careful discussion of the relation of the views of Heidegger, particularly the early Heidegger, and Husserl.[16] Marion, as will emerge below, has recently devoted intensive study to the relation of the early Heidegger and Husserl in the process of working out his own position.[17]

Heidegger's impact on Sartre's theory is arguably even more significant. Sartre's thought continues to attract attention elsewhere, particularly in the United States.[18] His near total eclipse in France at present is directly traceable to his loss of the philosophical battle with Heidegger for influence in the philosophical discussion.

Sartre was characteristically generous in assimilating his thought to Heidegger's, and in minimizing the importance of Heidegger's turning to National Socialism for the latter's position.[19] In view of Sartre's well known political commitment, his clement – some would say his overly clement – attitude toward Heidegger's Nazism, unusual in a thinker who quarreled with virtually everyone with whom he came into contact, is attributable to a double failure on his part.

On the one hand, there is his superficial reading of Heidegger's thought – precisely the point that Heideggerians constantly raise – typical of a thinker who apparently rarely read anyone's work with care. On the other hand, there is his questionable attachment to Heidegger's theory precisely when the latter was most overtly politically active, during Heidegger's period as rector of the University of Freiburg. Sartre, the apostle of intellectual responsibility, was simply not responsible enough to examine the link between Heidegger's theory and his Nazism with any care.

What I am depicting as Sartre's double failure significantly enabled him at the end of the Second World War to invoke Heidegger as someone who held views relevantly similar or even identical to his own. This is some-thing he could not have done had he been willing to put into question either his blindness to Heidegger's political activism or its link to Heidegger's philosophy.

Sartre, who was not disinterested, was generous in his appraisal of Heidegger's position; but Heidegger and the Heideggerians, who are also not disinterested, have not been generous to Sartre. After a period in which Sartre's theory was dominant in the French philosophical debate, particularly in French phenomenology,[20] its influence quickly declined. This decline was helped by at least three factors. One was Sartre's death in 1980 that brought to an end his phenomenal intellectual productivity. Another was the attack on his thought launched by Heidegger in the "Letter on Humanism", and later prolonged by Beaufret, Derrida and others. Finally, there is the emergence of French structuralism, with existentialism one of the two most significant French philosophical movements in the postwar period, in the revolt against Sartre's intellectual hegemony.

HEIDEGGER AND THE FRENCH INTERPRETATION OF THE HISTORY OF PHILOSOPHY

Heidegger's influence on the French reading of the history of philosophy is not confined to phenomenologists such as Husserl and Sartre, but extends to numerous other figures, including Nietzsche, Schelling, Descartes, Suarez, Aristotle, and Parmenides. The French discussion of Nietzsche began in the late nineteenth century. His writings were translated into French by Eli Halévy and Henri Albert as early as the end of the last century.[21] His thought influenced many French writers, including Gide and Valéry.[22]

Although there was a steady stream of works in French on Nietzsche's position, and an occasional book concerning Nietzsche's thought was even translated into French, his theory was not always held in high esteem. At the beginning of the century, for example, Emile Faguet suggested that Nietzsche was not a very original philosopher since all his views could be entirely reconstructed from those of La Rochefoucauld, Goethe and Renan.[23] The early French appreciation of Nietzsche was so coarse grained that as late as 1927 Julien Benda could refer in passing to Nietzschean pragmatism[24] and even later in 1946 Henri Lefebvre could classify him as an existentialist.[25]

Heidegger and Jaspers were both interested in Nietzsche. Jaspers's study of Nietzsche's thought attracted notice in the French discussion.[26] Yet the ongoing French Nietzsche discussion[27] was transformed by the publication in 1961 of Heidegger's two volume study of Nietzsche. The appearance of this study led to a revival of French interest in Nietzsche. This revival was fueled by a number of factors, including the relatively rapid translation of Heidegger's massive Nietzsche study into French in 1971, the impact of Nietzsche's theory, particularly as interpreted by Heidegger, on Pierre Klossowski,[28] the translator of Heidegger's study, as well as on Gilles Deleuze[29] and above all on Michel Foucault.

In the wake of Heidegger's study of Nietzsche's thought, the French philosophical interest in Nietzsche ran wide and deep.[30] Vincent Descombes believes that the entire generation of the 1960s in France was dominated by a Nietzschean perspectivism.[31] Most recently, a series of writers have used the vehicle of a collective work on Nietzsche to free themselves from the French philosophical assault during the 1960s, under the influence of Heidegger and then Derrida, on the ideals of the Enlightenment.[32]

In France, all observers agreed with Heidegger that Nietzsche was an important figure, although few follow Heidegger's tendency to read Nietzsche's theory with the same seriousness as if it were, say, Aristotle's.[33] Nietzsche's aphoristic style is at least partly responsible for the very wide range of opinions concerning his thought. Philippe Raynaud distinguishes three recent forms of French Nietzscheanism due respectively to Deleuze, Foucault, and to Nietzsche's wider impact on French culture.[34] Certainly, Nietzsche is a central theme in the writing of Georges Bataille.[35] An incomplete sample of recent French debate on Nietzsche includes a rightwing effort to recuperate Nietzsche on behalf of so-called individualism,[36] an interpretation of Nietzsche as completing the Copernican Revolution,[37] a study of Nietzsche and metaphor,[38] and so on. Many, but not all French students of Nietzsche are more or less strongly influenced, both positively and negatively, by Heidegger's Nietzsche interpretation.

As could be anticipated, as always Heidegger's closest follower was Jean Beaufret. As early as his first book concerning Heidegger's theory, Beaufret contends that since most French writers on Nietzsche incorrectly see him as having surpassed Platonism – although for Heidegger Nietzsche reestablished a form of Platonism – most French Nietzsche scholars have failed to understand either Heidegger's reading of Nietzsche or Nietzsche's thought.[39] Beaufret develops Heidegger's reading of Nietzsche's theory in detail throughout his four volumes of dialogues with Heidegger. Beaufret's reading of Nietzsche's theory has recently been restated in briefer fashion by Courtine.[40] Others who contest Heidegger's reading of Nietzsche's theory in various ways include François Laruelle, who criticizes Heidegger's supposed reduction of Nietzsche to an imperialist thinker in favor of an interpretation of Nietzsche as an antifascist,[41] and Derrida, who tries several times to "save" Nietzsche from Heidegger's interpretation.[42] In fact, Derrida can be said to attempt to turn Heidegger's interpretation of Nietzsche against Heidegger in maintaining that despite his later opposition to metaphysics Heidegger also remains a metaphysical thinker.

Francisco Suarez, the Spanish philosopher of the sixteenth century, is a key link in Heidegger's reading of the philosophical tradition. In *Being and Time*, he remarks that through Suarez's *Disputationes metaphysicae* the Greek metaphysical impulse is transmitted to modern philosophy, determining even Hegel's position.[43] Heidegger amplifies this statement in a lecture course from the same period. He claims that Suarez, whom he regards as more important than Duns Scotus or even Thomas Aquinas, provides a system for Aristotelian metaphysics that determines all the later discussion up to and including Hegel.[44] Heidegger points to Suarez's distinction between *metaphysica generalis*, or general ontology and *metaphysica specialis*, or special ontology, including the theories of the world, nature, psychology, and God. He points out that this distinction recurs widely in later thought, for instance, in Kant's *Critique of Pure Reason*.[45]

Courtine applies this Heideggerian scheme in a detailed, recent study of Suarez. The aim of the work, he tells us, is to situate Suarez in the history of metaphysics, or in still more Heideggerian language, to determine "the nature and the significance of the turning, 'the *historicality*,'" of Suarez's contribution.[46] Echoing Heidegger's view that Suarez is the author of the system lacking in Aristotle's *Metaphysics* – precisely that system that permitted its later influence in the modern philosophical tradition as well as the Heideggerian idea of ontotheology – Courtine states his desire "to contribute . . . to the general study of the *system of metaphysics*, that is the stages of its systematization, through the guiding thread of an elaboration, which is *historical*, of the logic of its ontotheological constitution."[47] In his conclusion, more than 500 pages later, Courtine offers the hypothesis, again following Heidegger, that the problem of the *analogia entis* is, as Heidegger seems to have suspected, unthought within metaphysics. And he underlines the importance of not conflating various Heideggerian distinctions.[48]

Throughout his career, Heidegger derives an important source of inspiration from his meditation on Greek philosophy and Greek poetry. In a sense, *Being and Time* is the form taken by a book on Aristotle originally planned by Heidegger but never written. Many of Heidegger's fundamental concepts can be understood as revisions of Aristotelian concepts.[49] Heidegger's interpretations of selected Greek philosophers, like other aspects of his thought, are controversial and have attracted criticism from some observers.[50] Others, particularly French writers, regard them as casting an important new light on ancient Greek philosophy.

In France, a Heideggerian approach to the interpretation of Greek philosophy has been fostered by Beaufret, who, unceasingly orthodox in all things Heideggerian, devotes an entire volume of his *Dialogues with Heidegger* to the latter's views of Greek philosophy,[51] and Pierre Aubenque, the influential Aristotle scholar. Aubenque was aided in making his case for a Heideggerian approach to Greek philosophy and to philosophy in general through his own important studies of Greek thought, his chair in Greek philosophy at the Sorbonne, and his presence in several key committees that influenced philosophical appointments in the highly centralized French educational system.

Aubenque's works on Aristotle's views of being[52] and prudence,[53] on which his scholarly reputation is mainly based, reflect more than a simple awareness of Heidegger's theory. Although frequently critical of Heidegger's specific readings of particular texts, he accepts a broadly Heideggerian approach to Greek thought. His study of the problem of being in Aristotle significantly begins with a citation from Heidegger about metaphysics as a designation for the philosophical predicament.[54] Following Heidegger's concern to destroy the history of ontology, his aim is nothing less than, as he writes, "to unlearn all that the tradition *has added* to the primitive Aristotelianism."[55] He holds that "the restitution of the living Aristotle" is important since the way in which Aristotle's thought was understood has decisively influenced its interpretation.[56]

Heidegger's understanding of Greek philosophy becomes even more important in Aubenque's later writings. In a recent article on the contemporary significance of Aristotle's thought, he describes its manifold influence on a series of propositions basic to later Western views of the world. These propositions form a structure that, following Heidegger,[57] he labels ontotheological.[58] And he follows Heidegger's view that the contemporary interest in metalanguage is the consequence of Aristotelian metaphysics.[59]

Aubenque acknowledges Heidegger's concept of ontotheology as an appropriate appellation for the metaphysical framework deriving from Aristotle's thought. Rémi Brague, the most important younger Aristotelian scholar in France today, presupposes Heidegger's concept for his discussion of Aristotle's idea of the world. With respect to Heidegger's understanding of Greek philosophy, the difference between these two Aristotelian scholars is that Aubenque was closer to his mature understanding of Aristotle before he encountered Heidegger whereas Brague – a student of Aubenque and the author of the most important French study of Aristotle since Aubenque's study of Aristotle's view of being – encountered Heidegger's view of Greek philosophy at an earlier point in his career, before his own views were fixed.

Brague draws insight from Heidegger's study of ontology to interpret Greek philosophy. Heidegger criticizes the traditional view of ontology, based on what he calls presence-to-hand (*Vorhandenheit*) in favor of his own alternative conception. For Brague, Heideggerian phenomenology is a mode of access to Greek philosophy, and Heidegger's corpus can be regarded as an effort to work out the original conception of ontology lying behind the ontology historically attached to Aristotle's name.[60]

Brague's study of the question of the world in Aristotle's thought applies Heidegger's conception of the world to the interpretation of the ancient Greek tradition. As part of his critique of Descartes, Heidegger develops a lengthy analysis of the worldhood of the world that he understands as neither the entities in the world, such as tables and chairs, nor as the being in general of these entities.[61] For Brague, Aristotle's position can be grasped through a relation of coimplication among concepts of ontology, anthropology, and cosmology within a presupposed but unthematized concept of the world. "World" is understood in a Heideggerian phenomenological sense as "that in which we are,"[62] a concept that Greek philosophy presupposes but does not explore.[63]

In a lengthy study that maintains a constant dialogue with Heidegger, Brague utilizes this concept unthought by Aristotle but explicated by Heidegger to illuminate the Aristotelian corpus. He discerns a deep parallel between Heidegger's ontotheology, or the name for traditional metaphysics, and what he calls, in an untranslatable neologism of his own devising, *katholou-prôtologique*.[64] The latter concept, which is wider than ontotheology, is present as well within the various domains of Aristotelian ontotheology.[65] In Brague's Heideggerian reading of Aristotle, the domains of ontology, anthropology and cosmology revolve around a central point running "from presence to the present, from being to the entity."[66] In short, Brague's reading of Aristotle's presupposes Heidegger's ontological difference, or a basic distinction between being in general and entities. According to Brague, the conception of being in the world, or Dasein, that is never thematized but latent in Aristotle, forms a whole with the "kathological-protological" structure of Aristotelianism.[67]

We can end this section on Heidegger's impact on the French study of the philosophical tradition with a remark on Beaufret's orthodox Heideggerian reading of Parmenides. In *Being and Time*, Heidegger indicates that his characteristic doctrine of truth as disclosure derives finally from Parmenides's thought. According to Heidegger, for whom Karl Reinhardt has finally solved the vexed problem of the unity of Parmenides's poem,[68] Parmenides's assertion of the identity of thought and being yields the thesis that truth is the beholding that founds Western philosophy.[69] Heidegger later elaborates his view of Parmenides's theory in a number of places, including a lecture course in 1942–1943,[70] and a lecture in 1957.[71]

In his writings on the master, Beaufret dwells frequently on Heidegger's reading of Parmenides's poem, most explicitly in two articles in the first volume of his *Dialogues*.[72] Beaufret asserts that it is not possible either to summarize or to expound Heidegger's thought.[73] This claim, if true, undermines the intention, even the possibility of his "dialogues" with Heidegger over some thirty years, "dialogues" intended to make available Heidegger's own view of his thought to the French. He develops a Heideggerian reading of Parmenides's view in detail in a translation and commentary on the latter's poem.[74]

Beaufret's introduction frequently adverts directly to Heidegger's interpretation, or defends it against possible misreadings. He dwells at length on why the overwhelming Platonism of the philosophical tradition impeded the correct understanding of the unity of Parmenides's poem until, as Heidegger notes,[75] Reinhardt's breakthrough.[76] For Beaufret, following Heidegger, there is an original unity of thought and being in Parmenides's poem prior to any artificial separation and later juxtaposition.[77] Parmenides presents the view of truth as disclosure[78] foreshadowed in the "Letter on Humanism" and developed elsewhere, the ideas that entities are sent to us, that they are literally mittances of Being.[79]

HEIDEGGER AND CONTEMPORARY FRENCH PHILOSOPHY

Heidegger's impact is strongly felt in the the positions of contemporary French philosophers. Numerous French philosophers are uninterested in Heidegger's theory; others oppose it, even frankly oppose it, often for reasons linked to his Nazi turning, including Nicolas Tertulian, the well known Lukács specialist, Luc Ferry and Alain Renaut, two young anti-establishment thinkers, Christian Jambet, a former *nouveau philosophe*, and others. Still others, sometimes after an initial enthusiasm, take a more nuanced, often critical line, including Janicaud, Ricoeur, Henry, Marion, perhaps Courtine, and in some of his moods Derrida. Yet it is fair to say that the vast majority of French philosophers since the war have been marked by their encounter with Heidegger, including, in no particular order, such well known thinkers as Lévinas, Kojève, Koyré, Hyppolite, Lyotard, Foucault, Janicaud, Brague, Courtine, Aubenque, Deleuze, and others.

Virtually everywhere one looks in the contemporary French philosophical debate, one espies ideas that owe something, often more than just a little, for some thinkers even the essence of their positions, to a "postmodern" reading of Heidegger's thought. Like others influenced by Heidegger's position, Lyotard is an original thinker, whose position is more than a pale copy, a simple restatement, an echo however distant of Heidegger's thought, but which takes shape in the horizon formed by Heidegger's study of being.

"Foundationalism," the main epistemological strategy of modern times, can be succinctly characterized as "the view, most prominently illustrated in Descartes's position, that knowledge can be based on an initial point known with certainty and from which the remainder of the theory can be deductively derived."[80] In *Being and Time*, Heidegger stakes out an antifoundationalist theory, consistent with his anti-Cartesianism, in his analysis of the hermeneutic circle of the understanding, in which knowledge in the classical philosophical sense yields to interpretation.[81] In his later studies of Nietzsche, he consistently interprets the slogan "God is dead" as signifying the advent of modern nihilism.[82] In his study of the modern condition, Lyotard, who seems immune to Heidegger's view that truth rests on the disclosure of being, carries forward the basic Heideggerian insight that knowledge in our time must assume another form, including another form of justification.

For Lyotard, a science is modern in virtue of its concern to justify itself. The history of modern science is a series of crises concerning the various overarching justifications (*grands récits*) proposed. Philosophy is nothing other than scientific discourse aimed at the justification (*légitimation*) of claims to know.[83] In the postmodern period, by implication that period beyond philosophy where perfect epistemological justification is no longer, or at least no longer thought to be, possible, knowledge has also changed.[84] At this late date, no overarching justication of any form is still credible.[85]

135

Yet a science that is not justified is no more than an ideology that represents a certain form of power.[86] Since in the postmodern period scientific knowledge is self-validating through immanent rules, by implication philosophy is over.[87] Even the idea of a common justification must be abandoned since the different forms of knowledge deriving from different language games have nothing in common.[88]

In his own way, Foucault argues a similar point. He is sometimes classed as a structuralist, and structuralism is widely thought to dispense with subjectivity, even to be "the philosophy of the death of man."[89] Yet, as his exchange with Derrida makes clear, Foucault does not so much dispense with as offer a novel analysis of the subject. In a typically lengthy discussion of Foucault's remark in passing on Descartes's thought,[90] Derrida objects, thereby adumbrating his own later view of textuality (*textualité*), that on Foucault's reading of Descartes there could be something outside of, or prior to, the realm of philosophical discourse.[91] Foucault's response, criticizing Derrida for reducing "discursive practices to textual traces,"[92] points to the need to go beyond the texts, or abstract philosophical discussion, through analysis. For Foucault, who is influenced by Nietzsche, this leads to analysis of the mechanisms of power within which the ideas of truth and of subjectivity are meaningful. Since truth is relative to the domain of power,[93] and since there is nothing outside of power structures, the problem is not to change people's consciousness but rather to change the regime that produces the truth within the particular relations of power.[94]

Heidegger's view that philosophy since Descartes has tended to privilege the subject at the expense of the object, by inference to make objectivity dependent on subjectivity, leads to his effort to decenter the subject.[95] For Foucault, the mechanisms of power are prior, not only to the analysis of truth, but also to subjectivity. He sees the alternatives as the idealist view of the subject as constitutive, for instance in the Kantian or Marxian senses, and the phenomenological view of subjectivity, even in historicized form, in which the subject evolves over time. His insistence that one needs to dispense with the constituent subject would lead to the death of subjectivity only if there were no other alternative. In an important passage linking his genealogical analysis to subjectivity, he insists on the need "to arrive at an analysis which can account for the constitution of the subject within a historical framework."[96] The result is to make subjectivity genuinely historical by inverting the relation between subjectivity and objectivity or history. Foucault continues:

> And this is what I would call genealogy; this is a form of history which can account for the constitution of knowledges, discourses, domains of objects, etc., without having to make reference to a subject which is either transcendental in relation to the field of events or runs in its empty sameness throughout the course of history.[97]

A student of French philosophy does well to remember the importance of religion, particularly Catholicism, throughout French life, including French philosophy. Perhaps because of the similarity between Heidegger's idea of being that in *Being and Time* took shape as an analysis of the meaning of the being of beings,[98] and the Thomist thesis that the being of beings is God, Heidegger has a special attraction for philosophers positively inclined towards Roman Catholicism. This natural attraction has only been strengthened by the theological turning in French phenomenology, including such important phenomenologists as Michel Henry, and Jean-Luc Marion, that Janicaud traces to Lévinas.[99] Janicaud's thesis receives indirect support in a recent collective volume on phenomenology and theology, presented by Courtine, and offering essays by Henry, Ricoeur, Marion, and Jean-Louis Chrétien.[100]

Although still not as well known as Lyotard, Foucault, and Derrida, Henry is certainly one of the most original contemporary French thinkers.[101] Like Sartre, Henry is both a successful writer as well as a philosopher.[102] A number of elements of his strikingly original material phenomenology are already in place in his first major work, *The Essence of Manifestation*.[103] His position can be described as resulting from a radicalization of the Cartesian theory, initially under Heideggerian and Husserlian influences[104] – although more Husserlian than Heideggerian – that later develops, in reaction against Heidegger, in a resolutely Husserlian direction. In his more recent thought, Heidegger's influence figures negatively in Henry's theory, as a kind of antithesis that he strives to surpass.

The views of Heidegger and Henry describe parallel, but separate trajectories in reaction to Descartes. Heidegger, who criticizes the Cartesian *cogito ergo sum* for neglecting the *sum*, addresses this problem in his theory of being through a conception of Dasein. Henry addresses the being of the cogito in order to describe the meaning of subjectivity. The problem of the being of the cogito belongs to first philosophy, which Henry identifies with universal ontology. The Cartesian beginning point is insufficiently radical, since it presupposes a more radical foundation that it does not explicate.[105]

Henry's theory of the subject can be regarded as an effort to overcome the dualism following from Descartes's inability to make the transition from the representation to the represented, from the transcendent to the immanent planes.[106] More generally, Henry deepens phenomenology through a theory of affectivity. He holds that entities manifest themselves only in the form of an "effective phenomenological offer" within a horizon. Since the manifestation of an entity supposes a horizon, its affect on us, in fact *"all ontical affection presupposes an ontological affection and finds within it its foundation."*[107] Yet Henry goes further when he maintains that in the various "tonalities" of existence, such as despair or suffering, the absolute is constituted and revealed.[108]

In his many writings, Henry works out his theory through studies of the body, Marx, psychoanalysis, Kandinsky, socialism, and so on. In a recent work he defines the task of material phenomenology as a radicalization of phenomenology intended to "interrogate the way in which it [i.e. pure phenomenality] originally [originellement] phenomenalizes its substance, its stuff, the phenomenological matter of which it is made – its pure phenomeno-logical materiality."[109] For Henry, the foundation of pure phenomenality is life understood not as a thing, but as the principle of everything that Heidegger is unable to capture in his ontological categories. In his study of *The Crisis of European Sciences and Transcendental Phenomenology*, Husserl argues that Kant's theory presupposes the unthematized concept of the life world.[110] Similarly, Henry understands his own material phenomeno-logy as engaging the absence in Husserlian phenomenology of "a phenom-enology of transcendental life" that apparently founds it.[111]

Marion is one of the most prolific and most interesting of the younger French philosophers. His work, like that of such younger scholars as Brague and Courtine, exemplifies a qualified return to the best traditions of French philosophical scholarship that have never ended but were temporarily sus-pended during the existentialist, structuralist and poststructuralist movements.

Marion has been influenced by Henry, Heidegger, Derrida, Husserl and Lévinas, as well as others. Like Henry, whose work he especially appreci-ates,[112] he is engaged in working out what can loosely be characterized as a phenomenology of the invisible, in his case a theory with Heideggerian, Cartesian, and religious components. Again like Henry, there is a distance to Heidegger, in Marion's case through his own theory of being.[113]

Marion's writings can be said to fall into three main categories, including works on God and love, as well as technical philosophical studies.[114] The latter include historical investigations as well as his own theory. In his scholarly writing, Marion has contributed important studies of Descartes, a traditional topic in French philosophy. His Descartes studies, among the very best in France at present, are distinguished by their quality and their frequent reference to Heidegger.[115]

More recently, he has published an impressive discussion of the problem of phenomenology in Husserl and Heidegger up to 1926, the year prior to the appearance of *Being and Time*, where his own ideas frequently intrude. Here he exploits the obvious connection between the theories of Descartes, Husserl, and Heidegger to examine the relation between Husserl and the early Heidegger, albeit from a perspective closer to the later Heidegger. He is concerned with the nature and significance of their respective attitudes toward Descartes[116] and toward intentionality.[117]

Marion's own phenomenological thought concerns the problem of given-ness.[118] Simplifying enormously, we can say that what Henry calls affectivity Marion calls givenness (*donation*). Phenomenology from his perspective is nothing other than the analysis of the given as it is given in order to complete metaphysics.[119] Marion locates the relation of Heidegger to Husserl in a further elaboration of the latter's critique of objectivation. The problem, then, is whether the return to things, or to things themselves, leads to their objectivity or to their being, or, as Marion also formulates the question, to a transcendental subject or to Dasein.

His most original idea concerns the relation of reduction and givenness. For Marion, an appearance (*apparition*) suffices for being only if, in appearing, it gives itself perfectly. Yet that entails a direct relation between reduction and givenness.[120] On this basis, Marion differentiates no less than three forms of reduction: a first, or transcendental reduction; a second, or existential deduction following from entities and concerning being, with obviously Heideggerian overtones; and a third reduction whose "call however does not come from the horizon of being (or objectification) but from the pure form of the call."[121] Like the later Heidegger who desires to be open to being, Marion wants to be open to the call that questions us.

DERRIDA AND HEIDEGGER

In comparison with others discussed in this chapter, a more extended treatment of Derrida is warranted because he is presently better known, certainly better known in the United States than other contemporary French philosophers. Like Lacan before him, for some years Derrida has been inventing his own persona in a series of carefully crafted, difficult texts, strewn with multiple distinctions and linguistic puns that often simply cannot be satisfactorily rendered into another language. Although Derrida's view must be addressed, it is probably not possible to do so in a way that will satisfy his readers, particularly those, always more numerous in the US than in France, who are his disciples.

In any discussion of Derrida, certain caveats are in order. I will leave to one side the difficult, but tangential question of whether Derrida is a philosopher or only a philosopher[122] in order to concentrate on his texts. Any discussion of what goes on in them is open to objection, hence must remain tentative, since Derrida prefers to apply his view rather than to describe it unambiguously. It might be thought, particularly by a Derridean, however that is defined, that I have failed to grasp Derrida's theory, even described it incorrectly. But that is hardly to be avoided since a central theme in Derrida's practice is precisely the effort to avoid being pinned down to any definite view or set of views. Such a reaction is all the more easy to understand since, if I am correct, Derrida is specifically concerned to provide a negative answer to the problem of reference, so important to analytic philosophy and which analytic philosophy has arguably failed to resolve,[123] and that he apparently regards as an impossible quest.

Suffice it to say that Derrida's relation to Heidegger requires special treatment in virtue of the size of Derrida's corpus – at present more than forty volumes – the attention it evokes, and its extreme complexity. His relation to Heidegger clearly overflows the artificial distinction in use in this chapter. For in an obvious way he is devoted to Heidegger's theory; he makes use of Heideggerian insights in his reading of the history of philosophy; and he is also a creative thinker.

This rarely studied[124] relation is highly controversial. From this angle of vision, Derrida's theory has been characterized as simple imitation differing only in Derrida's peculiar style, described as "Heidegger + Derrida's style"[125] and as leading to a highly original view whose very fidelity to Heidegger's theory paradoxically results in an opposition more important than any other thinker.[126]

Although the nature of the relation of Derrida's theory to Heidegger's is controversial, no one denies its existence. Our task will be to make a beginning toward an understanding of that relation, to show how it might be understood in more detail. In this respect, it is useful to look to the history of philosophy. It is not sufficiently noticed that chronologically later thinkers, who criticize their predecessors, often remain committed to their projects. Although Hegel is an original thinker of great power, his own position is inconceivable without Kant's. There is evidence that the young Hegel intended to develop further and even to complete Kant's Copernican Revolution in philosophy.[127]

In the same way, it is consistent to regard Derrida, despite his criticisms of Heidegger's theory, as finally remaining within the Heideggerian orbit. The point is neither to deny the originality of Derrida's theory nor to make of Derrida a sort of latter-day Beaufret. It is, then, consistent to acknowledge that Derrida has criticized Heidegger on a number of grounds, such as valorizing unity over difference, gathering over dispersal, nostalgia over the violence of the past, presence over representation, meaning over dissemination, and so on, while still regarding Derrida as committed to a form of the basic Heideggerean project.

Derrida's theory cannot be understood merely through its relation to Heidegger's. Suffice it to say that it is triply determined by the positions of the "three Hs" in recent French philosophy: Husserl, Heidegger, and Hegel. Derrida interacts with Heidegger's theory on at least four levels: as a reader and then as a defender of Heidegger's texts, as a critic of others from a Heideggerean angle of vision, and in the way that he draws on it in his own theory.

To begin with, Derrida is an unusual reader of the texts of many writers, including Heidegger. After Beaufret's death, Derrida maintains a similar fascination with Heidegger's thought that he continues to subject to the most careful textual analysis.[128] His analysis of the idea of sexual difference (*Geschlecht, différence sexuelle*) in a recent article indicates that, when he is finished reading Heidegger's texts, often nothing is challenged, nothing is changed.[129]

After noting that Heidegger speaks rarely if at all of sex,[130] Derrida proposes to study sexual difference through the word "Dasein."[131] In

Derrida's discussion, there is not even a single word devoted to a justification or explanation of the utility of this approach as if it were self-evident that Heidegger's theory provides the adequate basis for an understanding of sexual difference. Yet this assumption is implicitly challenged by his acknowledgment that Heidegger never directly addresses the topic. Typically, the entire article – which never mentions either men or women, whose relation is in question, or other writers specifically concerned with this question, or indeed any other theory, including a philosophical theory, that might bear on the theme – is solely taken up with the elucidation of the question of sexual difference from a Heideggerian standpoint through the analysis of Heideggerian texts.

The conclusion of Derrida's article raises more questions than it resolves. According to Derrida, who implicitly accounts for Heidegger's failure to consider problems relating to human sexuality, Dasein is a being without sex since for Heidegger sexual difference must be thought through the structures of Dasein.[132] Heidegger's texts do not contain more than the most elliptical references to sexual difference since his thought moves on a deeper level than merely existential concerns.

This conclusion is comforting to an orthodox Heideggerian although perhaps not to anyone else. Derrida is unperturbed by the utter lack of any comment that might be relevant to the issue that concerns him in Heidegger's text. Yet someone who holds that the master thinker must speak to every issue might be troubled, say, by Heidegger's apparent failure to comment specifically about the social world, or about men and women other than in the most general terms, or even by his failure to comment on sexual difference.

Derrida's conclusion is consistent with Heidegger's remark in the "Letter on Humanism" that his thinking is prior to theory and practice.[133] Heidegger's humble claim disclaiming anything so mundane as a practical motivation for "thinking" points to its utter irrelevance for the problem that is Derrida's concern in this text. Now if one's concern is sexual difference from a Heideggerian perspective, the realization that Heidegger's thinking is so deep as not to raise the question is hardly reassuring. This is still another example, if one is needed, of the incapacity of philosophical thought to find a way to take up the problems of the world in which we live, to which it prefers such topics as the worldhood of the world.[134] Someone who is not an orthodox Heideggerian might read the same inference as revealing the inability of the master thinker to say anything useful about the problem. What is startling is Derrida's own seeming lack of awareness that the master thinker has nothing to contribute to the topic of the discussion, no way to illuminate the problem, since there is nothing in his theory that is specifically relevant to the problem of sexual difference.

Second, Derrida is capable, as Beaufret was not, of defending Heidegger on a high philosophical plane as distinct from using ridicule to cast doubt on his opponents' views. Derrida is especially concerned to defend Heidegger for actions linked to his Nazi turning. In the famous Vienna lecture that grew into the *Crisis*, Husserl suggests that Western philosophy is basically European.[135] Derrida, who is interested in this idea as early as his own edition of Husserl's essay on "The Origin of Geometry,"[136] later used it in an invidious defense of Heidegger. He claims that although Heidegger has been criticized for his apparent abandonment of Husserl, from the spiritual perspective of European man not Heidegger but Husserl was at fault.[137] As we shall see in the next chapter, Derrida further utilizes the spirit of Heidegger's theory to defend it against its letter.

Third, Derrida presents a generally Heideggerian critique of other theories. This critique, inspired by the spirit of Heidegger's theory, is directed against other theories, including Heidegger's. For instance, Derrida's attack on Sartre in "Les Fins de l'homme"[138] creatively repeats, but repeats nonetheless, points previously raised by Heidegger in the "Letter on Humanism."

In his remarks on Sartre, whom he evidently respects, Beaufret is mainly concerned to draw an ever clearer, more radical distinction between Heidegger and his French admirer. The relative calm of Beaufret's remarks pales before the violence of Derrida's attack that manifests no respect and yields no quarter. Derrida has said that although none of his work would have been possible without Heidegger,[139] in everything that he writes there is a distance with respect to Heidegger's own themes.[140] Yet here the reputed distance is literally invisible in the midst of a veritable catalogue of Sartre's faults arising from an alleged failure to understand Heidegger's theory.

Derrida's lecture can be regarded as an application of Heidegger's effort, namely the effort to distance his own theory of Dasein from the sciences of human being, to the French philosophical concern with anthropological humanism at the end of the War. His point is simply to recall, against the initial French anthropological reading of Heidegger, Heidegger's own proscription of any conflation between philosophy and anthropology.

In his "Letter on Humanism," Heidegger responds to Sartre without ever coming to grips with any single Sartrean text. Following Heidegger in his lecture, Derrida offers an excoriating, clearly Heideggerian reply to Sartre, again without ever coming to grips with any single Sartrean text.[141]

The title of the lecture contains a triple reference to the humanist concept of man, as Derrida makes clear through three quotations placed in exergue concerning: Kant's view of human being as an end in itself, Sartre's remark that ontology enables one to determine the ends of human being, and Foucault's comprehension of human being as the result of a recent movement whose end is perhaps near. At the end of the war, Derrida notes, the French philosophical discussion was dominated by the humanist theme. Humanism peaks in Sartre's position based on "the monstrous translation" of Dasein as "human reality" adopted – according to Derrida, who momentarily forgets Kojève – under Sartre's influence, as a warrant of the tendency to read or not to read Heidegger.[142]

142

Following Heidegger's objection to Descartes, Derrida contends that Sartre fails to question the unity of human being and, worse still, collapses the distinction between the philosophical and the human subject. In this way, humanism and anthropology, the themes common to existentialists of all stripes, Marxists, spiritualists, as well as social democrats and Christian democrats, are linked to an anthropological reading of Hegel, Husserl and, "perhaps worst of all [un contresens, peut-être le plus grave]" to Heidegger.[143]

Derrida has written widely on the positions of Husserl, Heidegger, and Hegel. His writings on the theories of Hegel and Husserl apply Heideggerian insights, often very critically, to their positions. *Being and Time* presents incompatible views of transcendental phenomenological truth (*veritas transcendentalis*)[144] and a hermeneutical conception based on the circle of the understanding.[145] If truth is based on a hermeneutical circle, traditional philosophical claims for absolute truth cannot be sustained. In Derrida's writings on Hegel, one of the main themes is the application of this Heideggerian insight to questioning Hegel's idea of absolute knowledge.[146]

There is a strongly Heideggerian thrust to all of Derrida's writings on Husserl. An example is the lengthy introduction to his edition of Husserl's manuscript on the "Origins of Geometry,"[147] with which Derrida first broke into print. A prominent theme here is his complaint that Husserl fails to "problematize" history.[148] Another is his "Saussurian" approach[149] to the problem of the sign in Husserl's thought, centering on the question – present in the later Heidegger, prominently in the "Letter on Humanism" – of whether Husserlian phenomenology escapes or could even conceivably escape from a metaphysical presupposition.

In *Being and Time*, Heidegger notes the traditional approach to being as "presence" (*Anwesenheit*).[150] He amplifies this point in a late essay through the remark that metaphysics thinks entities in a representational manner through presence.[151] In a lengthy passage, in which the Heideggerian genealogy of his analysis of Husserl is manifest, Derrida writes:

> The most general form of our question is thus indicated: does pheno-
> menological necessity, the precision and the subtlety of Husserlian
> analysis, the demands to which it responds and that we must take into
> consideration, nevertheless dissimulate a metaphysical presupposition?
> Don't the demands hide a dogmatic or speculative adherence which,
> surely, would not keep phenomenological criticism outside itself,
> would not be a remainder of unthought naïveté, but would *constitute*
> phenomenology in its interior, in its critical project and the instituting
> value of its own premises: precisely in what it will soon acknowledge
> as the origin and guarantee of all value, the "principle of principles,"
> that is the originarily given evidence, the *present* or *presence* of
> meaning in a full and originary intuition. In other terms, we will not
> ask if this or that metaphysical inheritance was able, here or there, to

143

limit the vigilance of a phenomenologist, but whether the *phenomenological* form of this vigilance is not already ordered by metaphysics itself.[152]

Derrida's reading of Heidegger's theory as a nonanthropological humanism presupposes Husserl's objection to the conflation of philosophy and anthropology as psychologism. In this respect, the main difference between Heidegger and Derrida is that the latter generalizes the problem of how to read the former's theory to the positions of Hegel and Husserl as well. The anthropological reading that is incorrect for Husserl's, for Hegel's, as well as for Heidegger's views only echoes Husserl's misapprehension of *Being and Time* as "an anthropological deviation from transcendental phenomenology."[153] The result, despite progress in the French discussion, is to amalgamate the positions of Hegel, Husserl, and Heidegger as instances of the recurrence of humanist metaphysics. On behalf of Heidegger, Derrida affirms that "the thought of what is specific to human being is inseparable from the question or the truth of Being."[154] For Heideggerian humanism rejects an anthropological approach to human being that is properly understood in terms of being.

Derrida's various criticisms of Hegel and Husserl[155] depend on the later Heidegger's view that metaphysics and, for that reason philosophy, has come to an end. Heidegger develops this view in a number of places, notably in "The End of Philosophy and the Task of Thinking," where he maintains *inter alia* that metaphysics thinks beings as a whole, that metaphysics thinks presence through representational thinking, that metaphysics is Platonism, and that metaphysics, hence, philosophy, has come to an end.[156] Derrida's critique of Husserl in *La Voix et le phénomène* is intended to show that Husserlian phenomenology is vitiated by the metaphysical presupposition of presence.[157]

Hegel criticizes the critical philosophy while remaining true to its spirit in order to complete Kant's Copernican Revolution. Derrida has a similar relation to Heidegger's theory. In his criticisms of Heidegger's writings, Derrida invariably judges the letter of the theory by its spirit. In his examination of Heidegger's destruction of traditional ontology, Derrida maintains that despite Heidegger's intention, he nonetheless remains faithful to traditional metaphysics.[158] In Derrida's reading, Heidegger fails to realize the intrinsic aim of his own theory. Derrida makes the same point again, on a different level, in his defense of Heidegger's theory against its association with Nazism, when he concedes that, despite Heidegger's critique of metaphysics, Heidegger's early thought remains metaphysical. This critique of Heidegger's early theory means in essence that it is not consistent with its own intention, that Heidegger was untrue to his central insight; but it should not be taken as the suggestion, veiled or otherwise, that Heidegger's central insight is untrue.

Fourth, Derrida advances his own position that is consistent with, arguably inspired by, his understanding of the spirit of Heidegger's theory. Derrida, of course, is not a philosopher in any usual sense. He just never says anything as straightforward as "here is my position," or "here is the view that I mean to defend against all objections," or "here are the arguments that suppport my view." In fact, he could not do so since part of his strategy is to avoid taking a definite stance that, in turn, could be relativized with respect to the ongoing discussion. So in conjunction with Bennington's recent study of his thought, Derrida provides a text intended to show that it overflows, hence "evades," the ideas that the scholar of his view employs to "capture" it.[159]

Nonetheless, Derrida's writings contain ideas and practices that can be loosely labeled as his rather than someone else's. What we can informally refer to as Derrida's position is composed of close exegesis of Heidegger's writings, criticism of other theories in terms of the spirit of those writings, as he interprets it, and a number of characteristic doctrines that are invariably either borrowed from, consistent with, or extensions of Heideggerian doctrines.

Here we see clearly the limits of the analogy between Hegel's relation to Kant and Derrida's to Heidegger. Despite the Kantian impulse in his thought, Hegel finally moves very far beyond Kant on any reasonable reading, as in his reinterpretation of the thing-in-itself in a way that arguably contradicts not only the letter but also the spirit of the critical philosophy. This is also the case for Gadamer, aside from Derrida the other important contemporary Heideggerian. Although in some ways, Gadamer remains very close to Heidegger, in other ways he transforms Heidegger's theory into its opposite. In the working out of implications of the hermeneutic circle, Gadamer is led to revalorize the tradition that Heidegger precisely devalorizes in his supposed destruction of the history of ontology. Yet this is never the case for Derrida, whose ideas never conflict with the spirit of Heidegger's later thought.[160]

It is not easy, despite the very number of Derrida's writings, to specify even their main theme. Certainly, a persistent theme is his attack on so-called logocentrism that he, like Heidegger, associates with the metaphysical tradition. Derrida's ongoing attack on the very idea of logocentrism is waged through his deconstruction of texts within the metaphysical, logocentric tradition. The practice of deconstruction rests on a concept that remains elusive since it has never clearly been stated in any of his many texts, but has clear precedents.

There is major difference of opinion about the idea of deconstruction in Derrida's writings. Some writers regard Derrida as taking over and developing the Heideggerian idea of deconstruction.[161] Others point to Derrida's inconsistent claims and practice concerning the translation of "Abbau" as "déconstruction."[162] At least one observer regards deconstruction as a basically Kantian enterprise.[163] Another is impressed by the way that deconstruction breaks down the distinction between philosophy and literature.[164]

In the present context, I will emphasize the phenomenological background that seems the most prominent component in Derrida's thought. Suffice it to say that the idea of deconstruction (*Abbau*)[165] has solid roots in the writings of the later Husserl[166] and throughout Heidegger's thought.[167] In *Being and Time*, Heidegger insists on the importance of the destruction of the history of ontology.[168] In lectures from the same year in which his main treatise appeared, Heidegger maintains that phenomenological method consists of three basic components: reduction, construction, and destruction. Heidegger describes his proposed deconstruction of metaphysics as a de-construction (*Abbau*). He speaks of "destruction" as "a critical process in which traditional concepts that at first must necessarily be employed are de-constructed down to the sources from which they were drawn."[169]

Derrida's own view of deconstruction can be understood as an effort to carry out the proposed destruction of the history of metaphysics in a way that escapes the problems of Heidegger's own effort, compromised in Derrida's eyes by its residual metaphysical character. Were he to be successful, he would carry out the intended Heideggerian critique of the Cartesian dream of self-founding and self-justifying philosophy in a way that circumscribes its limits from a place beyond it.[170]

With respect to philosophy, Derrida is a sceptic if scepticism is understood as the claim that theory of knowledge and knowledge are impossible within the framework of the philosophical tradition as it has been understood until now and as it can possibly take shape. He is, however, not a sceptic from a postmetaphysical, later Heideggerian stance located somewhere beyond philosophy. His characteristic doctrine of textuality extends Heidegger's rather traditional form of textual deconstruction in new ways intended to realize its intrinsic aim: through the assertion that everything is a text or can be represented in textual terms adumbrated in his objection to Foucault's reading of Descartes, and in the related assertion that texts cannot yield knowledge. He argues for the first claim by maintaining that there is nothing outside the text, that writing has primacy over speech, and that texts refer only to other texts. He argues for the second claim by attempting a deconstruction ranging over any possible statement in a text.

The latter amounts to an attack on referentiality, never so far as I know simply stated but rather exemplified. This attack is multiply determined by the views of Hegel, Husserl, and Saussure, among others. These and other thinkers take up a continental analogue of the problem of reference. In the first chapter of the *Phenomenology of Spirit*, Hegel argues against sense certainty as knowledge, roughly on the grounds that you cannot say what you mean or mean what you say.[171] Saussure's theory of language rests on the distinction between the signifier and the signified. Like Frege, who created the analytic form of the problem, Husserl distinguishes between sense (*Sinn*) and reference (*Bedeutung*).[172] His theory turns on the possible correlation of one with the other.

It is apparently inspired in the first instance by the Hegelian view that language is inadequate to refer. Starting with his published text, his edition of Husserl's essay on the "Origins of Geometry," Derrida similarly argues that any effort to refer to a real object turns out to refer to an unknowable absolute origin as well.[173] Through his reading of Husserl's theory from a Heideggerian perspective, he comes close to the point that Hegel makes about sense certainty, a point that he then generalizes to cover any effort to know on the basis of his view of the failure of metaphysics, construed as logocentrism.

In sum, although Derrida correctly regards himself as questioning Heideggerian ideas, and although he depicts his reading of the master's doctrines as a form of dissidence to the point of claiming that in everything he writes there is "a *separation* [écart] with respect to the Heideggerian problematic,"[174] he remains mainly, perhaps even wholly within the Heideggerian fold. For if he occasionally rejects the letter of Heidegger's position, he invariably accepts its spirit as he understands it. In Derrida's writings, as in so many writings of orthodox French Heideggerians, everything happens as if Heidegger's thought and Heidegger's thought alone formed the horizon of the "philosophical" enterprise in general, of thinking as it is supposedly still possible after Heidegger in the space delimited by his thought.

8

HEIDEGGER'S POLITICS AND FRENCH PHILOSOPHY

This is the second of two chapters[1] intended to provide a concrete account of Heidegger's influence in recent French philosophy. The preceding chapter provided a selective account of the impact of Heidegger's thought in the postwar French debate. Heidegger's theory influences recent French philosophy on three levels, including the small army of philosophers occupied with the exegesis of his thought; the frequent tendency to appropriate Heideggerian insights in the reading of various theories in the philosophical tradition; and as a source of insight informing the positions of leading French philosophers.

The present chapter will further demonstrate the influence of Heidegger's theory in postwar French philosophy through an account of the current state of the French phase of the ongoing controversy raised by Heidegger's turning to National Socialism. The French phase of the discussion of this problem will be understood in a wide sense as including not only French writers but also those occasional non-French participants, such as Karl Löwith, a German, Georg Lukács, a Hungarian, and above all Victor Farías, a Chilean, whose intervention provoked a heated response from French writers.

AN OUTLINE OF THE PROBLEM

The problem posed by Heidegger's political turning is unique. It is without parallel in the prior philosophical tradition; no other major philosopher turned to National Socialism. Even Lukács's support of Stalinism,[2] which might be said to mirror Heidegger's endorsement of German fascism, does not really compare for a variety of reasons:

- although an important thinker, arguably the most important Marxist philosopher, Lukács is less important;
- although long committed to orthodox Marxism, his Stalinist episode came to an end through explicit criticism of Stalin whereas Heidegger, who never clearly broke with Nazism, despite vague claims by himself and his closest supporters that he did so, apparently remained committed at least to an ideal form of Nazism;

- Lukács did not later organize an effort to conceal the nature and extent of his attachment to Stalinism as Heidegger did for his own continuing attachment to Nazism;
- unlike Lukács, whose Stalinism has been routinely acknowledged and sharply criticized even by his close supporters,[3] a number of Heidegger's followers, most recently Nolte, have long sought to deflect any criticism based on Heidegger's Nazism.

Heidegger's decision to affiliate with National Socialism has been the topic of often heated discussion over many years that still continues.[4] It is useful to distinguish between the facts as they are now known, a situation which is obviously subject to change as new material emerges, and Heidegger's reaction to them. In a remark about a lecture course on Nietzsche, already noted, Heidegger claimed that the course itself was intended to confront National Socialism.[5] Yet he *never* publicly distanced himself from Nazism. In 1945, he composed an article, published only posthumously, in which he claimed that his period as rector was meaningless.[6] In an interview with the German weekly *Der Spiegel* in 1966[7] that was withheld at his request until his death ten years later, he maintained that after 1934 he no longer made favorable statements about Nazism. Earlier favorable statements include his public endorsement of the *Führerprinzip*, in Heidegger's version the acknowledgment that the Führer alone is "the source of all German reality and its law now and in the future"[8] – after 1934.

On the basis of this scant information about what Heidegger thought and did on the political plane, there is a widespread view that after an initial enthusiasm he later turned against Nazism. This view of the matter, due to Heidegger himself, what we can call the official view, has since gained currency in the debate on his philosophy and his Nazism, and has been maintained in various ways by his closest supporters. Yet the facts do not support that interpretation.

Heidegger's indication that his Nietzsche lectures were intended as a critique of National Socialism is contradicted by evidence of a continued enthusiasm that belies this claim. Statements apparently favorable to Nazism were removed from notes of later lecture courses when they were later published. Although textual interpretation is always subject to disagreement, a number of passages clearly indicate Heidegger's continued commitment to Nazism well after the war. The most prominent and clearest example is a statement in a lecture course published with his cooperation in 1953: "The works that are being peddled about nowadays as the philosophy of National Socialism but have nothing whatever to do with the truth and greatness of this movement . . ."[9]

Observers have further been troubled by Heidegger's continued silence about this entire period, including his silence about the Holocaust, and what even his closest followers have on occasion seen as his insensitivity to the problems of the Holocaust. Many writers have been especially bothered by

Heidegger's claim, excised from the published version of a lecture delivered in 1949, that "agriculture is now a mechanized food industry, in essence the same as the manufacturing of corpses in gas chambers and extermination camps, the same as the blockade and starvation of nations, the same as the production of hydrogen bombs."[10] The most obvious thing to say about Heidegger's failure to distance himself from the Holocaust or even to take a clear position on the Holocaust is that from the perspective of his theory it was not possible to do so.[11]

The facts of the matter are not inherently controversial. The interpretation of the link between Heidegger's philosophical thought and political action is exceedingly difficult and highly controversial. This interpretation, an important exercise in hermeneutics, has led to a special cottage industry in the Heidegger literature centered on this and allied problems. Heidegger's turning to National Socialism raises problems on a least three distinct levels, including the interpretation of his thought, its reception in an already enormous and steadily growing literature, and the traditional, normative philosophical view of philosophy.

One problem concerns the link between Heidegger's philosophical thought and his political engagement. Although certainly deplorable, it is not philosophically interesting to know that Heidegger became a Nazi since many other Germans, including the vast majority of the philosophers who remained in Germany during the war, joined the German Nazi party.[12] Yet Heidegger was neither an ordinary German, since he was a philosopher, nor even an ordinary German philosopher. Obviously, he was distinguished from all the other German Nazis as the author of an unusually important philosophical theory. It becomes philosophically significant if a link can be shown between Heidegger's philosophical position and his political commitment. It is important to know whether Heidegger's turning to National Socialism follows from, or is in some way motivated by, his philosophical position; or whether, on the contrary, it is merely a contingent fact unrelated to or at least not dependent on his philosophical position.

A second cluster of problems concerns the reception of Heidegger's turn to Nazism, including its reception in the French philosophical discussion. Heidegger had numerous grounds to disguise the reasons for as well as the extent of his adherence to National Socialism, including the understandable desire, in personally difficult circumstances, to conceal his continued adherence to his personal vision of Nazism even after real Nazism was defeated. Other factors arguably include his alleged personal moral weakness, the supposed "inauthenticity" of his life, and assorted character flaws.

In defense of Heidegger, one might argue that his life was inseparable from the difficult historical period in which he lived. This argument, which is possible on Heidegger's behalf, although not necessarily convincing, is neither convincing nor even possible with respect to Heidegger's later students, those who, after the war, turned to his thought. It is disturbing that at this late date, when so much is known about Heidegger's political engagement, when sordid details have emerged about his denunciation of colleagues,[13] so many writers interested in his thought are hesitant, reluctant, unwilling to take up the matter, concerned to warn against the very idea of studying the link between his thought and his political commitment.[14]

Such well informed writers as Jean Wahl believe that although we need to be aware of Heidegger's political misdeeds, his thought can be separated from his Nazism.[15] Yet Heidegger's Nazism is not irrelevant but precisely relevant to an appreciation of his philosophical theory. It is always difficult to come to grips with a novel body of thought. Novel theories require a process of reception before they can be assimilated and evaluated. On occasion this process can extend over centuries, for instance in the ongoing efforts to come to comprehend Kant's *Critique of Pure Reason* and Hegel's *Phenomenology*, to say nothing of his *Science of Logic*, surely the darkest work of German idealism. It is difficult enough to comprehend an important new theory; but it is impossible to do so if a fundamental, or even a significant, element in that theory is hidden from view. And it is difficult to take the Heidegger discussion seriously to the extent that it handles the problem of the relation of his philosophical thought and political commitment through such strategems as sheer denial, mere silence, or even admonitions not to raise the problem at all.

A third set of problems concerns the normative self-image of philosophy. There is a longstanding controversy within philosophy about its social relevance.[16] This controversy opposes those who maintain that philosophy is socially irrelevant and those who maintain the contrary opinion. On one view of the matter, philosophy is the source of truth and knowledge in an absolute sense and absolutely indispensable for the good life. This flattering view of philosophy is placed in jeopardy by the political engagements of such powerful thinkers as Lukács the Stalinist but above all by Heidegger the Nazi. A philosopher cannot be indifferent to the fact that an apparent philosophical genius like Heidegger adhered to Nazism. There is an obvious paradox that reflects on philosophy's flattering view of its own social relevance. For ordinary statements such as that Heidegger is a great philosopher, that philosophy is socially indispensable or at least socially useful, and that National Socialism is evil, the clearest example of absolute evil in our time, statements that appear true in isolation, are clearly incompatible with each other.

FRENCH DISCUSSION OF HEIDEGGER'S NAZISM

At the close of the Weimar Republic, many Germans, including many German intellectuals, turned to Nazism as a purported third way between the twin evils of liberalism and Bolshevism. Heidegger's turning to National Socialism was not exceptional, exceptional only in virtue of his unusual philosophical status as the author of an unusually important philosophical theory. Like the general banality of evil, Heidegger's Nazism was and seemed to be unremarkable. It only began to attract attention after the war when he was called to account for his actions and sought to defend himself. It is at that point that a philosophical debate about Heidegger's Nazism began that initially was largely conducted among members of the philosophical corporation, a rather exclusive society composed of those masters of blindness and insight. It is only recently, in the wake of the publication of Victor Farías's study, *Heidegger and Nazism* (1987)[17] that the debate has been brought to the attention of the wider intellectual public.

The problem – roughly how to understand the link between Heidegger's philosophical position and his allegiance to National Socialism – is simple to state. Yet its analysis, like that of most philosophical problems, is endlessly complex as each facet of the argument calls forth a counterargument. The resolution of philosophical concerns, reputedly like psychoanalysis, is interminable.

As an aid in grasping a complex controversy, a distinction can be drawn between Heidegger's critics, who think that the problem is real and significant, and his defenders, who think there is less than meets the eye. Heidegger's critics discern more than an accidental relation between Heidegger's philosophical thought and political commitment, and hence criticize Heidegger's thought for what seem to be its political consequences. His defenders maintain that Heidegger's philosophy and his politics have no more than an accidental relation so that his political misadventures reflect neither favorably but certainly not unfavorably on his philosophical position.

This disagreement illustrates the venerable concern with the relation of theory and practice that has aroused widespread discussion but no agreement throughout the philosophical tradition. The many variations put forward in the debate on Heidegger's Nazism can be collected around two main assertions: either the relation between Heidegger's thought and his political commitment, more precisely between fundamental ontology and National Socialism, is purely contingent, in which case there is no substantive problem, certainly no specifically philosophical problem; or the relation derives from his philosophy, in which case there is a serious philosophical problem on various levels, beginning with the way that his commitment to Nazism, on the assumption that Nazism is evil, reflects on his philosophy. Although Heidegger never wrote an ethics, in fact rejected the very idea of the philosophical analysis of values,[18] there would be a clearly ethical problem, whatever the philosophical interest of his theory, if it could be shown that his philosophical theory is linked in some basic way to fascist politics.

It is a matter of fact that up to now the debate on Heidegger's Nazism has mainly occurred in France. In retrospect, the French debate on Heidegger and politics occurred in three main phases or waves.[19] We can distinguish between the factual issue of who intervened in the debate, at what point, in which way, and what, for want of a better term, we can call the dialectic of the ensuing discussion.

The initial wave occurred in 1946 and 1947 in the pages of *Les Temps Modernes*, a leading French intellectual journal, founded and edited by Sartre and his close associates. The discussion included contributions by Karl Löwith, Maurice de Gandillac and Alfred de Towarnicki. Löwith, who was Heidegger's first graduate student and sometime colleague, is well known for his own philosophical work. Gandillac, who may have been the first French colleague to come in contact with Heidegger after the war, was later a professor of philosophy at the Sorbonne. Towarnicki is a journalist who was later close to Beaufret. They were answered by Eric Weil, a former assistant to Ernst Cassirer, and Alphonse De Waelhens. Weil, an emigrant to France from Nazi Germany, later had a distinguished career in French philosophy. De Waelhens, a Belgian phenomenologist, published the first French language study of Heidegger in 1942.[20] The discussion temporarily ended with rejoinders by Löwith and De Waelhens.

With respect to ongoing discussion of the problem, the importance of this initial wave of the discussion resides in the pioneering identification of some main issues and strategies that run throughout later phases of the ensuing debate. We can differentiate between contingentist and necessitarian analyses, roughly the claims that the link between Heidegger's fundamental ontology and his Nazism is merely contingent or not contingent but in some sense necessary.

In the first stage of the discussion, the contingentist reading of the relation between Heidegger's thought and politics is represented by Gandillac and Towarnicki who maintain that Heidegger was politically naive and only unknowingly attracted to National Socialism. They imply that Heidegger was drawn to Nazism because of his basically untutored lack of awareness of the outside world. This line of argument relies on the familiar view of the philosopher as uninterested in or at least unaware of social reality, a view illustrated early on by Aristotle's account of Thales's supposed fall into a well while looking at the stars, appropriate for a thinker who claims that all is water. On this view, the philosopher is competent only in the library. A similar view has recently been restated by Gadamer, who claims that a philosopher not only has no comparative advantage, in fact is actually at a disadvantage, in understanding politics.[21]

In the initial phase of the discussion, the contrary, necessitarian reading is represented by Löwith. He holds that Heidegger's turning to National Socialism is explicable only through a main principle of his position: existence reduced to itself reposes only on itself in the face of nothing. This is precisely the view that Koyré identified as Heidegger's basic contribution in his introduction to the first French translation of a Heideggerian text.[22]

In response to Löwith, De Waelhens unveils a main defensive strategy in asserting that Heidegger's detractors are insufficiently familiar with his theory. From this angle of vision, finally only specialists in Heideggerian exegesis, precisely those concerned only to explain but not to judge the master's thought, are capable of evaluating it.

In practice, most scholars of Heidegger's thought steadfastly reject any effort to associate his political convictions with his philosophy. Criticisms raised by such obvious defectors from the Heideggerian fold as Thomas Sheehan,[23] Rainer Marten,[24] Michael Zimmerman,[25] and to a lesser degree Otto Pöggeler[26] and Dieter Thomä[27] are countered by such equally knowledgeable Heidegger defenders as Friedrich-Wilhelm von Herrmann in Germany, in the United States by William Richardson, and above all in France by Beaufret and a host of others, including François Fédier and Pierre Aubenque, and in a restricted sense Jacques Derrida and Philippe Lacoue-Labarthe. In France, to the best of my knowledge at present Dominique Janicaud is the only philosopher strongly identified with Heidegger[28] who has taken an openly critical stance.[29]

In the space of a year, with the exception of Löwith's paper, the first wave unfolded as a calm debate among French colleagues. In retrospect, the very calmness of the initial phase of the French discussion was surprising in a country that was defeated in the Second World War by Nazi Germany with which Heidegger clearly identified. In comparison to the compact, civil, well defined nature of the first wave, the second wave of the French discussion was more amorphous, less compact, more international, and considerably more strident. Its limits can arbitrarily be fixed between 1948, when Lukács's belligerent, even bellicose defense of Marxism against the perceived threat of existentialism appeared in French, and 1968 when Jean-Michel Palmier's examination of Heidegger's political writings, the first such volume in French, was published.[30] Lukács criticized Heidegger's *Being and Time* as prefascist in the initial edition,[31] before expounding this criticism at greater length in a discussion of the "Letter on Humanism" later added in an appendix.[32]

In the initial wave of the French debate, the normally abstract character of philosophical discussion is compounded by relatively sparse reference to the relevant Heideggerian writings and their complete inaccessability in French translation. In the second wave, more than a dozen years later this lacuna was corrected by Jean-Pierre Faye. Faye, who was later derided by Beaufret as a mere sociologist,[33] published several Heideggerian texts relevant to any debate on the philosophical import of Heidegger's political turn. These include Heidegger's rectorial address, his public homage for Albert Leo Schlageter, a German executed for terrorist acts who was later transformed into a kind of Nazi saint,[34] and Heidegger's famous remark on supposedly authentic National Socialism.[35]

Obviously, academic careers were at risk in the commitment to the theory of a major philosopher. Since the personal stakes were high, it is not surprising that the second phase of the French debate on Heidegger's Nazism was tough, even unyielding, at a point in time before the relevent materials were readily accessible. It quickly assumed a more personal, *ad hominem* character when pertinent Heideggerian writings were made available in translation. The intensity of the debate was heightened by Faye and Fédier, who represent opposing points of view. Faye noted close parallels between Heidegger's language in the translated materials and Nazi terminology, due to the alleged Nazification of the German language. François Fédier rebutted perceived attacks on Heidegger.

At this point in the mid-1960s, Heidegger had for all intents and purposes already been naturalized as a "French" thinker. Fédier's defense was directed against writings due to three foreign writers: Guido Schneeberger, Theodor W. Adorno and Paul Hühnerfeld.[36] With the possible exception of Pierre Aubenque, at this late date, after the death of Beaufret, Fédier remains as the main, perhaps even the only important, proponent of the idea that from the appropriate perspective every objection raised against Heidegger's politics can be explained away.

In hindsight, the second wave of the debate produced an extension of the expert defense first raised by De Waelhens. This is the view that only a Heidegger expert is entitled to criticize Heidegger. In France, where mastery of the German texts provides a distinct comparative advantage, acceptance of this view has often led to the attempt to show that critics of Heidegger's turning to National Socialism are insufficiently versed in German, or in Heidegger's admittedly peculiar use of the German language. In appealing to this strategy, Heidegger's defenders are guided by the conviction that when we examine the texts it becomes apparent that what his critics have seen as problematic is only apparently so.[37] Fédier, for instance, routinely poses as someone who knows German in the appropriate manner, presumably but improbably better than such native German speakers critical of Heidegger as Löwith, or later Pöggeler, Marten and Thomä. Fédier suggests that a "real" translation of the rectorial address will remove the traces of Nazism injected into it.[38]

Heidegger's deep influence in French philosophy has led to an explicit tendency, naturally strongest among Heideggerians, to identify French philosophy with Heidegger's thought. Fédier, at present Heidegger's most uncritical representative in France after Beaufret's death, spoke for others as well in stating that "the interest for philosophy today is inseparable from the interest for Heidegger."[39]

The third, most recent wave of the French debate began with the publication of Victor Farías's study *Heidegger et le nazisme* in French in the fall of 1987. Numerous French philosophers regarded this work as tantamount to an attack on French philosophy. Hugo Ott, the author of a critical biography of Heidegger, accurately captured this reaction in the observation that "in France a sky has fallen in – *the sky of the philosophers*."[40] This reaction is understandable for two reasons: the extreme extent to which French philosophy since the end of the war has continued to identify with Heidegger's thought, and the well known French reluctance even now to reopen wounds caused by the war. It is common knowledge in France that at the end of the war there was in effect a tacit agreement among representatives of all political tendencies not to address the French defeat in 1940 and not to address the moral failures of the collaborationist Vichy government.[41] This desire has led to what has often been seen as a French inability to confront this phase of French history. An example among many is the recent decision of the French court system, later reversed, to reject an indictment for crimes against humanity brought against Paul Touvier, a French war criminal who was twice condemned to death in absentia and later pardoned.[42]

Since the third wave of the French debate may still be under way, any description must remain provisional, subject to change, as further publications emerge. What is clear is that it contains two subphases: an initial phase lasting several months, including an almost immediate, passionate, often raucous and strident series of reactions to Farías's study by writers who attacked and defended the book, Heidegger, and even each other; and a later subphase, still under way, in which scholarly studies have been appearing in response to the renewed controversy. Farías's study obviously changes the debate on the link between Heidegger's thought and political commitment. It transforms what was initially a staid, austere discussion, mainly between philosophers, differing from other such discussions only in that its theme was unusually important, into what for academic circles, even for French academic circles, is a very violent debate.

This part of the third wave was mainly played out in daily newspapers, as well as weekly and biweekly journals. It was provoked, even incited by the sharply worded preface to Farías's book by Christian Jambet, a former *nouveau philosophe*. Through a reference to the film *Night and Fog* (*Nuit et brouillard*), he drew a connection between Heidegger's thought and Nazi concentration camps: "Heidegger has the merit of making ontology the question of our time. But how can we accept that philosophy, born of Socrates's trial for leading a just life, ends in the twilight where Heidegger wanted to see the end of the gods, but which was only the time of *Night and Fog*?"[43]

The other subphase of the third wave is represented by a remarkable series of books devoted to the theme of Heidegger's thought and his politics. In retrospect, this phase can be held to begin in 1975 in the publication of a solid study by Pierre Bourdieu, of Heidegger's so-called political ontology against the background of the historical context. Farías's book was published in October 1987. After the shock caused by this event that rapidly became l'affaire Farías, Bourdieu quickly updated his work.[44]

In an extraordinary fit of French philosophical creativity, in the short period running from that October 1987 until May 1988, unusually short by philosophical standards, no less than five other books appeared on the general theme of Heidegger and politics. These books were due respectively to Lyotard,[45] Ferry and Renaut,[46] Fédier,[47] Derrida,[48] and Lacoue-Labarthe.[49] Since that time only Janicaud's book[50] on this theme has been published, although occasional journal articles have continued to appear as the controversy continues to simmer.

MAIN ASPECTS OF THE THIRD WAVE

Farías's controversial study forms an important link in the ongoing French debate on Heidegger's Nazism. It presents a form of the more general necessitarian thesis advanced earlier by others, such as Löwith, in the French Heidegger debate. Like Löwith, Farías sees a relation of continuity between Heidegger's life and times, his thought, and his political engagement.

Yet Farías's discussion differs in several main ways from Löwith's. One difference is that he is considerably less successful in drawing attention to, and certainly less able to analyze, the claimed continuity between Heidegger's philosophical thought and politics. Another difference is that through extensive archival research he was able to discover numerous, relevant details. Together with Ott's important biographical study, the result is to disclose a fuller, more rounded – and, in virtue of the comparatively richer detail, particularly in Ott's work, an even more disturbing – picture of the relation of Heidegger's political commitment and philosophical theory to his sociocultural background in a small town in Southwestern Germany in the late nineteenth and early twentieth centuries. Then there is the difference in tone between Löwith's sober discussion, on the usual high plane of philosophical abstraction, intended to link Heidegger's theory of being and his commitment to Nazism, and Farias's similar effort, in what has been described as the style of a criminal dossier. As a result, Farias has become a kind of official enemy for Heidegger's defenders in which attacks on his book tend to replace a careful consideration of the many issues arising from the link between Heidegger's philosophy and politics.[51]

The new phase of the debate, its most concentrated, philosophically richest form to date, is to an important extent composed of a series of reactions to Farías's book. In this debate, the works by Lyotard on the one hand and Ferry and Renaut on the other address peripheral issues. Lyotard's strangely vague book scores some points against other participants in the French debate concerning what he strangely insists is a French problem.[52] This suggestion is correct if taken to imply that it is above all a topic that has attracted attention in France. Yet it is difficult to comprehend if it is meant to suggest that France or French philosophy were separately or collectively somehow responsible for the Heideggerian entanglement of philosophy and Nazism.

As in some of their earlier studies,[53] the book by Ferry and Renaut is intended to call attention to a supposedly antihumanist tendency in recent

French philosophy and French thought in general, based on a reading of structuralism as a form of antihumanism. Yet this line of argument is problematic. For instance, Ferry and Renaut fail to analyze or even to acknowledge the differences in the various, so-called structuralist views of subjectivity that lead to the questionable classification, say, of Foucault not only as a structuralist, an appellation he explicitly contests,[54] but as an antihumanist.

The five remaining books can be grouped into three broad categories as variant analyses of the relation of Heidegger's philosophical thought and of his politics as either contingent or necessary. In general terms, Fédier maintains that this relation is merely contingent whereas Bourdieu and later Janicaud independently argue that it is necessary. A compromise in the form of a more limited version of the necessitarian analysis is sketched in related fashion by both Lacoue-Labarthe and Derrida.

The allergy of orthodox Heideggerians to Sartre's theory is matched, even exceeded, by their aversion to Farías's study. Fédier's discussion consists of two parts: a lengthy attack intended to refute every significant objection raised by Farías against Heidegger, and an alternative analysis intended to explain Heidegger's adherence to Nazism in a way that does not incriminate his philosophical theory. In Sartrean terminology, we can say that Fédier attributes Farías's critique simply to bad faith. His own, alternative explanation innovates in introducing a form of scepticism to account for the supposed inability in 1933, when Heidegger joined the Nazi party, to foresee what it would later become.[55] He strongly, but unconvincingly asserts that how Nazism would later evolve was clear only on September 1, 1939.[56] Yet this line of argument is problematic since the likelihood that Nazism would develop as it in fact did was considerably clearer than, say, the famous Aristotelian problem of whether a sea battle will occur tomorrow.[57] The main thrust of Nazism was already clear in the party program in 1920, restated in detail in Hitler's *Mein Kampf* and elsewhere, and, as Heidegger later explicitly conceded, understood by Jews and "liberal" politicians.[58] And if the standard for moral responsibility is anything resembling divine foreknowledge then no one, perhaps not even *deus absconditus*, is ever responsible for anything.

Bourdieu and Janicaud carry further the contextualist effort to understand Heidegger's Nazi turning against his sociocultural background and his philosophical position. In retrospect, Bourdieu's discussion that provided early, but important corrections on a number of details, including Heidegger's anti-Semitism that can now no longer be denied,[59] is doubly distinguished. One point is his methodological decision to refuse the distinction between philosophy and politics in favor of a double reading (*double lecture*) of Heideggerian texts. For Bourdieu, Heidegger's texts are elaborated and must be read as "inseparably political and philosophical through the reference to two social spaces to which correspond two mental spaces."[60] Bourdieu's refusal to isolate the philosophical and political components of Heidegger's corpus enables him – this is the other point – to provide an interpretation of Heidegger's thought against its sociocultural background. In this respect, he continues the task undertaken by Löwith, Farías, Ott and others, but rarely pursued in the French discussion, of providing a unitary interpretation of Heidegger's life and thought.

Bourdieu, who relates the political and philosophical aspect of Heidegger's corpus, is comparatively stronger in analyzing the former aspect. Janicaud, who also seeks to grasp Heidegger's thought in its context, is comparatively stronger in analyzing the texts themselves. For Janicaud, Heidegger's failure to elaborate a political doctrine – like many others in the French debate, such as Aubenque, he holds that *Being and Time* is not a political but an apolitical book[61] – is philosophically and politically significant, leading to the effort to found an authentic politics.[62] This effort is pursued in the rectorial address that Janicaud analyzes in detail. Janicaud sees the later Heidegger's radicalization of his earlier thought, roughly the destinal theory of being announced in the "Letter on Humanism" and other later writings, as impeding an understanding of the lessons following from his turn to Nazism.[63]

On the deepest level, as Fichte recognized, philosophy is a matter of personal commitment prior to rational justification. For that reason, it is about as amenable to change through reasoned argument as is religious conviction. When so much is known – except for a few philosophical dinosaurs, such Heideggerian true believers as Beaufret, Fédier and Aubenque in France, Richardson in America, von Herrmann and from a different perspective Gadamer in Germany, or Vattimo in Italy – for even the most ardent Heideggerian it is now too late simply to maintain that Heidegger never did anything that could justify the objections raised against him or that those who criticize him are simply mediocre thinkers.[64] In comparison, the works by Derrida and Lacoue-Labarthe represent a new effort by philosophers strongly influenced by Heidegger's position to find a way to "save," if not the man, or his entire theory, at least his later thought that has long been influential in French philosophical discussion.[65]

There are levels of possible Heideggerian interpretation of the link between his thought and politics, of which the first, suggested by Heidegger himself, is that his political episode is simply meaningless. Derrida and Lacoue-Labarthe, close students of Heidegger who disagree with him in regarding this episode as meaningful, exploit Heidegger's suggestion of a turning in his thought to "save" his later thought.[66]

Heidegger suggests that through the radicalization of his concern with being he was led beyond metaphysics that is identical with philosophy, hence led beyond philosophy. This suggestion clearly bears on the proper interpretation of the continuity or discontinuity of Heidegger's position as it develops over time. Where Heidegger sees continuity with difference in the development of his position through the later elaboration of his original beginning as the other beginning, Derrida and Lacoue-Labarthe see differ-ence without continuity, in other words a conceptual break. Their respective analyses turn on the reading of National Socialism as metaphysics – in Lacoue-Labarthe's case as metaphysical humanism – and the supposition that Heidegger's early thought, but not his later thought, was also metaphysical. From this angle of vision, each maintains that Heidegger's Nazi turning followed from the metaphysical character of his early thought that is left behind in the turning.[67] For both, as Heidegger turns away from metaphysics, he also turns away from National Socialism.

Derrida and Lacoue-Labarthe both follow the same line of argument. Both attempt to "save" Heidegger's later theory by reading it, against Heidegger's own self-understanding, as reflecting a basic discontinuity. Both rest their defense of Heidegger's later theory on the supposition of a break between Heidegger I and Heidegger II, between his early metaphysical theory and his later nonmetaphysical or postmetaphysical theory.

The line of analysis elaborated by Derrida is first stated by Lacoue-Labarthe who in turn later reworks it after it is taken up by Derrida. In a recent collection of papers,[68] Lacoue-Labarthe maintains that the rectorial address is an effort to found the conservative Nazi political revolution in philosophy. Heidegger's political engagement, leading to the collapse of Heidegger's fundamental ontology, was metaphysical, and his effort to lead National Socialism was basically spiritual.

Lacoue-Labarthe's less radical version of the same basic strategy accords full responsibility to Heidegger for the link between fundamental ontology and Nazism based on the hegemony of the spiritual and philosophical over the political[69] rooted in his early thought.[70] To an even greater extent than Derrida, Lacoue-Labarthe discerns a discontinuity between Heidegger's early and later texts in which he supposedly broke with Nazism.[71]

According to Lacoue-Labarthe, the link between Nazism, humanism and the early Heideggerian theory is not difficult to discern. He goes so far, in a simply incredible statement, as simplistically to equate Nazism and human-ism. Although philosophers have made all kinds of wild statements over the last two and half millenia, Lacoue-Labarthe, not to be outdone, straight-forwardly claims that "Nazism is a humanism in that it rests on a deter-mination of *humanitas* that it sees as more powerful, that is more effective, than any other."[72] If this is the case, then in basing the humanism in his early view on a determinate view of *humanitas*, what Heidegger calls the tradi-tional, metaphysical view of humanism, Heidegger and Nazism naturally came together. Yet it is exceedingly difficult to see how Nazism can reasonably be understood as humanism, anymore than, say, Stalinism is humanism. And to call Nazis humanists without qualification, in effect to equate humanism and Nazism, is to imply that anyone interested in another, more traditional form of humanism, such as Sartre, is a Nazi, or at least a potential Nazi. This is an obvious error. Further, this overly general way of using the concept of humanism fails either to explain how and why Heidegger turned to Nazism or to identify anything typical of Nazism.

Even more than Lacoue-Labarthe, Derrida illustrates the widespread tendency to separate Heidegger the thinker from Heidegger the Nazi enthusiast. Derrida, who has long portrayed himself as a member of the intellectual left wing, has recently used his important intellectual position to restrict discussion about the political involvements of both Paul de Man and Heidegger. In his recent writings, he has attempted to downplay the anti-Semitic leanings of Paul de Man as insignificant.[73] He has threatened legal action to prevent the republication of an interview he gave concerning Heidegger's Nazism.[74] And in a recent controversy played out in the pages of the *New York Review of Books*, he has raised a series of obstacles to publication of relevant materials, such as denying the threat of legal action and calling attention to points of translation, that taken together have the effect of deflecting attention away from the deeper, more important issue of Heidegger's Nazism.[75]

Derrida elaborates the supposedly limited connection between Heidegger's early theory and National Socialism – that is a connection limited to the early phase of his theory only – by emphasizing what he regards as a basic difference between Heidegger's early concern with metaphysics and later concern with postmetaphysical thought. According to Derrida, closely following Heidegger, there is a difference in kind between Heidegger's initially metaphysical position and the later position that is no longer philosophy. Derrida's variant of this line of argument turns on a reading of Heidegger's conception of spirit. In an ingenious meditation on Heidegger's use of the terms "Geist," "geistig," and "geistlich,"[76] he contends that Heidegger's spiritual commitment to Nazism was later overcome, for instance in an essay on Trakl,[77] by transcending metaphysics.[78]

Derrida's version of this argument is exceedingly radical since he holds that even in 1933 when Heidegger adhered to Nazism the latter understood this political movement in a spiritual sense. This is, I believe, at least partially correct since study of Heidegger's writings, such as the infamous rectorial address, shows Heidegger's frequent emphasis on the link between his own theory, philosophy, National Socialism, and the realization of the essence of the German people. The latter idea derives from the concept of the *Volk* that the Nazi ideologists took over from nineteenth-century, rightwing German *Volksideologie*. Yet there is clearly a political aspect to Heidegger's Nazi turning as well, for instance in his public acceptance of the infamous *Führerprinzip*, what may have been his adherence to the Hitler cult, his conviction that there is anything like an authentic essence of Nazism that the Nazis failed to realize and may not even have perceived, and so on.

For Derrida, the problem is simply Heidegger's spiritual concern with Nazism that is later overcome. Yet this adherence is not confined to his early writings, to his thought prior to the turning. For it is demonstrably present in his later thought as well. Derrida simply fails to realize that there are abundant references of the same kind, for instance in the *Beiträge zur Philosophie*, after Heidegger supposedly broke with Nazism, that is after he resigned as rector of the University of Freiburg and after the first series of Nietzsche lectures.[79] Further, it is inconsistent for Derrida to portray the early Heidegger as concerned with spirit, and, by inference, with the problem of humanism. For the basis of his attack on Sartre, as noted above, is his objection to Sartre's humanist reading of Heidegger's theory.

SOME REMARKS ON THE FRENCH DISCUSSION

The French debate on the link between Heidegger's philosophy and politics amply illustrates the influence, even the fascination that his theory has long exerted on French philosophy. This is doubly apparent: in the ease with which, despite widespread awareness of his Nazi turning, he became the leading French philosopher of the postwar period; and the capacity of his theory to counter objections based on its link to his politics.

The "Letter on Humanism," as has been pointed out, is a key element in understanding how Heidegger became and continues to be the French master thinker of this period. Above it was pointed out that Heidegger's concept of the turning in his thought is usually regarded from an anticontextualist angle of vision. But if we remember Heidegger's difficult personal situation when he wrote this text, then the turning appears in a different light as responding to both philosophical and political imperatives, in short as a mainly strategical move determined by his then difficult political situation as well as his continued adherence to a form of Nazism. Heidegger's suggestion in this text that he had turned away from any political commitment is in effect a simple but simply misleading reassurrance in the face of his apparently continued commitment to Nazism. But it was effective in France where the majority of intellectuals, like the population as a whole, were disinclined to rake over the coals of the recent past and also perhaps overly willing to accept on faith the idea that like other philosophers Heidegger was not worldly wise.

The philosophically interesting question, we have said, is not whether Heidegger was naive, which is possible, or a Nazi, since by any ordinary standard that point can no longer be reasonably denied, but rather whether his Nazism can be said to follow from, or to be based on, his philosophy. The Heidegger Archives in Marbach are not open to the public and his *Nachlass* is controlled by his family. Heidegger's defenders are well placed to obstruct the release of documents, to "censor" what has been released by removing politically incriminating passages, particularly in writings after the rectorate to perpetuate the fiction that Heidegger later broke with Nazism, and generally to impede efforts to arrive at a balanced judgment based on full and fair access to the relevant materials.

In the French debate to date, the two major lines of defense that have so far emerged include the related claims that Heidegger's detractors are insufficiently versed in his thought or in the German language. The latter claim explains the otherwise incomprehensible, vigorous struggle, with clear political implications, over the proper translation of key terms in Heidegger's theory. This type of linguistic defense is possible in France or in the US but not in Germany. It is further possible to hold that some of Heidegger's critics misunderstand him in whole or in part, although this must be shown in detail. Textual interpretation is difficult at best and Heidegger's texts present unusual interpretive difficulties. Yet it is implausible to contend that authorities on Heidegger's thought – such as Sheehan, Zimmerman and Kisiel in the US, Löwith, Pöggeler and Marten in Germany, and Janicaud in France – simply base their criticism on misunderstandings of it.

Efforts to demonstrate a merely contingent link between Heidegger's thought and politics are problematic. At this late date, it is about as convincing as suggestions that the earth is flat to maintain that there is no substantive link between Heidegger's thought and his political commitment. Defenders of this view have a doubly difficult task. First, it is necessary to clear away the obstacle raised by textual analyses pointing to a link. Second, even if adequate rejoinders could be found to objections raised by Janicaud, Bourdieu, Tertulian and others who identify the suggested link, no argument could demonstrate the nonexistence of a relation between Heidegger's philosophical theory and his political commitment.

Despite the improbable nature of the claim that Heidegger the Nazi philosopher is wholly without blame, it continues to be urged by some of his staunchest defenders. Heidegger's unconditional defenders, for whom he in effect can do no wrong, in the French discussion writers such as Beaufret, Fédier and Aubenque, attempt to do too much. They wish to rescue Heidegger's entire thought and life by insisting on a reading of Heidegger the thinker and Heidegger the man as wholly unrelated and each as wholly free from blame. If Heidegger's thought is not the source of his politics, then one cannot reason backward from his politics to impugn his thought. And if his greatest fault is to be naive in the way that all philosophers are supposedly naive, as conceptual country bumpkins visiting at the city slickers' carnival of life, then Heidegger the man is no more responsible for his adherence to Nazism than anyone else who was similarly deceived.

The comparatively more modest attempt, put forward in the French debate by Lacoue-Labarthe and Derrida in effect candidly concedes that his early thought leads to Nazism. Yet although this weaker, fallback claim by some of Heidegger's most ingenious defenders might seem advantageous in view of its concessions, its willingness to defend a smaller amount of terrain, it is open to significant objections.

One problem concerns the assumption of a difference – an assumption made by Derrida and Lacoue-Labarthe, for example – not only in degree but in kind between the earlier and later forms of Heidegger's theory as respectively metaphysics and nonmetaphysics or postmetaphysics. The two stages of

Heidegger's position are separated by a period of development during which the initial statement of the position, or fundamental ontology, is transformed by him into his later theory, or thinking, where the thinking that is to come is understood as being no longer philosophy. Through his distinction between the first beginning and the other beginning Heidegger insists on a radical change in his position; but his very distinction between these phases of his theory supposes a deeper level of continuity underlying its transformation.

Since authors do not have hermeneutical privilege with respect to their writings, it is conceivable that Heidegger misunderstands his texts. A number of existential factors might have led Heidegger to misrepresent the later development of his thought and its link to his early position. Yet since there is no single instance in the philosophical tradition of a conceptual rupture in the position of any important thinker, it is implausible to contend that there is a conceptual break, a radical discontinuity between Heidegger's early and later phases of Heidegger's thought as Lacoue-Labarthe and Derrida suppose.

The other problem concerns an assumption about textual interpretation. Lacoue-Labarthe and Derrida illustrate in practice a theory of textual interpretation formulated by Derrida and others. For Derrida there is nothing outside of texts and texts call forth other texts.[80] From a hermeneutical angle of vision, this is a version of the anticontextualist view that philosophical theories can be understood apart from and without reference to the contexts in which they emerge. To allow this thesis is tantamount to restricting the comprehension of a position, any position, merely to textual study since there is, literally, nothing else. Yet if this move is allowed, it leads to the removal from consideration of a whole host of factors possibly relevant to the study of any position but surely relevant to an understanding of Heidegger's thought and Nazism.

If no position, including Heidegger's, can be reduced to the circumstances in which it emerges, neither can it be wholly understood in isolation from its sociocultural context. Heidegger belongs to a generation of thinkers whose entire life and thought are circumscribed by the series of events leading up to and leading away from the Second World War. This is a point that is often clearer to historians such as Ott and Nolte than to philosophers who, in order to maintain the fiction of philosophy as the source of transhistorical truth, often deny its dependence on contextual factors. Ott exhibits the importance of a contextual approach in his study of Heidegger.[81] Following Ott, Nolte, unlike Ott a strong Heidegger defender, simply concedes the crucial need to interpret Heidegger's position, including his turning to National Socialism, from both a textual and a contextual perspective since each illuminates the other.[82] Further, a contextual approach to understanding Heidegger's thought is precisely Heideggerian. The Heideggerian perspective subordinates abstract theory to human existence within which it constitutes an aspect and against which it must be comprehended. From this angle of vision, the very idea of an interpretation of Heidegger's thought of being that fails to consider his own being is deeply mistaken.

Heidegger was, in Löwith's apt phrase, a thinker in a time of need (*Denker in dürftiger Zeit*),[83] whose theory emerged in the specific historical circumstances of the Weimar Republic: after the defeat suffered in the First World War, in a time of resurgent industrial development and increasingly strident nationalism, in a historical moment when many Germans sought to recover from the defeat by a new awakening of the German people; and he turned to Nazism as the Weimar Republic foundered, when National Socialism appeared to many to offer a viable third way between Bolshevism and discredited liberalism, as the German economy was reeling under the worldwide economic catastrophe. To fail to acknowledge this, not to relate Heidegger's thought and actions to the spirit of his times, to grasp his thought in isolation from its historical context, to consider Heidegger as Beaufret and some of his other students do as a thinker unrelated to his time or indeed to any other time, surely corresponds to the view that some thinkers like to hold of philosophical thought as in but not of time. But such an approach is also largely mythological. For it overlooks Heidegger's own view of the matter in his concept of Dasein as existence, as well as his rare statements after the second defeat of Germany, and, finally, the reality of Heidegger's own situation.

The deeper problem endemic in the French discussion of Heidegger's Nazism is the failure, widespread elsewhere as well, to consider its specific nature. It is widely but incorrectly assumed that Heidegger's commitment to Nazism was unremarkable and transitory. Writers as diverse as Fédier and Aubenque, orthodox Heideggerians, or Lacoue-Labarthe and Derrida, whose views are more nuanced, and even Janicaud, who is more overtly critical, uncritically assume that Heidegger's Nazism comes to an end with his service as rector of the University of Freiburg i. B. in 1934. This approach has the advantage of freeing his later thought from any political taint. But it is simply unable to account for the known facts. In particular, it cannot explain Heidegger's continued membership in the German Nazi Party until 1945, his later reaffirmation of his faith in Nazism in the *Introduction to Metaphysics*, his effort to develop further the supposed Nazi confrontation with technology in his own writings, and the disturbing remarks about the concept of the *Volk* in his *Beiträge zur Philosophie*.[84] And it cannot account for his continued silence on Nazism and the development of his later thought that is literally incomprehensible without an acknowledgment of his steady, stubborn commitment to his own ideal form of National Socialism.

THE FRENCH DISCUSSION AND HEIDEGGER IN FRANCE

The main concern of this book is neither the proper analysis of Heidegger's Nazism, nor the link between his philosophical thought and his commitment to National Socialism, but the reception of his thought in postwar French philosophy. Had the situation been normal, Heidegger's influence in postwar French philosophy would have been usual not unusual. Yet the situation was not normal but abnormal in virtue of the unprecedented affiliation of an exceptionally powerful philosopher with National Socialism.

The unusual extent of the influence of Heidegger's theory in French philosophy is manifest not only in its impact on contemporary French philosophy as well as his capacity to emerge and to remain as the master thinker in postwar French philosophy. It is manifest as well in the inability within the French philosophical discussion, still so strongly influenced by Heidegger's theory, for most thinkers to come to grips with the issues raised by the link between his theory and his Nazism in other than Heideggerian terms.

There is a parallel between Derrida's initial approach to the problem of sexual difference, on which Heidegger has nothing whatsoever to say, and the French analysis of the issues concerning the link between Heidegger's theory and his Nazism. The effort of Derrida the Heideggerian to grasp the problem of sexual difference is at least initially undermined by his decision to remain within the framework of Heidegger's theory. Similarly, it is striking that most efforts in the French discussion to understand the link between Heidegger's theory and his Nazism remain within the framework of Heidegger's own theory. The most striking example of all are the closely-related efforts by Derrida and Lacoue-Labarthe to come to grips with this link through Heidegger's own concept of the turning without any effort to situate this concept in Heidegger's own existential background.

We need to distinguish between Heidegger's philosophical position and its reception in French philosophy. There is a distinction to be drawn between Heidegger's position prior to and then after his adherence to National Socialism. There is a further, more complicated series of distinctions to be drawn between Heidegger's initial influence in French philosophy at the beginning of the 1930s prior to his adherence to National Socialism, then his emergence after the war as the master thinker of postwar French philosophy when his turning to Nazism was known and the French debate on the significance of his political turning was under way, and finally the more recent phase, roughly since Farías's book appeared, when there has been extensive debate on Heidegger's politics.

Heidegger is known to have turned toward Nazism as early as 1931 but he did not become a member of the NSDAP before 1933. The initial reception of Heidegger's theory in France occurred prior to his official membership in the National Socialist movement; it is, then, unrelated to his political turning. At this point, his theory was widely misunderstood, for instance by Sartre, Beauvoir and their associates who oddly attributed their own concern with responsibility based on freedom to their reading of Heidegger.[85] Although concerned in *Being and Time* with responsibility, there is no evidence that Heidegger ever held anything like the Sartrean theory that each of us is responsible for everyone. In *Being and Time*, where his understanding of the relation to others is highly undeveloped, Heidegger places the main emphasis on responsibility toward oneself, say, in his theory of authenticity.

In the immediate postwar period, Heidegger's thought and politics were widely misconstrued since his thought was taken out of context. In postwar France, the potential danger posed by Heidegger's Nazism was temporarily neutralized although not permanently defused for three main reasons: Heidegger's reassurances concerning his politics that were repeated by his supporters, above all Beaufret, and uncritically accepted; the lack of knowledge of the nature and extent of Heidegger's commitment to Nazism that was never clear and certainly not terminated at the end of the war; and the French disinclination to face up to Heidegger's National Socialism in order to avoid coming to terms with their own past. Certainly, the ability of Heidegger's supporters to make a convincing case for what was presented as a turning away from or even against Nazism rested on the way that his thought was literally read in isolation from its context.

If this analysis is correct, we can attribute Heidegger's rise to prominence in the French discussion to the perceived importance of his philosophical thought, the widespread appeal to the traditional anticontextual approach to philosophy as not linked to its time and place in the reading of Heidegger's theory, and a series of contingent factors. Together these factors made it plausible to ignore or at least to bracket Heidegger's association with Nazism. It then became plausible to accept as valid without scrutiny declarations intended merely to reassure. An example is Gilson's unsupported, unclarified, demonstrably incorrect remark that Heidegger's interest in politics was merely spontaneous.[86] This situation, favorable to Heidegger, in which his reassurances were accepted either as given or as reformulated by his closest supporters, no longer obtained when Heidegger's Nazism began to be subjected to increasing scrutiny and the question of its possible link to his philosophy was raised.

In France, where the debate has been extremely vigorous, it is fair to say that the peculiar role of Heidegger's thought has not so far been seriously "damaged" or called into question by renewed attention to his Nazism. Philosophers have long insisted on the social importance, indeed the indispensability of what they do for the good life. Yet few philosophers in France or anywhere else are more than casually concerned with an external world that, if certain deconstructionists are to be believed, does not even exist outside the texts. It is, then, not surprising that now as before there are those willing to accept Heidegger's reassurances, or their second-hand repetition by his closest students, without further scrutiny. Yet it is striking that as the historical events become more distant and recede increasingly into the past, as the information now available about Heidegger's Nazism increases and is examined, and as its possible links to his philosophical thought are probed, there is not the slightest hint that Heidegger's preeminence in French philosophy has so far been counterbalanced, destabilized, or even threatened. That Heidegger's thought has so far been able to maintain its preeminence in French philosophy in a situation significantly altered by the resurgent debate on his Nazism is another, striking indication, even more striking than his emergence as the central philosopher in France after the war, of his profound, indeed profoundly durable influence in contemporary French philosophy.

9

HEIDEGGER, FRENCH PHILOSOPHY AND THE PHILOSOPHICAL TRADITION

This book has been concerned with the reception of Heidegger's philosophical position in France, particularly in the postwar period when he became the master thinker of French philosophy. In modern times, a number of important positions have influenced, even strongly influenced, the course of philosophical debate, sometimes even for decades, but rarely more than that. Examples include the theories of C. S. Peirce, William James and John Dewey in American philosophy, G. E. Moore, Bertrand Russell, Gottlob Frege and Ludwig Wittgenstein in analytic philosophy, Georg Lukács in Marxism, and Edmund Husserl and Martin Heidegger in phenomenology. Yet in modern philosophy there are only four unusually influential philosophical theories that have continued to shape the debate not only over decades but throughout this entire period: those of Descartes, Kant, Hegel, and Hume.

Different thinkers exert their influence differently. For an exceedingly brief moment, Karl Leonhard Reinhold dominated the post-Kantian debate before rapidly receding, well within his lifetime, into obscurity. Peirce attracted the attention of James but few others during his lifetime although since his death his reputation has continued to grow. Nietzsche's philosophical reputation has been acquired almost entirely since his passing. Heidegger's theory that attained almost mythical dimensions during his lifetime has become even more important since his recent death. It is too early to determine if, like the views of others, say Fichte and Bergson, the influence of his theory will like a supernova shine intensely, even incandescently but relatively briefly only, to be nearly extinguished after a short moment, or whether, like the single star he claimed to follow in his lifelong concern with being, his thought will remain fixed in the philosophical firmament, to serve as a beacon for others as long as the philosophical discussion continues. It is too early, then, to know whether Koyré was correct in contending that Heidegger's theory is not only an important new step in the discussion but rather marks the inception of a new phase of the discussion.

UNDERSTANDING THE PHILOSOPHICAL TRADITION

An understanding of the way that any philosophical theory, including Heidegger's, is taken up in the philosophical tradition presupposes an understanding of the concept "philosophical tradition." It might seem that the writings in that tradition and the tradition itself are fixed, or stable entities, since they are in a sense always and necessarily already there as a necessary precondition for later discussion. In order to discuss the critical philosophy, there must already be a series of texts in which this theory is stated. And the Kantian tradition in philosophy presupposes the Kantian theory.

Both the writings that compose the philosophical tradition and the philosophical tradition itself are variables. Texts change, for instance when a particular text is accepted as genuine or rejected as spurious, or when better, philologically more adequate, even critical editions appear that in turn may influence the understanding of philosophical theories.

Our understanding of Heidegger's position may well change as the texts change. A complete edition of Heidegger's writings is now in progress that, since it is not being edited according to the current views of what is a critical edition, will need later to be redone. In this edition passages omitted from texts already published, including politically sensitive remarks, have been restored. An unexpected change has occurred with respect to Heidegger's second doctoral thesis, or *Habilitationsschrift*, concerning the text "De modis significandi" that was earlier attributed to Duns Scotus. Heidegger's text is called "Die Kategorien- und Bedeutungslehre des Duns Scotus." Today we know that the author of the text on which Heidegger comments was not Duns Scotus but Thomas of Erfurt.[1]

Such changes indicate that the past to which the writings belong and the writings themselves are not congealed, frozen as it were. If the very content of the philosophical tradition is never fixed but always mutable, then it takes on a strangely amorphous quality, as an admittedly extreme example will show. Reference to "The Question Concerning Technology" needs to specify which form of this text is intended: the censored, published version where Heidegger simply states that "Agriculture is now the mechanized food industry:"[2] or the still unpublished, uncensored version, in which these five words begin a longer, arguably scandalous passage, already quoted above. For a text analyzing modern technology from the perspective of being is not the same as one that, in the course of such an analysis, simply equates agriculture and extermination camps.

Our understanding of this text obviously changes when the censored passage is restored. A text offering an apparently innocuous, not particularly interesting observation about contemporary agriculture as motorized, or better mechanized, is neither insightful nor controversial. It might be taken as an indication that Heidegger has nothing much to say about agriculture from his perspective. A very different text that adds the comparison of mechanized agriculture to extermination camps is arguably also not insight-ful; but it is apparently so controversial that, although this incriminating passage has been in the public domain for nearly a decade, the original manuscript of the lecture has never been published and is still not available to scholars. The latter version of this passage raises issues about Heidegger's scandalous insensitivity to extraordinary human suffering and the Holocaust in general; and it raises further questions about his capacity, through his analysis of being, to comment intelligently on the tragic events of the century and, by extension, on modernity.

Even more obviously than the texts themselves, their understanding is a historical variable that is always subject to further modification. As our understanding of philosophical theories changes, our short list of the few significant philosophical texts composing the philosophical canon, so to speak, also changes. As we approach the end of this century, there has never been less agreement on the main thinkers or the most influential works of this period or about the wider philosophical tradition.

It has been said that the three most important philosophical works of this century are Heidegger's *Being and Time*, Wittgenstein's *Tractatus*, and Lukács's *History and Class Consciousness*.[3] Yet Husserl scholars might prefer to include Husserl's *Logical Investigations* or *Ideas I*, or *Cartesian Meditations*, or even the *Crisis of the European Sciences and Transcendental Phenomenology*. Wittgenstein scholars, who are often critical of his early writing, prefer his later thought. Lukács's thought, which was controversial even within Marxism, is now likely to attract less attention after the collapse of official Marxism. Since Ryle's early review of *Being and Time*,[4] Heidegger has long been regarded within Anglo-American analytic philosophy as an unusually obscure German thinker, for Carnap the author of a classic illustration of the meaningless use of language.[5] Yet philosophical modes change. Analytic thinkers (e.g. Hubert Dreyfus, John Hoageland, Mark Okrent, Robert Brandom, and others) are now turning to Heidegger in increasing numbers.

Not only the content but even the idea of the philosophical tradition is a historical variable. This idea, as now understood, is relatively recent, and seems to have been invented by Hegel. He was apparently the first writer to regard the history of philosophy as a sort of Platonic dialogue extending through time, in which later thinkers build, or attempt to improve, on earlier theories. Hegel maintains that philosophy has always been concerned with the problem of knowledge. He seeks to avoid the appearance of favoring a particular perspective by favoring them all. He implies that his own view of the philosophical tradition is without perspective, or aperspectival. Although Hegel claimed to take an aperspectival attitude towards prior thought in order to take up into his own anything of value, in practice he could only appropriate ideas compatible with his own.[6] He typically omits from consideration the views of the later Fichte[7] and the later Schelling.[8]

Hegel's underlying assumption of a single philosophical tradition concerned with the problem of knowledge is insightful, interesting, but finally mistaken. Although we can read the prior philosophical tradition through the problem of knowledge, other perspectives are possible. There are numerous theories in the history of philosophy, such as Heidegger's analysis of being, that are not primarily, on occasion not even remotely, assimilable to a theory of knowledge. Further, different views of knowledge lead to vastly different readings of the history of philosophy, and point toward vastly different ideas of the philosophical tradition.

Hegel's assumption of a single philosophical tradition is apparently shared by Heidegger. His proposed destruction of the history of ontology is meant to free up the original insights concerning being to which he means to return. This proposed return to the beginning of the philosophical tradition seems to presuppose a spatial understanding of the history of philosophy. Now it is only possible to return to early Greek thought if it is possible to go back behind the philosophical tradition as one can later return down a path one has traveled in order to take another turning in the forest. Yet it is simply mistaken to suppose that one can, from a later vantage point, strip away the veil constituted by some two and half millenia of discussion to grasp the original insights in their pristine form; even the urge to do so follows from a perspective based on the experience of the later discussion. Moreover, the underlying, rationalist assumption about the nature of the philosophical tradition as akin to a single path is mistaken; for it is more like a series of paths that cross at irregular intervals and angles.

THE FRENCH RECEPTION OF HEIDEGGER'S THEORY

The reception of important philosophical theories – roughly the way that they enter into the philosophical discussion in order to become part of the philosophical tradition – is rarely if ever based on anything as simple as correct interpretation or even on strictly philosophical criteria. If Heidegger's theory is typical, the reception of an important position invites, perhaps even presupposes, and probably cannot avoid a certain misunderstanding.

There is a distinction to be drawn between the texts that compose the philosophical tradition, the process of the reception of theories as they are taken up in the philosophical discussion, and their reading and rereading over a period of time in the complex debate that constitutes philosophy. Wittgenstein's lectures that led his students in effect to debate his unwritten doctrines represent a special case. Philosophical theories are mainly described in print prior to and as a condition of their being taken up into the wider philosophical debate. This process obviously requires interpretation and, if the texts are deemed sufficiently important, successive reinterpretations over a period of time.

If a "correct" reading is possible at all, then it is most likely to occur for those rather ordinary positions that merely add an idea or two but otherwise leave "everything in place." Yet it more difficult to understand the idea of a "correct" reading for a more novel position that creates a fundamental change in the debate. It is still more difficult to comprehend what a so-called "correct" interpretation would be for the unusual case of a theory that departs radically from the ongoing discussion by innovating in some deep manner and, for that reason, requires for its understanding a process of reception in which new ideas are assimilated and often even new vocabulary to express them is developed.

Moreover, even for the most banal philosophical writings, the very idea of a single, univocally-correct reading, like that of the philosophical tradition, dissolves under scrutiny. We can sometimes exclude proposed interpretations as insufficiently supported by, even as incompatible with, the texts as we know them. Yet there is usually a range of possible readings that, insofar as they find what can vaguely be called "adequate" support in the texts, are admissible, and, hence, can be said to be "correct." Different interpretations of the same theory or text obviously highlight different aspects and reflect different viewpoints, different evaluations, and so on.

In general important philosophical texts are notoriously difficult to interpret, arguably impossible to read in a single "correct" fashion. Typically, there is not and clearly could not be a single, univocally-correct reading either of Plato's theory or of Plato's *Republic*. The history of Plato scholarship consists in a series of readings of his thought from different angles of vision. There is probably no example of an important philosophical position or philosophical text for which a univocally correct reading can be specified. The very idea of the "correct" reading of an important philosophical theory or philosophical text is questionable. Rather than the "conservative" view of text reading like a problem in mathematics for which there is a "right" answer that excludes all others, there seems to be no alternative to espousing a more liberal view of interpretation according to which, like child rearing or politics, there is more than one, even many "correct" possibilities.

Even the most original thinker cannot simply begin again at the beginning. At most one can provide a departure from the prior discussion. It follows that even the most novel philosophical position must be read against the background of the philosophical tradition. Since one can only reinvent a new way of continuing the ongoing debate, new philosophical ideas necessarily arise in reaction to, and represent a departure from, prior debate. Descartes, Kant and Husserl, three of the most radical philosophical thinkers of modern times, share a basic dissatisfaction with the entire preceding philosophical tradition. Although each is a highly original thinker, each finally offers new ways to reinvent, but not to invent, philosophy.

Now it is not the unimportant but the important philosophical positions that structure the philosophical discussion and, for that reason, the philosophical tradition. Since important positions by definition innovate with respect to the debate, they are difficult to interpret and routinely mis-construed. If this is the case, it follows that at least initially the philosophical tradition is mainly based on substantive misunderstandings or misreadings.

This idea clearly runs against the grain of the traditional view of philo-sophy, widely propagated by philosophers themselves, hardly a disinterested party. Ever since Plato, philosophers have argued that philosophy is not only the unique source of absolute truth and knowledge, but a strictly rational enterprise, in fact the only example of reason itself. The view of philosophy as intrinsically rational, as the main form of rationality, runs throughout the entire modern philosophical tradition. It is formulated in the Cartesian view of ahistorical reason, and later dominates the Enlightenment period. It reaches its highpoint in the Kantian theory of pure reason, a wholly theoretical analysis carried out in utter abstraction from all practical con-cerns, in a form of reason unsullied by any admixture that Kant held to be intrinsically practical.

Perhaps the most persuasive argument for philosophy's rational self-image lies in its fascination with science going back into the Greek tradition. If science, particularly mathematics, is the embodiment of reason, and if philosophy is science in a sense deeper, say, than the particular sciences, then philosophy is the embodiment of reason. The conviction that philosophy is not only scientific or rigorous but actually is science is everywhere in modern thought. It extends from Kant's idea of philosophy as systematic science, and Hegel's conception of phenomenology as the science of the experience of consciousness, to Husserl's notion of philosophy as rigorous science and to Heidegger's early view of philosophy as the science of being.

Husserl and the early Heidegger are exceptions. For there is now wide-spread agreement that although philosophy must be rigorous, it cannot be science. Since the traditional view of philosophy as pure reason can no longer be defended through any version of the claim that philosophy is more than rigorous, the precarious distinction between philosophy and a *Weltan-schauung*, or worldview, takes on an added importance.

Kant understood philosophy as a worldview, or *conceptus cosmicus* (*Weltbegriff*), intrinsically relevant to the ends of human being.[9] Yet Schel-ling is already close to the modern idea of worldview in his distinction between intelligence as either consciously or unconsciously productive, as in a worldview.[10] More recently, the notion of a worldview is the theme of a dispute between Jaspers, Dilthey, Husserl, and Heidegger. Jaspers identifies a world view as composed of subjective ideas about life experience, and so on, as well as objective ideas about the shape of the world.[11] On one interpretation, Dilthey seems to identify philosophy with a worldview, for instance when he evokes "the task of coming to terms with the incessant need for ultimate reflection on being, ground, value, purpose, and their inter-connection in a *Weltanschauung*."[12] This idea is strongly opposed by Husserl and, following him, Heidegger. In response to Dilthey, Husserl maintains that as the source of truth philosophy is incompatible with either a worldview or naturalism.[13] His view is echoed in Heidegger's insistence that philosophy is not the construction of a worldview, but at most the basis of one.[14]

Apparently following Jaspers, Heidegger understands a worldview as a matter of coherent conviction that arises for a particular individual, as distinguished from universal science independent of any historical person.[15] He correctly points out that if the task of philosophy is to construct a worldview, then there is no distinction between them.[16] Yet the French reception of Heidegger's theory indicates that philosophy is not independent of the sociohistorical context. Although the evolution and reception of Heidegger's position cannot be reduced to the context in which it emerged, neither can it be understood in isolation from this context.

Through his concept of Dasein as existence, Heidegger insists on the contextuality of all thought, including his own. Yet there is a pronounced tendency in the Heidegger literature to ignore the background against which his theory emerged and evolved, in part to maintain the fictitious, but useful distinction between Heidegger the great philosopher and Heidegger the ordinary Nazi.[17] Like other philosophical theories, Heidegger's cannot be understood without reference to others that influence it or to which he desired to respond, or to the background in which it emerged. We cannot grasp his initial position without reference to the period of the Weimar Republic in which it was formulated; and it is even more difficult to grasp the later evolution of his thought without an awareness of his own existential situation at the end of the Second World War, his steady commitment to his own private form of Nazism, and so on.

Philosophers like to regard the philosophical discussion as responding merely to philosophical imperatives, to other philosophical ideas only. Yet like everyone else philosophers are children of their times, to which they respond in their own abstract ways. The distinction between philosophy and *Weltanschauung* is not absolute, for it is not possible to separate cleanly or finally between views held to be true and the existential conditions in which they are formulated. The formulation, evolution, and French reception of Heidegger's theory amply contradict his restatement of the traditional, theoretically-desirable, but practically-indefensible view of philosophy as utterly distinct from a worldview. Although philosophy likes to regard itself as the product of a wholly free, entirely rational activity, it is rooted at every remove in social existence.

SUBJECTIVITY AND HEIDEGGER IN FRANCE

It does not follow, because it is usually, perhaps always impossible to provide a single correct reading of important philosophical theories, that they cannot be read incorrectly. In fact, this is a frequent occurrence. Early on, Heidegger's view of the subject was read incorrectly in the French debate.

The French reception of Heidegger's theory illustrates how difficult it is to comprehend a novel philosophical position in a more than fragmentary manner. The initial French appropriation of Heidegger's thought through a reading of fundamental ontology as philosophical anthropology ran counter to his own reading of his position and the position itself. It is clear that although an anthropological interpretation of fundamental ontology has textual support, it is simply inadequate. In terms of the Kantian distinction between the spirit and the letter of a theory, although arguably faithful to the letter of the theory, an anthropological reading of fundamental ontology is simply not faithful to its spirit.

The early misreading of Heidegger's theory as philosophical anthropology, hence as anthropological humanism, contradicts his consistently antianthropological stance. Yet it correctly identifies the anthropological component of the theory of subjectivity as existence that Heidegger presents under the heading of Dasein. It follows that the initial French misreading of Heidegger's position points to the basic incoherence of his conception of the subject.

Heidegger was never interested in human being for its own sake. If we take Heidegger at his word, his entire position is dominated through his single-minded, some would say obsessive, concern with being. Even when he seems to be most interested in human beings, as in his occasional suggestion that Nazism will bring about an authentic gathering of the German people, arguably the central theme of the rectorial address, his main interest is being. His lengthy analysis of Dasein in *Being and Time* is not meant to elucidate human being; it is rather meant to elucidate human being understood through being as the vital clue to an understanding of being.

Since Heidegger's initial view of human being reaches a crisis as early as §10 of *Being and Time*, this paragraph merits detailed discussion. Here the anthropological misreading current in the early French reception of his thought appears as one aspect of an obviously dualistic conception of human being. The French reaction to the translation of "Dasein" as "réalité humaine," apparently a simple misrendering of a key term in his position, is hardly that. Derrida's pointed objection to this translation as "monstrous" is not just an excited Gallic reaction, although it is that as well. But above and beyond that, it signals the inadvertent identification of a fundamental inadequacy in Heidegger's position that is not overcome in its later evolution.

In *Being and Time*, in his analysis of Dasein, or *Daseinsanalytik*, Heidegger exploits his claim that all people have a nonspecific, unanalyzed conception of being as his clue to disclose being in general. "Dasein" designates human being as well as what it is about human being that is concerned with being. Heidegger's problem is to offer a theory of the subject adequate to his concern with being that avoids the problems he discerns in other views of subjectivity. In §10, in a discussion of the distinction between his own analysis of Dasein and the sciences based on a conception of human being, Heidegger argues for a difference in kind between his view of the subject and rival theories based either on philosophical anthropology or the Cartesian view.

A key to understanding Heidegger's position at this point is to realize that he is closely following as well as criticizing Husserl's general approach as he understands it. In remarks here on contemporary thinkers concerned with human being, he notes the agreement between Scheler and Husserl, and further notes Husserl's critique of Dilthey. For Heidegger, Husserl's basic view of personality (*Personalität*) is apparent in his famous *Logos* article, "Philosophy as Rigorous Science," and carried further in *Ideas, I*. Heidegger contends that Husserl correctly saw that a person is not an entity but a unity. He insists on the further elaboration of the Husserlian approach, or the "a priorism" that is "the method of all scientific philosophy" that must now be applied to the analysis of the everyday (*Alltäglichkeit*).[18]

Since Heidegger explicitly accepts the Husserlian a priori approach, he cannot simultaneously accept a merely empirical approach, for instance the empirical approach of philosophical anthropology starting from a proximally given subject. Husserl draws a distinction between empirical psychology and transcendental phenomenology. Similarly, Heidegger differentiates between concrete anthropology, the thematically complete ontology of Dasein,[19] other views that he rejects, and what he calls an existentially a priori anthropology.[20]

Heidegger's claim that the sciences presuppose an unanalyzed conception of subjectivity applies the Husserlian idea that the sciences lack a reflexive dimension provided only in philosophy.[21] His objection that the Cartesian theory fails to examine the "sum" is directed against the idea of a transcendental subject in abstraction from experience as well as its restatement in the views of Kant and Husserl. Against Descartes and those influenced by him, Heidegger maintains that since Dasein literally is existence, it is only on this basis that we can examine the theme of being. Yet he refuses any view of the subject as proximally given, as still presupposing the unexamined conception of the *subjectum*, or *hypokeimenon*. For Heidegger, Scheler and Dilthey understand that the subject is not an entity. And he notes that the problem of human being is covered up by philosophical anthropology, such as the ancient Greek or later Christian views of man.

If this is an accurate summary of Heidegger's view, then four points follow. To begin with, it is obvious that its early French readers construed it anthropologically, as philosophical anthropology, since this is the obvious reading. Philosophical anthropology has attracted many philosophers, including Max Scheler, the author of an important work from an anthropological perspective, *Man's Place in Nature*.[22] "Philosophical anthropology" has been understood as "an attempt to construct a scientific discipline out of man's traditional effort to understand and liberate himself."[23]

In §10 of *Being and Time*, an anthropological reading of Heidegger's position is suggested by such factors as the distinction between theoretical and practical approaches to the subject, the concept of Dasein as human being, the interpretation of Dasein as existence, and so on. This reading amounts to construing his conception of subjectivity as a form of anthropology, or philosophical anthropology, albeit of a new kind, one that raises the question of being.

Heidegger's analysis of Dasein with respect to its average everydayness sounds suspiciously like philosophical anthropology.[24] Heidegger specifically invites precisely an anthropological reading, more precisely an anthropological misreading of his view, through his remarks on what he refers to as traditional anthropology rather than on anthropology. In § 10, in rapid succession he objects no less than three times to traditional anthropology but significantly never to anthropology as such. To begin with, he objects to the understanding of human being through traditional anthropology in the ancient world and in Christian theology.[25] Then he objects to traditional anthropology that forgets the question of being.[26] Finally, he objects, in an apparent conflation between traditional anthropology and the Cartesian view – he later develops this point in his claim that the Cartesian conception of the cogito leads to modern anthropology – to the failure to reflect on the ontological foundations of anthropology.[27]

If Heidegger meant to protect his theory against an anthropological reading, then he did not do nearly enough to rule out that possibility. The fact that in §10 he objects to traditional anthropology but not to anthropology as such leaves the door open to an anthropological reading of his own view that could fairly be read as a nontraditional form of anthropology.

In later passages scattered throughout *Being and Time*, Heidegger only complicates the effort to insulate his view against an obvious reading as philosophical anthropology. His remark that a complete ontology of Dasein is needed for a philosophical anthropology suggests that in that respect his own effort is at best partial.[28] In a passage already identified he notes that although his aim is the study of being, what he has so far done could be extended as an existential a priori philosophical anthropology.[29] In later stating his desire to go beyond an existential a priori anthropology, he implies that this is the result so far of his analysis of Dasein.[30] A comment that the analysis of Dasein is not aimed at laying the ontological basis for anthropology does not rule out the compatibility between his analysis and that task.[31] This impression is only strengthened in the remark that we need to pass over anthropological, psychological and theological theories of conscience based on the concept of Dasein.[32]

An anthropological misreading of his position is further fostered by other factors as well. It is directly suggested in the next chapter of his book, comprising §§13–14, that is entirely devoted to "Being-in-the-world in general as the basic state of Dasein." This anti-Cartesian, even anti-Husserlian view implies a conception of human being as in the world, not as

transcendent to it. Yet in virtue of his acceptance of the Husserlian phenomenological view as basically correct, Heidegger is committed to a conception of the phenomenological subject as transcendent with respect to
the world.

An anthropological interpretation of Heidegger's theory is indirectly
suggested within § 10 by the remark on Descartes developed later in the book
in a detailed critique of the Cartesian theory. The objection that Descartes
fails to consider the nature of the "sum" of the cogito is misconstrued as a
refusal to conceive the subject as a strictly theoretical entity. For Heidegger
does not refuse but in fact welcomes a strictly theoretical approach to
subjectivity. He only refuses to accept a view of subjectivity, theoretical or
otherwise, in which its being is unexamined.

An anthropological interpretation of Heidegger's theory is again suggested
from a Cartesian angle of vision, familiar to Heidegger's French readers. For
a Cartesian, there are only two possible approaches to subjectivity: as either
theoretical or practical, passive or active, as a spectator or as an actor.
Heidegger's refusal of the Cartesian conception of the subject as a strictly
theoretical entity, in Cartesian terms the spectator view of subjectivity,
appears to commit him a view of the subject as an actor, as basically practical.

Second, this obvious, anthropological reading of Heidegger's theory is just
as obviously mistaken. For it conflates Heidegger's opposition to an unexamined conception of subjectivity that fails to examine the being of the
subject with an opposition, erroneously ascribed to Heidegger, to a theoretical
conception of subjectivity. Heidegger specifically suggests the need to
develop an analysis of what he calls the being of the whole man.[33] His own
view suggests the need to combine practical and theoretical elements in a
more general theory of human being. Understood as existence, human being
is the topic of philosophical anthropology; understood in relation to the
analysis of being, human being is the topic of a transcendental phenomenological analysis of being. But there is no way to combine these two
perspectives within a single conception of subjectivity.

In retrospect, an anthropological reading of Heidegger's theory exaggerates the disagreement between Heidegger and Husserl. The key problem is
the theme of psychologism running throughout the first volume of Husserl's
Logical Investigations. We recall Husserl's concern to avoid psychologism,
or roughly the confusion between the philosophical and the psychological
dimensions of experience, and Heidegger's contention that Husserl fell back
into psychologism.

To accept a view of the subject or subjectivity as merely human being in
an anthropological sense is to be guilty of psychologism. Husserl thought that
psychologism and phenomenology were incompatible. Heidegger agrees with
Husserl on this point. It follows that to allow psychologism, to propose an
anthropological view of subjectivity, is tantamount to suppressing the very
possibility of phenomenology. For this would amount to suppressing the

phenomenological analysis of the everyday world in the extended Husserlian sense that Heidegger still accepts, and that, he maintains, is required to understand being.

Third, it follows that Heidegger's view of subjectivity is radically inconsistent since he thinks Dasein as both immanent, hence as existent, and as transcendent. From the latter angle of vision, Dasein is able to do all the usual work of the transcendental subject, such as performing an analysis of Dasein, including an analysis of average everydayness, in short to disclose being that is transcendent through phenomenological knowledge.

Yet it is inconsistent to interpret Dasein as existence and as the subject of phenomenological truth, or *veritas transcendentalis*. Heidegger fails to unify human being as immanent and transcendent, a posteriori and a priori, practical and theoretical. For he fails to show that a being essentially defined as existence is capable of phenomenological truth. Husserl introduces the idea of phenomenological reduction in order to explain how it is possible to reach phenomenological truth, to go to the things themselves. Heidegger retains this Husserlian goal for which he substitutes the analysis of being. Yet Heidegger fails to address the central methodological point, roughly how it is possible to elicit phenomenological truth.

Fourth, it is just as obvious that Heidegger needs to deemphasize the immanent side of his concept of the subject in order to protect his phenomenological approach to the theory of being. For a claim to provide anything like a phenomenological disclosure of truth requires a view of the subject as transcendent. Husserl sees the minimum requirement for phenomenological truth as the ascent to the transcendental plane through the phenomenological reduction. In this way, Heidegger renews with a traditional view stretching from Plato over Descartes, Kant and many others to Husserl.

From Heidegger's distantly Husserlian perspective at this point, phenomenological truth rests on a double condition: an authentic reworking of the problem of being in the ancient Greek formulation that is scarcely accessible to the ordinary person; and a concept of the subject that discloses the a priori that, following Husserl, he regards as the meaning of the authentically philosophical "empirical" (*Empirie*). In other words, for Heidegger as for Husserl phenomenology, in Heidegger's case the phenomenological approach to being, requires a transcendental subject.

As his position evolves, Heidegger rethinks his conception of subjectivity in a way that brings it into line with the requirements of his own approach to being while eliminating any anthropological residue through the celebrated decentering of the subject. Yet this revision of his original theory in order to alleviate a basic problem merely creates another fundamental problem. In suggesting that the subject is passive in respect to being as active, Heidegger does not so much break with his early thought as refine or "purify" it by further refining one of its strands. In *Being and Time*, he already understands "phenomenology" as concerned with "that which shows itself."[34]

Heidegger's later decentering of the subject protects his phenomenological analysis of being only at the enormous cost of an evident and total collapse of his view of subjectivity. If the subject is merely transcendent but not imminent, then there is a unified view of subjectivity as that to which being is or can be disclosed. Yet if the precondition of the analysis of being is a unified view of a person, or a unified view of the whole man, in his decentering of the subject Heidegger has tacitly acknowledged his failure to grasp human subjectivity. If nowhere else, in Heidegger's later thought, in the decentering of the subject, in the turn away from the existential dimension of human being, Heidegger in effect bases his later theory of being on the death of man.

HUMANISM, ANTIHUMANISM AND HEIDEGGER IN FRANCE

It is clear that Heidegger is not a humanist, and his theory is not humanism in a traditional, anthropological sense. The early French reading of his theory as anthropological humanism – ingredient in Kojève's reading of Hegel's theory, influenced by the views of Heidegger and Marx, and taken up by Sartre – as philosophical anthropology, is a clear misreading. It remains to be seen whether Heidegger is, as he claims to be, a humanist in some other, say, postmetaphysical sense, whether his theory can fairly be called humanism, or whether, as some have said, it is antihumanism. I will argue that Heidegger's remarks on humanism are inconsistent and that his description of his theory as humanism is incompatible with the very idea of humanism.

In the French context, at least three factors suggest that Heidegger's theory is humanist: the initial French philosophical turning toward fundamental ontology, Heidegger's early thought, understood as a philosophical anthropology, or anthropological humanism; Heidegger's "Letter on Humanism," where he distinguished between traditional, metaphysical forms of humanism, such as Sartre's, and his own humanism, in which human being is understood through being; and the recent effort by some of his followers, such as Derrida and Lacoue-Labarthe, to defend his later thought by simply conceding that his early thought was a form of metaphysical humanism.

To understand Heidegger's view of humanism, we will need to sketch its development in his writings. Humanism is not discussed in *Being and Time*. To the best of my knowledge, this term does not occur in the book. The two main texts where Heidegger discusses this theme are his well known lecture, "The Age of the World Picture" and the "Letter on Humanism." In "The Age of the World Picture," Heidegger criticizes humanism that he links with anthropology as a mere worldview (*Weltanschauung*). Heidegger here rejects both anthropology as well as the idea of a worldview to which he links humanism.

In "The Age of the World Picture," Heidegger's objection to humanism is consistent with his objections to traditional anthropology in *Being and Time*. The result is to clarify the ambiguity in his discussion of Dasein in his initial book, where Heidegger left open the question of its anthropological status. Heidegger now insists on the nonanthropological status of a concept of the subject, taking Greek thought as his model. Forgetting the obvious humanist implications of Socratic questioning, he inconsistently maintains that humanism could never have gained ascendancy in Greek thought. Humanism has an essential connection with philosophical anthropology as revealed by the understanding of man and the world through man: "It [i.e. humanism] designates that philosophical interpretation of man which explains and evaluates whatever is, in its entirety, from the standpoint of man and in relation to man."[35] Humanism, he claims, is anthropology, when "anthropology" is understood as resting on an unreflective, dogmatic assumption concerning the nature of man.[36]

In "The Age of the World Picture" Heidegger links so-called traditional humanism to a worldview, or a philosophy of the worldview, as distinguished from postmetaphysical thinking. He suggests without argument that the traditional, or metaphysical form of humanism arises within metaphysics, or philosophy, that is in fact nothing more than a worldview, but not philosophy. Postmetaphysical thinking, although beyond metaphysics, is no longer a worldview. If the alternative lies in the choice between a worldview and philosophy, then postmetaphysical thinking, which is allegedly beyond philosophy, is only beyond that kind of philosophy not worthy of the name that fails to surpass a mere worldview. For postmetaphysical humanism, defined in terms of being, is intrinsically linked to thinking, or philosophy that is not a mere worldview.

In the "Letter on Humanism," Heidegger retreats from the view that philosophy culminates in his theory as part of his retreat from philosophy to thought. Here, at a point when Heidegger has abandoned any claims to philosophy, he does not exploit the implicit claim that in declining anthropology his own theory avoids the status of a mere worldview to realize philosophy. Yet the view of humanism that he now proposes is clearly inconsistent with his earlier criticism of humanism.

The inconsistency lies in the earlier rejection of humanism that he later claims for his own theory. In "The Age of the World Picture," he criticizes humanism as anthropology that fails to grasp the essence of human being. This criticism, which is consistent with the view in *Being and Time*, suggests a clear incompatibility between the grasp of human being and anthropology. Human being cannot be understood anthropologically, but only from a deeper remove, from the perspective of fundamental ontology.

Heidegger's description of his theory as a new, postmetaphysical form of humanism is inconsistent with his view of anthropology. In refusing anthropology that supposedly yields only a superficial view of human being, Heidegger refuses humanism as well. In suggesting in "The Letter on

Humanism" that his own theory is humanism, Heidegger takes a line inconsistent with his discussion in "The Age of the World Picture." It remains to be seen whether this line is consistent or inconsistent with the original position sketched in *Being and Time*.

In the "Letter on Humanism," Heidegger maintains that humanism necessarily implies metaphysics, and metaphysics fails to think man through man's essential human element, his *humanitas*.[37] If traditional humanism has so far failed to grasp man correctly, the solution is not to abandon humanism but to invoke a new humanism already available in fundamental ontology, namely a type of humanism that does not think metaphysically.[38] Returning now to his view of Dasein in *Being and Time*, Heidegger suggests that man is not merely human if this means "rational"; he is more than human since he is defined by his relation to being.[39] Heidegger sums up his new, nonmetaphysical view of humanism as a replacement for the old, allegedly metaphysical type:

> But – as you no doubt have been wanting to rejoin for quite a while now – does not such thinking [i.e. his own theory] think precisely the *humanitas* of *homo humanus*? Does it not think *humanitas* in a decisive sense, as no metaphysics has thought it or can think it? Is this not "humanism" in the extreme sense? Certainly. It is a humanism that thinks the humanity of man from the nearness to Being. But at the same time it is a humanism in which not man but man's historical essence is at stake in its provenance from the truth of Being. But then doesn't the ek-sistence of man also stand or fall in this game of stakes? So it does.[40]

Rather than a new position, or a new version of his position, in this passage Heidegger presents a reinterpretation of his original position as stated in *Being and Time*. Heidegger's claim now that his original position, earlier described as fundamental ontology, is humanism rests on a series of dichotomies, or exclusive alternatives, between: his early theory and his later theory, metaphysics and nonmetaphysics, humanism and nonhumanism, Nazism and non-Nazism, and so on.

It is obviously inconsistent for Heidegger to reject humanism as such and later to claim that his own theory is a form of humanism. If we grant that Heidegger's depiction of his theory as humanism in the "Letter on Humanism" is opportunistic and inconsistent with his depiction of humanism in "The Age of the World Picture," the more interesting question is whether, despite Heidegger's probable opportunism, he was correct in describing his theory as humanism.

There is a difference between Heidegger's later interpretation, in the "Letter on Humanism," of his original position in *Being and Time* and its redescription as humanism. What Heidegger calls a nonmetaphysical view of humanism in the "Letter on Humanism" is consistent with his original view of Dasein in *Being and Time* as human being understood through being. Yet it is misdescribed as humanism.

If Heidegger's reinterpretation of his original position is allowed to stand, then his thought was never metaphysical since it was always postmetaphysical. In other words, if his reinterpretation is correct then the break between his thought and metaphysics does not occur in the course of the evolution of his position, or in the later evolution of his thought. Rather, it occurs in the original formulation of his position that has always been beyond the metaphysical pale.

Heidegger's proposed reinterpretation of fundamental ontology creates more problems than it resolves. In *Being and Time*, Heidegger tries to return to the early Greek origins of the problem of ontology, or metaphysics, in order to carry it further than the point at which it was left in the Greek tradition. This concern is clearly inconsistent with the later effort to suggest that his theory has never been metaphysical. Either his concern with ontology commits him to metaphysics, as he still implied in his study of *Kant and the Problem of Metaphysics*, where he read his own theory as continuing the critical philosophy; or his theory is postmetaphysical and he was never concerned to renew the early Greek philosophical tradition. It cannot be both.

If we accept Heidegger's view of his position as outlined in the "Letter on Humanism," it follows that the effort by such French Heideggerians as Derrida and Lacoue-Labarthe to defend Heidegger's later theory by conceding the metaphysical status of his earlier view derives from a basic misreading of *Being and Time*. Yet to concede that Heidegger's later view of his theory as humanism after the so-called decentering of the subject is consistent with his original position but does not resolve and only deepens the problem which the supposed break in his thought was intended to resolve.

The problem is the well known political turning to Nazism. It is no longer possible to hold that since *Being and Time* is an apolitical book, a point on which all observers agree, it is not the basis of his attraction to Nazism. It is only possible to maintain that his later thought is unrelated to his earlier Nazism if the earlier theory was metaphysical, if the later theory is nonmetaphysical, and if there is a break between them. Yet it can no longer be denied that Heidegger was attracted to National Socialism and that this attraction was based on his theory. The implicit claim underlying the efforts of Derrida and Lacoue-Labarthe to show that Heidegger's development can be neatly separated into an early position, that of Heidegger I, and a later position, that of Heidegger II, was meant to show how Heidegger could become a Nazi in virtue of his theory, although his later theory was not thereby affected.

Heidegger's reinterpretation of his original position as beyond metaphysics and authentically humanist is internally consistent. Yet this way of reading Heidegger's theory fails to explain his attraction to Nazism. On his own account, metaphysics leads to "biologism," precisely the point that Derrida and Lacoue-Labarthe suggest. However, this kind of postmetaphysical reading of the Heideggerian theory is unsatisfactory. For if Heidegger's conception of Dasein is postmetaphysical, then his view of Dasein in terms of being can consistently be described as humanist in his special sense; but his turning to Nazism cannot be explained through his thought and remains inexplicable.

Heidegger's later description of his theory as postmetaphysical humanism is not inconsistent, although it fails to explain his attraction to Nazism. I believe that the interpretation of his position that Heidegger puts forward in the "Letter on Humanism" is self-consistent, not inconsistent, but unacceptable since at this late date any interpretation of Heidegger's position needs to understand the relation of his thought to National Socialism.

The suggestions by Aubenque or Fédier that Heidegger's turning to Nazism is due merely to his political naïveté or even, as Gadamer would have it, the political incompetence of philosophers in general, are inadequate since they fail to recognize the special status of a philosopher, particularly a singularly important philosopher. Heidegger's self-interpretation clearly fails if it is necessary to account for his political turning on the basis of his thought. Although I regard the efforts by Derrida and Lacoue-Labarthe as mistaken, they at least have the virtue of going beyond Heidegger, whose self-interpretation leaves his Nazi turning as inexplicable, to propose an explanation where Heidegger offers none.

Heidegger's later description of his theory as humanist is problematic. He is obviously free to define "humanism" as he desires since this term is solely normative. Yet this approach that might be open to someone else is not open to Heidegger since he claims consistently to grasp the essence, in this case the essence of human being, through his effort to think man's humanity with respect to being. It is appropriate to ask: does Heidegger grasp man's historical essence? Does he comprehend the essence of human being?

Although Heidegger's theory is superficially humanist, on a deeper level it is not humanist at all. The humanism of Heidegger's theory lies in stress on the importance of classical studies, particularly Greek literature and Greek philosophy, a theory of human being, and a version of the traditional claim for the social indispensability of philosophy. All of these features are stressed in the "Letter on Humanism."

The German philosophical embrace of Greek antiquity under way as early as the mid-eighteenth century, for instance in Johann Joachim Winckelmann's famous studies of Greek art, reached an early peak at the beginning of the nineteenth century in Hegel's thought.[41] Heidegger offers an extreme form of the typical German philosophical *graecophilia*. His familiar claim that the problem of being, originally raised in Greek philosophy, was later covered up leads to a series of other claims, including his conviction of the importance of the Greek conceptions of science and technology, his insistence that a defective translation of Greek philosophical terms into Latin deprived the later philosophical discussion of fundamental Greek philosophical insights, and so on. In a typical passage, after objecting to the situation in which "metaphysics persists in the oblivion of Being," he adds that

> the same thinking that has led us to this insight into the questionable essence of humanism has likewise compelled us to think the essence of man more primordially. With regard to this more essential *humanitas* of *homo humanus* there arises the possibility of restoring to the word "humanism" a historical sense that is older than its oldest meaning chronologically reckoned .... "Humanism" now means, in case we decide to retain the word, that the essence of man is essential for the truth of Being, specifically in such a way that the word does not pertain simply to man as such.[42]

Heidegger's theory is humanist according to its letter but not according to its spirit. We can distinguish between humanism, antihumanism, and non-humanism. If humanism is basically concerned with human being, then antihumanism opposes it, and nonhumanism is merely indifferent to, neither for nor against, human being. Consider, for a moment, the following passage on humanism taken from an article by Fernand Braudel, the great French historian. Braudel writes:

> Humanism is a way of hoping, or wishing men to be brothers one with another, of wishing that civilizations, each on its own account and all together, should save themselves and save us. It means accepting and hoping that the doors of the present should be wide open to the future, beyond all the failures, declines, and catastrophes predicted by strange prophets (prophets all deriving from black literature). The present can not be the boundary, which all centuries, heavy with eternal tragedy, see before them as an obstacle, but which the hope of man, ever since man has been, has succeeded in overcoming.[43]

Braudel's view of humanism is typical, typical of the use of the term to refer to an approach to the world and ourselves from an anthropological perspective. There are many types of humanism, but humanism of all kinds is, as the term suggests, oriented toward human being. All ways to understand "humanism" basically center on human being. Any other way of understanding this term is non-standard, different from, eventually unrelated to the way it has traditionally been understood in all the major Western languages.

If "humanism" is understood as essentially focused on human being, then Heidegger is not a humanist, despite his appeal to this term. For he employs the word in a way that breaks with its essential meaning for which he arbitrarily substitutes his own meaning. Heidegger's theory is oriented early and late, as he repeatedly claims, toward the problem of being. At no time in his long career, stretching over some six decades, was he concerned with human being other than as the clue to being. As early as his course on the hermeneutics of facticity in 1923, he argued that philosophy as such had no warrant to concern itself with universal humanity and culture,[44] and called for a reexamination of the misunderstood Greek view of being.[45] In *Being and Time*, his main work, he provides a theory of Dasein that he understood as concerned with being. In his infamous rectorial address, when he joined the Nazi party and in other documents of the period, he insisted on the realization of the German as German, "on the will that our people fulfill its historical mission."[46] This chauvinistic claim, which echoes National Socialist rhetoric, would be misconstrued as an interest in human being in general, since Heidegger's main concern is still being. Later, in the famous lecture on "The Age of the World Picture" he decenters the subject when he comes to believe that being does not need to be revealed since it reveals itself. Still later, in the "Letter on Humanism," he affirms that in his theory he thinks "the humanity of man from nearness to being,"[47] and reaffirms the message of his lectures on the hermeneutics of facticity in insisting that his theory is completely unrelated to practice.[48]

According to Heidegger, there is a reciprocal relation between revealing and concealing. In *Being and Time*, he maintains that covered-up-ness, literally concealment, is the counterpart of the phenomenon. In "On The Essence of Truth," he insists that concealment is undisclosedness, so that untruth is inherent in the notion of truth itself.

This view can be applied to Heidegger's theory and its French interpretation. The proposed link between Heidegger and humanism conceals more than it reveals. The fact that Heidegger is an unusually important thinker explains the widespread interest in his theory, including the interest among French philosophers. The perception that he is a humanist thinker goes further in specifically explaining his emergence as the master thinker in France in a way and to an extent unparalleled elsewhere.

The humanist reading of Heidegger's theory, so important in the French discussion, is obviously mistaken. If "humanism" is used in a way that retains a link with the Western humanist tradition, then it refers to "a way to understand human being centered on human being." Although Heidegger can use the term "humanism" as he wishes, his use of it has nothing other than the name in common with the term as used in the Western intellectual tradition. And wild claims that traditional humanism is Nazism meant to exculpate Heidegger's continuing commitment to a form of National Socialism do not justify a reading of his theory early or late as humanism in any recognizable sense of the term. For Heidegger's main commitment, as he indicates, is to being, hence not to human being, or to human being only as it concerns being. For this reason, Heidegger is not and should not be understood as a humanist thinker.

Sartre and other French readers of Heidegger have long been overly generous in detecting a convergence between Heidegger's theory and their own concerns around the theme of humanism when there is none. This supposed convergence is based on a misunderstanding of Heidegger's theory, initially as philosophical anthropology, or anthropological humanism, and later as postmetaphysical humanism. Yet in the final analysis Heidegger is neither an anthropological or metaphysical, nor a postmetaphysical humanist, in fact not a humanist at all; and the French reading, based as it was on the letter but not the spirit of the theory, misperceived a similarity between it and Heidegger's nonhumanistic thought.

RETURN TO DASEIN?

In writings after *Being and Time*, Heidegger rejects the early French reading of Dasein as philosophical anthropology. The later French reading of Heidegger as a postmetaphysical humanist significantly overlooks, in fact blocks access to, a central insight: his conception of human being as Dasein, or existence. In Heidegger's writings, being, his official topic, finally remains remarkably vague since he never tells us much about it. In his early writings, however, he does tell us a great deal, much of it still useful, about human being.

Postmetaphysical humanism is incompatible with philosophical anthropology, with the approach to the subject as a human being rooted in the world as the legitimate basis for an understanding of the world and ourselves. This insight, broached within Heidegger's concern with being, is important whether or not we are concerned with the problem of being. Yet it is lost in the later French reading of Heidegger as a postmetaphysical humanist. Since Heidegger later equates humanism with metaphysics, a postmetaphysical humanism goes beyond his insight into human being as existence, beyond the anthropological dimension of his insight into human being and human understanding.

In his later theory, Heidegger decentered the subject in order to concentrate on being that simply reveals itself. But as Descartes and Kant already knew, knowledge of all kinds, including phenomenological knowledge, can only be revealed to a subject. If this is correct, then the later Heidegger moved away from a central insight that has been simply overlooked in the more recent, poststructuralist reading of Heidegger as a humanist.

My suggestion is that it is useful, if necessary by reading Heidegger against himself, to make a qualified return to Heidegger's early view of Dasein read, as the early French Heidegger readers read it, from an anthropological angle of vision. This view carries forward the idea of human subjectivity that is the valid kernel in the theory of the subject that pervades modern philosophy. Heidegger is not a humanist, since he is basically unconcerned with human being. And although early thought, his Nazi turning and later thought, are inseparably linked, this is not a reason to reject his theory as a whole. Yet neither should his theory be accepted as a whole in uncritical fashion. Rather, it should be interpreted, as his own contextual approach to human being suggests, against the background of his life and times. When this is done, it

188

will be seen that there are aspects of Heidegger's theory that still speak to us in powerful ways. An example is his early, insightful conception of human subjectivity through the lens of its existence, which points to a useful way to develop the traditional, anthropological conception of humanism that has never been more necessary than at present, in the wake of Heidegger's own theory.

NOTES

INTRODUCTION

1 Martin Heidegger, *Aus der Erfahrung des Denkens* (Frankfurt/M.: Vittorio Klostermann, 1983), p. 76.
2 See Stephen W. Hawking, *A Brief History of Time: From the Big Bang to Black Holes* (Toronto: Bantam, 1988), pp. 91–92.
3 See Michael S. Roth, *Knowing and History: Appropriations of Hegel in Twentieth-Century France* (Ithaca: Cornell University Press, 1988), p. 60.
4 See Tom Rockmore, *On Heidegger's Nazism and Philosophy* (Berkeley: University of California Press, 1992).
5 Philippe Lacoue-Labarthe, *La Fiction du politique* (Paris: Bourgois, 1987), p. 138.
6 See Immanuel Kant, *Critique of Pure Reason*, trans. Norman Kemp Smith (New York: Macmillan, 1961), B xiii, p. 20.
7 See Otto Pöggeler, *Neue Wege mit Heidegger* (Freiburg: Alber, 1992), p. 11.
8 Alexandre Koyré, "Qu'est-ce que la métaphysique?," *Bifur*, no. 8 (1931), p. 5.
9 See François Fédier, *Heidegger: Anatomie d'un scandale* (Paris: Robert Laffont, 1988).
10 Cited in Frédéric de Towarnicki, "Traduire Heidegger," *Magazine Littéraire*, no. 222 (September 1985), p. 75.
11 See Victor Farías, *Heidegger et le nazisme* (Paris: Verdier, 1987). See also Victor Farías, *Heidegger and Nazism*, ed. Joseph Margolis and Tom Rockmore (Philadelphia: Temple University Press, 1989).
12 See "William James as Philosopher," in Arthur O. Lovejoy, *The Thirteen Pragmatisms and Other Essays* (Baltimore: Johns Hopkins University Press, 1963), pp. 88–89.
13 For recent discussion of Heidegger's politics, see *The Heidegger Case: On Philosophy and Politics*, ed. Tom Rockmore and Joseph Margolis (Philadelphia: Temple University Press, 1992).
14 For the most recent discussion, see Thomas Sheehan, "A Normal Nazi," *The New York Review of Books*, vol. 11, no. 1–2 (January 14, 1993), pp. 30–35.
15 See Richard Rorty, *Contingency, Irony, and Solidarity* (New York: Cambridge University Press, 1989).
16 This point is suggested by Sallis. See John Sallis, *Echoes: After Heidegger* (Bloomington: Indiana University Press, 1990), p. 11.
17 For this argument, see *Being and Time*, tr. John Macquarrie and Edward Robinson (New York: Harper & Row, 1962), §§ 31–33, pp. 182–195.
18 See Mikkel Borch-Jacobsen, *Lacan: Le maître absolu* (Paris: Flammarion, 1990).

19 See Michel Foucault, *Les Mots et les choses: Une archéologie des sciences humaines* (Paris: Gallimard, 1966).

20 See Jacques Derrida, *L'Ecriture et la différence* (Paris: Seuil, 1967), p. 95.

21 See Alexandre Kojève, *Introduction à la lecture de Hegel: Leçons sur la "Phénoménologie de l'Esprit" professées de 1933 à 1939 à l'Ecole des Hautes-Etudes*, ed. Raymond Queneau (Paris: Gallimard, 1947).

22 Jean-Paul Sartre, *L'Existentialisme est un humanisme* (Paris: Nagel, 1964).

23 See e.g. Jean Grondin, *Le Tournant dans la pensée de Martin Heidegger* (Paris: Vrin, 1987).

24 For a Heidegger defender who makes this point, see Ernst Nolte, *Heidegger: Politik und Geschichte im Leben und Denken* (Berlin: Propyläen, 1992), pp. 147, 153–169.

25 Martin Heidegger, *An Introduction to Metaphysics*, trans. Ralph Manheim (New Haven: Yale University Press, 1977), p. 199.

26 See Alfred North Whitehead, *Process and Reality: An Essay in Cosmology* (New York: Harper & Row, 1960), p. 63.

27 See Benedetto Croce, *What Is Living and What Is Dead in Hegel?*, trans. Douglas Ainslie (New York: Russell & Russell, 1969).

1 HEIDEGGER AS A "FRENCH" PHILOSOPHER

1 This statement occurs in the context of a remark on the adequacy of language to philosophy:

> I have in mind especially the inner relationship of the German language with the language of the Greeks and with their thought. This has been confirmed for me today again by the French. When they [i.e. the French] think, they speak German, being sure that they could not make it with their own language.

"Only a God Can Save Us: *Der Spiegel's* Interview with Martin Heidegger," *Philosophy Today*, vol. 20 (Winter 1976), p. 282.

2 For Heidegger's overture toward French philosophy, see "Wege zur Aussprache," in Martin Heidegger, *Aus der Erfahrung des Denkens*, ed. Hermann Heidegger (Frankfurt/M.: Vittorio Klostermann, 1983) pp. 135–139.

3 The main example is his discussion in *Being and Time*. See Martin Heidegger, *Being and Time*, tr. J. Macquarie and E. Robinson (New York: Harper & Row, 1962) §§ 14–15. See also "The Age of the World Picture," in Martin Heidegger, *The Question Concerning Technology and Other Essays*, tr. William Lovitt (New York: Harper & Row, 1977), pp. 115–154.

4 See "The Letter on Humanism," in Martin Heidegger, *Basic Writings*, ed. David Farrell Krell (New York: Harper & Row, 1977), pp. 189–242.

5 For instance, in a recent collection of essays on the fiftieth anniversary of Husserl's death, fully four of the sixteen articles directly consider Heidegger and Husserl, and this relation is discussed in passing in others as well. See *Phänomenologie im Widerstreit: Zum 50. Todestag Edmund Husserls*, ed. Christoph Jamme and Otto Pöggeler (Frankfurt/M.: Suhrkamp, 1989).

6 Pascal receives a canonical treatment in this work. On the uses of Pascal in this book, see Antoine Arnauld and Pierre Nicole, *La Logique ou l'art de penser*, intr. Louis Marin (Paris: Flammarion, 1970), pp. 17–18. See also the discussion of the infinite, in the first chapter of the fourth part that was inserted in the book in the edition published in 1664. Pascal was a Jansenist as were Arnauld and Nicole. For a discussion that relates Pascal's thought to Jansenism, see Nannerl O. Keohane,

Philosophy and the State in France: The Renaissance to the Enlightenment (Princeton: Princeton University Press, 1980), ch. 9: "Authority and Community in the Two Cities," pp. 262–282. For a recent discussion that examines the philosophical status of Pascal's thought, see Vincent Carraud, *Pascal et la philosophie* (Paris: Presses universitaires de France, 1992).

7 See "Philosophy as Rigorous Science," in Edmund Husserl, *Phenomenology and the Crisis of Philosophy*, tr. Quentin Lauer (New York: Harper, 1965).

8 In this respect, there is a parallel with the German classification of philosophy as a *Geisteswissenschaft*, a term that is often rendered as "human science" or "social science."

9 For a discussion of the concept of the French intellectual from the time of the Dreyfus affair to the present, see Pascal Ory and Jean-François Sirinelli, *Les Intellectuels en France de l'Affaire Dreyfus à nos jours* (Paris: Armand Colin, 1986). For a history of French philosophers in context, see Jean-Louis Fabiani, *Les Philosophes de la république* (Paris: Minuit, 1988).

10 V. Descombes, *Le Même et l'autre: Quarante-cinq ans de philosophie française (1933–1978)* (Paris: Editions de Minuit, 1979), p. 17.

11 It has been argued that the effort devoted to philosophy in the last years of the *lycée* and the first years of the university can usefully be seen as an attempt to indoctrinate all French students. See François Châtelet, *La Philosophie des professeurs* (Paris: Grasset, 1970).

12 See Stanley Hoffman, cited in Deidre Bair, *Simone de Beauvoir: A Biography* (New York: Simon & Schuster, 1990), p. 548.

13 This concern is easily apparent to foreigners. In a letter to Ralph Ellison (August 18, 1945), Richard Wright, who was then living in France, reports: "France is in ferment. Their discussion of the artist's responsibility surpasses anything I've ever seen." Cited in Bair, *Simone de Beauvoir*, p. 412.

14 See Jean-Paul Sartre, *Being and Nothingness: A Phenomenological Essay in Ontology*, tr. Hazel E. Barnes (New York: Washington Square Press, 1973), especially the discussion of "Freedom and Responsiblity," pp. 707–711.

15 Henri Bergson, *La Philosophie* (Paris: Larousse, 1915), pp. 5ff, cited in Franz Böhm, *Anti-Cartesianismus: Deutsche Philosophie im Widerstand* (Leipzig: Felix Meiner, 1938), p. 25 n5.

16 See René Descartes, *The Philosophical Works of Descartes*, vol. I, ed. and tr. Elizabeth S. Haldane and G. R. T. Ross (Cambridge: Cambridge University Press, 1970), p. 145.

17 See Michel Foucault, *Histoire de la folie* (Paris: Gallimard, 1972), pp. 56–59.

18 See "Cogito and Histoire de la folie," in Jacques Derrida, *L'Ecriture et la différence* (Paris: Editions du Seuil, 1967), p. 95.

19 For a study of Descartes's influence on French literature, see Gustave Lanson, "L'Influence de la philosophie cartésienne dans la littérature française," *Revue de métaphysique et de morale*, vol. 4 (1896).

20 Ernst Cassirer, *The Philosophy of the Enlightenment*, tr. Fritz C. A. Koelln and James Pettegrove (Princeton: Princeton University Press, 1968), p. 28.

21 A recent example is provided by the career of Jean-Luc Marion. Marion, who has also done much other work, has attained an impressive position in French philosophy in large part on the strength of his important studies of Descartes. See Jean-Luc Marion, *Sur l'ontologie grise de Descartes* (Paris: Vrin, 1981); *Sur la théologie blanche de Descartes* (Paris: Presses universitaires de France, 1981); *Sur le prisme métaphysique de Descartes* (Paris: Presses universitaires de France, 1986); *René Descartes: Règles utiles et claires pour la direction de l'esprit en la recherche de la vérité* (The Hague: Nijhoff, 1977); *Index des "Regulae ad directionem Ingenii" de René Descartes*, in collaboration with J.-R. Armogathe

(Rome: Edizione dell'Ateneo, 1976); *Questions cartésiennes* (Paris: Presses universitaires de France, 1991).

22 See Heidegger, *Being and Time*, pp. 122–134.
23 See "The Age of the World Picture," pp. 115–154.
24 See e.g. G. W. F. Hegel, *Faith and Knowledge*, tr. Walter Cerf and H. S. Harris (Albany: State University of New York Press, 1977).
25 See Jules Vuillemin, *L'Héritage kantien et la révolution copernicienne* (Paris: Presses universitaires de France, 1954), p. 301: "Or la philosophie moderne, que nous faisons commencer à la Révolution copernicienne, ne fait que décrire ce déplacement caractéristique d'une pensée théologique dans un monde athée."
26 See Cassirer, *Philosophy of the Enlightenment*, p. 134.
27 For a discussion of the relation between religion and philosophy in French philosophy, see Etienne Gilson, "La notion de la philosophie chrétienne," paper presented to the Société française de philosophie on March 21, 1931. The idea of philosophy in the light of faith is perfectly normal in the French context. See, for example, Etienne Gilson, *Introduction à la philosophie chrétienne* (Paris: Vrin, 1960).
28 For a recent example of this rightwing approach to Hegel, see Quentin Lauer, *Hegel's Concept of God* (Albany: SUNY Press, 1982).
29 For Hegel's view, see G. W. F. Hegel, *Werke in zwanzig Bänden*, vol. XX: *Vorlesungen über die Geschichte der Philosophie 3*, ed. Eva Moldenhauer and Karl Markus Michel (Frankfurt/M.: Suhrkamp, 1971), pp. 49–50.
30 See ibid., p. 120.
31 Ibid., p. 123.
32 See his treatment of religion in the chapter on "Absolute Knowledge" in *Phenomenology of Spirit*, tr. A. V. Miller (Oxford: Oxford University Press, 1977).
33 See Tom Rockmore, *Hegel's Circular Epistemology* (Bloomington: Indiana University Press, 1986).
34 For contrasting views of Roman Catholicism in France, see Antoine Arnauld, *Apologie pour les catholiques* (Paris, 1651) and Pierre Bayle, *Ce que c'est que la France toute catholique*, (Paris, 1686, rpt. Paris: Vrin, 1973).
35 Phenomenology is presently the main French philosophical tendency. For an analysis of the religious element in French phenomenology since the death of Merleau-Ponty in 1951, see Dominique Janicaud, *Le Tournant théologique de la phénoménologie française* (Combas: Editions de l'Eclat, 1991).
36 See Rémi Brague, *La Voie romaine* (Paris: Editions Criterion, 1992).
37 See e.g. Marion's analysis of the ontological proof, "L'argument relève-t-il de l'ontologie?," in Marion, *Questions cartésiennes*, pp. 221–258.
38 In the thirteenth of his *Principles*, he answers the question of in what sense the knowledge of all other things depends on knowledge of God with the statement that the mind "can have no certain knowledge until it is acquainted with its creator." Descartes, *Philosophical Works*, I, p. 224.
39 See Martial Gueroult, *Descartes selon l'ordre des raisons*, vol. II (Paris: Aubier-Montaigne, 1968), p. 272:

> D'abord réduit à un point au milieu de la nuit du doute, la lumière du Cogito, grandissant en quelque sorte sur elle-même, rencontre enfin le Dieu infini, autre que moi-même, qui détruisant la ténébreuse fiction de la tromperie universelle, illumine tout le ciel, d'un horizon à l'autre, par la splendeur souveraine de la véracité absolue.

40 See e.g. the fourth part of the *Discourse on Method*, where he writes:

For to begin with, that which I have just taken as a rule, that is to say, that all the things that we very clearly and very distinctly conceive of are true, is certain only because God exists, and that He is a Perfect Being, and that all that is in us issues from Him.

(Descartes, *Philosophical Works*, I, p. 105)

He makes a similar point in the *Reply to Objections II*, for instance in his denial that an atheist can really know:

That *an atheist can know clearly that the three angles of a triangle are equal to two right angles*, I do not deny, I merely affirm that, on the other hand, such knowledge on his part cannot constitute true science, because no knowledge that can be rendered doubtful should be called science.

(Descartes, *Philosophical Works*, II, p. 39; Descartes's emphases)

41 See Arnauld and Nicole, *La Logique ou l'art de penser*, p. 33.
42 See Alexandre Kojève, *Introduction à la lecture de Hegel: Leçons sur la "Phénoménologie de l'Esprit" professés de 1933 à 1939 à l'Ecole des Hautes-Etudes*, ed. Raymond Queneau (Paris: Gallimard, 1947).
43 For discussion of his view of religion, see George Kovacs, *The Question of God in Heidegger's Phenomenology* (Evanston: Northwestern University Press, 1990); see also Richard Schaeffler, "Heidegger und die Theologie", in *Heidegger und die praktische Philosophie*, ed. Annemarie Gethmann-Siefert and Otto Pöggeler (Frankfurt/M.: Suhrkamp, 1988), pp. 286–309.
44 See Etienne Gilson, *L'Etre et l'essence* (Paris: Vrin, 1987), pp. 372, 376.
45 This thesis is developed by Sluga. See Hans D. Sluga, *Gottlob Frege* (London: Routledge & Kegan Paul, 1980).
46 See Richard Rorty, *Essays on Heidegger and Others* (Cambridge: Cambridge University Press, 1991), p. 21.
47 See e.g. Jacques Rivelaygue, *Leçons de métaphysique allemande*, vol. I: *De Leibniz à Hegel* (Paris: Grasset, 1990), and vol. II: *Kant, Heidegger, Habermas* (Paris: Grasset, 1992).
48 On this point, see V. Descombe's useful study, *Le Même et l'autre: Quarante-cinq ans de philosophie française (1933–1978)* (Paris: Editions de Minuit, 1979).
49 See Michel Henry, *Phénoménologie matérielle* (Paris: Presses universitaires de France, 1990).
50 This is the view of Marion, who writes: "A l'évidence, depuis que la métaphysique a trouvé sa fin, soit comme un achèvement avec Hegel, soit comme un crépuscule avec Nietzsche, la philosophie n'a pu se poursuivre authentiquement que sous la figure de la phénoménologie." *Phénoménologie et métaphysique*, ed. Jean-Luc Marion and Guy Planty-Bonjour (Paris: Presses universitaires de France, 1984), p. 7.
51 For a brief account see Jean Hering, "Phenomenology in France," in *Philosophic Thought in France and the United States*, ed. Marvin Farber (Buffalo: University of Buffalo Publications in Philosophy, 1950), pp. 67–86. For a more detailed account, see H. Spiegelberg, *The Phenomenological Movement: A Historical Introduction* (The Hague: Martinus Nijhoff, 1982), pp. 425–452.
52 As recently as 1976, it was possible to publish an introduction to phenomenology that considered only Husserl's *Cartesian Meditations*. See Jean T. Desanti, *Introduction à la phénoménologie* (Paris: Gallimard, 1976).
53 The French-language Husserl discussion began quite early. For an early discussion of Husserl's opposition to psychologism, see L. Noël, "Les frontières de la logique," *Revue néoscolastique*, no. 17 (1910), pp. 211–233. Some time later, a fuller discussion of Husserl's theory was provided by Gurvitch. See Georges

Gurvitch, *Les Tendances actuelles de la philosophie allemande: E. Husserl, M. Scheler, E. Lask, N. Hartmann, M. Heidegger* (Paris: Vrin, 1930). Gurvitch describes Husserl as "le fondateur de la philosophie phénoménologique," and considers Heidegger's philosophy as both irrationalist and dialectical (ibid., pp. 11–66, 228).

54 See Emmanuel Lévinas, *Théorie de l'intuition dans la phénoménologie de Husserl* (Paris: Vrin, 1977). Derrida has edited Husserl and written widely on his thought. See Edmund Husserl, *L'Origine de la géométrie*, tr. and intr. Jacques Derrida (Paris: Presses universitaires de France, 1962, 1974); Jacques Derrida, *La Voix et le phénomène* (Paris: Presses universitaires de France, 1967); Jacques Derrida, *Le Problème de la génèse dans la philosophie de Husserl* (Paris: Presses universitaires de France, 1990). Lévinas is a cotranslator of Husserl's *Cartesian Meditations* into French.

55 For some examples, see "Husserl et Heidegger," in Jean-François Courtine, *Heidegger et la phénoménologie* (Paris: Vrin, 1990), pp. 161–282; Jean-Luc Marion, *Réduction et donation: Recherches sur Husserl, Heidegger et la phénoménologie* (Paris: Presses universitaires de France, 1989); Emmanuel Lévinas, *En découvrant l'existence avec Husserl et Heidegger* (Paris: Vrin, 1988).

56 For recent discussion between the relation of Husserl and Heidegger, see the articles by Manfred Riedel, Aldo Masullo, Otto Pöggeler, and Pier Aldo Rovatti in Jamme and Pöggeler, *Phänomenologie im Widerstreit*.

57 See Otto Pöggeler, *Martin Heidegger's Path of Thinking*, tr. Daniel Magurshak and Sigmund Barber (Atlantic Highlands: Humanities Press, 1989), p. 61.

58 On the question of the relation between Husserl and Heidegger, Merleau-Ponty writes:

> Voudra-t-on lever ces contradictions en distinguant entre la phénoménologie de Husserl et celle de Heidegger? Mais tout *Sein und Zeit* est sorti d'une indication de Husserl et n'est en somme qu'une explicitation du "natürlichen Weltbegriff" ou du "Lebenswelt" que Husserl, à la fin de sa vie donnait pour thème premier à la phénoménologie.
> (*Phénoménologie de la perception*, Paris: Gallimard, 1945, p. 1)

59 See "My Way to Phenomenology," in Martin Heidegger, *On Time and Being*, tr. Joan Stambaugh (New York: Harper & Row, 1972), pp. 74–82.

60 For an argument that Heidegger's later thought remains phenomenology, see "Réduction phénoménologique-transcendentale et différence ontico-ontologique," in Courtine, *Heidegger et la phénoménologie*, pp. 207–248.

61 For Wahl's claim that Hegel's logic is phenomenological, see Jean Wahl, *La Logique de Hegel comme phénoménologie* (Paris: Centre de documentation universitaire, 1969).

62 For Derrida's claim, see Husserl, *L'Origine de la géométrie*, p. 158.

63 For an instance of the French tendency to consider Hegel and Heidegger together, see Denise Souche-Dagues, *Hégélianisme et dualisme: Réflexions sur le phénomène* (Paris: Vrin, 1990).

64 The outstanding example of this in Heidegger's corpus is his dialogue with Kant. See Martin Heidegger, *Kant and the Problem of Metaphysics*, tr. Richard Taft (Bloomington: Indiana University Press, 1990).

65 See Heidegger, *Being and Time*, § 82, pp. 480–486.

66 See Michel Foucault, *Histoire de la folie* (Paris: 10/18, n.d.).

67 See "Joseph de Maistre and the Origins of Fascism," in Isaiah Berlin, *The Crooked Timber of Humanity*, ed. Henry Hardy (London: John Murray), 1990, pp. 91–174.

68 See Joseph-Arthur Gobineau, *Essai sur l'inégalité des races humaines* (Paris, 1853–1855).

69 It has become standard to emphasize the appeal of German philosophy for French thinkers. Against this tendency, Stoekl has recently stressed the importance of Emile Durkheim's thought for an understanding of contemporary French philosophy and literature. See Allan Stoekl, *Agonies of the Intellectual: Commitment, Subjectivity, and the Performative in the Twentieth-Century French Tradition* (Lincoln: University of Nebraska Press, 1992), esp. ch. 1: "Durkheim and the Totem Act," pp. 25–56.

70 See François Marie Arouet de Voltaire, *Lettres philosophiques* (Paris: Flammarion, 1964), esp. letters 13–17, pp. 81–117.

71 Hippolyte Taine, *Histoire de la littérature anglaise*, vol. V (Paris: Hachette, 1863–1864, 12th edn., 1911) p. 243, cited in Léon Brunschvicg, *Le Progrès de la conscience dans la philosophie occidentale* (2 vols., Paris: Félix Alcan, 1927), vol. II, p. 395.

72 See Luc Ferry and Alain Renaut, *La Pensée 68: Essai sur l'anti-humanisme contemporain* (Paris: Gallimard, 1988), p. 125.

73 See Eric Weil, *Logique de la philosophie* (Paris: Vrin, 1974).

74 See Fabiani, *Les Philosophes de la république*, p. 9.

75 See e.g. Paul Nizan, *Les Chiens de garde* (Paris: Rieder, 1932).

76 There is a large literature on the French system of elite schools. See R. J. Smith, *The Ecole normale supérieure and the Third Republic* (Albany: State University of New York Press, 1982). For further bibliography, see Pierre Bourdieu, *La Noblesse d'état: Grandes écoles et esprit de corps* (Paris: Editions de Minuit, 1989), pp. 329–330.

77 The *École normale* is a main source of future philosophers. For a detailed study of *normaliens* around the year 1920, see Jean-François Sirinelli, *Génération intellectuelle: Khagneux et normaliens dans l'entre-deux-guerres* (Paris: Fayard, 1988). For a series of articles by former students, see Alain Peyrefitte (ed.), *Rue d'Ulm, Chroniques de la vie normalienne* (Paris: Flammarion, 1963).

78 For comparative data, see Gustave Lanson, *L'Ecole normale supérieure* (Paris: Hachette, 1926), pp. 48–49.

79 This is the opinion of George Pompidou:

> On est normalien comme on est prince de sang. Rien d'extérieur ne le marque. Mais cela se sait, cela se voit, qu'il soit poli, et même humain de ne pas le faire sentir aux autres . . . . Cette qualité est consubstantielle. On ne devient pas, on naît normalien, comme on naissait chevalier. Le concours n'est que l'adoubement. La cérémonie a ses rites, la veillée d'armes se déroule dans des lieux de retraite placés comme il convient sous la protection de nos rois: Saint-Louis, Henri IV, Louis-le-Grand. Les gardiens du Saint-Graal, dont l'assemblée prend pour l'occasion le nom de jury, reconnaissent leurs jeunes pairs et les appellent à eux.
>
> (G. Pompidou, cited in Pierre Bourdieu, *La Noblesse d'état*, p. 534n)

80 See Pierre Bourdieu, "Epreuve scolaire et consécration sociale," *Actes de la recherche en sciences sociales*, no. 39 (September 1981), p. 30:

> On ne peut comprendre complètement les caractéristiques les plus significatives des "ecoles d'élite" (dans le cas particulier, les classes préparatoires aux Grandes écoles et les Grandes écoles elles-mêmes) qu'à condition d'apercevoir que la transformation qu'elles ont à opérer n'est pas seulement *technique* mais aussi sociale ou, si l'on veut, *magique*. Toutes les opérations *techniques* du processus éducatif sont surdéterminées symboliquement

parce qu'elles remplissent toujours par surcroît une *fonction de consécration* (ou de sociodicée) et qu'elles peuvent donc être décrites comme autant de moments d'un *rituel de consécration*: la sélection et aussi "l'élection" des "élus," l'examen est aussi "épreuve," la formation "ascèse" et la compétence technique, compétence sociale et qualification charismatique.

81 On unconditional loyalty to the system of which they are a product, see Pierre Bourdieu, *Homo Academicus* (Paris: Editions de Minuit, 1984), p. 134:

> Issus pour une très forte part du corps enseignant, et surtout de ses couches inférieures et moyennes, presque tous passés par la khagne et par l'Ecole normale supérieure, où ils enseignent encore très souvent, souvent mariés à des enseignantes, les professeurs canoniques des disciplines canoniques accordent à l'institution scolaire qu'ils ont choisie parce qu'elle les a choisis, et réciproquement, une adhésion qui, d'être si totalement conditionnée, a quelque chose de total, d'absolu, d'inconditionnel.

82 Bourdieu points out that for this reason, although Ricoeur and Hyppolite were on a roughly equal philosophical level, Hyppolite, the normalien, attracted many more doctoral students than did Ricoeur, who did not have this distinction. See Bourdieu, *Homo Academicus*, pp. 124–127, 201–203.
83 This criticism is unjust. See "Hegel and the Social Function of Reason," in Tom Rockmore, *Hegel and Contemporary Philosophy* (Atlantic Highlands, NJ: Humanities Press, forthcoming).
84 For the concepts of authentic choice and destiny, see Heidegger, *Being and Time*, § 74, pp. 434–439. For an analysis of the relation between Heidegger's philosophical thought and his Nazism, see Tom Rockmore, *On Heidegger's Nazism and Philosophy* (Berkeley: University of California Press, 1992).

2 HEIDEGGER AND THE MASTER THINKER IN FRENCH PHILOSOPHY

1 Passmore signals his awareness of the dominant roles played by Davidson and Dummett by devoting special consideration to their views and their views only. See John Passmore, *Recent Philosophers* (LaSalle: Open Court, 1990).
2 Heidegger is reported to favor speech over writing as part of his preference for the oracular utterance that is to be heard but neither interpreted nor tested. See Rainer Marten, *Heidegger Lesen* (Munich: Wilhelm Fink, 1991), p. 7. This is also a persistent theme in Derrida's corpus. See e.g. Jacques Derrida, *L'Ecriture et la différence* (Paris: Seuil, 1967).
3 Kripke writes:

> In January of 1970, I gave three talks at Princeton University transcribed here. As the style of the transcript makes clear, I gave the talks without a written text, and, in fact, without notes. The present text is lightly edited from the *verbatim* manuscript.
> (Saul A. Kripke, *Naming and Necessity*, Cambridge: Harvard University Press, 1980, p. 22; Kripke's emphasis)

Another example is Kojève's famous work on Hegel, which consists of the stenographic record of a course delivered orally and without notes. See Alexandre Kojève, *Introduction à la lecture de Hegel: Leçons sur la "Phénoménologie de l'Esprit" professées de 1933 à 1939 à l'Ecole des Hautes-Etudes*, ed. Raymond Queneau (Paris: Gallimard, 1947).

4 See Martin Heidegger, *Nietzsche*, vol. I (Pfullingen: Neske, 1961), p. 450.

5 This problem is a major concern in Derrida's work. See Jacques Derrida, *De la grammatologie* (Paris: Minuit, 1967).

6 One should distinguish between a *maître à penser*, which has a positive ring, and a *mâitre penseur*, a term that has a negative overtone. For a discussion of the latter, see André Glucksmann, *Les maîtres penseurs* (Paris: Grasset, 1977).

7 Descombes insists on Hegel as the master of the philosophical game. See Vincent Descombes, *Le même et l'autre: Quarante-cinq ans de philosophie française (1933–1978)* (Paris: Editions de Minuit, 1979).

8 For this model, see Nicholas Rescher, *Strife of Systems* (Pittsburgh: University of Pittsburgh Press, 1979).

9 Alfred North Whitehead, *Process and Reality: An Essay in Cosmology* (New York: Harper & Brothers, 1960), p. 16.

10 See Immanuel Kant, *Critique of Pure Reason*, tr. Norman Kemp Smith (New York: Macmillan, 1961), B 860, p. 653.

11 See David Hume, *An Inquiry Concerning Human Understanding*, ed. Charles W. Hendel (Indianapolis: LLA, 1955), pp. 29–30.

12 Kant, *Critique of Pure Reason*, B 802, pp. 654–655.

13 Ibid., B xliv, p. 37.

14 For Fichte's view of this discussion, see "Ueber Geist und Buchstabe in der Philosophie," in *Fichtes Werke*, vol. VIII, ed. Immanuel Hermann Fichte (Berlin: Walter de Gruyter, 1971), pp. 270–300.

15 For a reading of the later German idealist tradition as an effort to complete the Kantian revolution in philosophy, see Tom Rockmore, *Hegel's Circular Epistemology* (Bloomington: Indiana University Press, 1986), chs. 2–3, pp. 16–77.

16 See Martin Heidegger, *Kant and the Problem of Metaphysics*, tr. Richard Taft (Bloomington: Indiana University Press, 1990), p. xviii.

17 This is the theme of his well known study of Kant. In a reference to Kant's critical philosophy, he writes: "The task of the laying of the ground for metaphysics, grasped in a more original way, is therefore transformed into the elucidation of the inner possibility for the understanding of Being." Heidegger, *Kant and the Problem of Metaphysics*, p. 154.

18 See Kant, *Critique of Pure Reason*, B 370, p. 310.

19 Jean-Paul Sartre, *Search For a Method*, tr. Hazel E. Barnes (New York: Vintage, 1988), pp. 5–6.

20 Sartre, *Search For a Method*, p. 7.

21 This claim has often been made, but never in a more penetrating fashion than by Heine: "Our philosophical revolution is concluded; Hegel has closed its great circle." Heinrich Heine, *Religion and Philosophy in Germany*, tr. John Snodgrass (Albany: State University of New York Press, 1986), p. 156.

22 See Sartre, *Search For a Method*, p. 7.

23 In a recent interview with Jean-François Lyotard, Hegel was characterized as "[l]e maître incontesté de la philosophie moderne." *Le Figaro Littéraire*, (September 30, 1991), p. 6.

24 According to Lévinas, besides *Being and Time*, the most important philosophical works include Plato's *Phaedrus*, Kant's *Critique of Pure Reason*, Hegel's *Phenomenology of Spirit*, and Bergson's *Time and Free Will*. See Emmanuel Lévinas, *Ethique et infini: Dialogues avec Philippe Nemo* (Paris: Fayard, 1982), pp. 27–28.

25 For a recent discussion that stresses Wittgenstein's mesmerizing influence on the Cambridge University philosophers, see Ray Monk, *Ludwig Wittgenstein: The Duty of Genius* (New York: Free Press, 1990).

26 On the concept of a black hole, see Stephen W. Hawking, *A Brief History of Time: From the Big Bang to Black Holes* (Toronto: Bantam, 1988), pp. 81–82.

27 See Whitehead, *Process and Reality*, p. 63.

28 For recent discussion, see *Antifoundationalism Old and New*, ed. Tom Rockmore and Beth Singer (Philadelphia: Temple University Press, 1991).

29 For analysis of post-Hegelian philosophy as a series of reactions to Hegel, see Richard J. Bernstein, *Praxis and Action: Contemporary Philosophies of Human Activity* (Philadelphia: University of Pennsylvania Press, 1971).

30 In my view, Miller's tendency to see Foucault as assuming Sartre's mantle and as dominating French thought overstates the case. See James Miller, *The Passion of Michel Foucault*, (New York: Simon & Schuster, 1992).

31 For a critical discussion of his views, see "Le Marx d'Althusser," in Leszek Kolakowski, *L'Esprit révolutionnaire* (Brussels: Ousia, 1978), pp. 158–185.

32 For his discussion of Sartre's *Critique of Dialectical Reason*, see "Histoire et dialectique," in Claude Lévi-Strauss, *La Pensée sauvage* (Paris: Plon, 1962), pp. 324–357.

33 After Foucault's untimely death, Paul Veyne, a respected intellectual and an intimate friend, wrote: "L'œuvre de Foucault me semble être l'événement de pensée le plus important de notre siècle." Cited in Didier Eribon, *Michel Foucault* (Paris: Flammarion, 1991), p. 352.

34 For a highly favorable reading of Foucault's corpus after his death by an important contemporary philosopher, see Gilles Deleuze, *Foucault* (Paris: Editions de Minuit, 1986).

35 For this claim, see Elisabeth Roudinesco, *Jacques Lacan and Co.: A History of Psychoanalysis in France, 1925–1985*, tr. Jeffrey Mehlman (Chicago: University of Chicago Press, 1990), p. 117. According to Borch-Jacobsen, Lacan ruled over French psychoanalysis like an absolute master. See Mikkel Borch-Jacobsen, *Lacan: Le Maître absolu* (Paris: Flammarion, 1990). He incarnated in the French psychoanalytic movement the view of the thinker as a tyrant. For Kojève's famous claim that there is no essential difference between a philosopher and a tyrant, see Alexandre Kojève, *Tyrannie et sagesse* (Paris: Gallimard, 1954), p. 252. For the resonance of this remark in recent French philosophy, see Descombes, *Le Même et l'autre*, pp. 27–28.

36 See Edward S. Casey and Melvin Woody, "Hegel, Heidegger, Lacan: The Dialectic of Desire," in *Psychiatry and the Humanities* (New Haven: Yale University Press, 1983), vol. 6, pp. 75–111.

37 For the most recent and fullest discussion of Lacan's thought and life, see Elisabeth Roudinesco, *Jacques Lacan: Esquisse d'une vie, histoire d'un système de pensée* (Paris: Fayard, 1993).

38 On this point, see Roudinesco, *Jacques Lacan and Co.*, pp. 298–299.

39 See P. van Haute, "Lacan en Kojève: het imaginaire en die dialecktiek van de meester en de slaaf," in *Tijdschrift voor Philosophie*, 48 (1986), pp. 391–415.

40 See Jacques Lacan, "L'Etourdi," *Scilicet*, vol. I (Paris: Seuil, 1986), p. 33.

41 For an analysis, see Borch-Jacobsen, *Lacan: Le maître absolu*, p. 110.

42 See Dominique Auffret, *Alexandre Kojève: La Philosophie, l'état, la fin de l'histoire* (Paris: Grasset, 1990), pp. 274–278.

43 For a recent account, see "Paris: l'existentialisme est arrivé," in Annie Cohen-Solal, *Sartre, 1905–1980* (Paris: Gallimard, 1985), pp. 325–353.

44 Husserl's thought was already known in France when Sartre began to study. In the mid-1920s, Groethuysen devoted a chapter to Husserl in his presentation of contemporary German philosophy. See "Husserl," in Bernard Groethuysen, *Introduction à la pensée philosophique allemande depuis Nietzsche* (Paris: Librairie Stock, 1926), pp. 88–103.

45 See Jean-Paul Sartre, *La Transcendance de l'ego: Esquisse d'une description phénoménologique*, ed. Sylvie LeBon (Paris: Vrin, 1966).

46 See Jean-Paul Sartre, *Les Carnets de la drôle de guerre, Novembre 1939–Mars 1940* (Paris: Gallimard, 1983), pp. 225–227.

47 See Christopher M. Fry, *Sartre and Hegel: The Variations of an Enigma in "L'Etre et le Néant"* (Bonn: Bouvier, 1988); see also Klaus Hartmann, *Sartre's Ontology: A Study of Being and Nothingness in the Light of Hegel's Logic* (Evanston: Northwestern University Press, 1966).

48 Auffret, who insists that Sartre did not attend Kojève's lectures, reports that Sartre was influenced by an article Kojève published in *Mesures*. See Auffret, *Alexandre Kojève*, p. 238n.

49 Emmanuel Lévinas, "Un langage qui nous est familier," in *Les Cahiers de la nuit surveillée*, no. 3 (1984), p. 327, cited in Emmanuel Lévinas, *La Mort et le temps* (Paris: L'Herne, 1991), p. 139.

50 For a sketch of the main approaches, from a mainly rightwing perspective, see Emil L. Fackenheim, *The Religious Dimension in Hegel's Thought* (Boston: Beacon Press, 1970), pp. 75–105.

51 See Victor Cousin, *Cours de philosophie: Introduction à l'histoire de la philosophie* (1825, 1841, rpt.) (Paris: Fayard, 1991). For an account of Cousin's rationalist reading of Hegel without the conception of dialectic, see Roudinesco, *Jacques Lacan and Co.*, pp. 136–137.

52 For a discussion of the relation of Cousin to Hegel, see Jacques d'Hondt, *Hegel in His Time*, tr. John Burbidge with Nelson Roland and Judith Levasseur (Peterborough, Ontario: Broadview, 1988), pp. 132–161 and *passim*.

53 See Lucien Herr, "Hegel," in *La Grande Encyclopédie Larousse* (Paris: Larousse, 1890–1893), rpt. in Lucien Herr, *Choix d'écrits, II: Philosophie, Histoire, Philologie* (Paris: Editions Rieder, 1932), pp. 107–140. For Queneau, Herr's discussion was the only decent one available at the time. See Raymond Queneau, "Premières confrontations avec Hegel," *Critique*, nos. 195–196 (1963), p. 694.

54 See Victor Basch, *Les Doctrines politiques des philosophies classiques de l'Allemagne* (Paris: F. Alcan, 1904, 1927).

55 See Paul Roques, *Hegel, sa vie et ses oeuvres* (Paris: F. Alcan, 1912).

56 See Victor Delbos, "Les Facteurs kantiens de la philosophie allemande de la fin du XVIIIe siècle et du commencement du XIXe siècle, in *Revue de Métaphysique et de Morale*, nos. 26 (1919), pp. 569–593, 27 (1920), pp. 1–25, 28 (1921), pp. 27–47, 29 (1922), pp. 157–176, 32 (1925), pp. 271–281, and 35 (1928), pp. 529–551. The discussions in nos. 28 and 32 deal most closely with Hegel's thought.

57 See Emile Meyerson, *De l'explication dans les sciences* (Paris: Payot, 1921). For a summary of Meyerson's reading of Hegel, see Koyré, *Etudes d'histoire de la pensée philosophique*, pp. 215–220.

58 Léon Brunschvicg, *Le Progrès de la conscience dans la philosophie occidentale* (2 vols., Paris: Alcan, 1927). See vol. II, pp. 382–401.

59 See Brunschvicg, *Le Progrès de la conscience*, II, p. 396.

60 See ibid., II, p. 398.

61 See ibid., II, p. 395.

62 See Jean Wahl, *Le Malheur de la conscience dans la philosophie de Hegel* (Paris: Rieder, 1929).

63 See Jean Hyppolite, "Discours d'introduction," in *Hegel-Studien*, supplement 3 (1964), p. 11: "je dois dire que le premier choc véritable est venu de M. Jean Wahl et que la lecture de la *Conscience malheureuse dans la philosophie de Hegel* a été une sorte de révélation."

64 In his important study of appearance, Michel Henry, for instance, whose main

influences are Husserl and, to a lesser extent, Heidegger, discusses Hegel's conception of appearance in detail. See Michel Henry, "Appendice: Mise en lumière de l'essence originaire de la révélation par opposition au concept hégélien de manifestation (Erscheinung)," in *L'Essence de la manifestation* (Paris: Presses universitaires de France, 1990), pp. 863–906.

65 Despite the important tradition of English Hegel studies, Findlay begins his own study of Hegel with a comment that casts light on the comparative lack of attention to Hegel's thought: "[Prof. Ayer] has made me spend over two years in the close and constant company of one of the greatest and least understood of philosophical minds." J. N. Findlay, *Hegel: A Re-examination* (New York: Collier, 1962), p. 6.

66 "Hegel's Existentialism," in Maurice Merleau-Ponty, *Sense and Non-Sense*, tr. Hubert L. Dreyfus and Patricia Allen Dreyfus (Evanston: Northwestern University Press, 1964), p. 63. This idea is later echoed by others. According to Philippe Sollers, Nietzsche, Bataille, Lacan, and Marxism-Leninism result from "l'explosion du système hégélien." Philippe Sollers, *Bataille* (Paris: 10/18, 1973), p. 36, cited in Descombes, *Le Même et l'autre*, p. 23 n5.

67 For a discussion of Lacan's relation to Hegel, see Catherine Clément, "Lacan et l'obsession hégélienne," *Magazine littéraire*, no. 293 (November 1991), pp. 57–59.

68 See Jacques Derrida, *Glas* (2 vols., Paris: Denoël/Gonthier, 1981) Derrida goes so far as to claim unambiguously that it is impossible to finish reading Hegel and that, in a sense, that is all he is doing. See Jacques Derrida, *Positions* (Paris: Editions de Minuit, 1972), p. 103.

69 For a semipopular account of the rediscovery of Hegel in France, see Mark Poster, *Existential Marxism in Postwar France: From Sartre to Althusser* (Princeton: Princeton University Press, 1975), pp. 3–35.

70 See e.g. Claude Bruaire, *Logique et religion chrétienne dans la philosophie de Hegel* (Paris: Seuil, 1964).

71 See "The Age of the World Picture," in Martin Heidegger, *The Question Concerning Technology and Other Essays*, tr. William Lovitt (New York: Harper & Row, 1977), p. 140: "With the interpretation of man as *subiectum*, Descartes creates the kind of metaphysical presupposition for future anthropology of every kind and tendency."

72 This implication has been clearly seen. For a critical analysis of the Hegelian view of the master–slave relation, see Gwendoline Jarczyk and Pierre-Jean Labarrière, *Les Premiers Combats de la reconnaissance: Maîtrise et servitude dans la "Phénoménologie de l'Esprit" de Hegel* (Paris: Aubier-Montaigne, 1987). This analysis is intended, as the authors candidly point out, to refute Kojève. See ibid., pp. 9–12.

73 See Edmund Husserl, *Cartesian Meditations: An Introduction to Phenomenology*, tr. Dorion Cairns (The Hague: Martinus Nijhoff, 1960).

74 See e.g. Jean Wahl, *La Logique de Hegel comme phénoménologie* (Paris, 1965).

75 This analogy is developed in the French discussion by Kojève, Hyppolite, and Derrida. For Derrida's view, see his long introduction to Edmund Husserl, *L'Origine de la géométrie*, tr. and intr. J. Derrida (Paris: Presses universitaires de France, 1962, 1974), p. 58n.

76 Kojève provides an overly "Husserlian," descriptive interpretation of Hegel's view of phenomenology since he mistakenly regards Hegel's phenomenological method as a mere passive contemplation of the real. According to Kojève, thought only reflects a real that is itself dialectical. See Kojève, *Introduction à la lecture de Hegel*, p. 38. He goes so far as to identify the conceptions of method in Hegel and in Husserl. See ibid., p. 470.

77 His interpretation of Heidegger's relation to Hegel is curious and never uncritical, but he criticizes Heidegger for neglecting such themes as struggle and work found in Marx. See Kojève, *Introduction à la lecture de Hegel*, 566n and 575n. Auffret concludes that Kojève cannot be considered a Heideggerian reader of Hegel. See Auffret, *Alexandre Kojève*, p. 382.

78 Hyppolite limits the analogies he presents between Hegel and Husserl (see e.g. Jean Hyppolite, *Genèse et structure de la Phénoménologie de l'Ésprit de Hegel* (2 vols., Paris: Aubier Montaigne, 1946), vol. I, p. 15) and Hegel and existentialism (see ibid., I, p. 16). Like Kojève, he stresses the descriptive side of Hegelian phenomenology and underplays the dialectical aspect of Hegel's theory.

79 In a statement concerning the structure of Hegel's *Phenomenology*, Kojève declares:

>   La PhG est une description phénoménologique de l'existence humaine. C'est dire que l'existence humaine y est décrite telle qu'elle "apparaît" (erscheint) à celui-là même qui la vit. En d'autres termes, Hegel décrit la conscience de soi de l'homme qui est dominé dans son existence soit par une des attitudes existentielles types qui se retrouvent partout et toujours (1re Partie), soit par l'attitude qui caractérise une époque historique marquante (2e Partie).
>
>   (Kojève, *Introduction à la lecture de Hegel*, p. 576)

In Kojève's interpretation, the fifth chapter of the *Phenomenology*, officially entitled "Reason," is in fact concerned with the description of "les attitudes existentielles concrètes." Ibid., p. 583.

80 There is a direct line running from Kojève's to Hyppolite's own existential approach to Hegel. Hyppolite applies Sartre's definition of human being in *Being and Nothingness* to Hegel's conception of man. See Poster, *Existential Marxism in Postwar France*, p. 33–34. Kojève strongly influenced Sartre. See Descombes, *Le Même et l'autre*, pp. 50, 64–70.

81 For this kind of all-inclusive view of "existentialism," see Walter Kaufmann, *Existentialism From Dostoyevsky to Sartre* (New York: Meridian, 1956).

82 See Roger Garaudy, *Dieu est mort: Étude sur Hegel* (Paris: Presses universitaires de France, 1962).

83 D'Hondt stresses the interconnection of the views of Hegel and Marx to an unusual extent, as in the following passage: "Sa gloire posthume, Hegel la doit pour une grande part à Marx, parce que celui-ci ne renia jamais sa dette. Si Hegel apporta beaucoup à Marx, celui-ci le lui rend maintenant au centuple." Jacques D'Hondt, *Hegel et l'hégélianisme* (Paris: Presses universitaires de France, 1982), p. 54.

84 See Jean Hyppolite, *Studies on Marx and Hegel*, tr. John O'Neill (New York: Harper, 1969).

85 For discussion, see Tom Rockmore, *Irrationalism: Lukács and the Marxist View of Reason* (Philadelphia: Temple University Press, 1992), chs. 5 and 7.

86 See "Alienation and Objectification: Commentary on G. Lukács's *The Young Hegel*," in Hyppolite, *Studies on Marx and Hegel*, pp. 79–80.

87 See e.g. Alexandre Koyré, "Hegel à Iéna," *Revue d'histoire et de philosophie religieuses* (1934), rpt. in *Etudes d'histoire de la pensée philosophique* (Paris: Armand Colin 1961), pp. 247–289; see also Jean Hyppolite, "Les Travaux de jeunesse de Hegel d'après des ouvrages récents," *Revue de métaphysique et de morale*, vol. 42, nos. 3–4 (1935), and Jean Hyppolite, "Vie et prise de conscience de la vie dans la philosophie hégélienne d'Iéna," *Revue de métaphysique et de morale*, vol. 45, no. 1 (1938).

88 The two main studies of Hegel's *Phenomenology* in French are by Kojève and

Hyppolite. For a more recent reading, see Pierre-Jean Labarrière, *Structures et mouvement dans la Phénoménologie de l'Esprit de Hegel* (Paris: Aubier-Montaigne, 1968).

89 Andler gave two courses on Hegel at the Collège de France in 1928–1929. One course concerned Hegel's philosophy of religion; the other was apparently an analysis of the German text of Hegel's *Phenomenology*. For a brief description of Andler's courses, see Koyré, *Etudes d'histoire de la pensée philosophique*, pp. 226–227.

90 Apart from Kojève's work, the most significant Marxist study of Hegel is Georg Lukács's *The Young Hegel: Studies in the Relations between Dialectics and Economics*, tr. Rodney Livingstone (Cambridge: MIT Press, 1976). For discussion of Lukács's reading of Hegel, see Tom Rockmore, *Irrationalism*, pp. 153–174.

91 For a short, but objective account of Hegel in France, see Iring Fetscher, "Hegel in Frankreich," *Antares*, no. 3 (February 1953) pp. 3–15.

92 For a detailed summary of French interest in Hegel up to 1930, i.e. prior to Kojève's famous lectures, see Alexandre Koyré, "Rapport sur l'état des études hégéliennes en France," in *Verhandlungen des ersten Hegel-Kongresses* (The Hague, 1930, Tübingen, 1931), rpt. in Alexandre Koyré, *Etudes d'histoire de la pensée philosophique* (Paris: Armand Colin, 1961), pp. 205–230.

93 See G. W. F. Hegel, *Phenomenology of Spirit*, tr. A. V. Miller (Oxford: Oxford University Press, 1977), pp. 111–118.

94 Koyré was also interested in Hegel. For an appreciation of his role in French Hegel studies, see Jean Wahl, "Le rôle de A. Koyré dans le développement des études hégéliennes en France," in *Hegel-Studien*, supplement 3 (1964), pp. 15–26.

95 For a discussion of Kojève as a teacher, see Jean Desanti, "Hegel est-il le père de l'existentialisme?," in *La Nouvelle Critique*, vol. 6, no. 56 (June 1954), pp. 91–109. According to Desanti, reading Hegel through the eyes of Kojève retarded his own intellectual development. See ibid., p. 93.

96 On Bataille's complicated relation to Hegel, see Bruno Karsenti, "Bataille anti-hégélien?," *Magazine littéraire*, no. 293, (November 1991), pp. 54–57. For a recent discussion of Bataille as a reader of Hegel, see Allan Stoekl, *Agonies of the Intellectual* (Lincoln: University of Nebraska Press, 1992), pp. 283–301.

97 Different writers provide different lists. This composite list is drawn from Borch-Jakobsen, *Lacan: Le Maître absolu*, p. 285 n3. For a complete list of the participants in the seminar, year by year, see Michael S. Roth, *Knowing and History: Appropriations of Hegel in Twentieth Century France* (Ithaca: Cornell University Press, 1988), pp. 225–227. A somewhat different list is provided by Auffret, who denies that Sartre ever attended Kojève's lectures, but includes Jean Hyppolite. See Auffret, *Alexandre Kojève*, p. 238.

98 This theme has recently been revived in Fukuyama's thesis that the collapse of communism signifies the end of history. See Francis Fukuyama *The End of History and the Last Man*, (New York: Free Press, 1992).

99 For a discussion of Queneau's relation to Kojève, see Pierre Macherey, "Queneau scribe et lecteur de Kojève," *Europe*, nos. 650–651 (June–July 1983), pp. 82–91.

100 See, on this topic, Auffret's remarks on "La Dette envers Koyré," in Auffret, *Alexandre Kojève*, pp. 232–241.

101 See H. Spiegelberg, *The Phenomenological Movement: A Historical Introduction* (The Hague: Martinus Nijhoff, 1982), p. 167.

102 See ibid., p. 193.

103 See ibid., pp. 191–192.

104 Hering's suggestion that Koyré was an orthodox Husserlian is certainly mistaken. See Jean Hering, "Phenomenology in France," in *Philosophic*

Thought in France and the United States, ed. Marvin Farber (Buffalo: University of Buffalo Publications in Philosophy, 1950), p. 70.

105 See Kojève, *Introduction à la lecture de Hegel*, p. 527.

106 See ibid., pp. 75–76, 114, 119, 162f, 197f., 527.

107 See ibid., pp. 485f., 490.

108 See ibid., p. 470.

109 See ibid., p. 57.

110 In a recent article, Baugh argues that Koyré's Hegel interpretation anticipates Kojève's. See Bruce Baugh, "Subjectivity and the *Begriff* in Modern French Philosophy," *The Owl of Minerva*, vol. 23, no. 1 (Fall 1991), p. 75.

111 Despite the resemblance between their respective views of Hegel, it was not possible, according to Auffret, to deduce Kojève's reading from Koyré's. See Auffret, *Alexandre Kojève*, p. 234.

112 See Stanley Rosen, "Review of A. Kojève, *Essai d'une histoire raisonnée de la philosophie paienne*," *Man and World*, vol. 3, no. 1 (February 1970), p. 120.

113 For an objective, detached discussion, see Jean Wahl, "A Propos de l'Introduction à la lecture de la Phénoménologie de Hegel par A. Kojève," *Deucalion* 5 (1955), pp. 77–99.

114 See Jules Vuillemin, "Compte rendu de Kojève," *Revue philosophique de la France et de l'étranger*, vol. 40 (1950), pp. 198–200.

115 See Georges Bataille, "Hegel, la mort et le sacrifice," *Deucalion* 5 (1955), p. 21n.

116 See Auffret, *Alexandre Kojève*, p. 9.

117 See Henry, *L'Essence de la manifestation*, p. 871.

118 See Roudinesco, *Jacques Lacan and Co.*, p. 134.

119 See Raymond Aron, *Mémoires* (Paris: Juillard, 1984), p. 94.

120 See Patrick Riley, "Introduction to the Reading of Alexandre Kojève," *Political Theory*, vol. 9, no. 1 (1985), pp. 5–48.

121 See Descombes, *Le Même et l'autre*, p. 41.

122 For a critical article first published in 1948, see Georges Canguilhem, "Hegel en France," reprinted in *Magazine littéraire*, no. 293, (November 1991), pp. 36–39.

123 See Pierre Macherey, "Queneau scribe et lecteur de Kojève, p. 90.

124 See Pierre Macherey, "Kojève l'initiateur," *Magazine littéraire*, no. 293, (November 1991), p. 52.

125 For Lukács's later description of his famous breakthough to Marxism as "an attempt to out-Hegel Hegel," see his preface to the new edition of Georg Lukács, *History and Class Consciousness*, tr. Rodney Livingstone (Cambridge: MIT Press, 1971), p. xxiii.

126 For this description, see Auffret, *Alexandre Kojève*, p. 244.

127 In his otherwise excellent discussion, Descombes never seems to resolve or even to attend to the differences between Hegel and Kojève, or between Hegel and Hegel as read by Kojève, or, finally, between the views of Hegel and those of Kojève presented by the latter as a mere reading of Hegel. See Descombes, *Le Même et l'autre*.

128 For his important reading of Hegel, which remains influential in the French discussion, see Hyppolite, *Genèse et structure de la Phénoménologie de l'Ésprit de Hegel*.

129 Two examples will illustrate this point. In his list of works on Hegel, D'Hondt, a well known Hegel specialist, does not even list Kojève's book. See Jacques D'Hondt, *Hegel et le hégélianisme*, p. 126. Similarly, in his lengthy, authoritative introduction to the French translation of the *Encyclopedia*, Bourgeois, another well known Hegel specialist, does not even mention Kojève. See G. W. F. Hegel,

Encyclopédie des sciences philosophiques: La Science de la logique, tr. Bernard Bourgeois (Paris: Vrin, 1979).

130   The letter was addressed to Tran Duc Thao in 1948. See Auffret, *Alexandre Kojève*, p. 249.

131   For a discussion of this concept, see Besnier, *La Politique de l'impossible*, pp. 59–70. See also Barry Cooper, *The End of History: An Essay on Modern Hegelianism* (Toronto: University of Toronto Press, 1984).

132   Alexandre Kojève, "Le Concept et le temps," in *Deucalion* 5 (1955), p. 18.

133   See Jacques Derrida, *La Voix et le phénomène* (Paris: Presses universitaires de France, 1967), p.115.

134   See e.g. G. W. F. Hegel, *Werke in zwanzig Bänden*, vol. XX: *Vorlesungen über die Geschichte der Philosophie, 3*, ed. E. Moldenhauer and K. M. Michel (Frankfurt/M: Suhrkamp, 1971), pp. 460, 476.

135   For a study of this theme, see Reinhart Klemens Maurer, *Hegel und das Ende der Geschichte* (Freiburg i. B.: Karl Alber, 1980). For commentary on Kojève's view, see ibid., "Auseinandersetzung mit Kojève," pp. 139–156.

136   See Hegel's letter to Niethammer dated October 13, 1806, in *Hegel: The Letters*, tr. Clark Butler and Christiane Seiler (Bloomington: Indiana University Press, 1984), pp. 114–115.

137   See Aron, *Mémoires*, p. 96.

138   See Hegel, *Phenomenology of Spirit*, § 11, p. 6.

139   See G. W. F. Hegel, *Philosophy of Right*, tr. T. M. Knox (London: Oxford University Press, 1967), p. 13.

140   For a discussion of Kojève's and Hyppolite's readings of Hegel's *Phenomenology*, see Mikel Dufrenne, "Actualité de Hegel," in *Esprit*, (September 1948), pp. 396–408.

141   For comparison, see Gaston Fessard, "Deux Interprètes de la Phénoménologie de Hegel, Jean Hyppolite et Alexandre Kojève," in *Etudes*, no. 255 (1947), pp. 368–373.

142   See Findlay, *Hegel: A Re-Examination*, p. 5.

143   See Poster, *Existential Marxism in Postwar France*, p. 19.

144   Lukács continued to grapple with Hegel's thought throughout his lengthy Marxist period from 1918 to his death in 1971. In *History and Class Consciousness*, he emphasized the Hegelian roots of Marx's thought. In *The Young Hegel*, he stressed the economic element in Hegel's thought while emphasizing the anthropological element. In his last, uncompleted work, *Zur Ontologie des gesellschaftlichen Seins*, he underscored the tension in Hegel's thought between the commitment to conflicting forms of historical analysis based on philosophical anthropology and on logic. For discussion of Lukács's views on Hegel, see Tom Rockmore, *Irrationalism*, chs. 6, 7, and 9.

145   Engels's last, unfinished work deals with the dialectic of nature. See Friedrich Engels, *Dialektik der Natur*, in Karl Marx and Friedrich Engels, *Werke*, vol. XX, ed. Institut für Marxismus-Leninismus beim ZK der SED (Berlin: Dietz Verlag, 1975).

146   See Aimé Patri, "Dialectique du maître et de l'esclave," *Le Contrat social*, vol. 5, no. 4 (July–August 1961), p. 234, cited in Alexandre Kojève, *Introduction to the Reading of Hegel: Lectures on the "Phenomenology of Spirit"*, ed. Allan Bloom, tr. James H. Nichols, Jr. (New York: Basic Books, 1969), p. vii. Auffret claims that it is incorrect to regard Kojève as a Hegelian disciple of Heidegger. See Auffret, *Alexandre Kojève*, p. 178. In fact, Kojève was a Heideggerian and Marxian disciple of Hegel.

147   See Aron, *Mémoires*, p. 94.

148   See ibid., p. 731.

149 See Auffret, *Alexandre Kojève*, p. 9. Auffret bases his statement on Aron's interview with Brochier. See Jean-Jacques Brochier, "Le regard froid de l'analyste," *Le Magazine littéraire*, no. 198 (September 1983), p. 26.
150 See Aron, *Mémoires*, 100.
151 Ibid., p. 94.
152 See G. W. F. Hegel, *The Phenomenology of Mind*, tr. J. B. Baillie (New York: Macmillan, 1961).
153 His dissertation, written under the direction of Karl Jaspers, was entitled "Die Religionsphilosophie Wladimir Solowjews." A version of the dissertation was later published in French. See Alexandre Kojève, "La métaphysique religieuse de Vladimir Soloviev," *Revue d'histoire et de philosophie religieuses* vol. 14, no. 6 (1934), pp. 534–544, and vol. 15, nos. 1–2 (1935), pp. 110–152. Roth maintains that Kojève's concern in his dissertation to elucidate how a religious thinker reconciles his concerns with history with a commitment to the eternal decisively shaped Kojève's later study of Hegel. See Roth, *Knowing and History*, pp. 85–88. This reading of Kojève is explicitly contradicted by Kojève's own assertion that his reading of the *Phenomenology* is inspired by and derived from Alexandre Koyré's article on the concept of time in Hegel's discussion of the philosophy of nature in the Jena writings. See Kojève, *Introduction à la lecture de Hegel*, p. 367
154 See Frederick Engels, *Ludwig Feuerbach and the Outcome of Classical German Philosophy*, tr. C. P. Dutt (New York: International Publishers, 1941). Engels straightforwardly identifies Hegel's philosophy with the end of all history. See ibid., p. 13.
155 See Jacques Derrida, *Marges de la philosophie* (Paris: Editions de Minuit, 1972), p. 144.
156 See Kojève, *Introduction à la lecture de Hegel*, p. 434.
157 See ibid., pp. 434–437.
158 See ibid., p. 39.
159 See ibid., p. 454.
160 See ibid., p. 562.
161 See ibid., pp. 95ff, 145, 157.
162 See ibid., pp. 535–536n.
163 See Hegel, *Phenomenology of Spirit*, § 11, p. 6: "Besides, it is not difficult to see that ours is a birth-time and a period of transition to a new era."
164 Heidegger makes this claim in connection with his interest in Jünger's reading of Nietzsche. See Martin Heidegger, "The Rectorate 1933/34: Facts and Thoughts," in *Martin Heidegger and National Socialism: Questions and Answers*, ed. Günther Neske and Emil Kettering (New York: Paragon House, 1990), p. 17.
165 Alexandre Kojève, *Critique*, no 2–3 (1946), p. 366, quoted in Descombes, *Le Même et l'autre*, p. 21.

3 GERMAN PHENOMENOLOGY, FRENCH PHILOSOPHY, AND SUBJECTIVITY

1 For an interpretation of Heidegger's position in terms of his initial view of subjectivity and later rejection of it, see Dieter Thomä, *Die Zeit des Selbst und die Zeit danach: Zur Kritik der Textgeschichte Martin Heideggers 1910–1976* (Frankfurt/M.: Suhrkamp, 1990).
2 Descartes, for instance, writes: "In the matter of the cognition of facts two things alone have to be considered, ourselves who know and the objects themselves

which are to be known." René Descartes, *The Philosophical Works of Descartes*, vol. I, ed. and tr. Elizabeth S. Haldane and G. R. T. Ross (Cambridge: Cambridge University Press, 1970), p. 35.

3 See Ernest Barker, *Greek Political Theory* (New York: Barnes and Noble, 1961), p. 7:

> Although, as has been said, the Greek thought of himself as one who counted for what he was worth in his community – although he regarded himself as a moment in determining its action – the fact remains that in the political thought of Greece the notion of the individual is not prominent, and the conception of rights seems hardly to have been attained.

4 See Saint Augustine, *On Free Choice of the Will*, tr. Anna S. Benjamin and L. H. Hackstaff (Indianapolis: LLA, 1964).

5 See e.g. Etienne Gilson, *La Liberté chez Descartes et la théologie* (Paris: Alcan, 1913).

6 See Richard H. Popkin, *The History of Scepticism from Erasmus to Spinoza* (Berkeley: The University of California Press, 1979), p. 87:

> The wider popularity and application of the 'nouveau Pyrrhonisme' brought out more sharply its implications for both religious [sic] and science. This, in turn, gave rise to a series of attempts, culminating in the heroic failure of René Descartes, to save human knowledge by destroying scepticism.

7 See Edmund Husserl, *Cartesian Meditations: An Introduction to Phenomenology*, tr. Dorion Cairns (The Hague: Martinus Nijhoff, 1960), p. 157.

8 Augustine, *On Free Choice of the Will*, p. 40.

9 Ibid.; Augustine's emphases.

10 See the first four of the "Rules for the Direction of the Mind," in Descartes, *Philosophical Works*, I, pp. 1–9 *passim*.

11 Ibid., pp. 14–22.

12 For a collection of articles on this problem, *Antifoundationalism Old and New*, ed. T. Rockmore and B. Singer (Philadelphia: Temple University Press, 1991). For the distinctions between different forms of foundationalism and their relation to antifoundationalism, see the introduction to *Antifoundationalism Old and New*, pp. 1–12.

13 See Descartes, *Philosophical Works*, I, p. 10.

14 See ibid., p. 45.

15 Ibid., p. 101; Descartes's emphases.

16 Ibid., p. 144.

17 Ibid., p. 331.

18 Ibid., pp. 101–102.

19 He makes this point explicitly in the fourth of the *Meditations on First Philosophy*. See Descartes, *Philosophical Works*, I, p. 172.

20 See ibid., pp. 151–152.

21 See ibid., p.155.

22 See ibid., p. 107.

23 See Giambattista Vico, *The New Science of Giambattista Vico*, tr. Thomas Goddard Bergin and Max Fisch (Ithaca: Cornell University Press, 1970), § 331, pp. 52–53.

24 See "Discours sur les sciences et les arts," in Jean-Jacques Rousseau, *Du Contrat social ou Principes du droit politique* (Paris: Garnier, 1962), p. 3.

25 See Kant's letter to Beck of October 27, 1791, in *Immanuel Kants Werke*, ed. Ernst Cassirer (11 vols., Berlin: Bruno Cassirer, 1912–1922), vol. X, p. 98: "What

can be more fitting in addition to that and in fact for an entire lifetime, than to be concerned with the entire vocation [Bestimmung] of man, if one only had hope . . . that the least progress could be made in that regard."

26 See Immanuel Kant, *Critique of Pure Reason*, tr. N. Kemp Smith (New York: Macmillan, 1961), B 833, p. 635.

27 See Immanuel Kant, *Introduction to Logic*, tr. Thomas Kingsmill Abbott (New York: Philosophical Library, 1963), p. 15.

28 The whole first volume of the *Logische Untersuchungen* is taken up with this problem. See Edmund Husserl, *Logische Untersuchungen*, vol. I: *Prolegomena zur reinen Logik* (Tübingen: Max Niemeyer, 1980). Husserl has been accused of later falling back into psychologism. See Martin Heidegger, *On Time and Being*, tr. Joan Stambaugh (New York: Harper & Row, 1977), p. 76.

29 See Kant, *Critique of Pure Reason*, B 77–78, pp. 94–95.

30 For an interpretation of Kant's critical philosophy against Kant's explicit intentions as an ontology, see Martin Heidegger, *Kant and the Problem of Metaphysics*, tr. Richard M. Taft (Bloomington: Indiana University Press, 1990).

31 See Kant, *Critique of Pure Reason*, § 16, B 131–135, pp. 152–157.

32 See ibid., B xvii, p. 22.

33 See ibid., B xvi, p. 22.

34 See ibid., B xiii, p. 20.

35 See G. W. F. Hegel, *The Difference Between Fichte's and Schelling's System of Philosophy*, tr. H. S. Harris and Walter Cerf (Albany: State University of New York Press, 1977), p. 80.

36 See ibid., p. 79.

37 See J. G. Fichte, *Science of Knowledge (Wissenschaftslehre) with First and Second Introductions*, tr. Peter Heath and John Lachs, (New York: Appleton-Century-Crofts, 1970), p. 226; see also Hegel, *The Difference Between Fichte's and Schelling's System of Philosophy*, p. 81.

38 See Kant, *Critique of Pure Reason*, B 181, p. 183.

39 For an argument that Marx's theory is not materialist, see George L. Kline, "The Myth of Marx's Materialism," in *Philosophical Sovietology: The Pursuit of a Science*, ed. Helmut Dahm, Thomas J. Blakeley, and George L. Kline (Dordrecht: Reidel, 1988), pp. 158–203.

40 See Tom Rockmore, *Fichte, Marx and the German Philosophical Tradition* (Carbondale: Southern Illinois University Press, 1980).

41 See Fichte, *Science of Knowledge*, p. 97.

42 See ibid., §§ 1–3, pp. 97–119.

43 See Kant, *Critique of Pure Reason*, B 380, p. 317.

44 See G. W. F. Hegel, *Phenomenology of Spirit*, tr. A. V. Miller (Oxford: Oxford University Press, 1977), p. 9.

45 See ibid., p. 11.

46 See Georg Lukács, *History and Class Consciousness: Studies in Marxist Dialectics*, tr. Rodney Livingstone (Cambridge: MIT Press, 1973), pp. 149–209.

47 See Iso Kern, *Husserl und Kant* (The Hague: Martinus Nijhoff, 1964).

48 Husserl held that the phenomenological reduction enabled him to suspend the other sciences in order to attain the independence of phenomenology. For his view of the methodological importance of the phenomenological reduction, see Edmund Husserl, *Ideas: General Introduction to Pure Phenomenology*, tr. W. R. Boyce Gibson (New York: Collier Books, 1962), § 61, pp. 163–165.

49 For Husserl's view of subjectivity, see the fourth of his *Cartesian Meditations*, §§ 30–41, pp. 65–88.

50 The concept of constitution has attracted attention in the literature. Husserl scholars hold that there is a transition from an early view that objects constitute

themselves to a later view that the subject constitutes them. For discussion, see Herbert Spiegelberg, *The Phenomenological Movement: A Historical Introduction* (The Hague: Martinus Nijhoff, 1982), pp. 130–131. See also Maurice Natanson, *Edmund Husserl: Philosopher of Infinite Tasks* (Evanston: Northwestern University Press, 1973), pp. 93–94.

51 See Husserl, *Cartesian Meditations*, § 41, pp. 83–88.

52 See e.g. the following statement by Ebeling:

> Für die Philosophie Heideggers in *Sein und Zeit* möchte ich die Schlussfolgerung ziehen: Sie ist der brillanteste Versuch der Vernichtung neuzeitlicher Subjekttheorie und zugleich auch schon ein autodestruktives Wüten, an dessen Ende die Zerstörung der Philosophie wie die Zerstörung der Politik steht.
>
> (Hans Ebeling, "Philosophie auf Leben und Tod: Zum Verhältnis von Selbstbehauptung und Sterblichsein in Heideggers 'Sein und Zeit', in *Martin Heidegger – Faszination und Erschrecken: Die politische Dimension einer Philosophie*, ed. P. Kemper (Frankfurt/M.: Campus, 1990), pp. 149–150)

53 See Martin Heidegger, *Being and Time*, tr. J. Macquarie and E. Robinson (New York: Harper & Row, 1962), p. 62.

54 See ibid., p. 490 n1.

55 "Denken ist die Einschränkung auf einen Gedanken, der einst wie ein Stern am Himmel der Welt stehen bleibt." Martin Heidegger, *Aus der Erfahrung des Denkens* (Frankfurt/M.: Vittorio Klostermann, 1983), p. 76.

56 See Heidegger, *Being and Time*, p. 1

57 Heidegger, *Being and Time*, p. 62; Heidegger's emphases. Heidegger emphasizes the importance of this passage by quoting it again at the end of the book. See *Being and Time*, p. 437.

58 See Kant, *Critique of Pure Reason*, B 611–670, pp. 495–531.

59 Heidegger, *Being and Time*, p. 32.

60 See ibid., p. 32.

61 See ibid., p. 33.

62 See ibid., p. 83.

63 See ibid., p. 71.

64 This is a frequent theme in Husserl's texts. For a short text devoted merely to this problem, see Edmund Husserl, "Phenomenology and Anthropology," in *Husserl: Shorter Works*, ed. Peter McCormick and Frederick Elliston (Notre Dame: University of Notre Dame Press, 1981), pp. 315–323.

65 "Philosophie gilt mir, der Idee nach, als die universale und im radikalen Sinne strenge Wissenschaft. Als das ist sie Wissenschaft aus letzter Begründung, oder, was gleich gilt, aus letzter Selbstverantwortung, in der also keine prädikative oder vorprädikative Selbstverständlichkeit als unbefragter Erkentnisboden fungiert." Edmund Husserl, "Nachwort zu meinen Ideen," *Husserliana*, vol. V (The Hague: Martinus Nijhoff, 1950), p. 139.

66 See Heidegger, *Being and Time*, §10, pp. 71–75.

67 For instance, in the published version of the Nietzsche lectures, he maintains that the anthropological approach is so widespread and deep in modern metaphysics that it cannot even be thought from within that perspective. See Martin Heidegger, *Nietzsche*, vol. II (Pfullingen: Neske, 1961). p. 291.

68 See Heidegger, *Being and Time*, § 44, pp. 256–273.

69 See ibid., p. 265.

70 Ibid., pp. 56–57.

71 This difference has been widely noted. Lévinas, for instance, has emphasized the opposition between the concepts of subjectivity in Husserl and Heidegger as turning on the submergence of the Heideggerian subject in existence. See "L'Oeuvre d'Edmond Husserl," in Emmanuel Lévinas, *En découvrant l'existence avec Husserl et Heidegger* (Paris: Vrin, 1988), p. 25.

72 Lévinas emphasizes the continuity subtending the opposition between views of the subject as existence and as consciousness, since the former builds on the latter. See Lévinas, *En découvrant l'existence*, p. 52.

73 See Immanuel Kant, *Prolegomena to Any Future Metaphysics*, intr. Lewis White Beck (Indianapolis: LLA, 1950).

74 See "The Age of the World Picture," in Martin Heidegger, *The Question Concerning Technology and Other Essays*, tr. William Lovitt (New York: Harper & Row, 1977), p. 140.

75 Ibid., p. 153.

76 See Jean Wahl, "Heidegger et Kierkegaard: Recherche des éléments originaux de la philosophie de Heidegger," *Recherches philosophiques*, vol. 2 (1932–1933), pp. 347–370.

77 See Alexandre Koyré, "L'Evolution philosophique de Martin Heidegger," *Critique* (1946), rpt. in *Etudes d'histoire de la pensée philosophique* (Paris, 1961).

78 See Jean Wahl, *Vers le Concret: Etudes d'histoire de la philosophie contemporaine* (Paris: Vrin, 1932). Wahl provides an interpretation of Heidegger based on his syncretic appropriation of others' ideas in his own language and as a type of proto-existentialist. He understands Heidegger as providing an abstract statement of the views of Kierkegaard, pragmatism, Dilthey, and Spengler, and as "trying to join to the feeling of individual existence as experienced, for instance, by Kierkegaard the feeling of our existence in the midst of things as it has emerged in contemporary philosophy." Ibid., pp. 3–4.

79 The three articles, published over a period from 1953 to 1960, are reprinted in Jean Hyppolite, *Figures de la pensée philosophique*, vol. II (Paris: Presses universitaires de France, 1971). See "Note en manière d'introduction à *Que signifie penser?*", ibid., pp. 607–614; "Ontologie et phénoménologie chez Martin Heidegger," ibid., pp. 615–624; "Etude du commentaire de l'introduction à la *Phénoménologie* par Heidegger," ibid., pp. 625–642.

80 See Jean Hyppolite, *Logique et existence: Essai sur la logique de Hegel* (Paris: Presses universitaires de France, 1953).

81 See Michael S. Roth, *Knowing and History: Appropriations of Hegel in Twentieth-Century France*, ch. 3: "From Humanism to Being," pp. 66–80.

82 See e.g. Hyppolite, *Logique et existence*, p. 246: "L'être se fonde en lui-même, il est parce qu'il est possible, mais il est possible parce qu'il est." If there is a Heideggerian influence here, it is perhaps transmitted indirectly through Sartre's *Being and Nothingness*.

83 See Jean Hyppolite, *Etudes sur Marx et Hegel* (Paris: Marcel Rivière, 1955); tr. *Studies on Marx and Hegel*, ed. and tr. John O'Neill (New York: Harper & Row, 1973).

84 See Heidegger, *Being and Time*, pp. 279–311.

85 See A. Kojève, *Introduction à la lecture de Hegel*, ed. R. Queuneau (Paris: Gallimard, 1947), pp. 529–575.

86 See ibid., p. 539.

87 See ibid., pp. 572–573.

88 See ibid., 575n.

89 Descombes's claim that in France phenomenological existentialism is seen as beginning with Merleau-Ponty is incorrect since Sartre has always been regarded

as an existentialist. See Vincent Descombes, *Le Même et l'autre* (Paris: Editions de Minuit, 1979), p. 72.

90 Hollier says that French existentialism came into its own with the publication of Jean Wahl's work, *Études kierkegardiennes* in 1938. See *The College of Sociology (1937–39)*, ed. Denis Hollier, tr. Betsy Wing (Minneapolis: University of Minnesota Press, 1988), p. viii.

91 See Jules Vuillemin, *L'Héritage kantien et la révolution copernicienne* (Paris: Presses universitaires de France, 1954), pp. 227, 231.

92 In a reference to the French discussion after the Second World War, he writes:

> Et l'existentialisme français – peut-être Gabriel Marcel mis à part – est largement tributaire de la phénoménologie bien qu'il ne se soit nourri que de la partie anthropologique de la pensée heideggerienne, de cette philosophie de l'existence dont Heidegger ne veut pas pour lui.
>
> Lévinas, *En découvrant l'existence*, p. 5.

93 For his important critique, see "The Battle over Existentialism," in Maurice Merleau-Ponty, *Sense and Non-Sense*, tr. Hubert L. Dreyfus and Patricia Allen Dreyfus (Evanston: Northwestern University Press, 1964), pp. 71–82.

94 For Sartre's account of his apprenticeship in the writings of Husserl and Heidegger, see Jean-Paul Sartre, *Les Carnets d'une drôle de guerre* (Paris: Gallimard, 1983), pp. 225–230. There is no similar account of which I am aware of how Sartre acquired his knowledge of Hegel's writings. For an effort to elucidate this problem, see Christopher M. Fry, *Sartre and Hegel: The Variations of an Enigma in "L'Etre et le Néant"* (Bonn: Bouvier, 1988), pp. 3–9.

95 See Sartre, *Carnets d'une drôle de guerre*, p. 224.

96 Ibid., p. 228.

97 See ibid., p. 229.

98 On the clear link between Sartre's view of nothingness in *Being and Nothingness* and Kojève's reading of Hegel that does not address the further link between Kojève and Heidegger, see Descombes, *Le Même et l'autre*, pp. 64–70.

99 See Jean-Paul Sartre, *L'Existentialisme est un humanisme* (Paris: Nagel, 1964).

100 For this view, see Maurice Merleau-Ponty, *La Phénoménologie de la perception* (Paris: Gallimard, 1945); see also Maurice Merleau-Ponty, "Le Primat de la perception et ses conséquences philosophiques," in *Bulletin de la Société française de philosophie*, vol. 41 (1947), pp. 119–153.

101 See Maurice Merleau-Ponty, *Les Aventures de la dialectique* (Paris: Gallimard, 1955), "Sartre et l'ultra-bolchevisme," pp. 131–271.

102 The heterogeneity of the structuralist movement has led at least one observer to deny that there is anything in common between so-called structuralists. See François Châtelet, "Où est le structuralisme?," in *Quinzaine littéraire*, no. 31 (July 1–15, 1967), pp. 18–19.

103 For a wide-ranging analysis of structuralism, see Jean Piaget, *Le Structuralisme* (Paris: Presses universitaires de France, 1968).

104 See Peter Caws, *Structuralism: The Art of the Intelligible* (Atlantic Highlands, NJ: Humanities Press International, 1988), p. 1.

105 See Piaget, *Le Structuralisme*, p. 6.

106 See Michel Foucault, *Les Mots et les choses: Une Archéologie des sciences humaines* (Paris: Gallimard, 1966), pp. 220–221.

107 See Descombes, *Le Même et l'autre*, p. 89.

108 According to Caws, deconstruction is one of the forms of structuralism. See Caws, *Structuralism*, p. 162.

109 In his discussion, Piaget distinguishes between the conception of the human

individual as irrelevant and the idea of the "epistemic subject" or "cognitive nucleus." See Piaget, *Le Structuralisme*, p. 120.

110 Any list of structuralists is arbitrary, since there is no agreement about the nature of "structuralism." Goldmann can be counted as a structuralist since he calls his method "genetic structuralism."

111 See Piaget, *Le Structuralisme*, p. 58.

112 See Roland Barthes, "Death of the Author," in *Image, Music, Text*, ed. and tr. Stephen Heath (New York: Hill & Wang, 1977), p. 145:

> Linguistically, the author is never more than the instance writing, just as the I is nothing other than the instance saying I: language knows a "subject," not a "person," and this subject, empty outside the very enunciation which defines it, suffices to make language "hold together," suffices, that is to say, to exhaust it.

113 See Claude Lévi-Strauss, *La Pensée sauvage* (Paris: Plon, 1964), pp. 347–348.

114 In a famous passage, Kant described this activity as "an art concealed in the depths of the human soul. . . ." Kant, *Critique of Pure Reason*, B 181, p. 183.

115 See Claude Lévi-Strauss, *Anthropologie structurale* (Paris: Plon, 1962), p. 28.

116 See Paul de Man, *Blindness and Insight: Essays in the Rhetoric of Contemporary Criticism* (Minnesota: University of Minnesota Press, 1983), p. 11.

117 On the relation of structuralism and Marxism, see Lucien Sebag, *Marxisme et structuralisme* (Paris: Payot, 1964).

118 For a French humanist reading of Marx, see Jean-Yves Calvez, *La Pensée de Karl Marx* (Paris: Editions du Seuil, 1956, 1970).

119 This view is formulated in many places in his corpus, for instance in Friedrich Engels, *Ludwig Feuerbach and the Outcome of Classical German Philosophy*, ed. C. P. Dutt (New York: International Publishers, 1941).

120 For a critique of Althusser's antihumanist structuralism, see "Le Marx d'Althusser," in Leszek Kolakowski, *L'Esprit révolutionnaire* (Brussels: Editions Complexe, 1978), pp. 158–185.

121 Louis Althusser, *For Marx*, tr. Ben Brewster (New York: Vintage, 1970), pp. 228–229.

122 Michel Foucault, *Les Nouvelles littéraires*, June 28–July 5, 1984, cited in Luc Ferry and Alain Renaut, *La Pensée 68* (Paris: Gallimard, 1988), p. 129.

123 Deleuze, Foucault's close associate, correctly emphasizes this point. See Gilles Deleuze, "L'homme, une existence douteuse," in *Le Nouvel Observateur*, June 1, 1966, p. 33. In an interview published shortly after this article, Foucault points out that in *Les Mots et les choses*, he desired only to point out how the concept of human being was constituted at the end of the eighteenth and beginning of the nineteenth centuries. See "L'Homme est-il mort? Un entretien avec Michel Foucault," *Arts et loisirs*, no. 38 (June 15–21, 1966), p. 15.

124 For this reading, see Georges Canguilhem, "Mort de l'homme ou l'épuisement du cogito," *Critique*, no. 242 (July 1967), pp. 599–618.

125 For a recent study of Foucault's concept of the subject, see Stoekl, *Agonies of the Intellectual* (Lincoln: University of Nebraska Press, 1992), ch. 7: "Foucault and the Intellectual Subject," pp. 174–198. Stoekl argues that Foucault is doubly dependent on both Heidegger and Nietzsche, and that Foucault's Nietzschean affirmation of the death of man depends on the indissociable link between Nietzsche and Hegel.

126 See de Man, *Blindness and Insight*, p. 5.

127 See Foucault, *Les Mots et les choses*, p. 378.

128 The "romantic" view of the end of human being disseminated independently

by both Kojève and Heidegger echoed widely throughout French thought of the period. For instance, Sartre noted in his journal that Simone de Beauvoir thought that the human species came into being and would pass away at a future time. See Sartre, *Carnets de la drôle de guerre*, p.35.

129 See Foucault, *Les Mots et les choses*, p. 394.

130 See ibid., p. 397.

131 Interview with Michel Foucault, *Quinzaine littéraire*, no. 5 (May 15, 1966), cited in Didier Eribon, *Michel Foucault (1926–1984)* (Paris: Flammarion, 1991), p. 189.

132 See Foucault, *Les Mots et les choses*, p. 398.

4 HEIDEGGER, SARTRE, AND FRENCH HUMANISM

1 Marten has recently stressed Heidegger's almost mystical rhetorical capacities. See Rainer Marten, *Heidegger Lesen* (Munich: W. Fink, 1991).

2 For a version of this argument, see "Heideggers Übersetzung des 'je eigenen Daseins' in das deutsche Dasein," in Karl Löwith, *Mein Leben in Deutschland vor und nach 1933: Ein Bericht* (Frankfurt/M.: Fischer, 1989), pp. 32–42.

3 De Man, who is a seasoned observer of the continental scene, maintains that its rapid change is a sign of crisis. See Paul de Man, *Blindness and Insight: Essays in the Rhetoric of Contemporary Criticism* (Minneapolis: University of Minnesota Press, 1983), p. 3.

4 For a general survey, see Kate Soper, *Humanism and Anti-Humanism* (La Salle, IL: Open Court), 1986.

5 For discussion, see Ernesto Grassi, *Einführung in philosophische Probleme des Humanismus* (Darmstadt: Wissenschaftliche Buchgesellschaft, 1986), pp. 13–18. As early as the "Rules," Descartes drew a distinction between historical and systematic study in favor of a systematic procedure that in principle excluded any reliance on what others had previously thought. See the third of the "Rules for the Direction of the Mind," in René Descartes, *The Philosophical Works of Descartes*, vol. I, ed. and trans. E. S. Haldane and G. R. T. Ross (Cambridge: Cambridge University Press, 1970), pp. 5–8.

6 See "Letter on Humanism", in Martin Heidegger, *Basic Writings*, ed. D. F. Krell (New York: Harper & Row, 1977) pp. 189–242.

7 See Julien Benda, *La Trahison des clercs* (Paris: Grasset, 1975), pp. 153–154.

8 For a short discussion of Renaissance humanism, see the introduction to *The Renaissance Philosophy of Man*, ed. Ernst Cassirer, Paul Oskar Kristeller, and John Herman Randall, Jr. (Chicago: University of Chicago Press, 1971) pp. 1–20.

9 For an account, see Jacob Burkhardt, *The Civilization of the Renaissance in Italy*, ed. Irene Gordon (New York: New American Library, 1960). According to Grassi, humanism precedes Renaissance philosophy. See Grassi, *Einführung in philosophische Probleme des Humanismus*, p. 2.

10 See Jean-Claude Margolin, "Humanism in France," in *The Impact of Humanism in Western Europe*, ed. Anthony Goodman and Angus MacKay (London: Longman, 1990), p. 164: "In some respects, despite controversies, it might be accepted that European humanism, especially in Western Europe, oscillated between an enthusiastic practice of the *studia humanitatis* and a philosophy of man based on an acute awareness of his dignity."

11 Harald Höffding, *A History of Modern Philosophy*, vol. I, tr. B. E. Meyer (New York: Dover, 1955), p. 12.

12 Gay, who usefully considers humanism as the revival of classical letters, fails to

devote sufficient attention to its other dimensions. See Peter Gay, *The Enlighten-ment: An Interpretation*, (2 vols., New York: Norton, 1977), vol. I, pp. 257–322.

13 On Niethammer's classical humanism, see *Hegel: The Letters*, tr. Clark Butler and Christiane Seiler (Bloomington: Indiana University Press, 1984), pp. 138–139.

14 See Roland W. Henke, *Hegels Philosophieunterricht* (Würzburg: Königshausen & Neumann, 1989).

15 Pico della Mirandola, *Oration on the Dignity of Man*, § 3, cited in *The Encyclopedia of Philosophy*, vol. III, ed. Paul Edwards (New York: Macmillan, 1972), p. 70. For a discussion similar to Mirandola's, see Ludovicus Vives, "A Fable About Man," in *The Renaissance Philosophy of Man*, ed. E. Cassirer, P. O. Kristeller, and J. H. Randall, Jr. (Chicago: University of Chicago Press, 1971), pp. 387–393.

16 See Michel Foucault, "What Is Enlightenment?," in *The Foucault Reader*, ed. Paul Rabinow (New York: Pantheon, 1984), pp. 43–44.

17 See Ernst Cassirer, *The Philosophy of the Enlightenment*, tr. Fritz C. A. Koelln and James P. Pettegrove (Princeton: Princeton University Press, 1968).

18 See Gay, *The Enlightenment: An Interpretation*, and *The Party of Humanity: Essays in the French Enlightenment* (New York: Norton, 1971).

19 David Hume, *A Treatise of Human Nature*, ed. L. A. Selby-Bigge (Oxford: Clarendon Press, 1968), p. 273.

20 Ibid., p. xix.

21 Ibid., p. xx.

22 Ibid.

23 See Immanuel Kant, *Critique of Pure Reason*, tr. N. Kemp Smith (New York: Macmillan, 1961), B xxx, p. 29.

24 See Immanuel Kant, *Prolegomena to Any Future Metaphysics*, intr. L. W. Beck (Indianapolis: LLA, 1950), p. 8.

25 See "An Answer to the Question: What Is Enlightenment?," in Immanuel Kant, *Perpetual Peace and Other Essays*, tr. Ted Humphrey (Indianapolis: Hacket, 1985), p. 41.

26 See Tom Rockmore, "Subjectivity and the Ontology of History," in *The Monist*, vol. 74, no. 2 (April 1991), pp. 187–205.

27 Olson has recently argued that spirit understood in a specifically Lutheran sense is Hegel's central category. See Alan M. Olson, *Hegel and the Spirit: Philosophy as Pneumatology*, (Princeton: Princeton University Press, 1992).

28 See Kant, *Critique of Pure Reason*, B 508, p. 433.

29 Ibid., B 867, pp. 657–658.

30 Ibid., B 867, p. 658.

31 See Edmund Husserl, *Ideas: General Introduction to Pure Phenomenology*, tr. W. R. Boyce Gibson (New York: Collier Books, 1962), p. 166.

32 Hyppolite points to Hegel's implicit humanism when he writes that

> la *Phénoménologie* a eu dans tous les cas le mérite d'exposer les *fondements du fait humain* et de sa *rationalité* possible, de proposer une voie d'accès à ces fondements, quand le dogmatisme classique de la vérité éternelle aussi bien que la notion d'une conscience transcendentale étaient ébranlés par le devenir historique.
>
> (Jean Hyppolite, "Situation de l'homme dans la phénoménologie hégélienne," *Les Temps Modernes*, no. 19 (April 1947), p. 1289)

33 See Mikel Dufrenne, *Pour l'homme* (Paris: Seuil, 1968).

34 See Roger Garaudy, *Perspectives de l'homme: Existentialisme, pensée Catholique, structuralisme, Marxisme* (Paris: Presses universitaires de France, 1969).

35 See Heinrich Heine, *Religion and Philosophy in Germany*, tr. John Snodgrass (Albany: SUNY Press, 1986).

36 See Jean-Paul Sartre, *Being and Nothingness*, tr. by Hazel E. Barnes (New York: Washington Square Press, 1973), p. 792.

37 For a view of the Enlightenment as centrally concerned with a pagan conception of human being, see Gay, *The Enlightenment: An Interpretation*, vol. I: *The Rise of Modern Paganism*.

38 Henri de Lubac, *Le Drame de l'humanisme* (Paris: Cerf, 1983), p. 8.

39 For an illustration of this view, see Roger Daval, *Histoire des idées en France* (Paris: Presses universitaires de France, 1965), p. 122.

40 See André Bourde, "Les lumières, 1715–1789," in *Histoire de la France de 1348 à 1852*, ed. by Georges Duby (Paris: Larousse, 1988), p. 277.

41 See Etienne Gilson, "L'Etre et Dieu," *Revue Thomiste*, vol. 62 (April/June 1962), p. 181: "Il y eut un temps où le christianisme était mort et nul n'en doutait. Ce fut le temps des philosophes, illustré par le déisme rationaliste de Voltaire et les athéismes plus ou moins hésitants de d'Alembart et de Diderot."

42 Denis Diderot, "Epicuréisme," in *Oeuvres*, vol. XIV: *Encyclopédie*, p. 525, cited in Gay, *The Enlightenment*, vol. I, p. 305.

43 According to Margolin, in comparison with Italian humanism between 1480 and 1520 the French variety is characterized by a greater degree of continuity between the Middle Ages and the Renaissance, and a critical or even hostile reaction to certain Italian views on art, thought, and style. See Margolin, "Humanism in France," pp. 164–165.

44 See François Rabelais, *Pantagruel*, ed. Pierre Michel (Paris: Librairie Générale Française, 1972), bk. 2, ch. 8, pp. 119–132.

45 For an interesting effort to understand the views of Descartes and Pascal as opposing reactions to those of Montaigne, see Léon Brunschwicg, *Descartes et Pascal: Lecteurs de Montaigne* (New York and Paris: Brentano, 1944).

46 "Devant ce monde inconnu, l'homme cherche un refuge dans sa propre vie. Sa vie lui appartient comme une donnée toujours présente." Bernard Groethuysen, *Anthropologie philosophique* (Paris: Gallimard, 1952), p. 264.

47 Referring to Montaigne, Pascal mentions "Le sot projet qu'il a de se peindre." Blaise Pascal, *Pensées*, ed. L. Brunschvicg (Paris: Garnier, 1961), s. 2, no. 62. Voltaire, on the contrary, evokes "Le charmant projet que Montaigne a eu de se peindre naivement comme il l'a fait, car il a peint la nature humaine." Voltaire, *Lettres philosophiques*, lettre XXV: "Sur les pensées de M. de Pascal."

48 Michel Montaigne, *Les Essais de Michel de Montaigne*, ed. Pierre Villey (Paris: Presses universitaires de France, 1965), p. 3.

49 See Donald M. Frame, *Montaigne's Discovery of Man: The Humanization of a Humanist* (New York: Columbia University Press, 1955), p. 168:

> We may still call him a humanist in his late years. If we do, however, we are in fact declaring that he has changed the meaning of the term. He has given it a breadth and scope it had never had before. He has made it, even as he has made himself, fully human.

50 See Françoise Charpentier, *Essais, Montaigne* (Paris: Hatier, 1979), p. 50:

> Ce problème de la vérité plongera Montaigne dans la plus grave crise de sa vie, que retrace l'*Apologie de Raymond Sebond*. C'est pour être passé par ce tourniquet du doute, pour s'être mis "à rouet" comme il dit, que Montaigne, ayant compris qu'il n'est d'autre vérité qu'en soi-même, acceptera de regarder, de cultiver patiemment et doucement ce moi, jusqu'à devenir enfin capable de l'accepter totalement, d'en "jouir loyalement":

véritable philosophie de l'existence, au sens même que la pensée moderne de l'existentialisme donne à cette expression.

51 Descartes provides an original kind of foundationalism, but not the first version of foundationalism. Bacon says that "the fabric of human reason" is lacking a "foundation" and recommends "a total reconstruction of sciences, arts, and all human knowledge, raised upon the proper foundations." "The Great Instauration," in Francis Bacon, *The New Organon and Related Writings*, ed. Fulton H. Anderson (Indianapolis: LLA, 1960), pp. 3–4.

52 For a reading of Descartes as a humanist, see Roger Lefèvre, *L'Humanisme de Descartes* (Paris: Presses universitaires de France, 1957). According to Lefèvre, in virtue of his interest in humanism, Descartes anticipates later French existentialism. See Roger Lefèvre, *La Pensée existentialiste de Descartes* (Paris: Bordas, n.d.), p. 178.

53 See Lefèvre, *L'Humanisme de Descartes*, p. vii: "On découvre que le cartésianisme est, et a voulu être – répondant à son époque afin de la dépasser – un effort d'amélioration de la nature par la culture, un appel à l'épanouissement de la liberté . . . ."; and ibid., p. 246: "l'Humanisme cartésien appelle les siècles futurs à relever l'humanité." For other, recent discussion, see André Glucksmann, *Descartes, c'est la France* (Paris: Flammarion, 1987).

54 See *Discourse on Method*, in Descartes, *Philosophical Works*, I, p. 107.

55 See ibid., p. 87.

56 See ibid., p. 116.

57 See ibid., p. 401.

58 See "Cartesianism" in J. B. Bury, *The Idea of Progress: An Inquiry into Its Origin and Growth* (New York: Macmillan, 1932), pp. 64–77.

59 See André Bourde, "Les lumières," pp. 269–270.

60 Denis Diderot, *Rameau's Nephew and Other Works*, tr. Jacques Barzun and Ralph H. Bowen (Indianapolis: LLA, 1964), p. 293.

61 Rousseau maintains that the difference between animals and human beings lies in the fact that human beings can perfect themselves:

> Mais, quand les difficultés qui environnent toutes ces questions laisseraient quelque lieu de disputer sur cette différence de l'homme et de l'animal, il y a une autre qualité très spécifique qui les distingue, et sur laquelle il ne peut y avoir de contestation; c'est la faculté de se perfectionner, faculté qui, à l'aide des circonstances, développe successivement toutes les autres, et réside parmi nous tant dans l'espèce que dans l'individu.
>
> (J.-J. Rousseau, "Discours sur cette question proposée par l'Académie de Dijon: Quelle est l'origine de l'inégalité parmi les hommes et si elle est autorisée par la loi naturelle," in *Du contrat social* (Paris: Garnier, 1962), p. 48)

62 Condorcet, *Esquisse d'un tableau historique des progrès de l'esprit humain*, ed. Alain Pons (Paris: Flammarion, 1988), p. 266.

63 See Ludwig Feuerbach, *The Essence of Christianity*, tr. George Eliot (New York: Harper & Row, 1957).

64 See Søren Kierkegaard, *Fear and Trembling*, tr. Walter Lowrie (Garden City: Doubleday, n.d.).

65 Hegel famously held that the French Revolution was an example of abstract reason in the social sphere that in practice contradicted its theoretical aims. See the discussion of "Absolute Freedom and Terror," in G. W. F. Hegel, *Phenomenology of Spirit*, tr. A. V. Miller (Oxford: Oxford University Press, 1977), pp. 355–363.

66 Burke argued that the French Revolution was the result of the characteristic

Enlightenment contempt of tradition. See Edmund Burke, *Reflections on the Revolution in France*, ed. Thomas H. D. Mahoney, with an analysis by Oskar Piest (Indianapolis: LLA, 1955).

67 See e.g. Daniel Guérin, *L'Anarchisme* (Paris: Gallimard, 1965).

68 For a description, see Cornelius Castoriadis, "Les Mouvements des années soixante," cited in Luc Ferry and Alain Renaut, *68–86: Itinéraires de l'individu* (Paris: Gallimard, 1987), pp. 50–51.

69 See e.g. Maurice Blondel, "Le Christianisme de Descartes," *Revue de la métaphysique et de la morale*, 4 (1896), pp. 551–567.

70 Descartes, *Philosophical Works*, I, p. 145.

71 Ibid., p. 133.

72 See Daval, *Histoire des idées en France*, pp. 29, 38.

73 See the excellent "Introduction" by Alain Pons to Condorcet, *Esquisse d'un tableau historique*, pp. 36–37.

74 See ibid., p. 37.

75 See Blaise Pascal, *Pensées*, ed. Jacques Chevalier, intr. Jean Guitton (Paris: Librairie Générale de France, 1962), p. 185, § 384: "Le pyrrhonisme est le vrai." Ibid., § 387: "Le pyrrhonisme sert à la religion."

76 See Blaise Pascal, *Les Provinciales*, (Paris: Editions Garnier, 1965), "Dix-huitième lettre," pp. 354–380.

77 See Heidegger, "Letter on Humanism", pp. 193–242.

78 A fifth factor, whose role was probably slight, is Heidegger's attention to other philosophical figures, such as Nietzsche and Kierkegaard. The latter's thought was introduced into French at the beginning of the century by Henri Delacroix and Victor Basch. It is, then, significant that the discussion of Wahl's account of existentialism in a 1946 lecture turns in part on his account of the relation of Heidegger and Kierkegaard. See Jean Wahl, *A Short History of Existentialism*, tr. Forrest Williams and Stanley Maron (New York: Philosophical Library, 1949).

79 For details, see Georges Bataille, cited in *The College of Sociology (1937–1939)*, p. 299.

80 See Martin Heidegger, "De la nature de la cause," tr. A. Bessey, *Recherches philosophiques*, vol. 1, no. 1 (1931), pp. 83–125.

81 Alexandre Koyré, "Qu'est-ce que la métaphysique? Introduction," *Bifur*, no. 8 (June 1931), p. 5.

82 Ibid., p. 5.

83 Ibid., p. 6.

84 Ibid., p. 8.

85 See Alexandre Koyré, "L'Evolution philosophique de Martin Heidegger," *Critique* (1946); rpt. in *Etudes d'histoire de la pensée philosophique* (Paris: Armand Colin, 1961).

86 See Jean Wahl, "Heidegger et Kierkegaard: Recherches des éléments originaux de la philosophie de Heidegger," *Recherches philosophiques*, vol. 2, (1932), pp. 349–370.

87 See Martin Heidegger, *Qu'est-ce que la métaphysique?*, tr. Henry Corbin (Paris: Gallimard, 1938). This volume contains the first complete French translation of "Was ist Metaphysik?," a complete translation of "Vom Wesen des Grundes," §§ 46–53 and 72–76 of *Sein und Zeit*, §§ 42–45 of *Kant und das Problem der Metaphysik*, and a complete translation of "Hölderlin und das Wesen der Dichtung."

88 See Georges Gurvitch, *Les Tendances actuelles de la philosophie allemande* (Paris: Vrin, 1930).

89 See Emmanuel Lévinas, "Martin Heidegger et l'ontologie," *Revue philosophique*, (May–June 1932), pp. 395–431, rpt. in Emmanuel Lévinas, *En découvrant*

l'existence avec Husserl et Heidegger (Paris: Vrin, 1988). See also his early essay, "L'ontologie dans le temporel," originally published in Spanish, which appeared in French in 1949 in the first edition of this work.

90 It was published immediately. See Emmanuel Lévinas, *Théorie de l'intuition dans la phénoménologie de Husserl* (Paris: Vrin, 1930).

91 See Alexandre Kojève, "Compte rendu de Georg Misch, *Lebensphilosophie und Phänomenologie,*" *Recherches philosophiques*, vol. 2 (1932–1933), pp. 470–474; "Compte rendu de J. Kraft, *Von Husserl zu Heidegger,*" *Recherches philosophiques*, vol. 2 (1932–1933), pp. 475–477; "Compte rendu de *La Phénoménologie: Journées d'études de la Société Thomiste,*" *Recherches philosophiques*, vol. 3 (1933–1934), pp. 429–431; "Compte rendu de A. Sternberger, *Der verstandene Tod: Eine Untersuchung zu Martin Heideggers Existentialontologie,*" *Recherches philosophiques*, vol. 4 (1934–1935), pp. 400–402; "Compte rendu de A. Delp, *Tragische Existenz: Zur Philosophie Martin Heideggers,*" *Recherches philosophiques*, vol. 5 (1935–1936); "Compte rendu de A. Fischer, *Die Existenzphilosophie Martin Heideggers: Darlegung und Würdigung ihrer Grundgedanken,*" *Recherches philosophiques*, vol. 6 (1936–1937), pp. 396–397.

92 See Kojève, "Compte rendu de A. Fischer, pp. 396–397.

93 Gurvitch, *Les Tendances actuelles de la philosophie allemande.*

94 See E. Levinas, "Martin Heidegger et l'ontologie," in *En découvrant l'existence avec Heidegger et Husserl* (Paris: Vrin, 1988), pp. 53–76. This article first appeared in 1932.

95 See Lévinas, *En découvrant l'existence,* p. 89.

96 Heidegger is careful to reject any claim for a positive link between Hegel's thought and his own. See Martin Heidegger, *Hegels Phänomenologie des Geistes,* ed. Ingtraud Görland (Frankfurt/M.: Vittorio Klostermann, 1988).

97 See M. Heidegger, *Being and Time,* tr. J. Macquarie and E. Robinson (New York: Harper & Row, 1962), § 82: "A Comparison of the Existential-ontological Connection of Temporality, Dasein, and World-time, with Hegel's Way of Taking the Relation between Time and Spirit," pp. 480–486.

98 For a critical discussion of Heidegger's remarks on Hegel's view of force and understanding, see Denise Souche-Dagues, *Hégélianisme et dualisme: Réflexions sur le phénomène* (Paris: Vrin, 1990), pp. 20–32.

99 A. Kojève, *Introduction à la lecture de Hegel,* ed. R. Queneau (Paris: Gallimard, 1947), p. 527n.

100 See Heidegger's letter, dated March 10, 1937, to his French translator, Henry Corbin, in Martin Heidegger, *Questions I et II* (Paris: Gallimard, 1968), p. 10.

101 For Kant's analysis of the ontological proof of the existence of God, see Kant, *Critique of Pure Reason,* B 620–631, pp. 500–507.

102 Writing after the controversy concerning the proper rendering of *Dasein* into French, Aubenque maintains that it is better to leave the term in the original since any translation runs the risk of falsifying Heidegger's intentions. See his "Présentation" of Ernst Cassirer and Martin Heidegger, *Débat sur le kantisme et la philosophie (Davos, mars 1929)* (Paris: Beauchesnes, 1972), p. 9.

103 Michel Haar, a respected French Heidegger specialist, remarks in the preface to a recent edition of Heidegger's writings, that Corbin's initial translations provided the French public with access to Heidegger's writings. See Heidegger, *Questions I et II,* p. 7.

104 Kojève, *Introduction à la lecture de Hegel,* p. 11.

105 See Heidegger, *Being and Time,* p. 33.

106 See Heidegger, *Questions I et II,* pp. 9–17.

107 Ibid., p. 20.

108 See Jean-Paul Sartre, *L'Existentialisme est un humanisme* (Paris: Nagel, 1964).
109 See "A Propos de l'Existentialisme," in Jean Beaufret, *Introduction aux philosophies de l'existence: De Kierkegaard à Heidegger* (Paris: Denoël/ Gonthier, 1971), pp. 9–63.
110 Heidegger, *Questions I et II*, p. 14.
111 Jean-Paul Sartre, *Esquisse d'une théorie des émotions* (Paris: Hermann, 1965), p. 8; Sartre's emphases. Sartre maintained this translation of *Dasein* even in later writings; in his famous popular lecture on existentialism, for instance, he speaks of "l'homme ou, comme dit Heidegger, la réalité humaine." Sartre, *L'Existentialisme est un humanisme*, p. 21.
112 *Le Collège de sociologie (1937–1939)*, ed. by Roger Hollier (Paris: Gallimard, 1979), p. 187.
113 See Simone de Beauvoir, *La Force de l'âge* (Paris: Gallimard, 1960), p. 483.
114 See *Bulletin de la Société française de philosophie*, 1937, p. 168.
115 See ibid., pp. 168–172.
116 See Jean Wahl, *La Pensée de l'existence* (Paris: Flammarion, 1951), pp. 5–6.
117 See Jean Wahl, *Mots, mythes et réalité dans la pensee de Heidegger* (Paris: Les cours de la Sorbonne, 1962), p. 183.
118 See Otto Pöggeler, "Jean Wahls Heidegger-Deutung," *Zeitschrift für philosophische Forschung*, 1958, pp. 437–458.
119 See *Bulletin de la Société française de philosophie*, 1937, pp. 193–194.
120 Jean-Paul Sartre, "La république du silence," in *Situations, III*, pp. 11–12, cited in John Gerassi, *Jean-Paul Sartre: Hated Conscience of His Century* (Chicago: University of Chicago Press, 1989), p. 174.
121 According to Spiegelberg, more than anyone else Sartre created interest in Husserl in France. See Herbert Spiegelberg, *The Phenomenological Movement: A Historical Introduction* (The Hague: Martinus Nijhoff, 1982), p. 434.
122 For a short summary of Sartre's reading of the three H's, see Sartre, *Being and Nothingness*, "Husserl, Hegel, Heidegger," pp. 315–339.
123 Jean Beaufret, *Introduction aux philosophies de l'existence* (Paris: Denoël, 1971), p. 5.
124 See Jean-Paul Sartre, *Situations, X* (Paris: Gallimard, 1975), p. 110.
125 See Juliette Simont, "Sartre et la conscience malheureuse," in *Magazine littéraire*, no. 293 (November 1991), pp. 59–61.
126 See Christopher M. Fry, *Sartre and Hegel: The Variations of an Enigma in "L'Etre et le Néant,"* p. 3.
127 See Beauvoir, *La Force de l'âge*, p. 447.
128 Jean-Paul Sartre, *Critique de la raison dialectique* (Paris: Gallimard, 1960), p. 248.
129 Sartre seems on occasion not to be aware of the outside world. In reference to his journal, he writes: "Le carnet est une tâche, une humble tâche quotidienne et c'est plutôt avec humilité qu'on le relit." Jean-Paul Sartre, *Les Carnets de la drôle de guerre* (Paris: Gallimard, 1983), p. 90.
130 Ibid., p. 34.
131 See Immanuel Kant, *Fundamental Principles of the Metaphysics of Morals*, tr. by Thomas K. Abbott (New York: LLA, 1949), p. 67.
132 See Sartre, *Being and Nothingness*, p. 562.
133 See ibid., p. 568.
134 See ibid., p. 571.
135 Jean-Paul Sartre, *Lettres au Castor et à quelques autres* (2 vols., Paris: Gallimard, 1983), vol. II, p. 301, cited in Gerassi, *Sartre*, p. 170.
136 For a discussion of tradition, see Heidegger, *Being and Time*, § 74.

137 See Arthur Danto, "Thoughts of a Bourgeois Draftee," in *New York Times Book Review*, March 31, 1985, cited in Gerassi, *Sartre*, p. 168.

138 According to Sartre, he modified his initial view of absolute freedom by accepting as early as the early 1940s the idea that freedom is limited by the freedom of the other. See Simone de Beauvoir, *La Cérémonie des adieux*, suivi de *Entretiens avec Jean-Paul Sartre* (Paris: Gallimard, 1981), p. 453.

139 Jean-Paul Sartre, *Situations, I* (Paris: Gallimard, 1947), p. 33: Il faudra deux siècles de crise – crises de la Foi, crise de la Science – pour que l'homme récupère cette liberté créatrice que Descartes a mise en Dieu et pour qu'on soupçonne cette vérité, base essentielle de l'humanisme, l'homme et l'être dont l'apparition fait qu'un monde existe.

140 In a letter to Simone de Beauvoir dated January 9, 1940 he complains that in rereading his journal he became aware that the clearest ideas were due to Heidegger. The letter is cited in Annie Cohen-Solal, *Sartre* (Paris: Gallimard, 1985), p. 202.

141 One should distinguish sharply between Sartre's technical thought and his informal, public presentations of it. For a discussion of this lecture, see Thomas R. Flynn, *Sartre and Marxist Existentialism: The Test Case of Collective Responsibility* (Chicago: University of Chicago Press, 1984), pp. 31–48.

142 See Martin Heidegger, "The Self-Assertion of the German University," in *Martin Heidegger and National Socialism: Questions and Answers*, ed. G. Neske and E. Kettering (New York: Paragon, 1990), pp. 15–31. For an analysis of this text, see T. Rockmore, *On Heidegger's Nazism and Philosophy* (Berkeley: Unviersity of California Press, 1992), chapter 2, pp. 28–72.

143 In his lecture, where he insists on the need for action, he insists on his Cartesianism when he writes:

> Il ne peut pas y avoir de vérité autre, au point de départ, que celle-ci: *je pense donc je suis*, c'est là la vérité absolue de la conscience s'atteignant elle-même. Toute théorie qui prend l'homme en dehors de ce moment où il s'atteint lui-même est d'abord une théorie qui supprime la vérité.
>
> (Sartre, *L'Existentialisme est un humanisme*, p. 64)

144 For discussion of the compatibility of Sartre's thought and Marxism, see Tom Rockmore, "Sartre and 'the Philosophy of Our Time'," *Journal of the British Society for Phenomenology*, vol. 9, no. 2 (May 1978), pp. 92–101.

5 JEAN BEAUFRET AND THE "LETTER ON HUMANISM"

1 Pöggeler, one of the leading German Heidegger scholars, correctly recognized Sartre's role in the French Heidegger reception. "Durch den Einsatz Sartres ist Heidegger zu einem Denker geworden, der die Diskussionen der französischen Intelligenz entscheidend mitbestimmt". Otto Pöggeler, "Jean Wahls Heidegger-Deutung," in *Zeitschrift für philosophische Forschung*, 1958, p. 438.

2 For Deleuze's view of the deep impression made by this work, see James Miller, *The Passion of Michel Foucault* (New York: Simon & Schuster, 1993), p. 40.

3 See J. Gerassi, *Jean-Paul Sartre: Hated Conscience of His Century* (Chicago: University of Chicago Press, 1989), p. 30:

> No intellectual, no writer, no man is more hated by academics and newsfolk, by eggheads and politicians on both sides of the Atlantic than Jean-Paul Sartre. Nor is this new: Sartre has been hated by them for half a century.

NOTES

4 For a complete list, see Gerassi, *Sartre*, ch. 2: "L'Adulte Terrible," pp. 30–37.

5 See e.g. "Plaidoyer pour les intellectuels: Trois conférences données à Tokyo et à Kyoto en septembre et octobre 1966," in Jean-Paul Sartre, *Situations philosophiques* (Paris: Gallimard, 1990), pp. 219–281.

6 Michel points out that during the occupation, no one could publish without the approval of the Germans. He provides an impressive list of other writers, including Camus, Valery, Troyat, Gulloin, Cocteau, Mauriac, Gide and Paulhan who continued to publish in France rather than abroad, like Wahl and some others, during the occupation. See Henri Michel, *Paris allemand* (Paris: Albin Michel, 1981), ch. 9: "L'Activité culturelle: évasion ou soumission?," pp. 315–346.

7 This is the main message of Joseph's recent critical study. See Gilbert Joseph, *Une si douce occupation: Simone de Beauvoir et Jean-Paul Sartre, 1940–1944* (Paris: Albin Michel, 1991). For a similar study, mainly devoted to Simone de Beauvoir, see also Bianca Lamblin, *Mémoires d'une jeune fille dérangée* (Paris: Editions Balland, 1993).

8 "L'homme est-il mort?," *Arts et loisirs*, June 15, 1966, cited in D. Eribon, *Michel Foucault* (Paris: Flammarion, 1991), p. 189.

9 This view is elaborated by Descombes, who usefully relates it to Heidegger. See Vincent Descombes, *Le Même et l'autre* (Paris: Editions de Minuit, 1979), p. 93.

10 See Eribon, *Foucault*, p. 297.

11 See ibid., p. 188.

12 See Pierre Bourdieu, *Le Sens pratique* (Paris: Minuit, 1980), p. 8, cited in Eribon, *Foucault*, p. 188.

13 See Jean-Paul Sartre, *La Nausée* (Paris: Gallimard, 1938), pp. 164–179.

14 Kanapa rightly noted that everyone was for humanism although the different views of humanism did not necessarily share anything more than the term. See Jean Kanapa, *L'Existentialisme n'est pas un humanisme* (Paris: Editions Sociales, 1947), pp. 13–14.

15 "Tous les courants de pensée se recommandaient de l'humanisme au lendemain de la Seconde Guerre mondiale: Sartre démontrait que l'existentialisme est un humanisme, les marxistes l'utilisaient aussi à leur profit, et le P. Henri de Lubac reconnaissait à certains types d'athéisme un caractère humaniste." Jean-Claude Margolin, *L'Humanisme en Europe* (Paris: Presses universitaires de France, 1981), p. 6.

16 See Jean Lacouture, *Léon Blum* (Paris: Editions du Seuil, 1977), pp. 517–523.

17 See Tony Judt, *Past Imperfect: French Intellectuals, 1944–1956* (Berkeley: University of California Press, 1992).

18 See Judt, *Past Imperfect*, pp. 87–88, 90.

19 See Maurice Merleau-Ponty, *Humanisme et terreur: Essai sur le problème communiste* (Paris: Gallimard, 1947).

20 See Maurice Merleau-Ponty, *Les Aventures de la dialectique* (Paris: Gallimard, 1955).

21 See e.g. Drieu la Rochelle, *Socialisme fasciste* (Paris: Gallimard, 1934).

22 Joseph shows that the myth of Sartre's actual participation in the resistance movement is no more than that. See Joseph, *Une si douce occupation*, pp. 366ff. For a study of the role of intellectuals, see Jacques Débru-Bridel, *La Résistance intellectuelle* (Paris: Juilliard, 1970).

23 See Annie Cohen-Solal, *Paul Nizan: Communiste impossible* (Paris: Grasset, 1980).

24 See *Politzer contre le nazisme*, ed. Roger Bourderon (Paris: Editions sociales, 1984).

25 See Gabrielle Ferrières, *Jean Cavaillès: Un Philosophe dans la guerre, 1903–1944*

(Paris: Seuil, 1982); see also Georges Canguilhem, *Vie et mort de Jean Cavaillès* (Ambialet/Villefrance-Albigeois: Laleure, 1976).

26 Roger Garaudy, *Les Lettres françaises*, December 28, 1945, p. 89, cited in Cohen-Solal, *Sartre*, p. 381.

27 Jean Wahl, *Petite Histoire de l'existentialisme* (Paris: Club Maintenant, 1947), p. 12.

28 See *Bulletin de la Société Française de Philosophie*, 1937, pp. 193–194. In reaction to a paper presented by Jean Wahl, Heidegger writes (p. 193): "Vos remarques critiques au sujet de la 'philosophie de l'existence' sont très instructives. Je dois cependant redire que mes tendances philosophiques, bien qu'il soit question dans *Sein und Zeit* d' 'Existenz' et de 'Kierkegaard', ne peuvent être classées comme *Existenzphilosophie*."

29 For an account of the occasion, see Miller, *The Passion of Michel Foucault*, pp. 42–44.

30 In respect to Sartre's lecture, Burnier writes:

> l'importance prise par ces pages semble due à la paresse d'un bon nombre de critiques qui hésitaient à lire *l'Etre et le Néant* et qui furent heureux de pouvoir attaquer Sartre sans grande fatigue et avec bonne conscience après avoir parcouru 141 pages.
>
> (M. A. Burnier, *Les Existentialistes et la politique*, p. 31, cited in Michel Contat and Michel Rybalka, *Les Ecrits de Sartre: Chronologie, bibliographie commentée* (Paris: Gallimard, 1970), p. 131)

31 See Thomas Aquinas, *On Being and Essence*, tr. Armand Maurer (Toronto: Pontifical Institute of Medieval Studies, 1949).

32 See Jean-Paul Sartre, *L'Existentialisme est un humanisme* (Paris: Nagel, 1964), p. 17.

33 See ibid., p. 21.

34 See ibid., p. 62.

35 See ibid., p. 65.

36 See ibid., p. 92.

37 See ibid.

38 See ibid., p. 10.

39 See ibid., p. 64.

40 See ibid., p. 94.

41 See ibid., p. 95.

42 See Kanapa, *L'Existentialisme n'est pas un humanisme*, p. 27.

43 See ibid., p. 44.

44 See ibid., p. 61.

45 See ibid., p. 88.

46 See Henri Lefebvre, *L'Existentialisme* (Paris: Le Sagittaire, 1946).

47 For a brilliant French Marxist critique of French academic philosophy, originally published in 1932, see Paul Nizan, *Les Chiens de garde* (Paris: Maspero, 1960).

48 See Lefebvre, *L'Existentialisme*, p. 13.

49 For this perspective in the French discussion, see Georg Lukács, *Existentialisme ou Marxisme?*, tr. E. Kelemen (Paris: Nagel, 1948, rpt. 1961).

50 See Lefebvre, *L'Existentialisme*, p. 191.

51 Ibid., p. 211.

52 See ibid., p. 213.

53 See ibid., p. 221.

54 See ibid., p. 224.

55 For a French study of Jaspers, see Mikel Dufrenne and Paul Ricoeur, *Karl Jaspers et la philosophie de l'existence* (Paris: Seuil, 1947).

56 See Etienne Gilson, *L'Etre et l'essence* (Paris: Vrin, 1987), p. 354.

57 See ibid., p. 361.

58 See E. Lévinas, "L'Ontologie est-elle fondamentale?," *Revue de métaphysique et de morale*, vol. 56 (January–March 1951), p. 89.

59 See Henri Birault, "Existence et vérité d'après Heidegger," *Revue de métaphysique et de morale*, vol. 56 (January–March 1951), pp. 35–87.

60 See Henri Birault, *Heidegger et l'expérience de la pensée* (Paris: Gallimard, 1978), p. 9.

61 See Birault, "Existence et vérité," p. 39.

62 See Jean Beaufret, "A propos de l'existentialisme," in Jean Beaufret, *Introduction aux philosophies de l'existence: De Kierkegaard à Heidegger* (Paris: Denoël/Gonthier, 1971), pp. 9–77.

63 See ibid., p. 19.

64 See ibid., p. 16.

65 See ibid., p. 62.

66 See his "Martin Heidegger et le problème de la vérité," in Jean Beaufret, *Introduction aux philosophies de l'existence* (Paris: Denoël/Gonthier, 1971), pp. 111–146.

67 See ibid., p. 129.

68 See ibid., p. 131.

69 See ibid., p. 136.

70 Jean Beaufret, *Dialogue avec Heidegger*, vol. II: *Philosophie moderne* (Paris: Editions de Minuit, 1973), p. 18.

71 See ibid., pp. 49–50.

72 See ibid., p. 133.

73 See ibid., p. 147.

74 See Jean Beaufret, *Dialogue avec Heidegger*, vol. III: *Approche de Heidegger* (Paris: Editions de Minuit, 1974), pp. 41, 222.

75 See Jean Beaufret, *Dialogue avec Heidegger*, vol. IV: *Le Chemin de Heidegger* (Paris: Editions de Minuit, 1985), pp. 113–114.

76 Wahl, *Petite Histoire de l'existentialisme*, p. 52.

77 See ibid., p. 69.

78 See Tom Rockmore, *On Heidegger's Nazism and Philosophy* (Berkeley: University of California Press, 1992).

79 See "The Rectorial Address," in *Martin Heidegger and National Socialism*, ed. Günther Neske and Emil Kettering (New York: Paragon House, 1990), pp. 5–14.

80 This thesis is developed by Farías. See Victor Farías, *Heidegger and Nazism*, ed. Joseph Margolis and Tom Rockmore, tr. Paul Burrell and Gabriel R. Ricci (Philadelphia: Temple University Press, 1989).

81 See "Wege zur Aussprache," in *Alemannenland: Ein Buch von Volkstum und Sendung*, ed. Franz Kerber (Stuttgart: J. Engelhorns Nacht, 1937), pp. 135–139, rpt. in Guido Schneeberger, *Nachlese zu Heidegger: Dokumente zu seinem Leben und Denken* (Berne, 1962), pp. 258–262.

82 Brinkmann developed his analysis of art history, influenced by the racial views of Hitler and Mussolini, after the collapse of Germany in 1918. He regarded Italy, France and Germany as the three *Führernationen*. See Albert Erich Brinkmann, *Geist der Nationen: Italiener–Franzosen–Deutsche* (Hamburg: Hofmann & Campe, 1938), pp. 159–162.

83 Schneeberger, *Nachlese zu Heidegger*, p. 262.

84 Ibid., p. 258.

85 "Rectorial address – Facts and Thoughts," p. 497.

86 Schneeberger, *Nachlese zu Heidegger*, p. 260.

87 For this view in the early Marx, see his essay, "Contributions to the Critique of Hegel's *Philosophy of Right*: Introduction," in Karl Marx, *Early Writings*, tr. T. B. Bottomore (New York: McGraw-Hill, 1964), pp. 41–60. Lukács bases his own influential reading of Marx on the supposed efficacy of class consciousness. See Georg Lukács, *History and Class Consciousness: Studies in Marxist Dialectics*, tr. R. Livingstone (Cambridge: MIT Press, 1971).

88 Schneeberger, *Nachlese zu Heidegger*, p. 260.

89 Lukács's own effort to enlist Marxism as a revolutionary form of thought in the service of oppressed humanity, relevantly similar to Heidegger's view here, is a constant in his long Marxist period.

90 See "Lettre à Monsieur Beaufret," in Martin Heidegger, *Lettre sur l'Humanisme* tr. R. Munier (Paris: Aubier, 1964), pp. 179–185.

91 See Mikkel Borch-Jacobsen, *Lacan: Le Maître absolu* (Paris: Flammarian, 1990), p. 32.

92 For Jasper's report that led to Heidegger's "rustification" and later rehabilitation, see Hugo Ott, *Martin Heidegger: Unterwegs zu seiner Biographie* (Frankfurt/M.: Campus, 1988), pp. 315–317.

93 See Jaspers's letter to Heidegger of August 23, 1933, cited in Ott, *Martin Heidegger*, pp. 192–193.

94 For Croce's correspondence with Vossler concerning Heidegger, see Schneeberger, *Nachlese zu Heidegger*, pp. 110–112.

95 For Althusser's admission that his antihumanism was influenced by Heidegger's "Letter on Humanism," see Louis Althusser, *L'Avenir dure longtemps* suivi de *Les faits*, ed. Olivier Corpet and Yann Moulier Boutang (Paris: Stock/Imec, 1992), p. 168. For an effort to come to grips with Althusser in the wake of that work, see Stanislas Breton, "Althusser aujourd'hui," *Archives de philosophie*, vol. 56, no. 3, pp. 417–430.

96 Cousineau, who distinguishes four different interpretations of this text, maintains that it is so difficult to interpret because it is systematically ambiguous. See Robert Henri Cousineau, *Humanism and Ethics: An Introduction to Heidegger's Letter on Humanism with a Critical Bibliography* (Louvain: Edition Nauwelaerts, 1972), esp. pp. 65–66.

97 See Gerhard Krüger, "Martin Heidegger und der Humanismus," *Studia Philosophica*, no. 9 (1949), pp. 93–129, rpt. in *Philosophische Rundschau*, 1950, pp. 148–178.

98 Beaufret, *Introduction aux philosophies de l'existence*, p. 16.

99 See Heidegger, *Lettre sur l'humanisme*, pp. 182–183.

100 Martin Heidegger, *L'Etre et le Temps*, §§1–44, tr. R. Boehm and A. De Waelhens (Paris: Gallimard, 1964).

101 Martin Heidegger, *Etre et Temps*, tr. Emmanuel Martineau (Paris: Authentica, 1985).

102 Martin Heidegger, *Etre et Temps*, tr. François Vezin (Paris: Gallimard, 1986).

103 A partial translation by Joseph Rovan of the initial form of the "Letter on Humanism" was published in *Fontaine*, no. 63 (1947). A translation of the revised form of this text, published by Heidegger in 1947, appeared in 1953 in the *Cahiers du sud*, nos. 319–320, and was available in a bilingual edition in 1957.

104 See Heidegger, *Lettre sur l'humanisme*, pp. 182–183; Heidegger's emphasis.

105 Heidegger delivered three lecture series on Hölderlin in winter semester 1934/35, in winter semester 1941/42 and summer semester 1942. The first series is particularly important for an appreciation of Heidegger's turn to poetry. See Martin Heidegger, *Hölderlins Hymnen "Germanien" und "Der Rhein"*, ed. Susanne Ziegler (Frankfurt/M.: Vittorio Klostermann, 1980).

106 Heidegger delivered lectures on Nietzsche between 1936 and 1940. For a revised version of his lectures, see Martin Heidegger, *Nietzsche* (2 vols., Pfullingen: Neske, 1961).

107 See Martin Heidegger, *Die Grundbegriffe der Metaphysik: Welt–Endlichkeit–Einsamkeit* (Wintersemester 1929/30), ed. Friedrich-Wilhelm von Hermann (Frankfurt/M.: Vittorio Klostermann, 1985).

108 Heidegger's insistence on alienation here and in his main philosophical treatise has led some writers to see an influence of Marxism in his thought. Goldmann has argued that *Being and Time* is a response to Lukács's *History and Class Consciousness*. See Lucien Goldmann, *Lukács and Heidegger: Towards a New Philosophy*, tr. William G. Boelhower (London: Routledge & Kegan Paul, 1977).

109 Martin Heidegger, "The Letter on Humanism," in M. Heidegger, *Basic Writings* ed. D. F. Krell (New York: Harper & Row, 1977), p. 219.

110 See ibid., p. 208.

111 Ibid., p. 231.

112 See ibid., p. 220.

113 See ibid., p. 221.

114 See ibid., p. 222.

115 See ibid., p. 239.

116 See ibid., p. 231.

117 See ibid., pp. 239, 241–242.

118 See ibid., p. 220.

119 See ibid., p. 221.

120 See ibid., p. 220.

121 Blondel, a philosopher of action, recalls the religious view, illustrated by St. Jean of the Cross that the true form of action is the thought of God: "L'action qui enveloppe et achève toutes les autres, c'est de penser vraiment à Dieu." Maurice Blondel, cited in André Lalande, *Vocabulaire technique et critique de la philosophie*, vol. I (Paris: Presses universitaires de France, 1926), p. 17.

122 The date and nature of the turning is controversial. Beaufret situates it in 1927 as the other beginning, more radical than the first, after the publication of *Being and Time*. See Beaufret, *Dialogue avec Heidegger*, IV, p. 85.

123 See, for example, his remarks about atheism as intrinsic to philosophy in Martin Heidegger, *Phänomenologische Interpretationen zu Aristoteles: Einführung in die phänomenologische Forschung*, ed. Walter Bröcker and Käte Bröcker-Oltmanns (Frankfurt/M.: Vittorio Klostermann, 1985), p. 197.

124 See Beaufret, *Dialogue avec Heidegger*, IV, p. 112.

125 See George Kovacs, *The Question of God in Heidegger's Phenomenology* (Evanston: Northwestern University Press, 1990), p. 180 n27.

126 After an initial period of study in a Jesuit seminary, Heidegger's relation to organized religion became strained, even hostile. He consistently held that philosophy cannot be placed on a Christian basis. For a recent study, see Kovacs, *The Question of God*. In the French discussion, Beaufret has seen this point. See Beaufret, *Dialogue avec Heidegger*, IV, p. 111, and Eryck de Rubercy and Dominique Le Buhan, *Douze questions posées à Jean Beaufret à propos de Martin Heidegger* (Paris: Aubier Montaigne, 1983), p. 32.

127 In his reaction to Jean Wahl's paper on Heidegger before the French Philosophical Society in 1937, Lévinas, who has always been concerned to intertwine his philosophical theory and his religious belief, insisted on Heidegger's own efforts to distinguish between them. See "Lettre de M. E. Lévinas," in *Bulletin de la Société française de philosophie*, 1937, p. 194.

128 See Birault, "Existence et vérité," p. 87. He later changed his mind. In a later article, he pointedly distinguishes between Heidegger's ontology and

Christianity. See Henri Birault, "La foi et la pensée d'après Heidegger," *Recherches et débats*, no. 10 (May 1955), p. 132: "Mais la voix de l'Etre n'est pas la Parole de Dieu, c'est une voix qui nous livre à la stupeur originelle du 'il y a' obscur et clair séjour des dieux et des mortels."

129 Heidegger, "Letter on Humanism," pp. 207–208.
130 See *L'Endurance de la pensée* (Paris: Plon, 1969).
131 See "Preface by Martin Heidegger," in William J. Richardson, *Heidegger: Through Phenomenology to Thought* (The Hague: Martinus Nijhoff, 1967), pp. viii–xxiii.
132 See ibid., pp. xvi, xvii.
133 Those who take a contextualist approach, even among Heidegger's closest adherents, are less likely to take over his anticontextualist view of the turning, to the point of even doubting its existence. See Ernst Nolte, *Heidegger: Politik und Geschichte im Leben und Denken* (Berlin: Propyläen, 1992).
134 See Alberto Rosales, "Zum Problem der Kehre im Denken Heideggers," *Zeitschrift für philosophische Forschung*, 38 (1984), p. 243.
135 See ibid., p. 262.
136 See J.-F. Mattéi, "Le Chiasme heideggérien ou la mise à l'écart de la philosophie," in Dominique Janicaud and J.-F. Mattéi, *La Métaphysique à la limite* (Paris: Presses universitaires de France, 1983), p. 85.
137 See ibid., p. 93.
138 See Jean Grondin, *Le Tournant dans la pensée de Martin Heidegger* (Paris: Presses universitaires de France, 1987), p. 121.
139 See Martin Heidegger, *Metaphysische Anfangsgründe der Logik im Ausgang von Leibniz* (Sommersemester 1928), ed. Klaus Held (Frankfurt/M.: Vittorio Klostermann, 1978).
140 Martin Heidegger, "On the Essence of Truth," in M. Heidegger, *Basic Writings* ed. D. F. Krell (New York: Harper & Row, 1977), p. 139.
141 Martin Heidegger, *Schellings Abhandlung "Über das Wesen der menschlichen Freiheit" (1809)*, ed. Hildegard Feick (Tübingen: Max Niemeyer, 1971), p. 38.
142 Ibid., p. 79.
143 See Martin Heidegger, *The Will to Power as Art*, tr. David Farrell Krell (New York: Harper & Row, 1979), chs 5 ("The Structure of the 'Major Work': Nietzsche's Manner of Thinking as Reversal [Umkehrung]") and ("Truth in Platonism and Positivism: Nietzsche's Overturning [Umdrehung] of Platonism"), pp. 25–33, 151–161.
144 See ibid., pp. 29, 30.
145 See ibid., p. 210.
146 See Heidegger, *Nietzsche*, p. 654.
147 "Only A God Can Save Us: *Der Spiegel*'s Interview with Martin Heidegger," *Philosophy Today*, Winter 1976, p. 274.
148 See Hannah Arendt, *The Life of the Mind: Willing* (New York: Harcourt Brace Jovanovich, 1978), p. 173.
149 See Aubenque, "Encore Heidegger et le nazisme," *Le Débat*, no. 48 (January–February 1988), p. 121.
150 See Silvio Vietta, *Heideggers Kritik am Nationalsozialismus und an der Technik* (Tübingen: Max Niemeyer, 1989), ch. 4: "Heideggers Nietzsche-Lektüre: Kritik der Weltanschauungen und Nihilismusbegriff", pp. 48–68, esp. pp. 66–68.
151 See Otto Pöggeler, "Heidegger, Nietzsche, and Politics," in *The Heidegger Case: Philosophy and Politics*, ed. Tom Rockmore and Joseph Margolis (Philadelphia: Temple University Press, 1992), pp. 114–140.
152 Martin Heidegger, *Beiträge zur Philosophie*, ed. Friedrich-Wilhelm von Hermann (Frankfurt/M.: Vittorio Klostermann, 1989), p. 407.

153 Ibid., p. 408.
154 Martin Heidegger, *Die Technik und die Kehre* (Pfullingen: Neske, 1962), p. 42.
155 See Heidegger, *Hölderlins Hymnen*.
156 See Martin Heidegger, *Zur Bestimmung der Philosophie*, ed. Bernd Heimbüchel (Frankfurt/M.: Vittorio Klostermann, 1987), p. 75 and passim.
157 Rockmore, *On Heidegger's Nazism and Philosophy*.

6 HEIDEGGER'S "LETTER ON HUMANISM" AND FRENCH HEIDEGGERIANISM

1 For discussion of the reception of Kant's critical philosophy through the general problem of system, see Tom Rockmore, *Hegel's Circular Epistemology* (Bloomington: Indiana University Press, 1986), ch. 2: "Epistemological Justification: System, Foundation, and Circularity," pp. 16–43.

2 See Martin Heidegger, *Being and Time*, tr. J. Macquarie and E. Robinson (New York: Harper & Row, 1962), § 44: "Dasein, disclosedness, and truth," pp. 256–273.

3 See e.g. the series of essays in Martin Heidegger, *Gelassenheit* (Pfullingen: Neske, 1959).

4 See Martin Heidegger, "The Letter on Humanism," in M. Heidegger, *Basic Writings* ed. D. F. Krell (New York: Harper & Row, 1977), p. 197.

5 See ibid., p. 198.

6 See ibid., p. 207.

7 See ibid.

8 See ibid., p. 209.

9 See ibid., p. 210.

10 According to Heidegger's French translator, the "Letter," along with the introduction to the lecture, "What Is Metaphysics?," is the best introduction to *Being and Time*. See Roger Munier, "Introduction" to Martin Heidegger, *Lettre sur l'humanisme* tr. R. Munier (Paris: Aubier, 1964), p. 7.

11 The simple identification of metaphysics with philosophy, or Western philosophy, although useful for Heidegger's effort to portray his later position as beyond philosophy, is also controversial. For an objection in the French philosophical discussion, see Paul Ricoeur, *La Métaphore vive*, (Paris: Editions du Seuil, 1975), p. 395: "Le moment est venu, me semble-t-il, de s'interdire la commodité, devenue paresse de pensée, de faire tenir sous un seul mot – métaphysique – le tout de la pensée occidentale." For Beaufret's response to Ricoeur's criticism, see Jean Beaufret, *Dialogue avec Heidegger*, vol. IV: *Le Chemin de Heidegger* (Paris: Editions de Minuit, 1974), p. 41.

12 In the "Afterword to the Second Edition" of his well known study of Heidegger, Pöggeler wrote: "The *Beiträge* were for me Heidegger's major work." Otto Pöggeler, *Martin Heidegger's Path of Thinking*, tr. David Magurshak and Sigmund Barber (Atlantic Highlands, NJ: Humanities Press, 1987), pp. 286–287. In a more recent article, written after the publication of the *Beiträge*, Pöggeler wrote: "In dieser Einsamkeit schrieb Heidegger 1936–38 sein eigentliches Hauptwerk, die 'Beiträge zur Philosophie'." Otto Pöggeler, "'Praktische Philosophie' als Antwort an Heidegger," in *Martin Heidegger und das "Dritte Reich": Ein Kompendium*, ed. Bernd Martin (Darmstadt: Wissenschaftliche Buchgesellschaft, 1989), p. 85.

13 In reference to this work, Marten writes: "In ihr [that is, the *Beiträge*] hat er völlig unverblümt, ohne jeden Versuch zu argumentieren und zu entwickeln, seinen Überlegungen, Einfällen, Phantasien, prophetischen Vermutungen und Ahnungen freien Lauf gelassen und sie doch zugleich immer wieder sich selbst zugespielt.

Was herauskommt, ist das philosophisch am wenigsten Überzeugende und daher Unbefriedigenste, für den Philosophen Heidegger aber Typischste." Rainer Marten, *Heidegger Lesen* (Munich: Wilhelm Fink, 1991), p. 84.

14 For discussion, see Rockmore, *On Heidegger's Nazism and Philosophy* (Berkeley: University of California Press, 1992), ch. 5: "Nazism and the *Beiträge zur Philosophie*," pp. 176–203.

15 See Beaufret, *Dialogue avec Heidegger*, IV, p. 9.

16 Heidegger, *Basic Writings*, p. 242.

17 See E. de Rubercy and D. Le Buhan, *Douze questions posées à Jean Beaufret à propos de Martin Heidegger* (Paris: Aubier Montaigne, 1983), p. 17.

18 Pierre Bourdieu, "Aspirant philosophe: un point de vue sur le champ universitaire dans les années 50," in *Les Enjeux philosophiques des années 50* (Paris: Centre Georges Pompidou), p. 23n.

19 For instance, in a letter to Beaufret dated February 22, 1975 about the interviews with Beaufret on Heidegger's thought, Heidegger commends Beaufret's answers to questions 10 and 11 as "das eigentliche Meisterstück des Ganzen." De Rubercy and Le Buhan, *Douze questions*, p. 74.

20 Beaufret, *Dialogue with Heidegger*, IV, p. 80.

21 See ibid., p. 21.

22 See Jean Beaufret, "Heidegger et le problème de la vérité, in J. Beaufret, *Introduction aux philosophies de l'existence* (Paris: Denoël/Gonthier, 1971), p. 136.

23 Jean Beaufret, "Heidegger et le monde grec," in Beaufret, *Introduction aux philosophies de l'existence*, p. 154; Beaufret's emphases.

24 See Beaufret, *Dialogue avec Heidegger*, IV, p. 124.

25 See ibid., p. 126.

26 For a complete list, see ibid., p. 81.

27 See ibid., p. 82.

28 Ibid.

29 Ibid.

30 Pierre Aubenque, "Heideggers Wirkungsgeschichte in Frankreich," in *Martin Heidegger – Faszination und Erschrecken: Die politische Dimension einer Philosophie*, ed. Peter Kemper (Frankfurt/M.: Campus, 1990), p. 124.

31 See ibid., p. 115.

32 Beaufret notes that his academic career suffered because of his devotion to Heidegger. See Beaufret, *Dialogue avec Heidegger*, IV, p. 81.

33 See Martin Heidegger, "The Rectorate 1933/34: Facts and Thoughts," in *Martin Heidegger and National Socialism: Questions and Answers*, ed. G. Neske and E. Kettering (New York: Paragon, 1990), pp. 15–32.

34 See William J. Richardson, *Heidegger: Through Phenomenology to Thought* (The Hague: Nijhoff, 1963, 2nd edn 1967).

35 See Friedrich-Wilhelm von Herrmann, *Die Selbstinterpretationen Martin Heideggers* (Meisenheim am Glan: Anton Hain, 1974).

36 See Otto Pöggeler, *Der Denkweg Martin Heideggers* (Pfullingen: Neske, 1963). In subsequent editions, Pöggeler acquired a more critical distance.

37 See Richardson, *Heidegger*. For Pöggeler's more recent view, see Otto Pöggeler, *Neue Wege mit Heidegger* (Freiburg i. B.: Alber, 1992).

38 See Beaufret, *Introduction aux philosophies de l'existence*.

39 See Jean Beaufret, *Dialogue avec Heidegger* (4 vols., Paris: Minuit, 1973–1985).

40 See Parménide, *Le Poème*, ed. Jean Beaufret (Paris: Presses universitaires de France, 1991).

41 See Jean Beaufret, *Entretiens avec Frédéric de Towarnicki* (Paris: Presses universitaires de France, 1984); and de Rubercy and Le Buhan, *Douze questions*.

42 This information is taken from the "Essai de bibliographie de Jean Beaufret," in Jean Beaufret, *Introduction aux philosophies de l'existence* (Paris: Vrin, 1986, pp. 171–182).

43 See Beaufret, *Dialogue avec Heidegger*, IV, p. 82.

44 See Beaufret, *Introductions aux philosophies de l'existence*, p. 147.

45 Arendt, for instance, typically maintained that Heidegger taught us how to think, as if no one before Heidegger had ever thought. See Hannah Arendt, "Martin Heidegger ist achtzig Jahre alt," *Merkur*, 1969, pp. 893–902.

46 Beaufret, *Introduction aux philosophies de l'existence*, p. 62.

47 See Jean Beaufret, *Dialogue avec Heidegger*, vol. III: *Approche de Heidegger* (Paris: Editions de Minuit, 1974), p. 62.

48 See "Le chemin de Heidegger," in Beaufret, *Dialogue avec Heidegger*, IV, pp. 88–107.

49 See "En chemin avec Heidegger, in Beaufret, *Dialogue avec Heidegger*, IV, pp. 108–128.

50 This impression of a determined effort at hagiography is only strengthened by the inclusion in that volume of a wholly uncritical biographical note on Heidegger and of his letters to Beaufret and to the poet René Char. See de Rubercy and Le Buhan, *Douze questions*.

51 See ibid., p. 29. See also Beaufret, *Dialogue avec Heidegger*, IV, p. 94.

52 This sounds like a transparent reference to Heidegger's *Beiträge zur Philosophie*, which Beaufret may have seen or even have had in manuscript form. The only problem is that the manuscript was composed in 1936–1938, hence well after 1927. But perhaps Beaufret is confusing the movement of thought that began in 1927 with the work in which it is described in detail, which was composed later.

53 Beaufret, *Dialogue with Heidegger*, IV, p. 93.

54 Ibid.

55 Ibid., p. 126; Beaufret's emphases.

56 See Martin Heidegger, *Identity and Difference*, tr. Joan Stambaugh (New York: Harper & Row, 1969), p. 36.

57 See Beaufret, *Dialogue with Heidegger*, IV, p. 126.

58 Ibid., p. 127.

59 To take one example, Courtine, a former Beaufret student and who is one of the best and most faithful French Heideggerians, nevertheless clearly states that Heidegger's theory does not permit an analysis of the idea of political community and that *Being and Time* represents from one end to the other a real perversion of ethico-religious categories. See Jean-François Courtine, *Heidegger et la phénoménologie* (Paris: Vrin, 1990), p. 348.

60 Beaufret, *Dialogue avec Heidegger*, IV, p. 82.

61 See Alain Renaut, "La fin de Heidegger et la tâche de la pensée," *Etudes philosophiques*, no. 4 (October–December 1977), pp. 485–492.

62 See "A propos de *Questions IV* de Heidegger," in Beaufret, *Dialogue avec Heidegger*, IV, pp. 75–87.

63 For Beaufret, Renaut is a better philologist than someone like Jean-Paul Faye, a "mere" sociologist; according to Beaufret Renaut is so good that he "ne se trompe que sur les nuances." Ibid., p. 87.

64 See Jules Vuillemin, *L'Héritage kantien et la révolution copernicienne* (Paris: Presses universitaires de France, 1954).

65 See Jean Beaufret, *Dialogue avec Heidegger*, vol. II: *Philosophie moderne* (Paris: Editions de Minuit, 1973), pp. 96–97.

66 See Maurice Merleau-Ponty, *Phénoménologie de la perception* (Paris: Gallimard, 1945), p. 1.

67 Beaufret, *Dialogue avec Heidegger*, III, p. 62.

68 See Martin Heidegger, "The Age of the World Picture," in M. Heidegger, *The Question Concerning Technology and Other Essays*, tr. W. Lovitt (New York: Harper & Row, 1977), pp. 115–154.

69 Beaufret, *Dialogue avec Heidegger*, III, p. 57.

70 See "Heidegger et la théologie," in Beaufret, *Dialogue avec Heidegger*, IV, pp. 38–50.

71 See ibid., p. 41.

72 See ibid., p. 43.

73 See ibid., p. 41.

74 See ibid., p. 43.

75 See Karl Löwith, "Les Implications politiques de la philosophie de l'existence chez Heidegger," *Les Temps Modernes*, vol. 2, no. 14 (November 1946), pp. 343–360.

76 Beaufret, *Dialogue avec Heidegger*, IV, p. 113.

77 Ibid., p. 121.

78 For a former Beaufret student, who regards the link between Heidegger's thought and political commitment as a serious problem, see Dominique Janicaud, *L'Ombre de cette pensée: Heidegger et la question politique* (Grenoble: Millon, 1990).

79 See Beaufret, *Introduction aux philosophies de l'existence*, pp. 30–31.

80 Beaufret, *Dialogue avec Heidegger*, IV, p. 118.

81 See Beaufret, *Entretien avec Fréderic de Towarnicki*, p. 87.

82 See de Rubercy and Le Buhan, *Douze questions*, p. 37.

83 See ibid., p. 38.

84 For a dismaying report on Heidegger's denunciation of Staudinger, see Hugo Ott, *Martin Heidegger: Unterwegs zu seiner Biographie* (Frankfurt/M.: Campus, 1988), pp. 200–213.

85 See Hugo Ott, "Biographical Bases for Heidegger's 'Mentality of Disunity',", in *The Heidegger Case: On Philosophy and Politics*, ed. T. Rockmore and J. Margolis (Philadelphia: Temple University Press, 1992), p. 109.

86 See *Cahiers de l'Herne: Heidegger*, ed. Michel Haar (Paris: Editions de l'Herne, 1983).

87 This is the case for the articles by Janicaud and Schürmann, which concern Marxism and ecology, and the conception of action at the end of metaphysics respectively. See ibid.

88 See Jean-Marie Veysse, "Heidegger et l'essence de l'université allemande," in *Cahiers de l'Herne: Heidegger*, ed. M. Haar, pp. 497–511. A similar hermeneutical feat has recently been performed by Scott. For his reading of the rectorial address in much the same spirit, see Charles Scott, *The Question of Ethics: Nietzsche, Foucault, Heidegger* (Bloomington: Indiana University Press, 1990), pp. 178–192.

89 Jean-Michel Palmier, *Les Écrits politiques de Heidegger* (Paris: L'Herne, 1968).

90 See Jean-Michel Palmier, "Heidegger et le national-socialisme," in *Cahiers de l'Herne: Heidegger*, ed. M. Haar, pp. 409–447.

91 According to Ferry and Renaut, Derrida is typical of the French Heideggerian tendency to overinterpret minor Heideggerian texts. See Luc Ferry and Alain Renaut, *La Pensée 68: Essai sur l'antihumanisme contemporain* (Paris: Gallimard, 1988), p. 153.

92 See Luc Ferry and Alain Renaut, *Heidegger et les modernes* (Paris: Grasset, 1988), p. 117.

93 See Michel Haar, *Le Chant de la terre* (Paris: L'Herne, 1985).

94 See Michel Haar, *Heidegger et l'essence de l'homme* (Grenoble: Millon, 1990).

95 See Haar, *Le Chant de la terre*, p. 22.

96 Ibid., p. 23.
97 See ibid., p. 81.
98 See ibid., p. 82.
99 Ibid., p. 95.
100 See Haar, *Heidegger et l'essence de l'homme*, p. 20.
101 See Ulrich Sieg, "Die Verjudung des deutschen Geistes," *Die Zeit*, December 22, 1989, p. 50.
102 For Heidegger's public endorsement of the *Führerprinzip*, see Guido Schnee-berger, *Nachlese zu Heidegger* (Berne, 1962), pp. 135–136.
103 See Haar, *Heidegger et l'essence de l'homme*, pp. 10–11.
104 See ibid., p. 21.
105 Ibid., p. 248.
106 See ibid., p. 249.
107 Ibid., p. 250.
108 Ibid., p. 252.
109 See Reiner Schürmann, *Heidegger on Being and Acting: From Principles to Anarchy*, tr. Christine-Marie Gros (Bloomington: Indiana University Press, 1987). A shorter version of this book was originally published as *Le Principe d'anarchie: Heidegger et la question de l'agir* (Paris: Editions de Seuil, 1982).
110 Derrida takes pains to emphasize that de Man was always critical of Heidegger, and that he cannot be accused of propagating Heidegger's thought. See Jacques Derrida, *Mémoires pour Paul de Man* (Paris: Editions Galilée, 1988), p. 227.
111 See David Farrell Krell, *Daimon Life: Heidegger and Life-Philosophy* (Bloomington: Indiana University Press, 1992).

7 ON HEIDEGGER AND CONTEMPORARY FRENCH PHILOSOPHY

1 See Alain Boutot, *Heidegger* (Paris: Presses universitaires de France, 1989).
2 See Alain Boutot, *Heidegger et Platon* (The Hague: Nijhoff, 1970).
3 For critical discussion of the very idea of an absolute distinction between systematic and historical approaches to the history of philosophy, see Tom Rockmore, "Quines Witz und die Philosophiegeschichte," in *Annalen für dialektische Philosophie* vol. 9, ed. Hans Jörg Sandkühler (Zürich: Peter Lang, 1991), pp. 219–226.
4 See Dominique Janicaud, *Le Tournant théologique de la phénoménologie française* (Combas: Editions de l'Eclat, 1991).
5 Jacques Lacan, *Le Séminaire, livre XI: Les quatre concepts fondamentaux de la psychanalyse*, ed. Jacques-Alain Miller (Paris: Editions du Seuil, 1973), p. 227.
6 See Martin Heidegger, *On the Way to Language*, tr. Peter D. Hertz (San Francisco: Harper & Row, 1982).
7 See Lacan, *Le Séminaire*, XI, p. 240.
8 This remark occurs in the discussion following Wahl's lecture on existentialism. See Jean Wahl, *Petite Histoire de l'existentialisme* (Paris: Club Maintenant, 1947), p. 83.
9 See, for example, Denise Souche-Dagues, *Le Développement de l'intentionalité dans la phénoménologie husserlienne* (The Hague: Nijhoff, 1972). See also Jean T. Desanti, *Introduction à la phénoménologie* (Paris: Gallimard, 1976).
10 A recent example by someone close to Heidegger is Courtine's collection of essays all of which concern facets of the relation of Heidegger to Husserl. See Jean-François Courtine, *Heidegger et la phénoménologie* (Paris: Vrin, 1990).
11 See Paul Ricoeur, *A L'Ecole de la phénoménologie* (Paris: Vrin, 1986), p. 285.

12 For a recent discussion in French that emphasizes the arbitrary nature of Lévinas's Husserl interpretation, see Janicaud, *Le Tournant théologique*, pp. 26–29.

13 Marion's first book, *Sur l'ontologie grise de Descartes* (Paris: Vrin, 1981), is significantly dedicated to Ferdinand Alquié and Jean Beaufret, the then most important French Descartes and Heidegger scholars, thereby indicating the two main sources of his philosophical thought. For a critique of Marion's position from a broadly phenomenological perspective, see Janicaud, *Le Tournant théologique*, ch. 3, pp. 39–56.

14 Derrida has published extensively on Husserl. See his lengthy introduction to Edmund Husserl, the size of a small volume (170 pp. in a work of 219 pp.), in E. Husserl *L'Origine de la géométrie* (Paris: Presses universitaires de France, 1974); Jacques Derrida, *La Voix et le phénomène: Introduction au problème du signe dans la phénoménologie de Husserl* (Paris: Presses universitaries de France, 1967); and his, *Le Problème de la genèse dans la philosophie de Husserl* (Paris: Presses universitaires de France, 1990).

15 For his recent work, see "D'une idée de la phénoménologie à l'autre: 1. Husserl; 2. La réappropriation heideggérienne," in Jacques Taminiaux, *Lectures de l'ontologie fondamentale: Essais sur Heidegger* (Grenoble: Millon, 1989), pp. 17–88.

16 See Courtine, *Heidegger et la phénoménologie*, which contains fifteen essays on various aspects of this relation.

17 See Jean-Luc Marion, *Réduction and donation: Recherches sur Husserl, Heidegger et la phénoménologie* (Paris: Presses universitaires de France, 1989).

18 For a good recent study, see William L. McBride, *Sartre's Political Theory* (Bloomington: Indiana University Press, 1991).

19 There are at least three instances in which Sartre maintained that there is no philosophical connection between Heidegger's Nazism and his philosophical thought. See "Deux documents sur Sartre", in *Les Temps Modernes*, vol. 1, no. 4 (January 1946), p. 713; Sartre's article "A Propos de l'existentialisme: Mise au point," in *Action*, no. 17 (1944), p. 11; and Jean-Paul Sartre, *Search for a Method*, tr. Hazel E. Barnes (New York: Vintage, 1968), p. 38.

20 Although Sartre was not a Husserl scholar, and although French Husserl studies owe their decisive impulse to Lévinas, half a century later Janicaud still regards Sartre's short text on Husserlian intentionality – "Une Idée fondamentale de la phénoménologie de Husserl: L'Intentionnalité" – as the central French text. See Janicaud, *Le Tournant théologique*, pp. 8–11.

21 For a bibliography of Nietzsche, including translations of his works from 1891–1914, see Gabriel Huan, *La Philosophie de Frédéric Nietzsche* (Paris: E. de Boccard, 1917), pp. 345–360.

22 See Jean Beaufret, *Introduction aux philosophies de l'existence* (Paris: Denoël, 1971), p. 203.

23 See Emile Faguet, *En lisant Nietzsche* (Paris: Société française d'imprimerie et de librairie, 1904).

24 See Julien Benda, *La Trahison des clercs* (Paris: Grasset, 1975), p. 181n. The original edition of this work was published in 1927. Benda bases his comment on R. Berthelot, *Un Romantisme utilitaire* (Paris: F. Alcan, 1911).

25 See Henri Lefebvre, *L'Existentialisme* (Paris: Editions Sagittaire, 1946), pt 2, ch. 2: "L'existentialisme magique (suite): Nietzsche," pp. 143–159.

26 See Jean Wahl, "Le Nietzsche de Jaspers," in *Recherches philosophiques*, vol. 6 (1936–1937), pp. 346–362.

27 For a discussion of Nietzsche's influence on French writers from 1930 to 1960, see Pierre Boudot, *Nietzsche et l'au-delà de la liberté: Nietzsche et les écrivains français de 1930 à 1960* (Paris: Aubier-Montaigne, 1970).

28 See Pierre Klossowski, *Nietzsche et le cercle vicieux* (Paris: Mercure de France, 1969).

29 See Gilles Deleuze, *Nietzsche et la philosophie* (Paris: Presses universitaires de France, 1962); and Gilles Deleuze, *Nietzsche* (Paris: Presses universitaires de France, 1965).

30 For a representative survey of French readings of Nietzsche in the 1970s, see the proceedings of the Nietzsche colloquium held at Cerisy-la-Salle in July 1972, published as *Nietzsche aujourd'hui* (Paris: UGE, 1973).

31 See V. Descombes, *Le Même et l'autre* (Paris: Editions de Minuit, 1979), p. 218.

32 See *Pourquoi nous ne sommes pas nietzschéens*, ed. Luc Ferry and Alain Renaut (Paris: Grasset, 1991).

33 In a recent book, Kofman mocks those who doubt that Nietzsche is less significant than the "great philosophers." See Sarah Kofman, *Nietzsche et la scène philosophique* (Paris: Editions Galilée, 1986), p. 10.

34 See Philippe Raynaud, "Nietzsche éducateur," in *Pourquoi nous ne sommes pas nietzschéens*, ed. L. Ferry and A. Renault (Paris: Grasset, 1991), pp. 194–201.

35 For an account of Bataille's work from this perspective, see Allan Stoekl, *Agonies of the Intellectual* (Lincoln: University of Nebraska Press, 1992), ch. 10: "Sur Bataille: Nietzsche in the Text of Bataille," pp. 261–282.

36 See Pierre Chassard, *Nietzsche: Finalisme et histoire* (Paris: Copernic, 1977).

37 See Olivier Reboul, *Nietzsche, critique de Kant* (Paris: Presses universitaires de France, 1974).

38 See Sarah Kofman, *Nietzsche et la métaphore* (Paris: Editions Galilée, 1974).

39 See Beaufret, *Introduction aux philosophies de l'existence*, pp. 203–205.

40 Courtine recalls Heidegger's thesis that Nietzsche's effort to overturn Platonism makes him the most Platonic of thinkers against a long list of French philosophers who contest this view. See Courtine, *Heidegger et la phénoménologie*, pp. 130–131.

41 François Laruelle, *Nietzsche contre Heidegger* (Paris: Payot, 1977).

42 See Jacques Derrida, *Eperons: Les styles de Nietzsche* (Paris: Flammarion, 1978).

43 See Martin Heidegger, *Being and Time*, tr. J. Macquarie and E. Robinson (New York: Harper & Row, 1962), p. 43.

44 See Martin Heidegger, *The Basic Problems of Phenomenology*, tr. Albert Hofstadter (Bloomington: Indiana University Press, 1982), p. 80.

45 See ibid.

46 Jean-François Courtine, *Suarez et le système de la métaphysique* (Paris: Presses universitaires de France, 1990), p. 5; Courtine's emphasis.

47 Ibid.

48 See ibid., pp. 534–535.

49 For careful study of Heidegger's reappropriation of the Aristotelian concepts of *poiesis* and *praxis*, see J. Taminiaux, "La réappropriation de *l'Ethique à Nicomaque*: Poiesis et praxis dans l'articulation de l'ontologie fondamentale," in Taminiaux, *Lectures de l'ontologie fondamentale: Essais sur Heidegger* (Grenoble: Millon, 1989), pp. 147–190. See also Jacques Taminiaux, "Heidegger and Praxis," in *The Heidegger Case: On Philosophy and Politics*, ed. T. Rockmore and J. Margolis (Philadelphia: Temple University Press, 1992), pp. 188–207.

50 See ch. 5: "Die Griechen," in Rainer Marten, *Heidegger Lesen* (Munich: W. Fink, 1991), pp. 153–226. See also Rainer Marten, "Heidegger and the Greeks," in *The Heidegger Case*, pp. 167–187.

51 See Jean Beaufret, *Dialogue avec Heidegger*, vol. I: *Philosophie grecque* (Paris: Editions de Minuit, 1973).

52 See Pierre Aubenque, *Le Problème de l'être chez Aristote: Essai sur la problématique aristotélicienne* (Paris: Presses universitaires de France, 1962, 2nd edn 1966).
53 See Pierre Aubenque, *La Prudence chez Aristote* (Paris: Presses universitaires de France, 1963).
54 See Aubenque, *Le Problème de l'être chez Aristote*, p. 21.
55 Ibid., p. 3; Aubenque's emphasis.
56 See ibid.
57 For Heidegger's view of ontotheology, see "The Onto-theological Constitution of Metaphysics," in Martin Heidegger, *Identity and Difference*, tr. Joan Stambaugh (New York: Harper & Row, 1974), pp. 42–73.
58 See Pierre Aubenque, "La Philosophie aristotélicienne et nous," in *Aristote aujourd'hui*, ed. M. A. Sinceur (Paris: Unesco and Editions Eres, 1988), p. 321.
59 See Martin Heidegger, *Unterwegs zur Sprache*, ed. Friedrich-Wilhelm von Herrmann (Pfullingen: Neske, 1985), p. 160; and Aubenque, "La Philosophie aristotélicienne et nous," p. 323.
60 See Rémi Brague, "La Phénoménologie comme voie d'accès au monde grec: Note sur la critique de la *Vorhandenheit* comme modèle ontologique dans la lecture heideggérienne d'Aristote," in *Phénoménologie et métaphysique*, ed. Jean-Luc Marion and Guy Planty-Bonjour (Paris: Presses universitaires de France, 1984), pp. 247–273. See also Rémi Brague, "La Naissance de la raison grecque," in *La naissance de la raison en Grèce*, ed. Jean-François Mattéi (Paris: Presses universitaires de France, 1990), pp. 23–31.
61 See Heidegger, *Being and Time*, pt 1, ch. 3: "The Worldhood of the World," §§ 14–24, pp. 91–148.
62 Rémi Brague, *Aristote et la question du monde* (Paris: Presses universitaires de France, 1988), p. 6.
63 See ibid., p. 47.
64 See ibid., p. 110.
65 See ibid., pp. 513–514.
66 Ibid., p. 514.
67 See ibid.
68 See Heidegger, *Being and Time*, p. 494.
69 See ibid., p. 215.
70 See Martin Heidegger, *Parmenides*, tr. Richard Rojcewicz and André Schuwer (Bloomington: Indiana University Press, 1992).
71 See "The Principle of Identity," in Martin Heidegger, *Identity and Difference*, tr. J. Stambaugh (New York: Harper & Row, 1974), pp. 23–41.
72 See "Héraclite et Parménide" and "Lecture de Parménide," in Jean Beaufret, *Dialogue avec Heidegger*, vol. I: *Philosophie grecque* (Paris: Editions de Minuit, 1973), pp. 38–51, 52–85.
73 See Parménide, *Le Poème*, ed. and tr. Jean Beaufret (Paris, 1955), p. 7.
74 He thanks Heidegger for "the inestimable help [offered by] several discussions." See ibid., p. x.
75 See ibid., p. 27.
76 See ibid., p. 53.
77 See ibid., p. 67.
78 See ibid., p. 69.
79 See ibid., p. 70.
80 For a discussion of "foundationalism," see *Antifoundationalism Old and New*, ed. Tom Rockmore and Beth Singer (Philadelphia: Temple University Press, 1992), pp. 1–12.

81 See Heidegger, *Being and Time*, § 32: "Understanding and Interpretation," pp. 188–194.

82 See "The Word of Nietzsche: 'God is dead,'" in Martin Heidegger, *The Question Concerning Technology and Other Essays*, tr. W. Lovitt (New York: Harper & Row, 1977), pp. 53–112.

83 See Jean-François Lyotard, *La Condition postmoderne* (Paris: Editions de Minuit, 1979), p. 7.

84 See ibid., p. 9.

85 See ibid., p. 63.

86 See ibid., p. 64.

87 See ibid., p. 89.

88 See ibid., p. 105.

89 See ch. 3: "Le Structuralisme: De la méthode structurale à la philosophie de la mort de l'homme," in Roger Garaudy, *Perspectives de l'homme: Existentialisme, pensée catholique, structuralisme, marxisme* (Paris: Presses universitaires de France, 1969), pp. 231–250.

90 See Michel Foucault, *Histoire de la folie à l'âge classique* (Paris: Gallimard, 1972), pp. 56–59.

91 See "Cogito et histoire de la folie," in Jacques Derrida, *L'Ecriture et la différence* (Paris: Editions du Seuil, 1967), pp. 51–97.

92 Foucault, *Histoire de la folie*, p. 602.

93 See Michel Foucault, *Power/Knowledge: Selected Interviews and Other Writings, 1972–1977*, ed. Colin Gordon (New York: Pantheon, 1980), p. 131.

94 See Foucault, *Power/Knowledge*, p. 133.

95 See "The Age of the World Picture," in M. Heidegger, *The Question Concerning Technology and Other Essays*, tr. W. Lovitt (New York: Harper & Row, 1977), pp. 115–154.

96 Foucault, *Knowledge/Power*, p. 117.

97 Ibid.

98 See Heidegger, *Being and Time*, p. 1.

99 See Janicaud, *Le Tournant théologique*, p. 57.

100 See *Phénoménologie et théologie*, ed. Jean-François Courtine (Paris: Criterion, 1992).

101 For a study of his writings, see Gabrielle Dufour-Kowalska, *Michel Henry: Un Philosophe de la vie et de la praxis* (Paris: Vrin, 1980).

102 He is a novelist of distinction. See e.g. Michel Henry, *Le Fils du roi* (Paris: Gallimard, 1981).

103 See Michel Henry, *L'Essence de la manifestation* (Paris: Presses universitaires de France, 1963, 2nd edn 1990); tr. Gerard Etzkorn (2 vols., The Hague: Martinus Nijhoff, 1973).

104 Henry perceives a fundamental identity between Husserlian and Heideggerian phenomenology at a certain level. He specifically claims that "there is no difference between the philosophy of consciousness and the philosophy of being." Henry, *L'Essence de la manifestation*, p. 118.

105 See ibid., § 1, pp. 1–3.

106 See Jean-Luc Marion, *Questions cartésiennes* (Paris: Presses universitaires de France, 1991), pp. 161, 164. For an analysis of Henry's contribution to Cartesian studies, see ibid., "La Générosité et le dernier 'cogito,'" pp. 153–187.

107 Henry, *L'Essence de la manifestation*, p. 573.

108 See ibid., p. 858.

109 Michael Henry, *Phénoménologie matérielle* (Paris: Presses universitaires de France, 1990), p. 6.

110 See E. Husserl, *The Crisis of European Sciences and Transcendental Phenomenology*, tr. David Carr (Evanston: Northwestern University Press, 1970), § 28, pp. 103–110.

111 Henry, *Phénoménologie matérielle*, p. 10.

112 See Jean-Luc Marion, "Le Cogito s'affect-t-il? La générosité et le dernier *cogito* suivant l'interprétation de Michel Henry," in *Questions cartésiennes*, pp. 153–187.

113 See Jean-Luc Marion, *Dieu sans l'être* (Paris: Fayard, 1982).

114 For a brief mention of his *œuvre*, see Roger-Pol Droit, "Les paradoxes de Jean-Luc Marion," *Le Monde* (July 12, 1991), p. 24.

115 See Marion, *Sur l'ontologie grise de Descartes*; and his *Sur la théologie blanche de Descartes* (Paris: Presses universitaires de France, 1981).

116 See Marion, *Réduction et donation*, ch. 2: L'*ego* et le *Dasein*, pp. 119–162.

117 See Marion, *Questions cartésiennes*, pp. 158–164.

118 For an overview, see "A propos de réduction et donation de Jean-Luc Marion," a special issue of *Revue Métaphysique et de Morale*, no. 1 (1991).

119 Marion, *Réduction et donation*, p. 8.

120 See ibid., p. 303.

121 Ibid., p. 305.

122 For discussion, see "Is Derrida a transcendental philosopher?," in Richard Rorty, *Philosophical Papers, II: Essays on Heidegger and Others* (Cambridge: Cambridge University Press, 1991), pp. 119–128.

123 For this view, see Hilary Putnam, *Realism with a Human Face*, ed. James Conant (Cambridge: Harvard University Press, 1990), p. 51.

124 See e.g. Herman Rapaport, *Heidegger and Derrida: Reflections on Time and Language* (Lincoln: University of Nebraska Press, 1989).

125 See Luc Ferry and Alain Renaut, *La Pensée 68: Essai sur l'anti-humanisme contemporain* (Paris: Gallimard, 1988), pp. 201, 221.

126 See Geoffrey Bennington and Jacques Derrida, *Derrida* (Paris: Editions du Seuil, 1991), p. 254:

> L'originalité de Heidegger serait donc en partie produite par Derrida, qui serait à son tour l'une des originalités de Heidegger. Mais les paradoxes du même et de l'autre laisseraient soupçonner que la proximité même à Heidegger implique une altérité plus importante qu'avec tout autre penseur.

127 See Hegel's letter to Schelling, dated April 16, 1795, in *Hegel: The Letters*, tr. C. Butler and C. Seiler (Bloomington: Indiana University Press, 1984), pp. 35–36.

128 See e.g. his statement, in a recent article:

> Autre précaution, autre appel à votre indulgence: faute de temps, je ne présenterai qu'une partie ou plutôt plusieurs fragments, parfois un peu discontinus, du travail que je poursuis cette année au rhythme lent d'un séminaire engagé dans une lecture difficile et que je voudrais aussi minutieuse et prudent que possible de certain textes de Heidegger.
> (Jacques Derrida, *Heidegger et la question: De l'esprit et autres essais* (Paris: Flammarion, 1990), p. 176)

129 See Jacques Derrida, "Geschlecht: Différence sexuelle, différence ontologique," in *Cahiers de L'Herne: Heidegger*, ed. M. Haar (Paris: Editions de l'Herne, 1983), pp. 571–594, reprinted in Jacques Derrida, *Heidegger et la question*.

130 See Derrida, "Geschlecht," p. 571.

131 See ibid., p. 575.

132 See ibid., p. 594.

133 See Martin Heidegger, "The Letter on Humanism," in *Basic Writings*, ed. D. F. Krell (New York: Harper & Row, 1977), p. 240.

134 See Heidegger, *Being and Time*, ch. 3: "The Worldhood of the World," §§ 14–24, pp. 91–148.

135 See "Philosophy and the Crisis of European Man," in E. Husserl, *Phenomenology and the Crisis of Philosophy*, pp. 155–158.

136 See Husserl, *L'Origine de la géométrie*, pp. 45, 120, 162.

137 See Derrida, *De l'esprit*, pp. 94–100. See also J. Derrida, *L'Autre Cap* (Paris: Editions du Minuit, 1991), pp. 36–37.

138 See "Les Fins de l'homme," in Jacques Derrida, *Marges de la philosophie* (Paris: Editions de Minuit, 1972, pp. 129–164. For a recent, critical reading of Derrida's influential article, see Stoekl, *Agonies of the Intellectual*, pp. 209–217.

139 See Jacques Derrida, *Positions* (Paris: Editions de Minuit, 1972), p. 18.

140 See ibid., p. 73.

141 Stoekl not unfairly characterizes Derrida's attack on Sartre and French humanism as remarkably naive and thematic. See Stoekl, *Agonies of the Intellectual*, p. 209.

142 Derrida, *Marges de la philosophie*, p. 136.

143 Ibid., p. 139.

144 See Heidegger, *Being and Time*, p. 62.

145 See ibid., pp. 188–194.

146 See Jacques Derrida, *Glas* (2 vols., Paris: Denoël, 1981).

147 For an English translation, see Edmund Husserl, *The Crisis*, appendix 3, pp. 353–378.

148 See Husserl, *L'Origine de la géométrie*, p. 8.

149 Saussure was very influential in French philosophy during the structuralist period. See Ferdinand de Saussure, *Cours de linguistique générale* (Paris: Payot, 1968).

150 See Heidegger, *Being and Time*, p. 47.

151 See "The End of Philosophy and the Task of Thinking," in M. Heidegger, *On Time and Being*, tr. J. Stambaugh (New York: Harper & Row, 1977), p. 56.

152 Derrida, *La Voix et le phénomène*, pp. 2–3; Derrida's emphases. For a discussion of Derrida's criticism of the metaphysics of presence, see Marion, *Réduction et donation*, pp. 33–38

153 Derrida, *Marges de la philosophie*, p. 140.

154 Ibid., p. 148.

155 For a recent defense of Husserl against Derrida's criticism, see J. Claude Evans, *Strategies of Deconstruction: Derrida and the Myth of the Voice* (Minneapolis: University of Minnesota Press, 1992).

156 See Heidegger, "The End of Philosophy," pp. 55–73.

157 See Derrida, *La Voix et le phénomène*, p. 3.

158 Derrida, *Marges de la philosophie*, p. 54.

159 See "Circonfession," in Bennington and Derrida, *Derrida*, pp. 7–291.

160 Bennington's claim that Derrida is finally as opposed to Heidegger as to any other thinker is mistaken. See Bennington and Derrida, *Derrida*, p. 255.

161 See Reiner Schürmann, "Que faire à la fin de la métaphysique," in *Cahiers de L'Herne: Heidegger*, ed. M. Haar (Paris: Editions de L'Herne, 1983), p. 473 n2.

162 In *La Carte postale*, Derrida resists this translation. See Jacques Derrida, *La Carte postale* (Paris: Flammarion, 1980), pp. 285–287. In *De l'esprit*, he employs this translation without hesitation or further comment. See *De l'esprit*, p. 35. For discussion, see Rapaport, *Heidegger and Derrida*, pp. 3–9.

163 See Christopher Norris, *Derrida* (London: Fontana, 1987), pp. 94–95.

164 See "Deconstruction and Circumvention" in Rorty, *Philosophical Papers, 11*, pp. 85–106.
165 For discussion of Derrida's idea of deconstruction, see Rodolphe Gasché, *The Tain of the Mirror* (Cambridge: Harvard University Press, 1986), pp. 121–254.
166 See Edmund Husserl, *Experience and Judgment*, tr. James S. Churchill and Karl Ameriks (Evanston: Northwestern University Press, 1973), pp. 47–48.
167 The term "Abbau" occurs in lectures delivered in 1927, the year that *Being and Time* was published. See Heidegger, *The Basic Problems of Phenomenology*, p. 23.
168 See Heidegger, *Being and Time*, § 6.
169 Heidegger, *The Basic Problems of Phenomenology*, pp. 22–23.
170 See Gasché, *The Tain of the Mirror*, p. 176.
171 See G. W. F. Hegel, *Phenomenology of Spirit*, tr. A. V. Miller (Oxford: Oxford University Press, 1977), ch. 1: "Sense Certainty: or the 'this' and 'meaning,'" pp. 58–67.
172 See e.g Edmund Husserl, *Ideas: General Introduction to Pure Phenomenology*, tr. W. R. Boyce Gibson (New York: Collier, 1962), § 124, pp. 318–322. For discussion of the relation between these two thinkers, see J. N. Mohanty, *Husserl and Frege* (Bloomington: Indiana University Press, 1982).
173 See Derrida, *L'Origine de la géométrie*, § 11, pp. 155–171.
174 Derrida, *Positions*, p. 73.

8 HEIDEGGER'S POLITICS AND FRENCH PHILOSOPHY

1 This chapter is based upon, but differs significantly from, my earlier discussion of this issue. See ch. 7: "The French Reception of Heidegger's Nazism," in Tom Rockmore, *On Heidegger's Nazism and Philosophy* (Berkeley: University of California Press, 1992), pp. 244–281.
2 The analogy is limited in several ways, including Lukács's lesser philosophical status, and his later efforts to distance himself from Stalinism. Significantly, the study which Lukács intended to support democracy against totalitarianism was never completed. See Georg Lukács, *Demokratisierung heute und morgen*, ed. László Sziklai (Budapest: Akadémiai Kiadó, 1985). For an analysis of Lukács's Marxism, with discussion of his Stalinism, see Tom Rockmore, *Irrationalism: Lukács and the Marxist View of Reason* (Philadelphia: Temple University Press, 1992).
3 For strong criticism of Lukács's Stalinism, see the preface by István Eörsi to Georg Lukács, *Pensée vécue, mémoires parlés*, tr. Antonia Fonyi (Paris: L'Arche, 1986), pp. 9–29.
4 For a series of documents concerning Heidegger's Nazi turning, see Guido Schneeberger, *Nachlese zu Heidegger: Dokumente zu seinem Leben und Denken* (Berne, 1962).
5 For discussion, see Rockmore, *On Heidegger's Nazism and Philosophy*, ch. 4, pp. 122–175.
6 Martin Heidegger, "The Rectorate 1933/34: Facts and Thoughts," in *Martin Heidegger and National Socialism: Questions and Answers*, ed. Günther Neske and Emil Kettering, intr. Karsten Harries (New York: Paragon, 1990), pp. 15–32.
7 See "Only a God Can Save Us: *Der Spiegel*'s Interview with Martin Heidegger," *Philosophy Today*, (Winter 1976).
8 See Schneeberger, *Nachlese zu Heidegger*, p. 136.
9 Martin Heidegger, *An Introduction to Metaphysics*, tr. Ralph Manheim (New Haven: Yale University Press, 1977), p. 199.

10 The passage cited is given in Victor Farías, *Heidegger and Nazism*, ed. J. Margolis and T. Rockmore (Philadelphia: Temple University Press, 1989) p. 287; translation modified.

11 See Tom Rockmore, "Heidegger and Holocaust Revisionism," in *Martin Heidegger and the Holocaust*, ed. Alan Rosenberg and Alan Milchman (Atlantic Highlands, NJ: Humanities Press, 1994).

12 See George Leaman, *Heidegger im Kontext: Gesamtüberblick zum NS-Engagement der Universitätsphilosophen* (Hamburg: Argument Verlag, 1993).

13 See Hugo Ott, *Martin Heidegger: Unterwegs zu seiner Biographie* (Frankfurt/M.: Campus, 1988), pp. 201–213.

14 For a recent instance of the latter, see John Sallis, *Echoes: After Heidegger* (Bloomington: Indiana University Press, 1990). According to Sallis, if we raise the question of Heidegger's politics we prevent his texts from speaking to us. See ibid., p. 11.

15 See his review of Heidegger's *Einführung in die Metaphysik* under the title "Déclin ou floraison de la métaphysique," *Critique*, (April 1956), pp. 354–361.

16 For discussion, see Tom Rockmore, "Philosophy, Literature, and Intellectual Responsibility," *American Philosophical Quarterly*, vol. 30, no. 2 (April 1993), pp. 109–122.

17 See Victor Farías, *Heidegger et le nazisme* (Paris: Verdier, 1987). See also Farías, *Heidegger and Nazism*.

18 For his view of the relation between being and the ought, see Heidegger, *An Introduction to Metaphysics*, pp. 196–206.

19 For a factually more detailed account, see Rockmore, *On Heidegger's Nazism and Philosophy*, pp. 244–281.

20 See Alphonse De Waelhens, *La Philosophie de Martin Heidegger* (Louvain: Nauwelaerts, 1942, rpt. 1971).

21 See Hans-Georg Gadamer, "The Political Incompetence of Philosophy," in *The Heidegger Case: On Philosophy and Politics* ed. T. Rockmore and J. Margolis (Philadelphia: Temple University Press, 1992), pp. 364–372.

22 See Karl Löwith, "Les Implications politiques de la philosophie de l'existence chez Heidegger," *Les Temps Modernes*, vol. 2, no. 14 (November 1946), pp. 343–360.

23 See Thomas Sheehan, "Heidegger and the Nazis," *The New York Review of Books*, vol. 35, no. 10 (June 16, 1988).

24 See Rainer Marten, *Heidegger Lesen* (Munich: Wilhelm Fink, 1991).

25 See Michael E. Zimmerman, *Heidegger's Confrontation with Modernity: Technology, Politics, Art* (Bloomington: Indiana University Press, 1990).

26 See Otto Pöggeler, "Den Führer führen? Heidegger und kein Ende," in *Philosophische Rundschau*, vol. 32 (1985), pp. 26–67. See also Otto Pöggeler, "Heideggers politisches Selbstverständnis," in *Heidegger und die praktische Philosophie*, ed. Annemarie Gethmann-Siefert and Otto Pöggeler (Frankfurt/M.: Suhrkamp, 1988), pp. 17–63.

27 See Dieter Thomä, *Die Zeit des Selbst und die Zeit danach: Zur Kritik der Textgeschichte Martin Heideggers 1910–1976* (Frankfurt/M.: Suhrkamp, 1990).

28 His change of perspective is considerable and courageous. As late as 1983, he still maintained that it was too soon to judge Heidegger's thought. See Dominique Janicaud and Jean-François Mattéi, *La Métaphysique à la limite* (Paris: Presses universitaires de France, 1983), p. 218.

29 See Dominique Janicaud, *L'Ombre de cette pensée: Heidegger et la question politique* (Grenoble: Millon, 1990).

30 See Jean-Michel Palmier, *Les Ecrits politiques de Heidegger* (Paris: L'Herne, 1968). The tendentiously Heideggerian dimension of his earlier contribution has

entirely disappeared in Palmier's most recent discussion of the same theme. See Jean-Michel Palmier, "Postface" to Hugo Ott, *Martin Heidegger: Eléments pour une biographie* (Paris: Payot, 1990), pp. 379–413.

31 See Georg Lukács, *Existentialisme ou Marxisme?*, tr. E. Kelemen (Paris: Editions Nagel, 1948, rpt. 1961).

32 See "Anhang: Heidegger Redivivus," in Georg Lukács, *Existentialismus oder Marxismus?* (Berlin: Aufbau Verlag, 1951), pp. 161–183.

33 See Jean Beaufret, *Dialogue avec Heidegger*, vol. IV: *Le chemin de Heidegger* (Paris: Editions de Minuit, 1974), p. 87.

34 For these texts, see Jean-Pierre Faye, "Heidegger et la révolution," *Médiations*, no. 3 (Autumn 1961), pp. 151–159.

35 See Jean-Pierre Faye, "Attaques Nazies contre Heidegger," *Médiations*, no. 5 (Summer 1962), pp. 137–151.

36 See François Fédier, "Trois Attaques contre Heidegger," *Critique*, no. 234 (November 1966), pp. 883–904.

37 Scott manages to reread the rectorial address as a document concerning the German university and science only. See Charles Scott, *The Question of Ethics: Nietzsche, Foucault, Heidegger* (Bloomington: Indiana University Press, 1990), ch. 5: "These violent passions: The Rector's address," pp. 148–172.

38 See François Fédier, "A propos de Heidegger: Une lecture dénoncée," *Critique*, no. 242 (1965), pp. 672–686.

39 Frédéric de Towarnicki, "Traduire Heidegger," *Magazine littéraire*, no. 222 (September 1985), p. 75

40 Hugo Ott, "Wege und Abwege: Zu Victor Farias' kritischer Heidegger-Studie," *Neue Zürcher Zeitung*, no. 275 (November 27, 1987), p. 67.

41 See Lucette Valensi, "Présence du passé, lenteur de l'histoire," in *Présence du passé, lenteur de l'histoire: Vichy, l'occupation, les Juifs*," *Annales*, vol. 48, no. 3 (May/June 1993), p. 491.

42 See "French Angered at Ruling on Nazi Collaborator," *The New York Times* (April 15, 1992), p. 5.

43 Christian Jambet, preface to Farías, *Heidegger et le nazisme*, p. 14.

44 See Pierre Bourdieu, *L'Ontologie politique de Martin Heidegger* (Paris: Editions de Minuit, 1988).

45 See Jean-François Lyotard, *Heidegger et "les juifs"* (Paris: Editions Galilée, 1988).

46 See Luc Ferry and Alain Renaut, *Heidegger et les modernes* (Paris: Grasset, 1988).

47 See François Fédier, *Heidegger: Anatomie d'un scandale* (Paris: Robert Laffont, 1988).

48 See Jacques Derrida, *De l'esprit: Heidegger et la question* (Paris: Flammarion, 1990).

49 See Philippe Lacoue-Labarthe, *La Fiction du politique* (Paris: Christian Bourgois, 1987).

50 See Janicaud, *L'Ombre de cette pensée*.

51 See Victor Farías, "Foreword to the Spanish Edition, *Heidegger and Nazism*," in *The Heidegger Case*, pp. 33–34.

52 See Lyotard, *Heidegger et "les juifs,"* p. 16.

53 See especially Luc Ferry and Alain Renaut, *La Pensée 68: Essai sur l'anti-humanisme contemporain* (Paris: Gallimard, 1988).

54 For his objection, see Michel Foucault, *Power/Knowledge: Selected Interviews and Other Writings, 1972–1977*, ed. C. Gordon (New York: Pantheon, 1980), p. 114.

55 See Fédier, *Heidegger: Anatomie d'un scandale*, p. 37.

56 See ibid., p. 162.

57 See Aristotle, *De Interpretatione*, 9, 19b30–34, in *The Complete Works of Aristotle*, vol. I, ed. Jonathan Barnes (Princeton: Princeton University Press, 1984), p. 30.

58 See Heidegger's letter to Jaspers on April 8, 1950, in M. Heidegger and K. Jaspers, *Briefwechsel 1920–1963*, ed. W. Biemel and H. Sauer (Frankfurt/M.: Vittorio Klostermann 1990), p. 202.

59 In a recently published letter Heidegger complains of the "Jewification [Verjudung] of the German spirit." See Ulrich Sieg, "Die Verjudung des deutschen Geistes," in *Die Zeit*, no. 52 (December 22, 1989), p. 50. See also Bourdieu, *L'Ontologie politique de Martin Heidegger*, pp. 59 61n.

60 Bourdieu, *L'Ontologie politique de Martin Heidegger*, p. 10.

61 See Janicaud, *L'Ombre de cette pensée*, pp. 58–64.

62 See ibid., p. 63.

63 See ibid., p. 159.

64 According to Beaufret, "Heidegger n'a jamais rien fait qui ait pu motiver les allégations formulées contre lui," and the political scrutiny of his thought results from "la conspiration des médiocres au nom de la médiocrité." J. Beaufret, *Entretien avec F. de Towarnicki* (Paris: Presses universitaires de France, 1984), p. 87. See also ibid., p. 90.

65 For a recent, critical discussion of Derrida's view of Heidegger's politics, see Stoekl, *Agonies of the Intellectual*, pp. 217–232.

66 For Stoekl, Derrida is basically unable, in virtue of his Heideggerian approach, to criticize Heidegger's politics. See Stoekl, *Agonies of the Intellectual* (Lincoln: University of Nebraska Press, 1992), pp. 200, 228–229.

67 For the view that Lacoue-Labarthe makes "humanism the main culprit for Nazism," see Agnes Heller, "Death of the Subject?," in *Can Modernity Survive?* (Berkeley: University of California Press, 1990), p. 66.

68 See especially "La Transcendance fini e/t dans la politique" and "Poétique et politique," in Philippe Lacoue-Labarthe, *L'Imitation des modernes* (Paris: Editions Galilée, 1986).

69 See Lacoue-Labarthe, *La Fiction du politique*, p. 28.

70 See ibid., p. 43.

71 See ibid., p. 64.

72 See ibid., p. 138.

73 See Jacques Derrida, "Like the Sound of the Sea Deep Within a Shell: Paul de Man's War," in *Responses on Paul de Man's Wartime Journalism*, ed. Werner Hamacher, Neil Hertz, and Thomas Keenan (Lincoln: University of Nebraska, 1989), pp. 127–164.

74 See "Un Entretien avec Jacques Derrida: Heidegger, l'enfer des philosophes," *Le Nouvel Observateur*, no. 47 (November 27, 1987). For an account of the threatened legal action, see "Preface to the MIT Press Edition: Note on a Missing Text," in *The Heidegger Controversy*, ed. Richard Wolin (Cambridge: MIT Press, 1993), pp. ix–xx.

75 For Derrida's reply to a critical article by Thomas Sheehan and Sheehan's rejoinder, see *The New York Review of Books*, vol. 40, no. 4 (February 11, 1993), pp. 44–45.

76 See Derrida, *De l'esprit*, p. 11.

77 See "Die Sprache im Gedicht: Eine Erörterung von Georg Trakls Gedicht," in Martin Heidegger, *Unterwegs zur Sprache* (Pfullingen: Neske, 1959).

78 See Derrida, *De l'esprit*, p. 12.

79 For this argument, see Rockmore, *On Heidegger's Nazism and Philosophy*, ch. 5, pp. 189–199 and *passim*.

80 See Jacques Derrida, *De la grammatologie* (Paris: Editions de Minuit, 1967), pp. 227.
81 See Ott, *Martin Heidegger: Unterwegs zu seiner Biographie.*
82 See Ernst Nolte, *Heidegger: Politik und Geschichte im Leben und Denken* (Berlin: Propyläen, 1992).
83 See Karl Löwith, *Heidegger: Denker in dürftiger Zeit* (Stuttgart: J. B. Metzler, 1984).
84 For discussion, see Rockmore, *On Heidegger's Nazism and Philosophy*, ch. 5, pp. 176–203.
85 See Simone de Beauvoir, *La Force de l'âge*, p. 483.
86 See Etienne Gilson, *L'Etre et l'essence* (Paris: Vrin, 1987), p. 358.

9 HEIDEGGER, FRENCH PHILOSOPHY, AND THE PHILOSOPHICAL TRADITION

1   See Otto Pöggeler, *Martin Heidegger's Path of Thinking*, tr. Daniel Magurshak and Sigmund Barber (Atlantic Highlands: Humanities Press, 1989), p. 247.
2   "The Question Concerning Technology," in Martin Heidegger, *Basic Writings*, ed. D. F. Krell (New York: Harper & Row, 1977), p. 296.
3   See Herbert Schnädelbach, *Philosophy in Germany 1831–1933*, tr. Eric Matthews (Cambridge: Cambridge University Press, 1984), p. 1.
4   See Gilbert Ryle, "Review of Martin Heidegger's *Sein und Zeit*," *Mind*, vol. 38 (1929).
5   See Rudolf Carnap, "The Elimination of Metaphysics through Logical Analysis of Language," in *Logical Positivism*, ed. A. J. Ayer (Glencoe, IL: Free Press, 1959).
6   See "Hegel and the Hermeneutics of German Idealism," in Tom Rockmore, *Hegel and Contemporary Philosophy* (Atlantic Highlands, NJ: Humanities Press, forthcoming).
7   Fichte's staunchest defender in recent years has been Reinhard Lauth. See e.g. Reinhard Lauth, *Hegel vor der Wissenschaftslehre* (Stuttgart: Franz Steiner Verlag, 1987); see also Reinhard Lauth, *Die transzendentale Naturlehre Fichtes nach den Prinzipien der Wissenschaftslehre* (Hamburg: Meiner Verlag, 1984).
8   See e.g. Walter Schulz, *Die Vollendung des deutschen Idealismus in der Spätphilosophie Schellings* (Stuttgart: Kohlhammer, 1955).
9   See Immanuel Kant, *Critique of Pure Reason* tr. Norman Kemp Smith (New York: Macmillan, 1961), B 867, pp. 655–656.
10 See his introduction to *Entwurf eines Systems der Naturphilosophie* (1799), in F. W. J. Schelling, *Ausgewählte Schriften*, vol. I (Frankfurt/M.: Suhrkamp, 1985), p. 339.
11 See Karl Jaspers, *Psychologie der Weltanschauungen* (Berlin: Springer Verlag, 1925), pp. 1–2.
12 Wilhelm Dilthey, *Gesammelte Schriften*, vol. V, ed. Georg Misch (Stuttgart: B. G. Teubner, and Göttingen: Vandehoek und Ruprecht, 1914–1974), V, p. 416. See also "Die Typen der Weltanschauung und ihre Ausbildung in den meta-physischen Systemen," in Dilthey, *Gesammelte Schriften*, vol. VIII, pp. 73–118. For an excellent discussion of Dilthey's concept of *Weltanschauung*, see Rudolf Makkreel, *Dilthey: Philosopher of the Human Sciences* (Princeton: Princeton University Press, 1975), ch. 9: "The Weltanschauungslehre and the Late Aesthetics," pp. 345–384.
13 See "Philosophy as Rigorous Science," in Edmund Husserl, *Phenomenology and the Crisis of Philosophy*.

14 See § 2: "The concept of philosophy: philosophy and world-view," in M. Heidegger, *The Basic Problems of Phenomenology*, tr. A. Hofstadter (Bloomington: Indiana University Press, 1982), pp. 4–11.
15 See ibid., p. 6.
16 See ibid., p. 7.
17 This distinction is becoming ever harder to draw. Nolte has recently argued in effect that there is no distinction, although there is nothing reprehensible about being a Nazi. See Ernst Nolte, *Heidegger: Politik und Geschichte im Leben und Denken* (Berlin: Propyläeu, 1992).
18 M. Heidegger, *Being and Time*, tr. J. Macquarie and E. Robinson (New York: Harper & Row, 1962), p. 75n.
19 See ibid., p. 238.
20 See ibid., p. 227.
21 See § 14: "Precursory characterization of objectivism and transcendentalism: The struggle between these two ideas as the sense of modern spiritual history," in Husserl, *The Crisis*, pp. 68–70.
22 Max Scheler, *Man's Place in Nature*, tr. Hans Meyerhoff (Boston: Beacon, 1961).
23 See H. O. Pappé, "Philosophical Anthropology," in *The Encyclopedia of Philosophy*, vols. V–VI, ed. Paul Edwards (New York: Macmillan, 1972), p. 160.
24 See Heidegger, *Being and Time*, pp. 37–38.
25 See ibid., p. 74.
26 See ibid., p. 75.
27 See ibid.
28 See ibid., p. 38.
29 See ibid., p. 170.
30 See ibid., p. 227.
31 See ibid., p. 244.
32 See ibid., p. 336.
33 See ibid., p. 73.
34 Ibid., p. 58.
35 M. Heidegger, "The Age of the World Picture," in *The Question Concerning Technology and Other Essays*, tr. W. Lovitt (New York: Harper & Row, 1977), p. 133.
36 See ibid., p. 153.
37 See M. Heidegger, "The Letter on Humanism," in *Basic Writings*, ed. D. F. Krell (New York: Harper & Row, 1977), p. 204.
38 See ibid., p. 213.
39 See ibid., p. 221.
40 Ibid., p. 222.
41 See Dominique Janicaud, *Hegel et le destin de la Grèce* (Paris: Vrin, 1975).
42 Heidegger, "Letter on Humanism," p. 224.
43 Fernand Braudel, *On History*, tr. Sarah Matthews (Chicago: University of Chicago Press, 1980), p. 217.
44 See Martin Heideger, *Ontologie: Hermeneutik der Faktizität* (Sommersemester 1923), ed. Käte Bröcker-Oltmanns (Frankfurt/M.: Vittorio Klostermann, 1988).
45 See Heidegger, *Ontologie*, p. 108.
46 "The Rectorial Address," in *Martin Heidegger and National Socialism: Questions and Answers*, ed. Günther Neske and Emil Kettering, intr. Karsten Harries, tr. Lisa Harries and Joachim Neugroschel (New York: Paragon House, 1990), p. 13.
47 Heidegger, "Letter on Humanism," p. 222.
48 See ibid., pp. 236–240.

INDEX

181, 182, 184, 185, 187; and French counteroffensive 107–11, 130, 154, 159; and French Heideggerianism 104–25, 162; and French Heideggerian orthodoxy 104–7; and Jean Beaufret 81–103; and turning in Heidegger's thought 98–103
"Letter to Richardson" 99, 100, 112, 114
Lévi-Strauss, Claude xvi, 25, 26, 56, 57, 58, 82
Lévinas, Emmanuel xvii, 1, 12, 14, 27, 55, 72–3, 86–7, 128–9, 135, 137, 138
Locke, John 14, 20, 23, 24
Löwith, Karl 88, 115, 117, 148, 153, 154, 155, 157, 158, 163, 165
Logical Investigations 13, 171, 179
Logique de Port Royal 9
Lovejoy, Arthur Oncken xiii
Lubac, Henri de, 65
Lukács, Georg 31, 34, 35, 36, 57, 105, 148, 151, 154, 169, 171
Luther, Martin 64
Lyotard, Jean-François 1, 135–6, 157

Macherey, Pierre 34
Maimon, Salomon 21
Maistre, Joseph de 14
Mallarmé, Stéphane 29
Malraux, André 6, 82, 83
Man's Place in Nature 177
Marcel, Gabriel 12, 54, 55, 84
Marion, Jean-Luc 1, 11, 110, 129, 135, 137, 138–9
Maritain, Jacques 11
Marquet, Jean-François 11
Marten, Rainer 154, 155, 163
Martineau, Emmanuel 110, 127
Marx, Karl xiii, xviii, 14, 22, 23, 25, 28, 29, 30, 36, 47, 48, 49, 54–5, 57, 62, 63, 77, 91, 97, 98, 100, 105, 112, 113, 181
Marxism 13, 26, 30, 31, 38, 57, 63, 64, 77, 83, 85, 86, 87, 92, 97, 108, 112, 118, 122, 148, 154
Marxists 17, 18, 38, 82, 85, 105, 109, 113
master thinker: concept of 18–39, 40, 59, 85, 105, 124, 141; Descartes, Lacan, and Sartre 25–7; Hegel as French 27–31; Kojève as 31–9; Whitehead, Kant, and Sartre on 20–5
materialism 48, 49, 97, 98

Mattéi, Jean-François 100
Mauriac, François 82
"Meditations on First Philosophy" 43, 53, 65, 69,
Merleau-Ponty, Maurice xiii, 3, 7, 12, 20, 25, 26, 29, 33, 55, 77, 83, 86, 115, 116, 121
metaphysics xix, 7, 39, 53, 97, 98, 100, 106, 110, 116, 117, 131, 132–4, 144, 146, 159–60, 163, 182, 183, 184, 188
Metaphysics 132, 133
Meyerson, Emile
Miller, J. Hillis 124
Mitterand, François 25
Mollet, Guy 83
Montaigne, Michel de xvi, 40, 66–7
Moore, George Edward 10, 18, 169
Mounier, Emmanuel 70, 83
Myerson, Emile 28

Naming and Necessity 19
Nancy, Jean-Luc 2, 125
Napoleon Bonaparte 16, 35, 68, 126
National Socialism xiii, xvii, xix, 3, 17, 38, 60, 80, 86, 88, 89, 91, 92, 93, 94, 95, 98, 101, 102, 103, 104, 117, 118, 119, 120, 129, 144, 148–68, 175, 183, 184, 185, 187
Nausea 83
Nazism *see* National Socialism
Newton, Isaac 14
New York Review of Books, The 161
Nicole, Pierre 9,
Niethammer, Immanuel Hermann 61
Nietzsche, Friedrich 14, 29, 31, 55, 57, 88, 101–3, 111, 112, 130–1, 135, 136, 169
Nietzsche 101–2, 130, 162
Nizan, Paul 83
Nolte, Ernst 149, 164
Nouvelle Critique, La 85

Okrent, Mark 171
"On the Essence of Truth" 99, 101, 102, 114, 187
Ontologie: Hermeneutik der Faktizität 186–7
Oresteia 41
"Origin of Geometry, The" 142, 143, 147
"Origin of the Work of Art" 118, 121
Ott, Hugo 155, 157, 158, 164
Owen, G. E. L. 11